ENGAGING
MEN
IN COUPLES
THERAPY

Routledge
Taylor & Francis Group

The Routledge Series on Counseling and Psychotherapy with Boys and Men

SERIES EDITOR

Mark S. Kiselica
The College of New Jersey

ADVISORY BOARD

Deryl Bailey
University of Georgia

Chris Blazina
Tennessee State University

J. Manuel Casas
University of California –
Santa Barbara

Matt Englar-Carlson
California State University –
Fullerton

Ann Fischer
Southern Illinois University –
Carbondale

David Lisak
University of Massachusetts – Boston

William M. Liu
University of Iowa

James O'Neil
University of Connecticut

Steve Wester
University of Wisconsin – Milwaukee

VOLUMES IN THIS SERIES

ENGAGING MEN

in COUPLES THERAPY

EDITED BY

DAVID S. SHEPARD AND MICHÈLE HARWAY

Routledge
Taylor & Francis Group
New York   London

Routledge
Taylor & Francis Group
711 Third Avenue
New York, NY 10017

Routledge
Taylor & Francis Group
27 Church Road
Hove, East Sussex BN3 2FA

© 2012 by Taylor & Francis Group, LLC
Routledge is an imprint of Taylor & Francis Group, an Informa business

Printed in the United States of America on acid-free paper
Version Date: 20110617

International Standard Book Number: 978-0-415-87587-5 (Hardback) 978-0-415-87588-2 (Paperback)

Library of Congress Cataloging-in-Publication Data

Shepard, David S.
    Engaging men in couples therapy / David S. Shepard and Michele Harway.
        p. cm.
    Includes bibliographical references and index.
    ISBN 978-0-415-87587-5 (hardcover : alk. paper) -- ISBN 978-0-415-87588-2
    (pbk. : alk. paper)
        1. Marriage counseling. 2. Men--Counseling of. I. Harway, Michele. II. Title.

    BF636.7.G76S54 2011
    616.89'1562081--dc22   2011003324

Visit the Taylor & Francis Web site at
http://www.taylorandfrancis.com

and the Routledge Web site at
http://www.routledgementalhealth.com

D. S. dedicates this book to his wife, Debra, the love of his life.

M. H. dedicates this book to her brother and to her son for providing her with secondhand exposure to the pains and perils of growing up male.

Contents

Series Editor's Foreword

If you walk into any bookstore, you will likely find a wide selection of books, both fiction and non-fiction, in which men are portrayed as baffling creatures, comfortable as cave dwellers, devoid of feelings, and unable to connect with their wives and partners. This depiction of men is also found in movies, on television, and on the stage. A common story about this type of man told across these different media involves a couple in a crisis caused by the man's archaic and mysterious nature. Such dramas portray a woman desperately trying to connect with a clueless husband or boyfriend who is either unable and/or unwilling to commit to, compromise with, and open up to her. His behavior pushes her to the point of giving him an ultimatum that he change his ways or she will leave him. He responds to her demands by withdrawing further into himself and away from her, setting the stage for the demise of their relationship.

This popular plot about men and the way they sabotage their romantic bonds with their partners, though perhaps entertaining, is disturbing because it reinforces a simplistic stereotype about men, which places the blame for the problems couples experience squarely on the shoulders of men. Although such blame may be warranted in some cases, it is dangerous to view the problems of couples in this stereotypic way, especially if one is a couples therapist charged with the professional responsibility of helping couples in a nonjudgmental, unbiased manner.

I mention this latter concern because I am aware of some troubling research findings indicating that clinicians who ascribe to hypoemotional stereotypes about men are more likely than clinicians without such stereotypes to blame men for the problems they bring to couples therapy (Heesacker, Wester, Vogel, Wentzel, Mejia-Millan & Goodholm, 1999). It is highly unlikely that therapists who take a blaming posture toward men can be neutral in their work with couples because they are likely to align themselves with women in a way that alienates men from couples counseling (Heesacker et al., 1999). But imagine how different men might react to couples therapy if counselors looked for the good in them, sought and affirmed their positive intentions, and tapped men's strengths, while helping men and their partners to address their conflicts. Under these latter circumstances, a man is likely to feel welcomed in counseling and optimistic about exploring ways that he can work to resolve his relationship issues. Thus, if we really want to help men who are experiencing difficulties in the relationships they have with the women in their lives, we must divest ourselves of simplistic stereotypes about men and practice male-friendly couples therapy that is guided by a more complex view of men and involves an empathic and non-judgmental approach to helping men that builds upon their many strengths.

In *Engaging Men in Couples Therapy*, the latest volume of the *Routledge Series on Counseling and Psychotherapy with Men*, Drs. David Shepard and Michèle Harway, two national authorities on the psychology of men and masculinity, have pulled together contributions from a distinguished team of colleagues to produce a truly constructive approach to working with men in couples therapy. Moving beyond simplistic assumptions about men, Drs. Shepard, Harway, and their colleagues demonstrate how to employ a male-sensitive perspective to achieve "balance" in couples therapy. By balance, they mean helping both the woman *and* the man to feel comfortable and understood during the counseling process. To achieve these conditions with men, who are usually the more difficult partner to engage in couples therapy, Drs. Shepard, Harway, and their fellow authors argue that we must understand what it means to be a traditional man in a counseling environment; that the male socialization process places men at a disadvantage when it comes to participating in couples therapy; that men feel under-appreciated for the way they try to demonstrate caring; that men have their own ways for connecting with others, some of which are different from the ways women seek and show connection; that there is a mismatch between current approaches used by therapists in couples counseling and the skills sets and relational styles of traditional men; and that the counseling process must be adapted to address the needs of special populations of men. Based on this foundation of understanding, the contributing authors demonstrate how various theoretical approaches to couples work can be applied in a male-sensitive manner.

I am grateful to my dear colleagues and friends, Drs. Shepard and Harway, and their associates for giving us this gem of a book, and I am honored to have their fine work as a volume in this series.

Mark S. Kiselica, Series Editor
The Routledge Series on Counseling and
Psychotherapy with Boys and Men
The College of New Jersey
April 7, 2011

REFERENCE

Heesacker, M., Wester, S. R., Vogel, D. L., Wentzel, J. T., Mejia-Millan, C. M., & Goodholm, C. R. (1999). Gender-based emotional stereotyping. *Journal of Counseling Psychology, 46,* 483–495.

Acknowledgments

For the 20 or so years I have been doing couples work, I have never ceased to be amazed by the resolve of male clients to "be there" for their wives or partners. In many first sessions, I would hear these words: "I'm here to support her in any way I can," even as their face and eyes said, "I'm scared to death of her leaving me and I feel completely helpless." And so they would "soldier on" in therapy, doing what was asked, gradually letting go of their armor, learning to listen patiently, struggling to find words for emotions that for years had been kept inside. To these men, I would like to say, "I knew you often didn't want to be here in my therapy office, but you came, and you worked hard, and demonstrated your extraordinary capacity for love and tenderness. You inspired me and I am grateful."

Michèle Harway has made collaboration a pleasure. Our regular Skype sessions became much more than about editing a book: They evolved into dialogues about the very nature of couples counseling as we shared stories of our own strategies and struggles in our clinical work. Her prior experience as an editor was invaluable to the process, and she taught me much. Balancing this project with the demands of academic life, clinical practice responsibilities, and just the realities of life was never easy, but the more we worked, the more we came to believe in the value of this volume.

I want to thank Mark Kiselica, the series editor. His enthusiasm for the project began at the first moment I suggested it to him and never ceased. Dana Bliss, our Routledge editor, has been equally unflagging in his support and trusting of our process.

I am blessed to be part of a faculty at California State University, Fullerton who make going to work a pleasure. In particular, I want to acknowledge three colleagues and friends: Jeffrey Kottler, who taught me the meaning of "pride of ownership" when your name is on the cover; Matt Englar-Carlson, whose generous invitation to me to work with him on a journal article about engaging men in couples and family therapy was the starting point for this book; and Jose Cervantes for his support and his desire to contribute from the book's inception.

The contributors to this book have come through with exactly what I had hoped for when first envisioning this project. Collaborating with them has also challenged my ideas about couples therapy and, I believe, strengthened my own clinical work.

Finally, I want to thank my wife, Debra, who believed in this book from the beginning and whose emotional support has been unstinting. She knew intuitively when to reassure me, when to challenge me, when to listen to my worries, and when to say, "Give it a rest." She has taught me everything I know about love.

—DS

I too have many people to thank for the successful completion of this book. I first want to thank David Shepard for inviting me to work on this manuscript with him. As he describes above, our collaboration has been a good one: it's been a wonderful experience of together bringing to fruition a vision that David had right from the outset. I have learned so much about men and working with men through our frequent Skype conversations and quite a bit about David as well. I know him to be an intellectually demanding colleague, a brilliant clinician and a caring and compassionate human being. Thank you, David, for inviting me to participate in this project and for putting up with my sometimes-crazy work schedule.

Mark Kiselica, the series editor, has been an inspiration in interactions with me and others. He is the role model for younger professionals that I would like to be.

I have many years of working with couples as well as with individual clients both male and female. I particularly want to acknowledge the men I have seen over the years because of what they have shared about themselves and the trust they placed in me to interact with them in different ways than they expected. As the book explores, it takes bravery to enter a domain (psychotherapy) that fundamentally relies on skills men believe they lack.

Those colleagues at Antioch University, Santa Barbara who have been so supportive of me are always in my heart.

My grown children, Sasha and Alissa, are the joy of my life and I wanted them to know how much I appreciate them.

—MH

About the Editors

David S. Shepard, PhD, is an associate professor of counseling at California State University, Fullerton and a private practice psychologist in West Los Angeles, where he specializes in couples counseling and gender-sensitive individual therapy with men and women. Shepard has authored or coauthored numerous journal articles and book chapters, primarily in the areas of couples therapy, effective psychotherapy with men, and male development. He also regularly gives workshops and conferences presentation on couples therapy, men and intimacy, and teaching counseling. He is coauthor (with Jeffrey Kottler) of the textbook *Introduction to Counseling: Voices from the Field*. He is a long-standing member of the Society for the Psychological Study of Men and Masculinity, a division of the American Psychological Association (Division 51), and he is a codirector of the Center for Boys and Men: Research and Outreach, at California State, Fullerton. Prior to his career as a psychologist, Shepard was a television screenwriter, specializing in children's animation, most notably, the series, *Doug*. He resides in Pacific Palisades, California, with his wife, Debra.

Michèle Harway, PhD, ABPP, is founding chair of the clinical psychology doctoral program at Antioch University, faculty research specialist at Fielding Graduate University, and maintains a small private practice in Westlake Village, California, where she specializes in couples and family therapy and working with trauma survivors. She is board certified in couples and family psychology (American Board of Professional Psychology). Harway has authored or edited nine books and many book chapters and journal articles, and has presented at numerous professional conferences on couples therapy, domestic violence, trauma survival, gender, and family issues. Active in several divisions of the American Psychological Association (APA), she is a fellow of four divisions, a former president of Division 43 (Family Psychology), former treasurer of Division 51 (Men and Masculinity), and current representative to APA's Council of Representatives from Division 43. She has worked and lived overseas, and maintains an interest in international issues. She currently resides in Southern California with her adult daughter and a feisty Jack Russell terrier.

About the Contributors

Brian Baucom, PhD, is a National Institutes of Health (NIH) postdoctoral fellow, lecturer, and clinical supervisor in the Department of Psychology at the University of Southern California. He studies couple conflict and couple therapy with a particular focus on the role of emotional expression during couple interaction. He is currently working on a longitudinal study of families (with Gayla Margolin and colleagues) and on a longitudinal study of German couples (with Kurt Hahlweg and colleagues).

Karl Bergenstal, PhD, is a certified clinician and trainer in the Gottman method of couples therapy and he has presented the Gottman method at couples workshops, to professional organizations, and in graduate classes at several local universities. He holds a diplomate status in clinical psychology from the American Board of Professional Psychology (ABPP) and has a private practice in Camarillo, California. His previous research is on attachment theory applied to family relationships.

Alisa A. Breetz, MA, is a doctoral candidate in clinical psychology at American University in Washington, DC. She has collaborated with Barry McCarthy on multiple articles and book chapters focused on sexual functioning, couple therapy, and sexual trauma.

Gary R. Brooks, PhD, is a professor in the Doctor of Psychology Program at Baylor University, after having been employed for 28 years as a psychologist with the Central Texas Veterans Health Care System. He is a Fellow of the American Psychological Association (APA) and has been president of APA's Division of Family Psychology and Society for the Psychological Study of Men and Masculinity. He received the 1996 and 2010 Distinguished Practitioner Award of the APA Division of Men and Masculinity, the 1997 Texas Distinguished Psychologist Award, and the 2002 Outstanding Researcher Award of the APA Division of Men and Masculinity. He has authored or coauthored six books, the latest of which is *Beyond the Crisis of Masculinity: A Transtheoretical Model For Male-Friendly Therapy* (APA Books, 2010).

Jon Carlson, PsyD, EdD, ABPP, is a distinguished professor of Psychology and Counseling, at Governors State University and a psychologist at the Wellness Clinic in Lake Geneva, Wisconsin. Carlson has served as editor of several periodicals including the *Journal of Individual Psychology* and *The Family Journal*. He is a diplomate in both family psychology and Adlerian psychology. He has authored 150 journal articles and 50 books including *Time for a Better Marriage* (Impact Publishers, Inc., 2002), *Adlerian Therapy* (APA, 2005), *Inclusive Cultural Empathy* (APA, 2008), *The Mummy at the Dining Room Table* (Jossey-Bass, 2005), *Bad Therapy* (Routledge, 2002), *The Client Who Changed Me* (Routledge, 2005), *Their Finest Hour* (Crown House Publishing, 2008), *Creative Breakthroughs in Therapy* (Wiley, 2009), and *Moved by the Spirit* (Impact Publishers, Inc., 2007). He has also created over 250 professional trade videos and DVDs with leading professional therapists and educators.

Joseph M. Cervantes, PhD, ABPP, is a professor in the Department of Counseling at California State University, Fullerton and holds diplomate certification in the areas of clinical and couples and family psychology from the American Board of Professional Psychology. He is the immediate past president of the National Latina/o Psychological Association and past chair of the Committee on Ethnic Minority Affairs (CEMA), American Psychological Association. Aside from his full-time faculty appointment, Cervantes is also in independent practice as a forensic child and family psychologist.

Matt Englar-Carlson, PhD, is an associate professor of counseling at California State University, Fullerton. He is a Fellow of the American Psychological Association (Division 51) and as a scholar, teacher, and clinician, Englar-Carlson has been an innovator and professionally passionate about training and teaching clinicians to work more effectively with their male clients. Englar-Carlson coedited the books *In the Room with Men: A Casebook of Therapeutic Change* (APA, 2006) and *Counseling Troubled Boys: A Guidebook for Professionals* (Routledge, 2008), and was the featured professional in the APA DVD *Engaging Men in Psychotherapy*. With his father, Jon Carlson, he is the series editor of the *Theories of Psychotherapy* (APA) book series, including the coauthor of the book on Adlerian therapy. In 2007 he was named the Researcher of the Year by the Society for the Psychological Study of Men and Masculinity. He is also a member of the APA Working Group to Develop Guidelines for Psychological Practice with Boys and Men. As a clinician, he has worked with children, adults, and families in school, community, and university mental health settings.

George Faller, MS, is a lieutenant in the NYC Fire Department and is a licensed marriage and family therapist (LMFT) in New York. He is the founder and director of the New York Center for Emotionally Focused Therapy (EFT). After September 11, 2001, Faller received extensive training from Dr. Susan Johnson in using emotionally focused therapy with traumatized couples. He is a clinical member of AAMFT and is an approved EFT supervisor. Faller is helping to spread EFT in the tristate area, running numerous supervision groups and is teaching an EFT course at the Ackerman Institute in Manhattan. Faller is also currently working with the U.S. Army to help repair returning veterans' marriages and train Army chaplains in using EFT. He has a private practice in Westchester and provides training throughout the country.

Paul S. Greenman, PhD, is a professor of clinical psychology at the Université du Québec en Outaouais in Gatineau, Québec, and a practicing psychologist at the Ottawa Couple and Family Institute and Montfort Hospital in Ottawa, Ontario. He specializes in emotionally focused therapy for couples in his teaching and clinical practice, and he conducts research on the emotional and interpersonal lives of children and adults. Greenman is also the leader of a research team at the Diabetes and Cardiovascular Rehabilitation Clinic at Montfort Hospital, designing, implementing, and testing a new psychological treatment tailored for individuals suffering from depression and posttraumatic stress as a result of coronary disease. Greenman and his team are currently testing an adaptation of emotionally focused therapy for couples with patients recovering from cardiac illnesses and their spouses.

Lori H. Gordon, PhD, is founder, president, and training director of the PAIRS Foundation, Inc., and has served as chief executive officer of the executive board. She has a private practice through the Family Relations Institute, Falls Church, Virginia, and consults through the Tequesta Consulting Services, Ltd., in Fort Lauderdale, Florida. She is the author of three popular books: *Love Knots, Passage to Intimacy,* and *If You Really Loved Me.* She is also coauthor of several professional articles on the PAIRS program as well as a range of professional training curricula, articles, and materials. She continues to develop relationship programs designed to sustain healthy marriages and stable families through the PAIRS Foundation. Gordon trains health care professionals and paraprofessionals to teach the PAIRS programs worldwide.

Susan M. Johnson, PhD, is the founding director of the Ottawa Couples and Family Institute (OCFI) and the director of the International Center for Excellence in Emotionally Focused Therapy (ICEEFT). For over 10 years she was also the director of the Marital and Family Clinic at the Civic Hospital in Ottawa and is recognized as an international expert and trainer in the field of couple and family therapy. Johnson is the primary proponent of the emotionally focused model of couple therapy, which has demonstrated its effectiveness in over 15 years of clinical research. Johnson is the author of several seminal books and numerous articles on couple and family therapy. She is the year 2000 recipient of the Outstanding Contribution to Marriage and Family Therapy Award given by the American Association of Marital and Family Therapy.

Steven M. Kadin, PhD, ABPP, is a core faculty member in the Doctor of Psychology program at Antioch University, Santa Barbara with over 25 years experience teaching and training advanced degree students. He is licensed both as a psychologist and a marriage and family therapist. In addition, he is a diplomate in couples and family psychology of the American Board of Professional Psychology. Kadin maintains a private practice in San Luis Obispo, California, with over 30 years of experience working with couples and families. His research interests include men and gender, and factors promoting healthy intimate relationships.

Supavan Khamphakdy-Brown, PhD, is currently completing her post-doctoral internship at the Professional Renewal Center in Lawrence, Kansas. She received her PhD in counseling psychology from the University of Missouri–Kansas City and interned at Kansas State University's Counseling Services. Brown's interests include assessment, mindfulness, and multicultural issues.

Wade Luquet, PhD, is an associate professor of sociology and human services, and program director of the human services degree program at Gwynedd-Mercy College in suburban Philadelphia. He is the author of *Short-Term Couples Therapy: The Imago Model In Action* (Routledge, 2006) and coeditor of *Healing in the Relational Paradigm: The Imago Relationship Therapy Casebook* (Routledge, 1998) and *Imago Relationship Therapy: Perspectives on Theory* (Jossey-Bass, 2005). He is on the academic faculty of Imago Relationships International. Luquet maintains a private practice in couples therapy in North Wales, Pennsylvania.

Don-David Lusterman, PhD, ABPP, is a licensed psychologist practicing couples and family therapy in Baldwin, New York. He is board certified in couples and family psychology. Lusterman is the author of *Infidelity: A Survival Guide* (New Harbinger Publications, 1998); *Integrating Family Therapy: Handbook of Family Psychology and Systems Therapy* (with Susan McDaniel) (APA, 1995); and *Bridging Separate Gender Worlds: Why Men and Women Clash and How Therapists Can Bring Them Together* (with Carol Philpot, Gary Brooks, and Roberta Nutt) (APA, 1997). He has also authored journal articles, been a frequent media guest, appearing on the *Today Show* and *Oprah*, and been the subject of many print and radio interviews.

Barry McCarthy, PhD, is a professor of Psychology at American University and a certified sex and marital therapist who practices individual, couple, and sex therapy at the Washington Psychological Center in Washington, DC. He has authored more than 90 professional articles, 22 book chapters, and 13 books, including *Enduring Desire* (Routledge, 2010), *Discovering Your Couple Sexual Style* (Routledge, 2009), *Men's Sexual Health* (Routledge, 2008), *Coping with Erectile Dysfunction* (New Harbinger, 2004), *Coping with Premature Ejaculation* (New Harbinger, 2003), and *Rekindling Desire* (Routledge, 2003). In addition to clinical practice and teaching, McCarthy has presented at more than 300 professional workshops locally, nationally, and internationally.

Ellen Purcell is a PAIRS master teacher and trainer and a certified relationship life coach through The Coaches Training Institute. She has served as executive director of the PAIRS Foundation and has lectured at George Mason University, James Madison University, and George Washington University on the PAIRS process. Purcell has been a contributing author in several books, and appeared on television and radio shows discussing PAIRS in the past 15 years.

Fredric E. Rabinowitz, PhD, is professor of psychology and the associate dean at the University of Redlands. Since 1984, his private psychology practice in Redlands, California, has specialized in individual and group psychotherapy with men. Rabinowitz has coauthored numerous articles and books, including *Deepening Psychotherapy with Men* (APA, 2002), *Men and Depression: Clinical and Empirical Approaches* (Academic Press, 1999), and *Man Alive: A Primer of Men's Issues* (Brooks Cole, 1994). He is a past president of the Society for the Psychological Study of Men and Masculinity (Division 51) of the American Psychological Association.

John M. Robertson, PhD, is the director of psychological services at the Professional Renewal Center in Lawrence, Kansas, working with men (mostly in the medical field) mandated to seek treatment for maladaptive behavior in their work settings. Robertson also has conducted research and written about various concerns men bring to psychotherapy. He is past president of the Society for the Psychological Study of Men and Masculinity (Division 51) of the American Psychological Association.

David B. Wexler, PhD, is a clinical psychologist in San Diego and the executive director of the nonprofit Relationship Training Institute. He has received the Distinguished Contribution to Psychology award from the California Psychological Association and the Practitioner of the Year award from the Society for the Psychological Study of Men and Masculinity (Division 51) of the American Psychological Association. Wexler is the author of many books and has appeared on hundreds of radio and TV programs throughout North America to help educate the public about relationships in conflict and how to resolve them.

1

Introduction

Setting the Stage

DAVID S. SHEPARD AND MICHÈLE HARWAY

The need for effective couples therapy has never been stronger. As Gurman has observed, "Divorce and marital problems are among the most stressful conditions people face. Partners in troubled relationships are more likely to suffer from anxiety, depression and suicidality, and substance abuse: from both acute and chronic medical problems" (2008, p. 3). Long and Young (2007) note the following sobering facts about the state of marriage: (a) one-half of all marriages end in divorce; (b) marital distress contributes to nearly 50% of admissions to mental hospitals; (c) couples issues can cause or worsen severe psychological and behavioral problems for children. Although similar statistics are not available for the impact of relationship distress on nonmarital couples, it is likely that the same kinds of negative outcomes can be obtained for them as well.

On the one hand, couples therapy has become the treatment of choice for distressed couples (Sperry, Carlson, & Peluso, 2006). At the same time, the success rate of couples therapy is alarmingly low, at least according to John Gottman, perhaps the preeminent researcher in the field. He reviewed the efficacy research and concluded that only 35% of couples report gains during treatment, and just 11% to 18% of couples are able to maintain their progress after ending therapy (Gottman, 1999). The premise of this book is that a crucial and overlooked reason for treatment failures may be the couples therapist's inability to respond to the needs and psychological issues particular to the male partner. Thus, it is important to note that this is not a volume about therapy with a special population, but one designed to help the reader succeed in the endeavor of working with couples. Simply put, it is about doing couples therapy well.

For couples therapy to succeed, three conditions must be met: both partners must feel equally comfortable in the therapeutic setting; both partners need to feel understood; and both partners must be convinced the therapy is "balanced," that is, the counselor is not aligned with the views and interests of a particular partner. When the process is not balanced, therapy is likely to end prematurely (Mack, 1989). These essential core conditions can be met, and specific, theory-based interventions can be effective, only when they are applied from a male-sensitive perspective, that is, when the psychology of men and masculinity is taken into account. Issues related to engaging women in therapy have been addressed long ago (Fitzgerald & Nutt, 1986; Gilligan, Rogers, & Tolman, 1991; McGoldrick, Anderson, & Walsh, 1991; Rawlings & Carter, 1977; Worrell & Remer, 1997). Most couples therapists are knowledgeable about how to engage their female clients, and the therapy process itself essentially capitalizes on skills that women more than men have been socialized to develop. As a result, engaging women in therapy will not be the primary focus of this book. Our goal for this book is to provide a research-informed practitioner's guide to conducting male-sensitive couples therapy, whether in private practice, community mental health, or university settings. This approach will benefit both the male clients who present because of relationship distress and also their female partners who will benefit from the work that will ensue.

WHY MALE-SENSITIVE COUPLES THERAPY IS ESSENTIAL

A number of factors contribute to the challenge couples therapists face in making the process male sensitive.

Men's socialization experiences can make couples therapy an unfriendly environment. Over 20 years of research on the psychology of men has explored men's reluctance to utilize mental health services (Addis & Mahalik, 2003). It has become well documented that male gender role socialization emphasizes self-reliance; restrictive emotionality, specifically the vulnerable affects; and denial or suppression of dependency needs (Good & Robertson, 2010). Many men are reluctant to engage in a process that presumes the failure of self-reliance, that values accessing and expressing tender feelings, and that facilitates contact with yearnings for dependence on another human being, whether the therapist or partner.

This tension between the values of psychotherapy and the male role have been thought to explain men's underutilization of mental health services in general; imagine, then, what it may feel like for a man to participate in couples therapy. Not only are core identity-related values being challenged by the therapeutic situation, but his female partner is likely to be far more at ease with the process, not to mention, able to display a capacity to engage in the language of feelings that surpasses his own, leaving him feeling incompetent and "one down." Women's socialization trains them in the language of psychotherapy, but the language of therapy is often a different language than the one men have learned to speak throughout their lives (Shay, 1996). Couples therapy can thus be a place where a man's self-esteem is challenged, and if counselors fail to maintain sensitivity to this vulnerability, the therapy—and, concomitantly, the relationship itself—may be at risk.

Men often feel underappreciated for their contribution to the relationship. Generally, women initiate couples treatment, voicing the complaint that their male partner does not understand their feelings. At the same time, note Shay and Maltas, "men feel misunderstood and unappreciated for their contributions to the relationship and criticized for demonstrating the kinds of traits that lead to their succeeding professionally and being good providers" (1998, p. 98). Character strengths like emotional calmness in a crisis, persistence when faced with challenges, and problem-solving skills can be sources of pride for many men, and yet may be of little help in deepening their intimate relationship with their partner. The active listening, "relationship talk," and disclosure of vulnerable emotions that the female partner defines as intimacy-enhancing may not be part of the male partner's relational repertoire. Couples therapy that does not affirm a man's strengths while focusing on his perceived weaknesses can leave a male client feeling at once devalued by both therapist and partner, and incompetent in satisfying his partner's intimacy requests.

The newest intervention models in the couples therapy field emphasize the skills many females already have and many men do not. In previous decades, behavioral marital therapy was the most popular and evidence-supported intervention model, and its problem-solving approach may have been well suited to the action-oriented styles of male clients. However, there has been a virtual revolution over the last 20 years in both research and practice (Kottler & Shepard, 2007). Models such as emotionally focused couples therapy (Greenman, Faller, & Johnson, this volume; Johnson, 2004), integrated behavioral couples therapy (Baucom, this volume; Jacobson & Christensen, 1996), and Imago Relationship Therapy (Hendrix, 1988; Luquet, 2005, this volume) have received empirical support, and are being widely adopted by therapists. All of these models emphasize expression of vulnerable feelings and increased levels of empathic connection—client tasks that can run counter to the gender role socialization experiences of many men. Given the research support they have demonstrated, the practitioner-developers of these models are presumably doing something right in making counseling male friendly. One purpose of this volume, then, is to present chapters by practitioners associated with the development of these models who can answer the question directly and through illustrative case studies: How are they adapting their conceptualizations and interventions to the needs, backgrounds, and styles of the male partner?

Both of us are couples therapists as well as teachers, and we see the results of couples therapists' lack of knowledge in male-sensitive couples counseling in our own clinical practice. A significant portion of our clients report a previously negative experience in couples therapy, usually manifesting in a complaint by the male partner that "the therapist took my wife's side." When we explore the man's frustration in the introductory session, we often learn that what really happened is not that the previous therapist openly agreed with the wife and contradicted the husband, but instead, fell into one of the following traps: (a) Without realizing it, the counselor sent signals that the female partner's expressions of emotion were much appreciated; the male partner, who may be less openly feeling, received fewer approving nonverbal gestures and empathic responses. (b) The female client complained that her partner seemed distant and disconnected, and therapy became focused on getting the man to be more openly expressive and empathic; the man received the message that he was the "problem" in the relationship. (c) The male partner's tendency to problem solve was labeled as dysfunctional, whereas the female partner's desires for increased communication were supported. (d) A female couples counselor may have failed to appreciate a male client's unexpressed fears that a woman-to-woman coalition was forming against him.

Couples therapists need help in understanding the psychology of men and masculinity as it relates to the practice or couples therapy; the goal of this book is to provide that assistance. To that effect, we invited authors who are deeply immersed in the development of male-sensitive clinical treatments to share how they conceptualize and intervene with couples from this gender-aware perspective. Some of these authors have a particular expertise in the area of men and masculinity research and clinical practice, some are associated with the development of well-known couples therapy models, and some are specialists in working with specific populations (e.g., men of color and veterans) or specific issues (e.g., infidelity, issues of fathering, sexual dysfunctions).

The reader will notice a particular theme that runs through many of the chapters in the book and plays a central role in why many men struggle in couples therapy; that theme is the role of shame in men's lives. The issue of shame manifests in both the male member's vulnerability to experience shame in sessions and in the presenting problem that brought the couple into therapy. It is critical, then, that the couples therapist knows how to use interventions and choose words that avoid inadvertently shaming the male partner.

Clearly a better understanding of the dynamics of shame in the lives of men and how these dynamics developed is necessary for effective clinical practice. Shame has been described as a public sense of inadequacy (Osherson & Krugman, 1990) and a feeling of deep worthlessness and helplessness, "a piercing awareness of ourselves as fundamentally deficient in some vital way as a human being" (Kaufman, 1985, p. 8). Boys learn to feel that sense of deficiency when they fail to conform to the rules of masculinity, resulting in repeated acts of embarrassment and humiliation from their male peers. Hartley (1959) observed this phenomenon of boys being shamed over 50 years ago. Pollack's more recent research (1998) with boys suggests that shame is still a powerful mechanism enforcing the Boy Code (don't cry, don't show neediness, dominate others, and demonstrate bravado and aggression). Krugman, a specialist in the relationship between male development and psychological trauma, wrote, "Boy culture is competitive, insensitive, and often cruel. Being chosen last, or not at all, is a vivid memory for many men. Being picked on, afraid to fight, or forced to fight generates a welter of intense feelings, with shame at the core" (1995, p. 93).

Feelings of shame lead a boy to negative self-talk where he exaggerates how he operates in the world and where he might tell himself that "I am unacceptable, weak, a loser, inferior, ..." This self-negating voice leads to increased self-consciousness and perhaps even to rage, which may serve as a protection to keep at bay others who might shame him again. As a result of early experience around shame, boys may also learn to mask (and in some cases, deny) their emotions, particularly their vulnerable ones, and instead adopt a false self of toughness and independence. Some may isolate themselves to avoid further shaming experiences. Some turn the feelings outward, becoming bullies. Any or all of these defensive maneuvers designed to prevent feelings of shame may later become part of adult men's inner life, understandably leaving them vigilant to protecting themselves from being shamed by their partners as well as by their therapist. It is for this reason that clinicians who treat men (whether individually or in couples therapy) must be particularly sensitive to not revictimizing male clients, especially when the presenting issue is already a profoundly humiliating one. In many of our subsequent chapters, authors focus on the shame that men present with (whether it be their lack of skills in the couple arena, or a personal problem such as one related to sexual functioning or infidelity) and demonstrate how the therapist can deconstruct the male partners' shame-bound experiences that keep them from fully knowing their feelings and keep both partners from knowing the joys of relationships.

CONTENTS OF THE BOOK

In conceptualizing this volume, we decided early in our process that counseling gay men in relationships, while bringing forth many of the same issues we are addressing here, warranted its own book and we concluded that providing a single chapter on this specific population would be doing a disservice to the many varied types of relationships present in the gay community and the complexity of gay relationships in their own right. Thus, the reader will notice that our focus is exclusively on heterosexual couples.

The book that we have developed includes three distinct sections. Part I, "Foundations of Male-Sensitive Couples Therapy," sets the stage for the chapters that follow. Its goal is to identify and discuss the critical issues regarding engaging men in couples therapy and making this modality a place where men feel as comfortable and free to be vulnerable as their female partners. In this initial chapter, we have identified the need for this book, and set forth its goals. In Chapter 2, we consider the five most critical challenges that men present in couples therapy, and which, if left unattended, may undermine the work of well-meaning clinicians. Although the chapter is framed around the pitfalls of conducting therapy that is uninformed by knowledge of male psychology, we essentially are laying out our clinical recommendations for effective, male-sensitive couples therapy, based on our years of experience striving to bring gender sensitivity to our clinical work.

In Chapter 3, Fredric E. Rabinowitz reviews the most current scholarship on effective counseling with men, emphasizing a developmental perspective that helps explain why men have difficulties with their intimate relationships as well as with the tasks of participating in couples work. Rabinowitz then incorporates this perspective into a "primer" on conducting therapy with men.

Part II, "Theoretical Models," presents the work of well-known clinicians representing a number of theoretical orientations to couples therapy. In each chapter, case material is presented and the authors have focused on how their approach might provide male-sensitive therapy. In Chapter 4, John Robertson and Supavan Khamphakdy-Brown, coming from a psychoanalytic perspective, propose a model of couples therapy that makes use of early life recollections in a manner that engages the male partner while uncovering his childhood memories relevant to the couples' distress. Although the authors present a psychodynamic model, their use of childhood memories can be integrated into a variety of therapeutic approaches. Matt Englar-Carlson and Jon Carlson, authors of Chapter 5, discuss how to blend Adlerian therapeutic ideas with their understanding of the psychology of men and masculinity. Wade Luquet, in Chapter 6, focuses on the use of Imago Therapy and its couple exercises, with specific emphasis on how clinicians can help men embrace the approach's use of empathic listening. Chapter 7's authors, Paul Greenman, George Faller, and Susan Johnson, introduce the idea that emotionally focused therapy (EFT) is inherently a male-sensitive approach to couples therapy because of its emphasis on the universal human needs for safety, closeness, and comfort. EFT practitioners insist that partners access their most vulnerable emotions in sessions, an approach that would seem to be counter to the male partner's socialization; in their chapter, these authors demonstrate how EFT-oriented clinicians engage men in their deepest emotional experiences and that of their partner's. Brian Baucom in Chapter 8 presents integrative behavioral couple therapy (IBCT), Jacobson's and Christensen's synthesis of promoting acceptance of each partner's differences, with traditional behavioral marital therapy exercises. Baucom demonstrates IBCT's focus on changing couple polarization, in particular the demand–withdraw pattern of relating, which IBCT theorists consider to be a major source of relationship problems. In Chapter 9, Karl Bergenstal reports on Gottman's research and clinical work with couples, with its emphasis on men's tendency to "stonewall" in difficult conversations as well as get caught up in adrenaline-fueled anger. His case illustrations demonstrate how practitioners of this model respond to these particularly male tendencies. Finally, Part II concludes with Lori Gordon and Ellen Purcell's discussion of PAIRS, a group psychoeducational approach to healing distressed couples and preventing future relational problems. As they present a sequence of experiential activities they ask the attendees of PAIRS programs to participate in, they argue that this type of intervention by its very nature is experienced by men as less threatening than traditional psychotherapy or relationship counseling. PAIRS exercises can also be adapted to more traditional couples counseling settings.

Part III, "Special Populations and Issues," begins with a rich case study in Chapter 11 by Barry McCarthy and Alisa Breetz that demonstrates male affirmative sex therapy with a male partner experiencing low sexual desire. The authors highlight both the masculinity issues inherent to their case as well as their therapeutic techniques for engaging men in what is often a most challenging and shame-provoking area of couple functioning. Another difficult area for couples is that of infidelity; in Chapter 12, Steven Kadin and Don-David Lusterman present a model for addressing infidelity caused by the male partner in a way that promotes healing by incorporating an understanding of men's psychology, without minimizing the emotional impact of infidelity on the female partner. In Chapter 13, Joseph Cervantes addresses the role of past racial wounds in the relational difficulties encountered by couples of color, specifically Latino and African American couples. Cervantes notes how micro- and macroaggressions, experienced throughout a man of color's childhood, can fuel anger and acting out; addressing both requires a high level of gender and multicultural sensitivity on the part of the therapist if effective couples work is to occur.

No other issue is as pressing and relevant as the difficulties encountered by the families of veterans when the male partner returns from his deployment; the challenges for the male and female partner are intense, not only because of the role of posttraumatic stress disorder (PTSD) but also because of the adjustment of the male partner from the hypermasculine military culture to the altogether different tasks of being in an intimate male–female relationship. Thus, in Chapter 14, Gary Brooks, who has worked extensively with veterans of Vietnam, both Iraqi wars, and the Afghanistan campaigns, describes the issues couples therapists must consider in working with this population. Finally in Chapter 15,

David Wexler reviews how to conduct male-sensitive counseling with men who are struggling with fathering issues. We have deliberately placed Wexler's chapter last, because as he explores how the issues of fathering play out in couples work, Wexler also effectively summarizes many of the main tenets of male-sensitive couples therapy, previously infused throughout the chapters in this volume.

We have been privileged that so many leaders in the field of couples therapy and working with men have volunteered to contribute to this book. We have asked all of them to emphasize *how* they work, illustrated with a case study, in addition to presenting the rationales behind their interventions. Additionally, readers will note that throughout the book, many of the chapter authors have addressed the issue of how the sex of the therapist affects conducting male-sensitive couples therapy. It is our hope that clinicians who work with men and their female partners will be greatly enriched by reading their insights, their case studies, and their clinical recommendations. Male-sensitive couples therapy is really just doing good therapy, but does require a particular set of clinical skills, theoretical knowledge, and therapeutic self-awareness. Our goal is that readers of this book can apply what its authors have discussed in a way that raises their clinical work to higher and more satisfying levels, integrating their prior knowledge of female-sensitive therapy with the contributions of our authors, so that couples therapy becomes a truly gender-sensitive endeavor.

REFERENCES

Addis, M. E., & Mahalik, J. R. (2003). Men, masculinity and the contexts of help seeking. *American Psychologist, 58*, 5–14.

Fitzgerald, L. F., & Nutt, R. (1986). Counseling/psychotherapy of women: Rationale and implementation. *The Counseling Psychologist, 14*, 180–216.

Gilligan, C., Rogers, A. G., & Tolman, D. L. (1991). *Women, girls & psychotherapy: Reframing resistance.* New York: Haworth Press.

Good, G., & Robertson, J. (2010). To accept a pilot? Addressing men's ambivalence and altering their expectancies about therapy. *Psychotherapy: Theory, Research & Practice, 47*, 306–315.

Gottman, J. M. (1999). *The marriage clinic: A scientifically-based marital therapy.* New York: Norton.

Gurman, A. S. (2008). A framework for the comparative study of couple therapy: History, models, and applications. In A. S. Gurman (Ed.), *Clinical handbook of couple therapy* (pp. 1–30). New York: Guilford Press.

Hartley, R. E. (1959). Sex role pressures and the socialization of the male child. *Psychological Reports, 5*, 457–468.

Hendrix, H. (1988). *Getting the love you want: A guide for couples.* New York: Harper Perennial.

Jacobson, N. S., & Christensen, A. (1996). *Acceptance and change in couple therapy: A therapist's guide to transforming relationships.* New York: Norton.

Johnson, S. M. (2004). *The practice of emotionally focused couple therapy: Creating connection* (2nd ed.). New York: Brunner-Routledge.

Kaufman, G. (1985). *Shame: The power of caring.* Rochester, VT: Schenkman Books.

Kottler, J. A., & Shepard, D. S. (2007). *Introduction to counseling: Voices from the field* (6th ed.). Belmont, CA: Thomson Brooks/Cole.

Krugman, S. (1995). Male development and the transformation of shame. In R. F. Levant & W. S. Pollack (Eds.), *A new psychology of men* (pp. 91–128). New York: Basic Books

Long, L. L., & Young, M. E. (2007). *Counseling and therapy for couples* (2nd ed.). Belmont, CA: Thomson Brooks/Cole.

Luquet, W. (2005). Introduction: A theory of relationality. In H. Hendrix, H. L. Hunt, M. Y. Hannah, & W. Luquet (Eds.), *Imago relationship therapy: Perspectives on theory* (pp. 1–10). San Francisco: Jossey-Bass.

Mack, R. N. (1989). Termination of therapy. In G. R. Weeks (Ed.), *Treating couples: The intersystem model of the marriage council of Philadelphia* (pp. 119–141). New York: Brunner/Mazel.

McGoldrick, M., Anderson, C. M., & Walsh, F. (1991). *Women in families: A framework for family therapy* New York: W. W. Norton & Co., Inc.

Osherson, S., & Krugman, S. (1990). Men, shame, and psychotherapy. *Psychotherapy, 27,* 327–339.

Pollack, W. S. (1998). *Real boys: Rescuing our sons from the myths of boyhood.* New York: Henry Holt and Company.

Rawlings, E. I., & Carter, D. K. (1977). *Psychotherapy for women: Treatment toward equality.* Springfield, IL: Charles C. Thomas Publisher.

Shay, J. J. (1996). "Okay, I'm here, but I'm not talking!" Psychotherapy with the reluctant male. *Psychotherapy, 33,* 503–513.

Shay, J. J., & Maltas, C. P. (1998). Reluctant men in couple therapy: Corralling the Marlboro man. In W. S. Pollack & R. F. Levant (Eds.), *New psychotherapy for men* (pp. 97–126). New York: Wiley.

Sperry, L., Carlson, J., & Peluso, P. R. (2006). *Couple therapy: Integrating theory and technique* (2nd ed.). Denver, CO: Love.

Worrell, J., & Remer, P. (1997). *Feminist perspectives in therapy: An empowerment model for women.* Newbury Park, CA: Sage.

Foundations of Male-Sensitive Couples Therapy

2

The Challenges of Conducting Male-Sensitive Couples Therapy
Common Pitfalls and Clinical Recommendations

DAVID S. SHEPARD AND MICHÈLE HARWAY

Couples therapy can be extremely challenging work, and a number of authors have noted the numerous clinical mistakes therapists can make, including failing to structure sessions, giving up on relationships prematurely, allowing arguments to escalate, timing interventions poorly, overcontrolling emotional expression, and accepting unfounded myths about the nature of healthy relationships (Doherty, 2002; Gottman, 1999; Weeks, Odell, & Methven, 2005; Weeks & Treat, 2001). After highlighting common therapeutic errors, these authors offer their own solutions, and in this chapter, we will follow that same sequence. Our particular focus is on where treatment can go awry when the clinician is not male sensitive. We define *male-sensitive therapy* as conceptualizing and intervening with an awareness of the particular fears, expectations, vulnerabilities, and strengths male partners bring into the treatment process. Our own thinking on male-sensitive couples therapy has been strongly influenced by the past two decades of scholarship on men and masculinity, much of it authored by researchers and theorists associated with the New Psychology of Men studies movement (Levant & Pollack, 1995). However, our thoughts are also drawn from our combined experience of over 50 years of clinical practice with couples and our long-standing efforts to bring a gender-aware perspective to our work.

Needless to say, over the course of our careers, we have made clinical errors too numerous to mention, many related to unintended insensitivity to the male partner. From our backlog of mistakes, we have identified five pitfalls we believe are the most salient for the couples therapist: failure to sustain the therapeutic alliance by inadvertently taking sides against the male partner; failure to monitor countertransference reactions against the male partner; failure to recognize male avoidance and withdrawal behaviors as symptoms of depression; failure to recognize the therapist's own internalization of traditional gender role norms; and failure to correctly assess intimate partner violence. The first four failures are related in that they are likely to stem from the clinician's lack of familiarity with current scholarship on the psychology of men and masculinity. On the other hand, we have included the need to assess for intimate partner violence (IPV) with a full appreciation that most couples therapists have received at least some training in this area. However, although both men and women can commit acts of violence toward their partner, it is still mainly men who are the perpetrators, and it is a challenge for even experienced clinicians to assess and respond effectively. We would be remiss if we did not include failure to address IPV as a critical pitfall in male-sensitive couples counseling.

CHALLENGE 1: MAINTAINING THE THERAPEUTIC ALLIANCE AND SUSTAINING BALANCE

Bordin (1994) defined the therapeutic alliance as an emotional bond between clinician and client, a connection based on trust, shared goals, and clearly defined tasks; it is a relationship that is at once conscious and collaborative. As in individual therapy, the quality of the therapeutic alliance in treating couples is critical to the outcome of treatment (Knobloch-Fedders, Pinsof, & Mann, 2007). To form and maintain that alliance, the couples therapists must maintain a position of balance in relation to both partners: The therapist interacts with both partners similarly, using empathic and challenging statements for both, demonstrates an equal commitment to understanding both, and shifts attention from one partner to the other in an ongoing process that ensures both partners stay engaged in the therapy. Additionally, the therapist conceptualizes marital distress from a perspective that avoids identifying one partner as the source of the presenting problem, instead using a systemic lens for viewing each partner's behaviors as a reaction to the other's (Garfield, 2004). What destroys the alliance is when therapists take one partner's side or are even perceived to have taken one partner's side; this outcome is most likely to occur when therapists fail to demonstrate equivalent empathy for both partners' emotions and viewpoints, challenge one partner more frequently or with more intensity than the other, and assign causality to one of the partners in their case conceptualizations.

When we look at just a few of the common reasons couples come in for therapy, it quickly becomes apparent why male partners can challenge therapists' capacity to maintain balance—it sometimes seems that men *are* the cause of the couple's problems. For example, men are unfaithful significantly more frequently than women (Kadin & Lusterman, this volume; Peluso, 2007). Men have a more difficult time containing their anger when they are physiologically aroused, and are also more likely to withdraw and stonewall in difficult conversations (Bergenstal, this volume; Gottman, 1999). Men are more likely than women to struggle with identifying, verbalizing, and disclosing vulnerable emotions, processes critical to fostering intimacy (Levant, 1995; Rabinowitz, this volume; Wexler, 2009). Men are more likely to begin therapy with ambivalence, which requires therapists to attend to their conflicted feelings and resolve any negative transference, in turn robbing the female partner of time spent on relating to her (Englar-Carlson & Shepard, 2005). We point out this list of issues men bring to the therapeutic process not to suggest men are the problem or women bear less responsibility for troubled relationships, but rather to highlight how strong the temptation is for therapists to stray from a balanced position in both their thinking and their interventions.

Therapists also have to deal with the risk of a countertransferential identification with the female client: Whether the therapist is male or female, he or she is likely to share certain values with the female client. For example, it is good to talk about relationships, express emotions, allow for dependence on others for help, verbalize emotional needs, and see intimacy as an essential prelude to sex. Thus, while therapists may be likely to agree that conceptualizing the couples' difficulty from a systemic perspective, avoiding blame, and sustaining equivalent empathy for both sexes are essential to achieving balance, doing so is no easy feat. The following vignette illustrates how these temptations can play out in a session:

Mark and Annette were in their mid-30s and had been married for 5 years, with two small children. Six months ago, Annette sought individual therapy to deal with her growing dissatisfaction with the marriage. In therapy, she realized the extent to which she had settled for a relationship with an emotionally reserved man who was unlikely to communicate on a level that satisfied her needs for closeness. Her weekly sessions gave her the opportunity to vent her frustrations without "dumping" them on Mark, but this well-intentioned strategy wasn't working, as Mark noticed her becoming increasingly irritable with him and escalating fights over petty issues. It was Mark who insisted they seek couples counseling, but Annette readily agreed.

Mark and Annette presented as intelligent, insightful people who had a palpable connection to each other. In the initial session, Annette described her frustrations with Mark in soft language; tears flowed easily as she disclosed her fears that the marriage could not survive if Mark didn't work on expressing his emotions so she would know what was going on inside of him, and hopefully, feel closer as a result. As she cried, the therapist leaned forward, softened her voice, and gently indicated she understood her pain. The therapist thought, "I like this woman; she is in touch with her deeper emotions and risks sharing them; she works hard not to be harsh toward her husband; she owns her own role in their distress by admitting she failed to demand more from him. She makes it easy for me to empathize with her. I feel like I am doing good work when I talk to her."

Mark presented as a kind man, certainly overregulated in his affect, and the first to admit he has trouble talking about his emotions. He grew up in a family environment characterized by a cordial superficiality between his parents, where the rule was people should be pleasant but avoid strong emotions. Mark quickly agreed with Annette that he needed to work on learning how to express his emotions better. With a chuckle, he said, "It won't be easy for me, you know." Annette reacted sharply to his light tone. "Mark, this is very important to me. I don't know if I can stay married if you don't do this." Mark immediately assumed a serious look on his face, though finding it difficult to make eye contact with her, and said to the therapist, "I do want to change." The therapist thought, "I like Mark, too. I'm going to enjoy helping him learn how to own his feelings and share them. This case is going to go very well."

The therapist subsequently proceeded to help Mark loosen his restricted emotionality and found numerous strategies in the literature for achieving this goal (e.g., Johnson, 2004; Rabinowitz & Cochran, 2002; Wexler, 2009). Initially, Mark positively responded to the interventions and truly got better at expressing his emotions in therapy. However, one month into the treatment, the couple reported that they had had a terrible fight, after which Mark had completely shut down emotionally, Annette was about to give up on the marriage, and the relationship was in crisis. The therapist thought, "What happened? It was going so well. Did I miss something?"

Several clinical errors events occurred in the first session that disrupted the therapeutic alliance and led to relationship deterioration: (a) The therapist's focus on Mark stirred up both resentment and an underlying shame at being labeled as the source of the problem, which he kept under wraps in sessions but eventually led him to shut down his emotions at home—his habitual strategy when faced with conflict. Mark's eager acceptance in therapy of the notion that his restricted emotions were dysfunctional represented his sincere desire to do whatever it takes to "fix" the relationship. But inwardly, this focus on his emotional life was both wounding and frightening, challenging a lifetime of socialization experiences teaching him that the expression of vulnerable feelings ran counter to the masculine ideal. (b) The therapist had challenged the partners unequally, pressuring Mark to change without confronting Annette's need to control him, a behavior that had manifested in how she defined the couple's problem in the initial session. Mark had silently watched the therapist respond soothingly to Annette's tears, observing the therapist's compassionate voice and approving head nods. The Annette he knew could be so different at home—demanding and argumentative to the point that Mark would withdraw in order to cool down his surging, adrenaline-fueled anger. (c) Finally, Mark had entered therapy fearful that a female therapist would ally with his wife, and focus on female-associated skills, which meant the strengths he brought to the relationship would be minimized. Not only were these fears realized, but the therapist failed to bring out into the open the possibility that Mark might have understandable anxieties about a female–female coalition forming against him.

Garfield (2004) recommended that in order to maintain balance and strengthen the alliance, the therapist needs to spend more energy connecting with the male partner at the beginning of therapy, while still keeping the female partner engaged. Her issues will certainly be addressed, and in future sessions given the attention they need, but the therapeutic alliance paradoxically becomes more secure when the therapist focuses on engaging the male in the first sessions. Indeed, two research studies did find that the strength of the bond between the male partner and the therapist was more important than the female–therapist alliance in predicting outcome (Bourgeois, Sabourin, & Wright, 1990; Symonds & Horvath, 2004). Nevertheless, we would modify Garfield's recommendation by suggesting that both partners need to experience balanced attention from the very beginning, but it may require additional effort to engage the male (e.g., noting his strengths, inviting him to talk about his work), especially if he has a tendency to withdraw. We have also found it useful to frame the emotional expressivity versus restrictiveness issue as processing-style differences; this approach removes the implication that the therapist values an expressive style and relieves the male partner of his fear that the therapist prefers his wife's personality over his. We might say, for example, "Annette, you tend to feel first and then think about your emotions, which is valuable in getting you guys to feel close. Mark, your style is to think first and take longer to tune in to your emotions; that's a real strength in making critical decisions in the marriage, plus, I'm guessing it's a strength for you at work. What are your thoughts about how it affects your marriage?"

When the therapist is female, it is especially important that she ask the male partner whether he has any concerns about working with a woman counselor. She can elicit a discussion of his fears, reassure him, and encourage him to give her feedback if at any time during therapy he is feeling ganged up on (Englar-Carlson & Shepard, 2005). When the therapist is a man, he can have a similar conversation with the female

partner, but also recognize that the male partner still may have anxieties about a therapist–female partner coalition, and they need to be
addressed openly. In both cases, transference issues need to be monitored: The female therapist may be perceived as the abandoning mother
and the male therapist, the competitive, even emasculating, father. The
degree to which the therapist discusses transference issues depends upon
theoretical orientation, but regardless of the model the therapist uses, it
is important that male withdrawal behaviors be recognized as possible
signs of a rupture in the therapeutic alliance and a loss of balance.

CHALLENGE 2: MONITORING COUNTERTRANSFERENCE TOWARD THE MALE PARTNER

A very different presenting problem illustrates the challenge to sustaining balance when the therapist experiences a strong negative reaction
to the husband, and a number of situations can trigger conscious or
unconscious hostility and judgment on the part of the therapist. Trust
violations and displays of aggression are obvious ones, but even more
subtle male behaviors can elicit countertransference (e.g., toward men
who persist in using an emotionally detached cognitive style despite
therapeutic encouragement to do otherwise). In the following vignette,
the therapist monitored her negative reactions and successfully finds
male-sensitive empathic language to ensure a balanced position is maintained and the alliance not damaged.

When Rod and Karla came for their first session, Karla was already
seething, ready to explode with pent-up anger. Rod was calm, congenial,
articulate. As they sat on the couch, Karla made no eye contact with
Rod and quickly pulled her hand away when Rod reached out for it. The
counselor's immediate thought was "They seem like a couple where the
husband has had an affair." Karla spoke first, explaining why they were
there: Their marriage had never recovered from an event that occurred
6 months ago. Karla's mother had died after her third bout with cancer.
The final ordeal had lasted for 2 weeks, during which time Rod, "by
choice," Karla emphasized, went road biking in Italy with a group of male
friends. The therapist felt an awareness of shock and heard herself think,
"He did what!?" Karla didn't know which hurt more: her mother's death
or Rod's leaving her alone when he was fully aware her mother might die
at any moment. "So Karla, you felt abandoned that Rod was away during this terrible time for you, and you still are hurting." (Empathizing
with Karla while being careful to word it as Karla's experience rather
than Rod's actual abandonment.) Karla's eyes welled with tears as she
nodded. Rod interjected forcefully, pleading for understanding from the
counselor. "You've got to understand. I'm a very responsible guy. I made
sure her mother had the best possible care. I invited Karla's sister to stay
in our house. And I'd been training for this trip for two years. It would

have made no difference if I'd have stayed home, but it would have been terrible if I missed out on this once-in-a-lifetime opportunity." The counselor thought, "Is he incredibly narcissistic, or just clueless about how he hurt her?" What she said is, "Rod, it makes complete sense to you that you would go on the trip. (Letting Rod know she recognizes that Rod thought this through and made a rational choice, implying appreciation for how Rod thinks; also, immediately making it clear she was not judging him or taking Karla's side.) It was really important to you—probably something you'd been dreaming about for years (empathizing with Rod's value system and making contact with Rod's deeper yearnings)—and you stepped up by make sure her mother got good care at the end." (Using a sports metaphor associated with courageous male behavior; making positive use of a maternal transference by praising him.) Rod's shoulders relaxed in relief, but Karla was in shock hearing the counselor say this. "And Karla, you're still stunned—it's like, how come he doesn't understand why you feel so betrayed." (Immediately reestablishing an empathic connection with Karla, using words that reflect the intensity of her emotional experience.)

The art of staying balanced in couples work in general is a kind of dance, where "the therapist needs to be able to move freely back and forth between members of the couple, always attending to the invitations to join one against the other" (Rait, 2000, p. 214). The case of Rod and Karla demonstrates how the art of maintaining a therapeutic alliance in male-sensitive couples therapy is staying equally empathic to both partners when the man is pushing the therapist's buttons.

CHALLENGE 3: ASSESSING FOR MALE DEPRESSION

For over 20 years, a number of researchers in men and masculinity have speculated that many men with a subclinical level of depression either hide or act out their symptoms in such a way that intimate partners, friends, and even health professionals, do not recognize that these men are depressed (Cochran & Rabinowitz, 2000; Rabinowitz & Cochran, 2008; Shepard, 2002). The notion is that men may mask their depression because overt expressions of sadness and emotional pain conflict with such traditional male role norms as stoicism, strength, and self-reliance (Pollack, 1998). Whether deliberately or unconsciously hidden, the depression does manifest itself in a number of forms, including irritability, expressions of anger, and increased interpersonal conflict; self-medication through alcohol or substance use; and withdrawal from partners and other close connections (Rabinowitz & Cochran, 2008).

The construct of a masked or hidden depression has been difficult to prove empirically (Addis, 2008). Nevertheless, we have found it to be heuristically invaluable in our work with couples, helping us distinguish between couples' distress rooted in repetitive negative interactional sequences or dysfunctional communication processes, and distress actually caused by the depression of the male partner. What makes correct assessment especially challenging is that depression can lead to these other, typical problematic couple interactions, and we suspect many couples therapists may find themselves treating these derivative symptoms rather than the true problem. The following brief vignette illustrates why masked depression is easy to miss.

Kate and Roger are a couple in their late 20s, married 5 years with a satisfying relationship for most of that time. When their first child was born 6 months ago, Kate expected Roger to take care of more of the household chores so she could concentrate on attending to the baby's needs. Instead, Roger spent increasing time glued to his computer, spending hours on stock trading sites, and significantly less time engaged in the kind of meaningful, close conversations the two of them had previously enjoyed. Kate found herself becoming a nag, constantly pointing out to her husband that chores needed to be done; Roger would initially complain about her nagging, and then withdraw into his home office, leaving Kate increasingly frustrated, angry, and exhausted taking care of both baby and house. As for sex, it stopped completely.

Therapists treating this couple and not appreciating the role of depression might attend to the pursue–withdraw cycle, perhaps reframing Kate's nagging as an "abandonment protest" (Greenman, Faller & Johnson, this volume; Johnson, 2004) or Roger's withdrawal as "stone-walling" (Bergenstal, this volume; Gottman, 1999). They might facilitate improved communication skills, so both partners can articulate their frustrations and truly hear their partner. They might address the challenge to homeostasis triggered by the new baby, and help the couple negotiate new rules in their system. What they might *not* do is understand that Roger is depressed; he had yearned to be a father, but watching Kate's intuitive mothering skills left him feeling useless and incompetent. Roger had managed for years to submerge doubts about his competence and value as a man, and when his hopes that fathering would eliminate those fears were dashed, the result was an emotional crash—a depression that manifested as withdrawal; workaholism; loss of sexual desire; and a gradual, painful "shutting down."

The pattern of male withdrawal accompanied by female pursuit via complaining is obviously an insufficient basis for assessing for male depression, let alone diagnosing it; it is hard to think of couples who do not feature this sequence to some degree. We have learned instead to be alert to additional evidence that may enable us to conceptualize that male depression is playing a central role in the couple's distress. These include the following:

- Physical expressions of shame (e.g., frequent turning away from the partner and looking down)
- Narcissistic vulnerability (a proneness to anger despite the fact that the partner's criticisms are mild or delivered softly)
- Self-critical comments that have a harsh, punishing quality

- Evidence of self-medication
- A withdrawal that seems more like hiding from the partner than normal attempts at increasing relationship distance
- A personality style characterized by marked cynicism, bitterness, and pessimism
- Unusual difficulty for us as therapists to facilitate the man's engagement with his partner

Once we have assessed that depression exists, the challenge becomes how to address it in treatment. To be sure, there are a number of mine-fields: if we raise the issue of depression, the man may hear us as saying, he is "the problem"; labeling him risks a rupture in the therapeutic alliance and unbalancing our relationship with the couple; we may indeed find ourselves over-focusing on the male partner in our treatment interventions, which may increase his self-blame and shame; we may be sending the message that the female partner no longer needs to examine her role in the couples' struggles.

When we bring up the possibility that the male partner is depressed, rather than present a diagnosis, we try to do so in a way that engages both partners' curiosity and desire for information, at the same time making it clear that we are open to being wrong in our assessment. The conversation might go like this:

> Roger, I'm just wondering. Do you see yourself as depressed? (Immediately assesses client's level of self-awareness.) OK. Let me just share some research findings with the both of you. (Engages partners' curiosity; minimizes defensiveness.) Roger, please tell me if any of this fits, or if it doesn't. (Empowers client to refute the therapist). Kate, I'd like to hear your thoughts as well. (Ensures female partner stays engaged and potentially adds valuable information to therapists' assessment.) Researchers have found that a lot of guys who know they are stressed, don't feel like being with people as much, and are just having a hard time enjoying life the way they used to may actually be experiencing a depression. You don't have to be miserable, crying all the time, and feeling suicidal to be depressed. There are other ways people can be depressed and not even realize it. (Presents concrete information; normalizes male partner's lack of awareness regarding his depression.) This is especially true for men, because they are taught since elementary school that it's not cool to feel sad or afraid. I'm guessing, Roger, that you learned pretty quickly that men don't say, "Hey, guys. I'm feeling pretty sad right now. I need some help. Let's talk." (Uses humor and exaggeration to engage male partner in discussion of painful material.) Roger, I'm wondering if you could explain to Kate how you learned to hide feelings? (Initiates dialogue with man leading conversation; facilitates male partner's self-exploration.)

The desired outcome is that the male partner becomes increasingly intrigued by his own experiences and wants to talk about them with his female partner. She, in turn, develops empathy and compassion for the male partner, as well as greater insight into his life narrative. She also feels relieved, because her intuitive sense that her partner was unhappy has now been validated. At this point, the therapist needs to add, "I want to make it clear that I don't see Roger's depression as the problem here—it's just a factor. Both of you play a role in the negative cycle that's been so hard for you to break. But it's an important factor, and we can do something about it."

CHALLENGE 4: RECOGNIZING ONE'S OWN GENDER ROLE SOCIALIZATION

There is an abundance of literature that a man's or woman's rigid adherence to a stereotypical definition of masculinity and femininity can have deleterious consequences on the person's mental and physical health (Wexler, 2009). Moreover, even as men and women increasingly experiment with behaving in ways that conflict with traditional norms, there is evidence they will encounter social and economic penalties (Moss-Racusin, Phelan, & Rudman, 2010). It is probably safe to suggest that most couples therapists, even if not aware of the research, recognize the negative impact inflexible adherence to gender role norms has on clients' lives, for themselves and their partners.

Nevertheless, whether we are female or male, we have all learned the classic hallmarks of the male role—stoicism, dominance over others, aggressiveness and bravado, and avoidance of the tender emotions associated with femininity (David & Brannon, 1976). When male partners deviate from these norms, we need to be careful to monitor our own cognitive and emotional reactions, appreciating the risk of forming negative judgments that stem from our own socialization experiences. Assuming we are free from those judgments can lead to clinical errors.

For couples therapists, perhaps the most damaging stereotype when it comes to conducting male-sensitive therapy is that men are hardwired to have limited abilities in sustaining committed intimate relationships, requiring more autonomy than connection. John Gray's "Mars–Venus" books have been popular since they first appeared in the 1990s, and have promulgated the message that men are fundamentally different than women when it comes to relationships (e.g., Gray, 1992). Although these books may have played a helpful role for some couples in facilitating acceptance of each other's differences, they also may be spreading notions largely unsupported by empirical research (Heesacker, Tiegs, Lawrence, Smith, Cawood, & Mejia-Millan, 2006). At the same time, evolutionary psychology theories on sex differences have argued that men are hardwired to seek multiple sex partners while women strive for committed relationships—both in the interest of passing on their genes (Buss & Schmitt, 1993).

While psychological sex differences certainly do exist, we would argue that the couples therapist who believes that men do not desire closeness as much as women do are both buying into stereotypes and confusing the idea of *innate tendencies* with *inability due to gender-role learning experiences*. In other words, we believe men not only desire closeness as much as women, but are equally capable of talking about their desires when the therapist helps them to do so. True, some men prefer to avoid analyzing issues of closeness and distance in a partnership, but it is because they do not feel competent at it and are trying to avoid the shame of failing at it, not because they are incapable of articulating their needs (Shepard, 2005). The clinician sensitive to any of these constraints can assist the male partner in finding the courage to express his most profound and deepest feelings and yearnings regarding connection to his partner.

The particular pitfall inherent to seeing men through the prism of stereotype is that the therapist may unwittingly act out, via lost opportunities for empathy, judgmental confrontations, or loss of objectivity, his or her negative reactions toward the man when he behaves in atypical gender role fashion. The following vignette illustrates what happens when a therapist (in this case, a male) deals with a situation in which the female partner has become the primary breadwinner, a dynamic occurring with increasing frequency in this era of two-income families and stressful economic conditions. It also demonstrates how male shame can trigger strong reactions on the part of the therapist.

Jason was a self-employed computer consultant whose business had fallen off dramatically in the last year. On the other hand, Erin's career as an executive coach was taking off, helped by her outgoing personality, work ethic, and strong organizational skills. In their late 30s with two children, they had been fighting continuously for months, almost always over money issues, and sought counseling to improve their "communication skills."

Both partners agreed that they were caught in a repetitive cycle where Erin would accuse Jason of not doing everything possible to earn more, and Jason would defend himself. The therapist watched them play out this pattern in the second session. Erin, her voice calm and firm, said to Jason, "Look, honey, I'll help you develop a business plan. I want you to succeed. But you've got to get yourself out there—you've got to call people every day. You've got to do the legwork." The therapist thought, "She's making a reasonable request and she's being supportive." Jason snapped back with unexpected anger, "Nothing I ever do is good enough for you. Just get off my back." The therapist thought, "He's highly reactive. She wasn't accusing him of anything. I need to monitor his narcissistic vulnerability."

Before the therapist could respond, Erin jumped in, this time with steel in her voice. "Jason, you've got take a hard look at yourself. You're not pulling your own weight. You've just got to man up." The therapist thought, "That was delivered too harshly, but she's not wrong." He observed Jason withering, wrapping himself into the couch. "Just back off, Erin, really—just leave me alone … for chrissake, what would you like me to do? You want me to get a job at Staples? Fine. I'll call them in the morning." The therapist thought, "I feel something weak about him, too. I can't put my finger on why, but I'm not liking him right now. I need to be careful in what I say and focus on the system, rather than on him." The therapist said to both of them, "Here's what I see. Erin, you demand that Jason be strong, and Jason, you react by pulling away, and Erin feels unheard and even more angry. That's the system you're stuck in. Jason, I'm wondering if we can change this pattern if you actually stand up to her. Tell her how she makes you feel, right now."

Jason looked in horror at the therapist. He stood up to his full height and paced before the therapist, muttering "I can't believe this is happening." The therapist thought, "He's trying to intimidate me, and I'm losing control of the session." "Jason," the therapist said, "I want to help the two of you, but you've got to sit down." He complied. "OK, OK, I'm sitting. But here's what you've got to know. You know how it feels to make less money than her? I can you tell you—it sucks! But I'm still there for her in every possible way. I have dinner ready when she comes home. I listen to her vent about her tough day. I'm there for the kids 24/7. I'm doing all of that and I'm trying to make more money, goddamit, but have you looked at the economy lately?" Erin stepped in, more softly this time: "Jason, all of that is true. You have been wonderful. I just feel ... I just feel so untaken care of." The therapist was now feeling completely ungrounded. "She's right, he's right, I'm confused ..."

Everyone in this vignette—clients and therapist—was caught up in a conflict-riddled web of emotions arising out of the couple's shifting gender roles. Erin was in the midst of a tug-of-war between the part of her committed to her career and another part that yearned to be taken care of in the more traditional feminine role learned throughout childhood and adolescence. Through that same socialization process, she had internalized the belief that men are supposed to be strong and the main provider, and when Jason failed at this, she inevitably judged him as weak. Underlying this judgment was a self-condemning voice in her head, saying, "What's wrong with me! I married a weak man."

Jason, of course, had internalized the same values and in his darker moments, thought of himself as weak. He struggled to maintain self-regard in the relationship by defending himself and fighting with her. The therapist was confused, because he (and it would be the same with a female therapist) also had internalized these gender role norms, and sensed his own condemnation of Jason, even as his "clinical superego" warned him against it. Ironically, neither Erin nor the therapist was entirely wrong. Jason may very well be weak, not as they have framed it with its pejorative gender role connotations, but in a psychological sense: shame, stress, discouragement, disappointment in himself, and the knowledge that he has disappointed his wife have sapped his emotional resources, leaving him drained of confidence and energy.

The therapist had in this moment lost his ability to decenter, the capacity to step back from his emotional reactions toward his clients and instead think about what the clients are feeling (Basch, 1988).

The same socially constructed definitions of masculinity and femininity constraining both partners' capacities for seeing their way outside
of their distress were also handcuffing the therapist. Moreover, his
countertransference reactions to male shame were playing a role, as his
instinctive negative reaction to Jason stirred up his internal struggle to
maintain objectivity.

The challenge this therapist was trying to deal with is one we experience frequently when our male clients' failure to embody traditional
masculinity leads to shame. We sense the male partner's desperation,
and summon our compassion and empathy, yet find it eludes us; there
is something about him we just don't like. While trying not to ally with
the female partner as we hear her blame and criticize, another voice
within us identifies with her frustration. As a result, we risk not seeing
and responding to his pain in not living up to male role norms. We miss
sensing, for example, his feelings of inadequacy and the expectation
that his partner judges him. We miss noticing the feelings of failure and
shame (in Jason's case, the failure of his career aspirations and shame
at not taking care of his family as a "man" should). We miss observing
how disconnected the man feels from his wife, retreating from her, or
pushing her away with aggressiveness as he tries to reassert his masculinity and shore up his weakened self (as Jason did when he stood up and
paced). Finally, we miss the chance to validate the courage and strength
it can take for some men to behave in nontraditional ways.

In addition to monitoring our personal emotional responses to a man
who deviates from role norms, we have found several interventions that
have helped us in situations such as the one the therapist experienced
with Erin and Jason. First, we may introduce the concept of gender role
socialization, and invite both partners to explore how they learned in
childhood and adolescence what it means to be male and female. This
step immediately shifts the focus out of a tense, blame-withdrawal pattern and into safer ground. Moreover, bringing in the experiences of
the male and female partner ensures balance and increases opportunities for reciprocal empathy. We may self-disclose our own experiences here, as a way of facilitating the conversation and sending the
message that no one is immune from these powerful developmental
forces. Second, we invite the couple to explore the costs on both their
relationship and psychological well-being of adhering to or deviating
from traditional norms.

Third, we use this discussion as an opportunity to help the male client verbalize emotions, especially when he is the kind of man who has
difficulty with identifying or expressing affect. Discussions of socialization experiences, rather than remaining sterile intellectual exercises,
can be used as a safe format for the male to describe intensely painful
experiences. When he talks about hurtful moments (e.g., failures in
sports, rejections by a girl, humiliation by a male authority figure), we
help him focus on his emotional reactions, and if given the opportunity,
introduce the concept of shame.

Therapist: Jason, can you sit with that feeling for a moment longer? What's going on inside you as you talk about that memory of trying to ask a girl to go out with you and getting turned down? (*Helping Jason focus on the emotional experience in the present.*)

Jason: I really was pretty scared when I called that girl. It's weird, isn't it, how when you're 14, girls can have such power over you?

(*The therapist brings the focus back to his emotion.*)

Therapist: Jason, stay with that feeling of fear when you dialed the phone till you can start to touch it again. Now, tell me where in your body you are experiencing it. What's going on for you?

Jason: I can remember what it was like when I hung up the phone as soon as I heard her voice. I'm feeling it again right now—in my gut—all the air going out of it.

(*The therapist uses this opportunity to explain to both partners that the emotion being described is shame.*)

Therapist: The word for that feeling is, shame, and so now when you feel it again, you'll know that's what's going on. Erin, do you know what that feeling is like? (*Reengaging the female partner and facilitating a connection between them as Jason reexperiences shame.*)

Erin (softly): Do I ever. (*She grabs his hand and holds it, strengthening the connection and implicitly letting him know shame is tolerable when you verbalize it with your partner.*)

The tendency for therapists to have a visceral negative reaction to a man's experience of shame in part may derive from therapists' disowning of or disgust with their own shame. Observing "weakness" in a male partner can activate within us an association first, with his shame, then with our own. By appreciating this process within ourselves, we gain a greater empathy for both the male client and his wife or female partner, who may be undergoing a negative reaction to the male similar to our own. We are then in a position to facilitate an empathic connection between man and woman, where the man has the novel experience of having his shame seen and not judged by his partner—a moment that might help heal wounds from his own male socialization humiliations, but just as importantly, help to heal the wounds in the relationship.

CHALLENGE 5: ASSESSING FOR DOMESTIC VIOLENCE

One of the most challenging aspects of working with couples is that interpersonal violence may be present in the relationship and not made known to the therapist. Since the majority of cases involving intimate partner violence (IPV) include a male perpetrator and a female recipient of the violence, it seems an important topic to include here. The failure to assess for IPV in all couples presenting for therapy constitutes a large pitfall in our clinical work that may have disastrous consequences. Assessment for IPV specifically is critical because couples who are experiencing violence in their relationships are unlikely to volunteer this information and thus the couples therapist must do an appropriate assessment to rule out partner violence. Couples therapists do not always do this

At the same time, couples for whom violence is an aspect of their relationship often do not report this at intake (Ehrensaft & Vivian, 1996). For one, couples experiencing violence do not see it as an issue of concern, as they might see their problematic or nonexistent communication, their sexual issues or even the infidelity, which may have been the incentive for seeking therapy. The violence, which is usually intermittent in its occurrence, is seen as secondary to the other issues and not the root cause of the couple's difficulties nor of particular importance to resolving the couple's difficulties. As a consequence, some couples may not even think to mention that this is an issue with which they struggle. Other couples may not mention the violence because of the shame that its admission elicits: the perpetrator (usually but not always the man) feels deep shame at having beaten his partner, the recipient (who often takes responsibility for eliciting the violence because she has been told that it is her fault) experiences shame for being in that predicament. Moreover, the recipient of the violence, wisely, may not mention the violence since doing so would violate a sometimes unspoken rule that it is to be kept secret and would potentially expose her to renewed beatings.

If the couple does not mention the violence to the couples therapist, then how is the therapist going to find out about the violence? This is where doing a proper assessment to rule out partner violence is important to do in any instance involving couples no matter what they describe as the issue that brings them into therapy. Asking a question directly about physical violence is not likely to yield information about the existence of underlying violence and consequently is not going to rule out its nonexistence. Instead, the properly trained clinician will screen all couples for partner violence using a systematic process such as we demonstrate in the following vignette:

Tony and his wife, Susan, were referred to a therapist for couples therapy because they were having some serious communication problems and were in considerable distress. As is usually the case, the wife called to set up the first appointment. The therapist asked her to describe the issues that brought them to therapy and while she indicated that they were communicating with great difficulty, she emphasized that both she and Tony were eager to get some help. Although IPV had not been mentioned on the phone, because of the high incidence of this issue with couples seeking therapy, the therapist, well trained in IPV assessment, wanted to set up appropriate expectations for the first session. Therefore, she described the intake process she takes with all couples presenting for couples therapy and describing difficult communications. The reason for using this process with all couples is because of the incidence of abusiveness in couples and the fact that couples do not volunteer to the therapist information about IPV (if there is any). Failing to do a thorough assessment at intake ruling out the possibility of IPV may result in the therapist treating a couple for a simple communication issue when something more complicated and more dangerous may underlie the case.

As a consequence, the therapist described her intake process during the initial phone call. She told Tony and Susan that her intakes with couples consist of four parts: an initial brief segment with the two of them together, a few minutes spent alone with Susan, a similar time alone with Tony, and then a final few minutes to make recommendations for the treatment.

When Susan and Tony arrived for their intake session, the therapist assessed whether Susan appeared to be afraid of Tony or seemed to be doing things to avoid angering him. Since in most cases, the root of IPV is control, the therapist examined whether she is feeling controlled by Tony; she listened for complaints of jealousy, especially those that seem exaggerated; she paid attention to whether there is a pattern where Tony seems to always focus on what Susan has done wrong (victims usually blame themselves); she assessed whether the couple or Susan seem isolated from family and other social support; and she evaluated whether Tony seems to want to be right at any cost. All of these would suggest that this may be an abusive relationship.

With these pieces of information about the couple's interaction style, the therapist proceeded to the next part of the intake, which involves spending a few minutes alone with Susan. As the possibly abused one, she was more likely to disclose incidents of violence if they exist. Then armed with that information, the therapist could speak with Tony with the goal of getting him to admit to abuse. The specific procedure she uses entails asking a series of more and more specific questions about how the couple handles disagreements with the same questions being asked of both, in a sequence described in Harway and Hansen (2004). It uses the *freeze-frame procedure* in which the therapist asks Susan to describe in great detail how a disagreement has been dealt with.

Therapist: I asked Tony to describe how the two of you have talked about the problem he sees with the children and he didn't seem to want to talk about that. Can you think back to a recent time when the two of you discussed this issue?

Susan: Well, last Tuesday, Tony came home from work and yelled at the children. Then he turned to me and told me what a lousy mother I am that I can't control the children. We had a big argument over this but we made up the next day.

Therapist: Hold on a second, this is going too fast for me. I'd like to go back over each piece of what happened and go really slowly so

I can understand what happened. So Tony walked in the door. What did he say when he first got home? (*Susan responds that he yelled at the children.*) What specifically did he say? Where were you when that happened? What if anything did you say to him? And then what did he say or do? (*Susan responds to each of these questions.*) What did you say in response to that? What happened next? And so what did you say or do then? What did Tony say or do?

The purpose of each of these questions is to break down the interactions in a freeze frame way, freezing each interaction as one might slowly freeze each frame of a movie so as to better understand the details of each scene. Doing so allows the therapist to discern whether any violence may have occurred during the interaction, a detail that often gets glossed over in the client's initial description of the situation. Note that in Susan's original description, one gets very little information about the argument itself or the specific behaviors or words of either Tony or Susan.

A little later in the intake if the freeze frame has not yielded information about any violent interactions.

Therapist: I know this is probably difficult for you, but I wonder whether during the argument you described in some detail just now Tony ever pushed or shoved you? (*Followed by a long list of other physically abusive behaviors, for example, slapping, kicking. The long list is important because there is evidence that some of those behaviors may not be construed as battering or even abuse if a more general question were to be asked.*)

After Susan answers the question, the therapist may also ask whether Susan has ever felt afraid as fear is the single best indicator that abuse is a factor. At the end of her time with Susan the therapist should have a fairly clear idea of whether violence is an issue in this relationship. If it is, she must provide Susan on the spot with information as to how she can get some help. If Susan has indicated any existing violence, the therapist is better prepared to ask Tony similar questions, allowing her to be even more persistent with him than she might otherwise be. It will be important to have him own some aspect of the abuse, even if he underplays its significance or intensity. If he discloses that information, the therapist can then make a recommendation for treatment of the domestic violence. She would do so rather than focus on a couple's communication issue as this may not be the central issue at all.

Therapist: I'd like to go over with you the argument you and Susan had over the problem with the children.

Tony: There really was no issue. We discussed it a little, disagreed, and then we moved on.

Therapist: Tony, I'd like to be a fly on the wall and get a sense of what each of you said and did, in detail. So, tell me more slowly now, what happened?

Tony: When I got home from work last Tuesday, the children were out of control. I told Susan that I was tired and that it was her job to control them.

Therapist: What did she say or do? (*As Tony responds to this, the therapist uses the freeze-frame approach previously discussed asking about individual interactions and words. She gets to the heart of the argument.*) ... So what did you do next when she said that to you?

Tony: I called her a bitch!

Therapist: So, then what happened?

Tony: She didn't like it.

Therapist: How do you know that?

Tony: Because she started to cry.

Therapist: So what did you do next ...?

Tony: I was pretty upset ...

Therapist: Yes?

Tony: Just that, I was upset.

Therapist: So what did you do?

Tony: I don't know ... I was upset.

Therapist: Is it possible that you may have pushed her a little?

Tony: Is that what she told you?

Therapist: I'm really interested in your view of what happened here.

Tony: Well, I may have pushed her a little ... but I didn't hurt her. She stormed out of the room and went to make dinner.

This admission on Tony's part is important as the therapist cannot acknowledge that she has gotten any information from Susan about abuse without further endangering her.

Also while some would disagree, most clinicians would concur that doing couples therapy when domestic violence is a factor is not indicated. Most would recommend that the perpetrator be referred to some type of batterer's treatment group and that the abuse recipient should get therapeutic support during this time.

During the final phase of the intake, the therapist presents the couple with the results of her inquiry. If violence has emerged during intake and she has been successful in getting Tony to admit to having used it, the following may ensue.

Therapist: Tony, you told me that when you and Susan had that disagreement last week, you got pretty upset and pushed her a little. Right?

Tony: Well, it really wasn't much of a push, but I guess so.

Therapist: Given that and also the fact that you, Susan, told me about some of your issues which are impeding the progress of this marriage, I would like to recommend that we put off working on the issues that you have as a couple and first deal with these individual issues. So, Tony, I am going to refer you to a group that a colleague of mine does for men who have issues similar to yours. (*The therapist never mentions abuse or battering by name.*) And, Susan, you should probably consider individual counseling. I can provide you with some names of therapists. At the appropriate time, we may then want to take up the issue of couples counseling again.

Tony: Hold on a second … what's this group you want to send me to?

Therapist: Most of the men in the group are in difficult relationships and they are having a hard time getting what they want in the relationship without getting really angry. The group is focused on helping them develop a better and safer relationship. (*The therapist reframes treatment for anger/abuse as increasing relationship skills, making it easier for Tony to embrace the idea of individual treatment.*)

Tony: Is it one of those anger management groups?

Therapist: I think of the group as more of a relationship building one although learning to control anger may be a piece of what is covered there. It's difficult to have a good relationship if one person is angry all of the time.

Tony: I'm not one of those out-of-control angry guys!

Therapist: I know that Tony. I also know that you love Susan and want your relationship to work. (*The therapist avoids confronting Tony or demonstrating judgment; instead, the therapist appeals to his aspirations for a better relationship.*) I think this group could help you a great deal. I hope you will seriously consider it. (*The therapist's phrasing avoids commanding Tony, which would challenge his masculinity and need for control; instead, the therapist uses the word "hope," which leaves the choice up to him.*)

The therapist was able to reduce Tony's defensiveness because she was able to understand the roots of abusive behavior for men. Abusive men were often shamed as children (Dutton, 1995) or feared losing their parents' love. Like most men, they were socialized from an early age to ignore or avoid feelings, especially those related to painful experiences. As adults in intimate relationships, abusive men may experience the cycle of feeling avoidance (Harway & Evans, 1996, p. 363). This cycle suggests that when a difficult interaction occurs between an abusive man and his partner, he may unconsciously interpret the partner's behavior as a rejection, may fear losing her love and simultaneously deflect the feelings, using abusiveness as a way of essentially "self-medicating" against the painful underlying feelings.

In a great majority of cases, referrals to individual treatment—psychotherapy for the female and group work for the male—do not result in the couple getting the help they need. Tony may, in fact, leave the therapist's office muttering about that therapist's incompetence and determined to find a "better" couples therapist who may help with their communication issues. They are likely to find someone who will not assess for the violence and treat their communication problem instead. That is why it is important to ensure that all therapists are adequately trained in this area. If violence does not seem to be present with the couple, then the therapist can proceed with doing more standard couples work focusing on their communication problems.

CONCLUDING THOUGHTS

This chapter has reflected five very different pitfalls in engaging men in couples therapy. Although suggestions for how to deal with these pitfalls have varied, there are two common themes we would like to highlight: the importance of the use of language and the existence of shame as an underlying mechanism in many couples presentations.

Use of language. The first theme underscores the need to carefully use language in dealing with the men in the therapy room, in particular, language that avoids shaming, highlights strengths, and presumes the male partner yearns for closeness as much as his female partner does. The therapist treating Mark failed to appreciate how talking about his emotional inexpressiveness made him feel isolated in the therapy room and judged by his therapist, leading him to eventually shut down. Rod's therapist was more agile with language and, in spite of her own countertransference, was able to attend to his needs for understanding his choices and to use sports metaphors and other male-oriented language to join with him. Roger's therapist, after identifying his masked depression, presented research findings to the couple, appealing to his intellectual curiosity instead of labeling him as depressed. With Jason, the therapist's countertransference around gender issues muddied the waters and prevented him from seeing his male client's shame and desperation. However, talking about gender role socialization and costs of adhering to traditional gender norms provided a safe holding environment in which Jason could start to open up. Finally, Tony's therapist's careful use of language to avoid shaming him about his fears of abandonment (which underlie his abusive behaviors) were the key to get him the treatment referral he needed.

Shame. One thread that ties together much of what will be presented in the chapters to come is the important role that shame has in many of the issues with which men present for couples therapy. Helping the female partner to avoid shaming the male partner thus becomes one goal of the therapy; a second goal is to ensure that neither the woman nor the therapist contributes to shaming the male member of the couple during the treatment process. Shame underlies a wide range of issues that male clients bring into therapy, starting with the feeling of incompetence many of them feel in relation to doing the work of therapy, to the incompetence they may feel in relating to their partners. Other examples of shame were portrayed in many of the cases presented in this chapter. The cases include that of Mark whose shame was oriented around his feeling that "his restricted emotions were dysfunctional (and that) this focus on his emotional life was both wounding and frightening." Roger's shame was directed at his inability to instinctively know how to father his newborn. Jason was a man whose self-perceived failure to fulfill the male role of provider for his family (and his wife's endorsement of the same) brought him great shame. Not least was Tony's shame about his fears of abandonment, which underlie his abusive behaviors.

Although this chapter focused on the challenges of working with men, our goal is not to make the couples therapist feel that men present a host of minefields that require extraordinary sensitivity to avoid. Indeed, if anything, the opposite is true: when the clinician can sustain a strong therapeutic relationship, he or she earns the latitude to make the inevitable mistakes that are inherent to our profession and afford us the opportunity to model the elements of all successful relationships: acknowledging mistakes, listening even harder, connecting through successful empathy, and continually demonstrating a generous curiosity about the complex individual sitting across from us.

REFERENCES

Addis, M. (2008). Gender and depression in men. *Clinical Psychology: Science and Practice, 15*, 153–168.

Basch, M. F. (1988). *Understanding psychotherapy: The science behind the art*. New York: Basic Books.

Bordin, E. S. (1994). Theory and research on the therapeutic working alliance: New directions. In A. O. Horvath & L. S. Greenberg (Eds.), *The working alliance: Theory, research and practice* (pp. 13–37). New York: Wiley.

Bourgeois, L., Sabourin, S., & Wright, J. (1990). Predictive validity of therapeutic alliance in group marital therapy. *Journal of Consulting and Clinical Psychology, 58*, 608–613.

Buss, D. M., & Schmitt, D. P. (1993). Sexual strategies theory: An evolutionary perspective on human mating. *Psychological Review, 100*(2), 204–232.

Cochran, S. V., & Rabinowitz, F. E. (2000). *Men and depression: Clinical and empirical perspectives*. San Diego, CA: Academic Press.

David, D. S., & Brannon, R. (1976). *The forty-nine percent majority: The male sex role*. Reading, MA: Addison-Wesley.

Doherty, W. J. (2002, Nov/Dec). Bad couples therapy: Getting past the myth of therapist neutrality. *Psychotherapy Networker*, pp. 26–33.

Dutton, D. G. (1995). *The batterer: A psychological profile*. New York: Harper Collins.

Ehrensaft, M. K., & Vivian, D. (1996). Spouses' reasons for not reporting existing marital aggression as a marital problem. *Journal of Family Psychology, 10*(4), 443–453.

Englar-Carlson, M., & Shepard, D. S. (2005). Engaging men in couples coun-
    seling: Strategies for overcoming ambivalence and inexpressiveness. *The
    Family Journal, 13*, 383–391.
Garfield, R. (2004). The therapeutic alliance in couples therapy: Clinical consid-
    erations. *Family Process, 43*, 457–465.
Gottman, J. M. (1999). *The marriage clinic: A scientifically based marital therapy.*
    New York: W.W. Norton & Company.
Gray, J. (1992). *Men are from Mars, women are from Venus.* New York: Harper-
    Collins.
Harway, M., & Evans, K. (1996). Working in groups with men who batter. In
    M. Andronica (Ed.), *Men in groups: Insights, interventions, and psychoedu-
    cational work* (pp. 357–375). Washington, DC: American Psychological
    Association.
Harway, M., & Hansen, M. (2004). *Spouse abuse: Assessing and treating battered
    women, batterers, and their children* (2nd ed.) Sarasota, FL: Professional
    Resource Press.
Heesacker, M. Tiegs, T. J., Lawrence, A. W. Jr., Smith, M. B., Cawood, R. L., &
    Mejia-Millan, C. M. (2006). *Was Donna Julia right? An analysis of the mag-
    nitude and stability of sex differences in romantic relationships.* Department of
    Psychology, University of Florida, Gainesville, FL.
Johnson, S. M. (2004). *The practice of emotionally focused couple therapy* (2nd ed.).
    New York: Brunner-Routledge.
Knobloch-Feddrs, L. M., Pinsof, W. M., & Mann, B. J. (2007). Therapeutic alliance
    and treatment progress in couple therapy. *Journal of Marital and Family
    Therapy, 33*, 245–257.
Levant, R. F. (1995). Toward the reconstruction of masculinity. In R. F. Levant
    & W. S. Pollack (Eds.), *A new psychology of men* (pp. 229–251). New York:
    Basic Books.
Levant, R. F., & Pollack, W. S. (Eds.) (1995). *A new psychology of men.* New York:
    Basic Books.
Moss-Racusin, C., Phelan, J., & Rudman, L. (2010). When men break the gender
    rules: Status incongruity and backlash against modest men. *Psychology of
    Men & Masculinity, 11*, 140–151.
Peluso, P. R. (2007). Infidelity: Introduction and overview. In P. R. Peluso (Ed.),
    Infidelity: A practitioner's guide to working with couples in crisis (pp. 1–10).
    New York: Routledge.
Pollack, W. S. (1998). Mourning, melancholia, and masculinity: Recognizing and
    treating depression in men. In W. S. Pollack & R. F. Levant, *New psycho-
    therapy for men* (pp. 147–166). New York: Wiley.
Rabinowitz, F. E., & Cochran, S. V. (2002). *Deepening psychotherapy with men.*
    Washington, DC: American Psychological Association.
Rabinowitz, F. E., & Cochran, S. V. (2008). Men and therapy: A case of masked
    male depression. *Clinical Case Studies, 7*, 575–585.
Rait, D.S. (2000). The therapeutic alliance in couples and family therapy. *JCLP/
    In Session: Psychotherapy in Practice, 54*, 211–224.
Shepard, D. (2002). A negative state of mind: Patterns of depressive symptoms
    among men with high gender role conflict. *Psychology of Men & Masculinity,
    3*, 3–8.

Shepard, D. S. (2005). Male development and the journey towards discon-
    nection. In D. L. Comstock (Ed.), *Diversity in development: Critical con-
    texts that shape our lives and relationships* (pp. 133–160). Belmont, CA:
    Thomson Brooks/Cole.
Symonds, D., & Horvath, A. O. (2004). Optimizing the alliance in couple therapy.
    Family Process, 43, 443–455.
Weeks, G. R., Odell, M., & Methven, S. (2005). *If only I had known ... Avoiding
    common mistakes in couples therapy.* New York: W. W. Norton & Company.
Weeks, G. R., & Treat, S. R. (2001). *Couples in treatment: Techniques and approaches
    for effective practice* (2nd ed.). New York: Brunner-Routledge.
Wexler, D. B. (2009). *Men in therapy: New approaches for effective treatment.* New
    York: W. W. Norton & Co.

3

Behind the Mask

A Primer on Understanding the Male Partner in Couples Therapy

FREDRIC E. RABINOWITZ

He seems preoccupied. I want us to feel close but I can't seem to get through to him. I wish he could share more with me about what is going on with him. I know he cares about me, but I'd like to feel some connection. I feel like we have drifted apart. This isn't what I bargained for.

—A female client in couples therapy speaking about her relationship
with her male partner

This is the painful end of a long unfolding of relationship dynamics, but not an uncommon scenario many therapists see in their practice. Each of us might have an immediate professional opinion about who is at fault and most likely we would be pointing our finger at the man for being unexpressive. But before we try to take sides and intervene, let's rewind the process and start at the beginning.

By better understanding the way that many men have been raised to be in relationships, counselors can better comprehend some of the presenting problems couples bring to therapy. For instance, male difficulty with verbal expression of inner emotional states can be a barrier for counselors who are expecting an open discussion of issues in their couples sessions. When men do share vulnerable aspects of their lives, counselors often underestimate the impact of shame on this disclosure. By taking male stoicism at face value, counselors can miss the unworthiness and embarrassment that makes self-disclosure so difficult for many men. Ultimately, effective couples counseling requires a thorough understanding of how male socialization impacts men in the interpersonal realm. Applying this knowledge in clinical practice and implementing interventions designed to engage men in counseling is crucial for couples work to be successful.

THE CHALLENGE TO BE INTIMATE: MEN'S DEVELOPMENTAL JOURNEY

Problems with relational intimacy for many men have origins in childhood. In families where the primary childcare duties fall on the mother or female caretaker, a special dynamic exists around gender. Usually, it is when the child is able to move around and explore that caretakers may start to differentiate their expectations of expressive behavior based on the sex of the child (Lytton & Romney, 1991). Boys often are reinforced for their rough and tumble play, whereas girls are often reinforced for their interpersonal verbal skills and emotional displays. In the developmental phase when children begin to separate psychologically, it seems to be easier for girls to maintain an interpersonal connection with the mother or female caretaker because they identify with mother's gender identity (Chodorow, 1978). In contrast, little boys experience relational discontinuity in their developmental progression from attachment through separation, forming their identities on being different than mother and identifying with father or a male figure (Pollack, 1990).

This early identification with the father has implications for the development of relational capacities in many men. While it might seem like second nature for a female client to express herself verbally and make an interpersonal connection with the therapist, a male client is more likely to be reticent in his disclosures. His discomfort with intimacy and closeness is not necessarily conscious but rather a reaction to the dangers that this kind of connection stirs in him. These dangers are twofold: There is the shame of not behaving like his father, who likely modeled some degree of emotional inexpressiveness himself; and there is the pain of reexperiencing the loss of closeness to his mother, an abandonment grief he first felt (and learned to repress) when he started the separation process as a small child. This particular pain was first identified by Pollack (1995), who theorized that in Western culture, with its emphasis on autonomy and separateness, little boys are pushed prematurely from connection to their mothers. He calls this a "traumatic abrogation of the early holding environment, an impingement in boy's development—a normative life-cycle loss—that may, later in life, leave many adult men at risk for fears of intimate connection. This traumatic experience of abandonment occurs so early in the life course that the shameful memory of the loss is likely to be deeply repressed" (Pollack, 1995, p. 41).

Adult interpersonal situations, in particular ones that involve increasing closeness with an intimate partner, can activate unconscious recollections of this childhood abandonment experience, and thus are often avoided or approached with caution. Bids by an intimate partner for closeness may therefore be rebuffed or stir up a defensive attitude in a man. This is also true in the counseling relationship, where intimacy is a strong part of the therapeutic process. By staying distant or emotionally unavailable, a man can sidestep the shame and sadness that can come from having and then losing intimacy. Because the process occurs at an unconscious level, most men are unaware of why they often maintain emotional distance in relationships. It is important to realize that this psychological pain of premature separation from mother, combined with society's norms for male autonomy, leads men in adulthood to avoid emotional intimacy or expressing their need for it. It may also explain why many men who have made a strong attachment to a female partner get overwhelmed when a primary relationship is threatened. It is like a reopening of the painful separation that occurred when a boy moved away from the warm feelings of dependency on his mother and into the autonomous world of men. Rage, despair, and paralysis represent reactions to a reopening of this earlier, forgotten trauma.

Couples therapists who explore their clients' early childhood experiences with an ear toward the male partner's early wounds may illuminate for both partners the sources of the man's pain. In the following vignette, the therapist first uncovers how the male partner learned as a child to suppress both soft emotions and needs for closeness with his mother, and then the therapist links these experiences to his anger issues in the relationship. The vignette also illustrates how conducting history taking early in treatment can be turned into a healing moment for the couple.

Susan and Harold came to therapy initially to deal with Harold's bursts of anger that were triggered when he felt ignored or dismissed by Susan. In gathering history about the couple, the counselor had asked Harold about his own childhood upbringing.

Harold: I was the youngest of four and the only boy. I had three older sisters. My dad seemed really pleased to have a son. Because I was babied a bit by my mom and sisters, my dad thought I was getting too feminized so he would go out of his way to toughen me up.

Counselor: What do you mean "toughen you up"?

Harold: He played rough with me. He made sure I played organized sports. He took me camping. I was never allowed to cry around him. I remember having to be strong, even when I was feeling scared or lonely. One time he brought me on a fishing trip with his buddies. I must have been 6 or 7 years old. At first it felt really great to be hanging out with the guys. They told stories, drank beer, but then they all passed out. I was still awake. I started feeling panicky and wanted my mom.

Counselor: So what did you do?

Harold: I started crying and tried to wake up my dad. Bad move.

Counselor: Why was that?

Harold: My dad half woke up, saw me crying and just had a disgusted look on his face. He then said something I can never forget. He called me a "little girl." He told me to shut up and quit crying. He said I knew I had spent too much time with my mom and sisters and that I needed to grow up. It was clear to me at that moment, if I wanted to be a man, I was going to have to stop crying and stop wanting my mom. I don't know if it was my mom or me, but I stopped telling her stuff after that camping trip. Even though I felt like I still needed her, it felt dangerous to get close to her or my sisters.

Counselor: You were only 6 or 7? Seems a little young for you to have to give up mom.

Harold: Yes. It didn't feel like I had much of a choice. My dad's approval was important.

Counselor: Do you think this connects at all to your anger at Susan?

Harold: I never really put these pieces together, but when she ignores me, it feels a lot like the cold place I had to go to keep a safe distance from my mom.

Counselor: Like an abandonment?

Harold: Yes. That is what it feels like. Not a good feeling.

Counselor: Susan, you have a puzzled look on your face.

Susan: Well, it's a lot to take in. I guess it's kind of a relief to know there's a reason he reacts so strongly sometimes. It's not just that he's got "anger issues."

MEN AND EMOTIONAL EXPRESSIVITY

Although young boys up to age 5 are actually more emotionally expressive than girls, most boys are brought up in well-meaning families to not cry, to not express tender or sad emotion, and to be tough in the face of pain. These masculine values contrast with traditional feminine norms that allow for emotional expression. As adults, the prohibition on emotional expressivity underlies the core of traditional masculine norms: not showing too much emotional vulnerability; keeping a rational attitude in the face of chaos; and ignoring physical and emotional pain.

Difficult and complex problems at work, interpersonal conflict in relationships, and unexpected life situations do result in sadness, a desire to be comforted, fear, disappointment, and shame. But, according to traditional gender role norms, this spectrum of emotion must be suppressed (Levant, 1995). Sadness, for instance, is only acceptable in its public form when there is a significant, tangible loss that a man deems big enough to warrant tears. To be comforted means to acknowledge one's weakness or vulnerability; sharing the soft emotions is often perceived as a feminine activity. Fear, a natural reaction to new and potentially dangerous situations, is also taboo in the traditional masculinity code. Even realistic fears such as the threat of losing one's job or a serious health-threatening medical diagnosis must be converted to a tough stoicism or counterphobic aggressiveness.

Unable to cope with psychological distress through appropriate emotional release or requests for comfort, many men will manifest it in less direct ways. A partner, spouse, or lover is often the recipient of the impact of this distress, which dislodges the equilibrium of the relationship. Sometimes it appears as a change in typical behavior, from someone who appeared confident, satisfied, and capable to one who seems distracted, sad, anxious, irritable, or angry. Other times it manifests as interpersonal distancing through absences from the relationship. This might take the form of excessive alcohol or drug use, too much working, preoccupation with pornography, or an emotional or physical affair outside the relationship (Cochran & Rabinowitz, 2000).

Carl and Lorraine came to couples therapy after Carl engaged in extramarital sex. Lorraine was a high-level human resources administrator. Carl had recently been laid off from his job as a sales representative for construction tools. Carl had begun to frequent massage parlors and play poker at a local casino during the day. Lorraine had been working long hours and was unaware of Carl's response to being unemployed. She assumed he was looking for work. It wasn't until Carl began to ask for extra cash and was absent from home when she returned from work that her suspicions had been raised. She soon saw charges for Asian massages on the credit card bill. She threatened divorce unless he entered therapy with her. The counselor explored Lorraine's and Carl's feelings about the situation and each other.

Carl: At first I was fine with having some down time. I have worked my whole life. It is what defines me. I've been salesman of the year at the company several times. The layoff hit me harder than I thought.

Counselor: What do you mean?

Carl: I just got bored. I started playing online poker and then hit the Indian casino down the road. Lorraine was working all the time. I wanted to take my mind off the reality of my life. I started getting into poker and then stopped at the massage parlor.

Lorraine: Why didn't you just tell me? We could have avoided all this.

Carl: It's not that easy. I was embarrassed. I hate to admit it, but I felt
    less than a man not having a job.
Lorraine: So you felt more like a man playing poker and having sex?
Carl: What can I say? I did. I am not saying it's right. I just couldn't stand
    hanging at home without anything to do.
Counselor: You sound like you were feeling pretty down.
Carl: I just felt edgy. I needed to do something. I just won't let myself
    get too down. It scares me to go there.
Lorraine: You could have asked for help.
Carl: Come on. You know that's not how I operate.
Counselor: This may be an opportunity to not only deal with the feel-
    ings you are experiencing but also to work on communicating
    in the relationship.
Lorraine: Carl, you heard what he said. We've got to work on communi-
    cating better if this marriage has a chance.
Carl: I get it. Really. I'll try anything at this point. It's just not going to
    be easy.

INDEPENDENCE VERSUS INTIMACY

Implied in developmental and male gender role analysis is a boy's identification with the world of men, a place primarily occupied by his father
or a male caretaker. If a father figure holds a traditional male gender role
orientation, a boy will see this as the norm. For many boys, this male
world reinforces an avoidance of intimacy and an overvaluing of independence. Often boys are shamed when they express emotional neediness,
leading many to disavow even the most basic of psychological needs—
the need to depend on another person for love, support, and nurturance.
Any relationship that evokes a man's dependent needs is often viewed as
threatening and potentially humiliating (Osherson & Krugman, 1990).
Many men focus instead on the less emotionally charged, more practical, rational, and factual aspects of life. When male emotional energy is
present, it is more likely to be channeled toward more competitive and
aggressive pursuits, fortified by the reinforcing emphasis in our society around sports, power, and financial gain. Relationships from this
perspective are by definition competitive, guarded, or team-based "us
versus them."

    Yearning for intimacy thus becomes an underground activity that
leaves many men unaware of how to meet their relational needs in relationships. This lack of awareness is one reason why some men pressure
partners for more sex in the relationship; they were socialized to learn
that an acceptable path for men to achieve closeness is sexual connection. Sex is within their relational comfort zone; intimate dialogue,
while consciously recognized as important to the relationship, can be
a challenging, even stressful experience. The vocabulary, nuance, and
sensitivity that many women grow up with in their interpersonal lives

is often not present for men, who have been busy competing and maintaining a safe distance in their relationships.

What are the implications of these issues for how men present themselves to a counselor or therapist? When a man arrives with his partner, he is out of his comfort zone in an interpersonal situation that is unfamiliar. Bergman (1995) argues that male identity at its core is based on "turning away from the whole relational mode," and couples therapy represents an intense immersion in this relational mode. That is one reason why it is a fact that very few men willingly come to couples therapy. Another reason is that self-sufficiency, strength, and control define masculinity. Often a man coming to counseling feels he is not living up to the masculine ideals of our culture. Even though a man may have deep emotional pain, the idea of going to a psychotherapist feels like an anathema, an admission of defeat, and a further sign of weakness. Typically, then, counseling is a last resort (Addis & Mahalik, 2003). Therefore, it is often the partner who suggests the idea of counseling or therapy. When he and his partner do arrive for the first session, it is not uncommon for the man to present a façade of strength, to cover his shame for having to be there in the first place (Scher, 1990). The therapist must remain sensitive to these dynamics of wanting to go at life alone, avoiding interpersonal vulnerability, and feelings of failure as a man—or risk alienating the male client he or she is trying to help.

As an illustration in a first session, the counselor gently probes to get a sense of the issues in the relationship from each partner's perspective. Despite the clarity of the female partner's view, the counselor is sensitive and nonjudgmental of the male partner's words, knowing how hard this is for him.

Counselor: I would like to hear from each of you your assessment about the relationship.

Rea: Why don't you go first John?

John: I'm not sure. I'd rather you went first.

Rea: This is part of the problem. He doesn't initiate things. I am always the one to do that. I think John is trying hard to please me, but I'm not sure he is aware of what he wants in the relationship.

Counselor: John?

John: Maybe she's right. I can't seem to do anything right in her eyes.

Counselor: What do you mean?

John: I'm a good provider. I make good money. I'm stable. I'm a good guy. I guess I don't know what else I need to be doing to make her happy. I don't really see what the big problem is.

Rea: You are a good guy. I just want you to listen better. Hear me. Tell me what you want.

John: I do hear your complaints. I'm not sure what you want me to do. I just want to be happy.

Counselor: It seems like you both see the relationship differently. Rea,
   for you it is about you feeling that you have to make all the
   decisions. John, seems like you feel you are doing all you can
   and it still isn't enough in Rea's eyes.
John: That is how I feel a lot.

THE PHYSICAL ENVIRONMENT

The space where counseling occurs can have an impact on a male client's
disposition coming for couple's therapy. Because counseling is more congruent with traditional female socialization, where feelings and problems are discussed, the environment may initially seem uncomfortable.
By noticing how a male client might perceive the therapeutic space, a
counselor can take steps to rearrange the physical environment to make
it more male friendly. From the magazines in the waiting room to the
pictures on the wall, the male client is taking in information about how
he will be perceived.
   It is important for the waiting room to have some male-oriented magazines relating to sports, men's health, or cars, along with the traditional
copies of women's magazines. Some of the pictures on the walls might
have some male themes related to action-oriented activities or outdoor
environments. This sends a subtle message that men come to this environment. This is especially important since men are reticent about coming to counseling in the first place. In the therapy room, furniture might
be arranged in a way that allows for side-by-side interaction or include
a swivel so that a man doesn't always need to be face to face with the
counselor. The demand of face-to-face interaction can be intimidating
and make opening up for a man more difficult. While each counselor
decorates his or her room based on personal preferences, attention to
potential gendered perceptions is worth assessing. By making a room
more gender neutral or thinking about how men and women might
perceive one's space, both male and female clients can feel relatively
comfortable and safe upon initial entry. If possible, the therapist's chair
should be centered, at an even distance from both partners; men may
be vigilant about whether the therapist will be allying with the female
partner, and chair placement helps reduce men's fears. Ultimately, the
room becomes representative of the holding environment, making it a
familiar, significant space for those in therapy.

MALE-SENSITIVE WAYS OF TALKING

Therapist self-disclosure is another way a therapist can convey some
normalcy to the interaction. The face-to-face intimacy of the therapy
relationship can lead to hesitation to share any fears if the therapist
moves too quickly. If a man is to feel comfortable sharing his inner

world, he needs to know that the therapist is human and can understand his conflicts. This often occurs when the counselor self-discloses and speaks the male client's language (Rabinowitz & Cochran, 2002). Sharing commonalities or current events make the counselor seem more human and less intimidating. How the therapist inquires about the couples' presenting issues can also be critical. Instead of starting the conversation with "What is the problem?" starting with "So how did it happen that you made it to my office? Feel free to tell me the story wherever you want to begin," conveys trust in his perspective. When a man says, "My wife thought it would be a good idea," it is important to counter with, "What's your take on things?" This allows the male client to frame his experience with his words and regain control over his sharing of himself. Finally, reflecting a man's strengths, as they emerge in the initial conversation, can reduce the shame-based narrative many male clients bring to counseling (Englar-Carlson & Shepard, 2005). This also reinforces a man's sense of competence.

THE VALUE OF EMPATHY

Those who have studied the therapeutic relationship suggest that an overarching attitude of nonjudgmental acceptance combined with empathy for the male experience often leads male clients to feel less anxious and more understood by the therapist (Englar-Carlson & Shepard, 2005). What does it mean to have empathy for the male experience? Knowing that most men are not comfortable sharing, a counselor must use this information to make the setting male friendly. This means not reinforcing the shame but instead normalizing the interaction. Rather than acting as an inquisitor, realize that the male client feels one down in the situation. Well-meaning empathy statements about the tender feelings that underlie a man's emotional state may be ineffective because they expose too much shame too fast (Osherson & Krugman, 1990; Shay, 1996). Direct statements that reflect "courage for coming in" or "it takes a lot of strength to reach out" are more effective as strength-based empathizing with his dilemma.

Men who have been in counseling often admit that engaging in the relational quality of psychotherapy is extremely challenging but a necessary part of the process (Rabinowitz & Cochran, 2002). By nonjudgmentally analyzing a man's reactions to the therapeutic relationship, a counselor can help the client make sense of troubling behaviors. When defenses arise, they can be explored. For instance, Rex, 42, went blank when he was asked about the death of his father at age 14. He had little to say and found it hard to articulate what he felt at the time or even now as he looks back at it. The empathic therapist can use this as an opportunity to say, "If it was me, I'd feel really sad. I wonder what might be holding you back from feeling this right now?" By helping a man out with emotional words, a therapist gives him permission to touch base with a part of his past in a more meaningful way (Englar-Carlson & Shepard, 2005). Metaphors also seem to resonate with many men (Shay & Maltas, 1998). Without training in labeling feelings, an image can unblock access to emotion. By reflecting to a male client who was surprised by his partner's desire for a divorce "it seems like it has been a slow motion train wreck you couldn't stop," a counselor can stimulate a more comprehensive emotional response than the traditional "you must be feeling sad about your divorce." By using therapist self-disclosure and metaphors to explore a man's relational trauma, it may be possible to bring to the surface a neglected inner world of images, memories, and the emotions connected to them (Rabinowitz & Cochran, 2002).

THE THERAPIST'S GENDER

When the therapist is male, there are additional issues to address, especially in early sessions. A male client might frame his concerns as minor or show very little affect describing a painful situation. Chris, 45, and recently separated from his partner of 20 years, described his current situation as "a little rough." When the male therapist asked what happened, Chris responded, "You know, the usual scenario. She told me I worked too much. I tried to cut back on my hours, but with this economy, I had to put even more time in. I came home one day to an empty house. Game over." This minimization of emotional expression is often a statement about not wanting to show too much vulnerability in the presence of a man he doesn't know (Wong & Rochlen, 2005). Like a game of chess, it is not unusual for the counseling relationship to begin with caution. Often these interactions can take on the quality of vying for control. A male client might brag about his success or question why someone like you (the therapist) would want to listen to people's problems all day. "Guess this is pretty much par for the course for you Doc. I don't know if I could listen to the stuff you must hear all day. You guys should get paid more. I guess I went into the right business. All I have to do is convince people they need insurance to make my stack," replied Dan, a 57-year-old man who had consulted the therapist for unexplained anxiety. This initial competitiveness and minimization of his issues, understood as a way a man is used to handling threat, needs to be responded to in a nondefensive way so that a male client can maintain a sense of competence, autonomy, and safety. He may just be trying to get comfortable in this foreign space. The therapist replied, "I'm not sure anyone has it easy. Sounds like your business is pretty stressful. I'm not so sure how well I would hold up under those conditions." Eventually the competitiveness will give way to more openness and authenticity when the client realizes that the therapist is an ally, not a threat (Rabinowitz & Cochran, 2002).

Initial interactions with female therapists will have a different quality. Depending on the age of the therapist, it is not uncommon for a male client to initially enact a mother or potential girlfriend transference to reduce the anxiety associated with intimacy (Johnson, 2001). For some men, a mother represents someone with whom they can let down emotionally, but for others she might represent betrayal, intrusiveness, and a lack of safety. Greg and Louanne, both in their early 30s, consulted a 60-year-old female counselor for difficulty Greg was having being able to take constructive criticism from Louanne. In trying to find out more about the nature of the relationship, the counselor asked, "What kinds of things seem to set you off?"

Greg: Why is that my problem? If she gave a little more positive feedback when I do a good job, I might not be sitting here.
Counselor: Do you feel like I am not appreciating your struggle?
Greg: You certainly ask a lot of questions. I do wish you would try to be more supportive.
Louanne: That is exactly what you say to me all the time.
Counselor: Is it possible my asking you questions feels like I'm getting in your face a lot? Maybe that's something you've been through before. And it didn't feel very good. What do you think?
Greg: My mother used to ask a lot of questions and I always felt there was a judgment there. Sorry if I am a little sensitive about this.
Counselor: I think this is an important issue for you. Let's talk about it further.

In the potential girlfriend transference scenario, the male partner may engage in some seductive behavior to form an alliance with the female therapist. It is important for the counselor to be aware of how a male client might use his charm, wit, and attractiveness to disarm the potential confrontation of his issues. In the following sequence, Gabe distracts the counselor with compliments and tries to persuade her to focus more on Amy than him.

Gabe: It is always nice to come to your office. It has a certain natural, inviting smell that makes me feel comfortable.
Amy: Can we get back to talking about the relationship?
Gabe: Amy, there is nothing wrong with my sharing how I feel about coming here. I think Dr. Morrison appreciates my comments.
Counselor: It's nice that you feel comfortable, but I am wondering if you may be ambivalent about confronting issues in the marriage, Gabe.
Gabe: I've said this before. Amy is the one who is more upset with the marriage. I want to be supportive of her needs and wishes. That is why I am here. I feel like most women would be happy to be with a guy like me.
Amy: I do have concerns, but one of them is that Gabe doesn't take me seriously.

Gabe: I do take you seriously or I wouldn't be here. I believe we should really be listening to Dr. Morrison and her wealth of experience.

Counselor: Gabe, this is about both you and Amy. It is important for both of you to look at what part you are playing in the dynamics of the relationship.

Because counselors and therapists bring their own issues to the consulting room, it is important for them to be aware of their own countertransference reactions. If one is reacting to a challenge, it is hard to be objective and focused on what lies beneath the behavior. Engaging in a competitive relationship with a client will hinder the therapeutic process and reduce the safety in the room. Mothering a male client will usually result in less honest self-disclosure by the client in the long run because of the activation of his shaming defenses. For the female therapist, there is a risk of unconsciously forming an alliance with the male partner in the form of agreeing with his viewpoint or being less challenging. This may be a way to feel validation from a male or to express some hostility toward the female partner. On the other hand, rejecting or avoiding a male client's attempts at seduction, rather than exploring the nature of this relational style, will often result in defensiveness and a withholding of relevant disclosures. By responding nonjudgmentally, a therapist can use the transference relationship with both partners as a means to understand the dynamics of their relationship and the defenses each has learned to employ to reduce interpersonal anxiety.

STAYING POSITIVE

To come full circle, let's look again at the description that opened this chapter. The way the female partner describes the man in her life can now be seen through a lens that embodies the core conflicts that most men must traverse. "Not talking" is a fairly normative way for many men to express feelings of confusion, ambivalence, and shame (Real, 1997). If he doesn't know what is going on internally or how to express his inner world in a way that he feels he might be understood, it makes sense that he might want to wait until it becomes more clear. A counselor who tries to interrogate a male client may end up doing more harm than good. By trying to understand the ambivalence and potential shame of being truthful, a counselor can instead focus on the positive side of a man's struggle. Often he is trying to protect those close to him from being hurt as he struggles to figure himself out. By asking a male client to talk about what benefits come from having a drink or wanting sex, a man might be more open to talking about the stresses in his life and his need for some relief. By showing empathy for his struggles in a nonjudgmental manner, the male client is more likely to feel less resistant to sharing his concerns. Finally, by asking the female partner about her expectations and disappointments, the focus can come off of the man as the sole problem, and back to her issues about the relationship, and how she might have partially contributed to his discomfort in sharing himself.

THE FIVE THEMES: GUIDANCE FOR ASSESSING AND INTERVENING

In developing a model for deepening individual psychotherapy with men, Rabinowitz and Cochran (2002) suggested that a man's narrative can be distilled into five overarching themes. They recommended that by utilizing these themes, a counselor can assess major influences on a man's personality structure and receive guidance for what interventions might be most effective. The themes are the conflict between independence and dependence in relationships; dealing with grief and sadness; the impact of male socialization; the conflict between being and doing; and identifying the emotional wounding that is a potential catalyst for change (Rabinowitz & Cochran, 2002). Although the model was initially designed for individual work, attending to how these themes emerge in the male client's narrative in couples therapy can be invaluable in deepening the process in this modality as well. The case of Gus and Gina illustrates how each of these five themes plays out in couples treatment.

The first of these themes concerns the relational aspect of a man's life, specifically the dynamics of a man's socially learned tendency toward independence and his often hidden dependence in his significant relationships. The process of therapy brings to light the contradictions between giving in to dependent connection and fleeing toward independence and separateness. For many men, independence and autonomy have been rewarded by cultural masculine norms, whereas dependence on others has been perceived as shameful. In relationships, it is not uncommon for couples work to be centered on this pattern with the female partner pushing for more dependence and the male partner toward more independence.

Gus and Gina, in their late 40s, were coming to weekly sessions despite their 2-month separation. The couple had been together since high school. They had three children, who were now grown and out of the house. Gus and Gina had divided the family labor in a fairly traditional manner with Gus working full-time and Gina staying home. Gus had his own contracting business and during the past 20 years had maintained long hours and been wedded to his work. The business was successful, but he and Gina led very separate lives. Without children to tend to, Gina had become aware of how separate the two of them were and how much she felt disconnected. When Gus continued to commit his time to the business, she continually confronted him about how they should spend more time together. Gus agreed verbally, but his actions suggested that he preferred spending his time at work. Fed up, Gina told Gus to get his own place if he didn't want to be with her. Without much fanfare, he got his own apartment but agreed to come to counseling to work on the marriage. In reviewing what happened in his marriage, Gus revealed that although he really missed Gina, he also felt relieved to not have to report his coming and going to her. "Since the kids left the house, you were so critical, I stopped telling you what I was doing. I guess that is not a good way to communicate," he shared. Shamed-based defenses, whose purpose is to reduce exposure and push away connection, were activated by his feeling judged. After Gina replied that she didn't mean for it to come out like that, Gus added, "I have to admit I like being on my own but really miss the good times we shared."

This couple seems to have gotten stuck in a pursue–withdraw cycle because of Gus's conflict about dependence and independence. He may have attempted to resolve this conflict by seeking more distance from her, and she responded with criticisms in hopes of engaging him and reducing distance. But because Gina used criticism, she actually pushed him away rather than bring him close, leading her to end up feeling helpless and despairing about the marriage. So did Gus, who used her criticisms as a rationale for resolving his inner tension about dependency. A separation seemed like a break from the distress both were feeling. Gus did miss the closeness he felt with her, but also experienced a sense of safety in the distance created by the separation.

The second theme involves a man's avoidance of the "depressive position," an emotional state that accompanies the many experiences across the life span of grief, loss, and disappointment. By listening carefully for these experiences, a therapist can begin to assess what the client has had to do to avoid feeling sadness and depression in his life. Many men are successful at defending against this type of pain for much of their lives, but then unexpectedly being overwhelmed by profound emotion with an unexpected loss or trauma, such as divorce, or the death of a parent or sibling. This sets up the fear that the sadness will be reactivated when there are strong conflicts in the current relationship and the threat of being left by his partner. He may use the same male-acceptable coping strategies from childhood (e.g., repression of sadness and grief, withdrawal and isolation, acting out with aggressiveness); but in the marriage, these strategies exacerbate the female partner's frustration, worsening the couple's distress. This occurred when Gus and Gina would fight over petty issues. Gus's particular coping strategy was illuminated in treatment when the therapist asked Gus to recall his parents' divorce when he was a boy.

Gus: I don't think it affected me that much. I think it was better for my parents to be split up so I didn't get caught up in their fighting.
Counselor: What did you do to get away from the fighting?
Gus: I don't know. I watched a lot of television alone in my room.

Counselor: Do you think that might be connected to how you chose to handle the conflicts you were having with Gina?

Gus: I don't hide in my room and watch TV, if that's what you mean.

Gina: No … but you do disappear on me.

Gus: It's true that I can go into my own world, sometimes. Yeah, I guess I've always done that. But Gina, it never seemed to bother you. You didn't even seem to notice.

Gina: I noticed, but I chose to focus my energies on the kids. I figured when they left the house, you and I would deal with each other. But we're not. You're still in some other world when things get emotional.

Counselor: Does what Gina is saying make sense to you Gus?

Gus: Yeah … she's right. I don't like difficult emotions. And it's been tough since the kids have left. I mean, it's been really hard on me. The house is so damn quiet, now. So, yeah, I guess I've been spending a lot of time at work … maybe even more than I need to. It's my escape when things get me down.

The third theme to note is the nature of the masculine self-structure; how a man's identity has been formed from the influence of early family interpersonal interactions, cultural norms, and the gender role demands of masculine socialization. By paying close attention to the way a man describes himself in his actions and attitudes, the therapist can begin to assess the impact of family and personal relationships as well as those that have been culturally learned. All of these influences are intertwined and related. The traditional male socialization process also exerts a powerful influence on how men act, think, and feel. David and Brannon (1976) articulated in poignant metaphors the four major rules of real masculinity: no sissy stuff, be the big wheel, be the sturdy oak, and give 'em hell. No sissy stuff is the proscription against anything feminine or risk being ridiculed as homosexual, or being less than a real man. The big wheel is the rule that says real men achieve their status by winning and competing. The sturdy oak tells men that they are to remain stoic, unemotional, and not ask for help in the face of desperation or pain. Give 'em hell reinforces the belief that men should seek adventure and solve their problems with toughness and aggression.

These rules of masculinity can be played out in relationships in a way that could cause conflict. The no sissy stuff leads many men to avoid housework or anything deemed to be a woman's job, including relationship maintenance. The big wheel leads a man to feel like he should feel in control in the relationship, including winning arguments and being supported fully in this position by his partner. This can result in unspoken resentments and power struggles. The sturdy oak manifests as quietness and inexpressiveness, often leading to communication difficulties. Give 'em hell encourages men to use anger as the main tool to deal with frustration in the relationship, often resulting in toxic arguing that does not reflect the deeper and more subtle emotional issues.

Counselor: I wonder how your upbringing as a man has impacted your relationship with Gina.

Gus: Never thought about that. I was like most guys. I felt a need to prove myself, especially since I didn't see my dad that much. I played sports all through out high school. It was good to have status at the school. Inside I felt pretty inferior—doesn't every teenager?—but on the football field, I could express everything pent-up inside. One of my frustrations after graduating was where to get my anger out. I guess I took it out on Gina a few times, but I didn't know what else to do.

Gina: I felt like I was the only person you talked to in high school. I also let you express everything. I think we ended up together because you could be open with me. I don't know what happened to that over the years.

Gus: Yes. I felt whole with you. Not broken. You were my escape from my family. When you became family, I guess I needed to escape again. Work was good for that. I felt productive and could provide for the family at the same time.

Counselor: Gus, seems like you found ways to cope with your difficult emotions by following the rules of masculinity that allowed you to be independent and a good provider.

Gus: Yes. It was a path I could follow, but this definitely had a down side. Now, I know I need to find some other ways to express myself. I'm just struggling with how.

The fourth theme to attend to in assessment is the conflict many men experience between "being" and "doing." How has a man handled problematic situations? It would be important to observe how anxious a man is about staying with a feeling or body awareness and how eager he might be to move into an action mode within the therapy relationship. In couples therapy, the focus on understanding one's actions and reactions leads to a heightened awareness of the body and emotions. How individuals experience this slowed down process can give a counselor a sense of how the doing–being continuum works in a man's life.

In the relationship with Gina, Gus tended toward doing when faced with uncomfortable emotions. His tendency to engage with work during emotionally difficult times is an example of his tendency toward the doing end of the spectrum. In response, the counselor tries to move him more toward the being mode by asking him to be in touch with his body in reviewing events that caused distress in the marriage.

Counselor: Gina, what do you want to ask of Gus?

Gina: I just want him to feel comfortable being around me. It would be nice if we could sit and watch TV together or share a glass of wine in the backyard.

Counselor: How does it feel in your body when Gina shares her request?

Gus: I don't know. I think she's right about doing it.
Counselor: But what does your body say?
Gus: I feel some tightness in my chest.
Counselor: Stay with the tightness. What is it trying to tell you?
Gus: It is uncomfortable. Threatening in some way.
Gina: What could be threatening about hanging out with me?
Gus: Not sure, but it feels like if I slow down to do what you want, I won't be able to breathe. Not sure if this is it.
Counselor: Sounds like just being with Gina with no active agenda is unfamiliar.
Gus: I guess it is unfamiliar. This never happened in the house I grew up in. Even with kids in our house, there was always action and not a lot of time to just be. I'm not used to it.

The fifth theme is gaining an in-depth understanding of the nature of the precipitating circumstances that brought the man in the couple to therapy. Often, a narcissistic injury or "wound" has pierced the defenses. This wound is the catalyst for a man to move toward a new solution, and by implication, face his emotional depth. Since men rarely come to therapy on their own without having been emotionally wounded or threatened, it is the counselor's job to decipher how this wound has impacted the nature of a man's self-identity. When Gina told Gus to leave the house, it activated abandonment anxiety he hadn't felt since his father left the family.

Counselor: What did you feel when Gina told you she didn't want you in the house anymore?
Gus: I was overwhelmed. It reminded me of when my dad left my mom. He just walked out and I thought he was coming home in a little bit. No one talked to me about it. Eventually my dad called the house about two weeks later. I had thought he was dead.
Counselor: Really abandoned.
Gus: Yes. It was terrifying.
Gina: I'm sorry I played it out this way Gus, but you weren't really listening to me. I needed to do something drastic.
Gus: I know. I'm not sure I'd be dealing with any of this if you hadn't done that. I hope we can get through this.
Gina: Me too. I have missed being with you.

CONCLUSION

Couples counseling is complex. Men are often initially reluctant clients. By making the physical and psychological aspects of the counseling environment male friendly, male clients are likely to be more engaged and less threatened. By knowing how men have been socialized and taught to communicate, a counselor can adapt his or her style to facilitate the therapeutic process. By having empathy for the male experience and the difficulties that arise from male socialization, a counselor can use this sensitivity to navigate difficult emotions with male clients. Being aware of male shame-based defenses gives the couple's therapist a roadmap for intervention. By attending to the language a man uses and by being nonjudgmental in responding to his words, a couple's counselor can facilitate a man's self-awareness and improve his communication skills. Counselor awareness of transference and countertransference reactions is essential in responding positively and effectively to male clients in couples work. Finally, by assessing the five themes that influence male behavior, couples counselors can anticipate roadblocks and design interventions that help men use counseling effectively.

REFERENCES

Addis, M. E., & Mahalik, J. R. (2003). Men, masculinity, and the contexts of help-seeking. *American Psychologist, 58,* 5–14.

Bergman, S. J. (1995). Men's psychological development: A relational perspective. In R. F. Levant & W. S. Pollack (Eds.). *A new psychology of men* (pp. 68–90). New York: Basic Books.

Chodorow, N. (1978). *The reproduction of mothering.* Berkeley, CA: University of California Press.

Cochran, S. V., & Rabinowitz, F. E. (2000). *Men and depression: Clinical and empirical perspectives.* San Diego, CA: Academic Press.

David, D. S., & Brannon, R. (Eds.). (1976). *The forty-nine percent majority: The male sex role.* Reading, MA: Addison-Wesley.

Englar-Carlson, M., & Shepard, D. S. (2005). Engaging men in couples counseling: Strategies for overcoming ambivalence and inexpressiveness. *The Family Journal: Counseling and Therapy for Couples and Families, 13,* 383–391.

Johnson, N. C. (2001). Women helping men: Strengths and barriers to women therapists working with male clients. In G. R. Brooks & G. E. Good (Eds.), *The new handbook of psychotherapy and counseling with men* (pp. 696–718). San Francisco, CA: Jossey-Bass.

Levant, R. F. (1995). *Masculinity reconstructed: Changing the rules of manhood—At work, in relationships, and in family life.* New York: Dutton.

Lytton, H., & Romney, D. M. (1991). Parents' differential socialization of boys and girls: A meta-analysis. *Psychological Bulletin, 109,* 267–296.

Osherson, S., & Krugman, S. (1990). Men, shame, and psychotherapy. *Psychotherapy, 27,* 327–339.

Pollack, W. (1990). Men's development and psychotherapy: A psychoanalytic perspective. *Psychotherapy, 27,* 316–321.

Pollack, W. (1995). No man is an island: Toward a new psychoanalytic psychology of men. In R. Levant & W. Pollack (Eds.), *A new psychology of men* (pp. 33–67). New York: Basic Books.

Rabinowitz, F. E., & Cochran, S. V. (2002). *Deepening psychotherapy with men.* Washington, DC: American Psychological Association.

Real, T. (1997). *I don't want to talk about it.* New York: Fireside.

Scher, M. (1990). Effects of gender role incongruities on men's experience as clients in psychotherapy. *Psychotherapy, 27,* 322–326.

Shay, J. J. (1996). Okay, I'm here but I'm not talking: Psychotherapy with the reluctant male. *Psychotherapy, 33,* 503–513.

Shay, J. J., & Maltas, C. P. (1998). Reluctant men in couple therapy: Corralling the Marlboro man. In W. S. Pollack & R. F. Levant (Eds.), *New psychotherapy for men* (pp. 97–126). Hoboken, NJ: John Wiley & Sons.

Wong, J. Y., & Rochlen, A. B. (2005). Demystifying men's emotional behavior: New directions and implications for counseling and research. *Psychology of Men and Masculinity, 6,* 62–72.

Theoretical Models

CHAPTER

4

Early Life Memories

A Male-Friendly Approach to Facilitating Couple Collaboration

JOHN M. ROBERTSON AND SUPAVAN
KHAMPHAKDY-BROWN

Longshoreman-philosopher Eric Hoffer did not think much of human memory. With characteristic wit, he observed, "We can remember minutely and precisely only the things which never really happened to us" ("Thoughts," 1971).

Childhood memories take many forms. Some are recalled as fleeting images, ethereal and imaginative. Others appear as complete stories, vivid and lifelike. Most childhood events disappear entirely from conscious memory, never to be reviewed again. Given their variability and insubstantiality, how can early recollections have any relevance for a man in therapy? More to the point of this book, how can remembering early life events appeal to men who typically ask counselors for actions plans and skill-building exercises? Why would an emotionally reserved man want to dredge up old stories from childhood, and then talk openly about them? In this chapter, we offer some thoughts about these questions, describe a tool that assists men in recalling childhood events, and then provide a case history of a male–female couple who used early life memories as an approach to understanding and improving their relationship.

DANDELION BOUQUETS AND THE
MEANING OF EARLY MEMORIES

More than a century ago, Sigmund Freud wrote about an event from his own childhood. In the memory, he was collecting bouquets of yellow dandelions in a meadow with two cousins, a boy and a girl. All three children are 3 or 4 years old. Freud recalls:

> We are picking the yellow flowers and each of us is holding a bunch of flowers we have already picked. The little girl has the best bunch; and as though by mutual agreement, we—the two boys—fall on her and snatch away her flowers. She runs up the meadow in tears and as a consolation the peasant-woman gives her a big piece of black bread. Hardly have we seen this than we throw the flowers away, hurry to the cottage, and ask to be given some bread too. And we are in fact given some; the peasant-woman cuts the loaf with a long knife. In my memory the bread tastes quite delicious ... (1899/1989, p. 119)

Memory of the incident was then "concealed" from young Sigmund for more than a decade. When he was 17 years old, he returned home from secondary school for a holiday, and suddenly found himself strongly attracted to a young woman in a yellow dress. In the midst of emotional turmoil over this woman, the memory of the dandelion incident came out of hiding, so to speak. Much later, this recollection led Freud to reflect on the development of adolescent sexuality and the changeability of early memories more generally. Just a few pages after telling this story, he reflects on the historicity of early memories:

> It may indeed be questioned whether we have any memories at all *from* our childhood: memories *relating to* [italics added] our childhood may be all that we possess. Our childhood memories show us our earliest years not as they were but as they appeared at the later periods when the memories were aroused. In these periods of arousal, the childhood memories did not, as people are accustomed to say, *emerge*; they were *formed* [italics added] at that time. And a number of motives, with no concern for historical accuracy, had a part in forming them, as well as in the selection of the memories themselves. (Freud, 1899/1989, p. 126)

Freud suggests that it is not the accuracy of the early memory that matters. Instead, it is the wealth of meaning that can be found in the recollection at a subsequent time and place. Freud titled this essay "screen memories" or "concealing memories" (Freud, 1901/1938, p. 62) because the recollections are "repressed" (Freud, 1899/1989, p. 124) until subsequent events make their appearance more likely and fruitful. Although these memories may seem hidden, their meaning can be uncovered.

Seventy years ago, Alfred Adler expanded this concept. Although he agreed with Freud that early memories are reconstructions of early life events, he proposed that what was known and reliably reported was just as valuable as what was concealed. Moreover, these reports are functional in everyday life. A person's early memory is a "story he repeats to himself to warn him or comfort him, to keep him concentrated on his goal, to prepare him, by means of past experiences, to meet the future with an already tested style of action" (Adler, 1931/1998, p. 73). A skilled clinician, then, can use these memories to understand a person's outlook on life (Adler, 1937). Adler's theoretical heirs continue to explore aspects of this concept (Clark, 2004; Hawes, 2007).

Forty years ago, Marty Mayman added an overtly object relations dimension to this developing view that early life memories have significance and value:

> I hope to show that early memories are not autobiographical truths, nor even "memories" in the strictest sense of the term, but largely retrospective inventions developed to express psychological truths rather than objective truths about the person's life; that early memories are expressions of important fantasies around which a person's character structure is organized; that early memories are selected (unconsciously) by the person to conform with and confirm ingrained images of himself and others around object relational themes. ... In short, I propose that a person's adult character structure is organized around object-relational themes which intrude projectively into the structure and content of his early memories *just as they occur repetitively in his relations with significant persons in his life* [italics added]. (1968, p. 304)

Mayman (1968) argues that adulthood relational patterns "intrude" into recollections of early life events. This makes all early memories, whether factual or embellished, a rich source of personal information for both client and clinician. For a male client, these early life stories speak with authority because they come from his own storehouse of memories. His own words become his teacher. The clinician's role is to help him organize the memories into relational themes that become clear, compelling, and heuristic. The same process occurs for female clients.

Mayman's views are not novel. They "express perhaps the core tenet of object relations theory; images of self, others, and self–other relationships are internalized in early development, and when uncovered in psychoanalytically informed psychotherapy, manifest as recollections of childhood experiences" (D. S. Shepard, personal communication, March 8, 2010). This idea has direct implications for psychotherapeutic work. To help a man identify his current relational tendencies with his partner, it can be highly instructive for him (and emotionally persuasive) to see these patterns in his own accounts of events he reports from childhood.

Substantial research has indicated that the use of early memories has high clinical value. Fowler, Hilsenroth, and Handler (2000) cite numerous studies demonstrating that a patient's memories of childhood experiences provide the clinician with valuable information about a person's personality, relationship patterns, depression, borderline pathology, aggression, and dependency. Other studies have examined the utility of early memories to understand delinquency (Davidow & Bruhn, 1990), suicide (Monahan, 1983), trauma (Parks & Balon, 1995), social problem-solving (Goddard, Dritschel, & Burton, 1996), social phobia (Wenzel, Jackson, & Holt, 2002), narcissistic personality disorder (Shulman & Ferguson, 1988), and even schizophrenia (Cuervo-Lombard et al., 2007).

Mystery writer Agatha Christie might have agreed with Freud, Adler, and Mayman about how to regard early life memories. Commenting on her own experiences with memory, she offered this reflection in the introduction to her autobiography: "I think, myself, that one's memories represent those moments which, insignificant as they may seem, nevertheless represent the inner self and oneself as most really oneself" (Christie, 1977, p. xiii).

The present chapter extends the work of Mayman and his coworkers, and reports on a particular application of early memories work to couple therapy. We have worked as a male–female therapist team using this approach consistently in conjoint therapy for several years.

One final introductory note: This is *not* a chapter about repressed memories, that is, the notion that long-forgotten and unknown traumatic memories can be deliberately recovered through certain therapy techniques. The professional controversies and legal wrangling that surrounded the topic in the 1980s and '90s have been addressed elsewhere (Loftus, 1993; Spiegel, Butler, & McConkey, 1997). In contrast with repressed memories techniques, the approach described here uses only memories that are readily available and reportable.

TO DO *AND* TO FEEL: THAT IS THE CHALLENGE

Two aspects of traditional masculine socialization make psychodynamic therapy with male–female couples especially challenging. The first is the expectation that men must "do something" to improve problematic situations. In a variety of work settings, being an effective problem-solver brings many rewards. So it is common for men to bring this strategy into the psychotherapy room. It is not surprising, then, that many male clients feel vulnerable and cautious about participating in self-revealing conversations with therapists who offer only insight-oriented approaches. Numerous authors and researchers have underscored the significance of this task-oriented tendency in men, and its potential for therapy (Addis & Mahalik, 2003; Hurst, 1997; Rabinowitz & Cochran, 2002; Robertson & Fitzgerald, 1992).

A second theme that affects therapy with men in couple counseling is the long-held view that men are socialized to avoid much emotional expressiveness (e.g., Balswick, 1988). This theme is relevant to our model because relationship repair requires that patients own and express the often intense affect that accompanies recollections of early child-hood experiences. Although vigorously challenged by some (e.g., Shields, 2002), evidence from both social constructivist (e.g., Mahalik, 2000; Wong, 2008) and neuroscience perspectives (e.g., Koch et al., 2007) suggests that therapists are not simply fabricating the idea that many men are reluctant or unskilled in verbally expressing their emotions in therapy (cf. Levant, 2001). The challenges posed by this socialized incli-nation are addressed by Rabinowitz and Cochran (2002) in their outline of approaches to "deepen" the psychotherapy experiences of men. These authors argue that in spite of intense socialization pressures, men can engage in therapy that is emotionally intense, personal, and revealing.

We have found in our clinical work that in spite of early life develop-mental deprivation and emotional injury, most men (a) want to engage in structured tasks that mobilize their problem-solving skills to find expla-nations and resolutions for their relational difficulties and; (b) want to become more emotionally accessible and expressive in their conversa-tions with their partners. We have found the approach described below to be comfortable for many men. It offers a structured way to "do" and "feel" their way toward more effective and satisfying relationships. We also have observed men *can* make these changes when they have ample time, sufficient motivation, and an emotionally safe holding environ-ment in which to pursue these adaptations.

"THE PAST IS NEVER DEAD. IT'S NOT EVEN PAST"

William Faulkner's line for one of his characters in *Requiem for a Nun* (Faulkner, 1951) expresses a familiar human truth: past actions rever-berate down the corridors of time, and actually shape present behavior. This awareness has been explored for decades by therapists who work with couples. In the Adlerian tradition, for example, therapists have pro-posed several uses of early life memories in couples work (Bettner, 2007; Curran, Hazen, Jacobvitz, & Feldman, 2005; Deaner & Pechersky, 2005; Harris & Dertsch, 2001; Hawes, 2007; Watts, 1997, 2000). Multiple strategies for collecting the memories have been developed as well (cf. Bruhn, 1992a, 1992b; Williams, 2003; Williams & Broadbent, 1986).

Like these authors, we have found that when a couple steps back from the immediacy of current quarrels and demands, and instead moves toward a broader understanding of the early life back-stories that contribute to their present conflicts, predictable consequences follow. The intensity of their interpersonal conflicts moderates, broader under-standings of their problematic patterns emerge, and therapeutic change becomes more likely. This requires, of course, that representative early memories must be recalled and that relevant developmental themes in those memories can be identified.

Psychodynamic therapists have elicited early life remembrances in a number of ways, including taking oral histories, asking probing-style questions at key moments in partner interactions, offering speculative interpretations, or using assessment instruments administered early in treatment. We have taken this latter approach and developed a public domain tool called Summary of Themes from Early Memories (STEM; available from Robertson & Khamphakdy-Brown, 2007). The STEM is a questionnaire that elicits memories of specific events from early life. Some of the probes are similar to queries used successfully over the last 40 years and reported in the references cited earlier, and others are original. The STEM has been refined over several years of multiple uses each week at an intensive day treatment program that serves professionals in health care, law, and business. About 9 of 10 of our clients are male (Professional Renewal Center, 2008). The STEM is given as a standard part of a week-long multidisciplinary, multimodal assessment for each client. As often as possible, the spouses are invited to come for intensive conjoint therapy for those who remain for treatment.

The memories are revealed in a face-to-face interview with a therapist who transcribes the stories verbatim. Administration takes about 90 minutes. The following questions are asked: What is your earliest memory of anything at all? What is your earliest memory of your mother/father? And your next earliest? As a child, how did you experience your mother/father as a person? Can you remember any comments your mother/father made to you about what he/she actually thought of you? These questions are followed by several other queries: earliest memory of school, an event in childhood that had significant impact on your life, a memory of anything now regarded as traumatic, a favorite story or book as a child, and a memory that illustrates what you thought of yourself as a child. Following the reporting and recording of each memory, several clarifying observations are sought: (a) impressions of yourself in the memory; (b) impressions of any other people in the memory; (c) the predominant mood, emotion, or feeling tone of the memory; and (d) the most vivid scene in the memory.*

As clinicians, we then read the transcripts multiple times and identify a tentative list of developmental themes illustrated with supportive quotations from the memories. Confirmation and reinforcement of the themes come from client responses to the Rotter Incomplete Sentences Blank (Rotter & Rafferty, 1950), from consultations with each other, and from subsequent conversations with the client.

Presentation of Findings

After we both have reviewed the memories and identified some developmental themes, we bring written summaries to the couple and read them aloud during an early session in the cojoint therapy cycle. When

---

* The STEM is copyrighted by J.M. Robertson, 2009, and may be used & freely copied if the author is identified on all copies, no changes are made to the wording, and if it is not sold for profit.

they hear an organized presentation of their own childhood memories read back to them, they are given an opportunity see the parallels between the "moral of the story" revealed in the early memories and their current troubles. They can see their presenting issues from a longitudinal, not cross-sectional, point of view. This leads, almost inevitably, to serious reflections about many aspects of their current problems: relational missteps, dysregulated behavior, emotional instability, ineffective coping styles, unchallenged self-concepts, or unsatisfying world views. The discussions become personal, compelling, intense, and informative. Although we have personally found the STEM process to be highly effective in gathering and organizing recollections, we suspect that other approaches cited in the literature can elicit memories that stimulate similar therapeutic self-reflections by both partners in a coupleship.

MEMORIES THAT LEAD TO CHANGE: THE CASE OF ANDREW AND JULIE

This case study presents our assessment of Andrew and Julie's relationship using their early life memories, and summarizes the underlying theory that we believe makes this approach work in therapy. We shall offer several personal observations and reflections along the way.

Assessment

Andrew, a hard-driving and successful corporate lawyer, was mandated by the partners in his law firm to seek intensive treatment. If he refused, they would activate the morals clause in his contract and dismiss him from the firm. The precipitating incident was a claim by a female client that Andrew had asked her for sexual favors in return for additional legal services. But the firm's concerns about his behavior had been building for quite some time. He had been making sexualized jokes to paralegals, missing days from work for mysterious reasons, attending staff meetings unprepared, falling behind in billing clients, requesting salary advances, and occasionally slurring slightly some of his words.

Andrew was a middle-aged European American of average weight, build, and height. He dressed in jeans and a t-shirt. In most settings, his presentation would not have stood out. But in the therapy room, his nonverbal behavior was striking. He frequently appeared shamed, with his body seeming to convey an apology for his very existence. He appeared nothing like the hard-nosed lawyer we had anticipated when hearing about his situation. He seemed more like a chagrined child who was having trouble staying in a timeout.

At his intake, Andrew reported that his central concern was a loss of interest in his work. He felt stressed and burned out. He agreed with some of the concerns raised by his firm, especially that his productivity had declined and his management of his personal income had become problematic. He acknowledged that although his 10-year sobriety from alcohol was still in place, he occasionally had been misusing anxiolytics. As he talked, it became clear that he had struggled for years with poor impulse control and a need to self-medicate in various ways. In all areas of his life, his behavior displayed high levels of risk taking and poor judgment. Andrew took Mahalik et al.'s (2003) Conformity to Masculine Norms Inventory, and his scores revealed patterns he acknowledged were maladaptive: his need to win every case, his pursuit of risk-taking behavior, his push for dominance, his playboy behavior, his need to maintain power over women, and his pursuit of status.

First impressions are instructive. To me (JR), Andrew seemed like a tightly compressed spring during our first one-on-one conversation. He squirmed. His eyes darted. His face flushed and his forehead was slightly sweaty. He clearly was a frightened man, even curling his body into a semifetal position on the couch at one point. He feared that his lucrative and successful law career was in jeopardy, as was his marriage. He felt profoundly humiliated and deeply shamed by his professional boundary crossing. The telling of his story was punctuated by sobbing, which came in wrenching waves. But he also spoke with clarity and honesty, owning up to the allegations directed against him.

As he talked, I was moved by his pain and his terror for the future. But at the same time, I was encouraged for his course of his therapy. In our clinic, we have found that most professionals are not as open as Andrew at the beginning of their assessment and treatment. More often, mandated clients defend their maladaptive behavior in ways that avoid, blame, obfuscate, or mislead us. But none of this was apparent in Andrew's presentation of his story. He admitted all of it—his failure to complete routine tasks at work, his frequent use of sexual innuendos with staff, his inappropriate behavior with a client, his reckless spending. These admissions were offered with a sense of confusion and alarm. He wondered how all of this could have happened. His general lack of eye contact was interspersed with intense gazing at me (JR), which seemed to plead for understanding. In addition to completing the other portions of his multidisciplinary assessment (cognitive and personality testing, social and spiritual histories, medical and psychiatric functioning), he reviewed his early life with me, using the STEM approach outlined earlier.

Several weeks into treatment, Andrew's wife, Julie, agreed to participate in intensive couple's therapy with her husband. The switch to couples work was intentionally timed to occur after Andrew had begun to address the reality that his behavior had harmed others, including his wife. Given Andrew's fears about losing his marriage, it became important to help him find ways to discuss his fears and hopes about the future of the relationship. In this sense, the marital therapy functioned as an adjunct to his individual work. However, the idea of examining their relationship was appealing to her, as well. After all, she had been injured by his behavior and had some things to say about what had happened. Therefore, the goals of marital work were (a) to give Andrew an opportunity to deepen his empathy for the impact his behavior had on Julie; (b) to give him a chance to try his newly developing skill of talking openly and honestly about difficult emotions; (c) to assist both Andrew and Julie in understanding how their current relational difficulties could be seen as a function of patterns with roots that extended back into their childhoods; and (d) to help them clarify how they might "do" their relationship differently.

Before the first couple session, I (SKB) met with Julie alone. She made an arresting impression. She was fashionably dressed, bejeweled, and groomed. For all outward appearances, she looked very well put together. A very attractive European American woman in her early 50s, she appeared physically much younger than her age. She was warm, polite, and a little reserved. However, the weight of her concerns and her emotional fatigue seemed to have aged her, making her put together presentation seem just that—a presentation. I felt a need to offer her reassurance and encouragement at the start, emphasizing that she had much to offer and much to gain from the couple's therapy process.

Julie reported that they had been married for over 20 years and were raising two teenage children. As she became more comfortable talking about years of conflict with Andrew, a flood of emotions poured out, as though washing over the top of a dam that could no longer contain them. Her composed exterior washed away with the mascara. It was clear that this experience was novel for her, as she appeared both startled and embarrassed by the intensity of her emotional responses. She warned me that she could not talk to Andrew with this much vulnerability and frankness. I found myself also near tears as she shared her pain over Andrew's sexual behavior, his substance use, and his habitual emotional withdrawal. It was easy to normalize her emotions as well as highlight her courage in sharing so openly.

Julie indicated that as a paralegal in her husband's large law practice, she had observed many of his inappropriate actions firsthand. She was humiliated that all her colleagues knew about his recent sexual indiscretion. It was evident in our discussion that her discomfiture minimized her willingness to engage socially both in the workplace and in her personal life, leaving her feeling isolated and alone.

In addition, Julie was resentful of the impact Andrew's misbehavior was having on larger family issues, such as their financial future and their children's welfare. She told me that Andrew would make an impulsive decision such as buying an expensive car without consulting her. This caused much stress for her, as she was left to sort out the financial consequences alone.

She acknowledged with shame that she had erupted in a rage over his behavior. Shortly before Andrew left for treatment at our facility, she went into a tirade over his sexual bargaining with client. She screamed at him, and threw a lamp that missed him and hit the wall instead. Andrew had retreated behind the safety of their locked bedroom door and refused to talk. She was infuriated by his passive response and also frightened by the intensity of her own anger. During this initial meeting, it was apparent that Julie was ambivalent about their marriage, but also wary about what a divorce might mean for their children. To her, couples therapy was an opportunity to see if her husband had indeed made changes in the early days of his therapy that might make their continued marriage possible.

I explained that Andrew had completed a review of his early life memories during his assessment, and that I hoped to explore with her some of her own early reminiscences for two purposes. It would provide us an opportunity to understand her better, and it also would give the two of them a chance to see how themes from their early lives might help us all understand the current relational crisis they faced. She was open to this process and was tearful as she described significant memories from her childhood, most of which she had not thought about for years. As she cried, I was struck by both her vulnerability and her resilience. She appeared incredibly burdened, tired, and depleted. Her patience for Andrew's behaviors had been exhausted. Her anger was intense and palpable. However, I also admired her courage and endurance, evident in her attempts to hold together her marriage and family for many years. Her openness and tentative hopefulness suggested to me that we had fertile ground in which to work.

Treatment

After using the STEM to collect memories from both Andrew and Julie, the two of us (JR and SKB) met to review their stories and to find the imbedded developmental themes. Two of Andrew's early memories illustrate how these themes can be used. In one, he recalled an event illustrating his belief that the world can be a dangerous place. "I remember playing in a sandbox and I found a piece of corn and it had started to sprout roots and grow. I was just amazed. I think I wanted to show people but I was afraid to. It was something I had discovered, alone. I buried it back I think." He reported feeling satisfaction in his discovery, but also fear "because (others) wouldn't understand and might take it away from me and destroy it and mess it up." He added that he remembered being very shy, "afraid to interact with other kids." A second example illustrates an embryonic version of a theme that had become dominant in his life: Achievement improves poor self-esteem. He recalled a nice teacher who took the children outside regularly to let them engage in a long race. He remembers, "She'd make the whole class run out in this field. I always prided myself in coming in first, way ahead of the others. Maybe they weren't trying hard enough. I felt a source of pride or self-worth maybe. It was an accomplishment. I felt happy." Encouraged to describe his view of himself during that memory, he states, "It gave me ... *made* me, feel better about myself. I was worth something. I could do something well." Most vivid was the experience of running up to his teacher and having her pat him on the back and say "good job, you did it again." He adds, "I was somebody."

For Andrew, we reviewed more than 15 memories, and produced a list of five developmental themes:

- I have poor self esteem (a self concept).
- I am not strongly attached with my parents (a relational pattern).
- The world is dangerous, and others might hurt me (a relational pattern).
- I isolate myself from others (an adaptive strategy).
- Self-worth can be gained through achievements (a lesson learned).

It was helpful to notice (and eventually point out to him) how directly these themes reflected masculine social norms that have become prominent in North America more generally: difficulty with attachment and commitment, a fear of being hurt, emotional isolation, and the expectation that high levels of achievement will have significant personal rewards.

A similar process identified several themes in Julie's stories. One portrayed her tendency to be patient and responsible, regardless of the provocation. She described waiting for her mother to come home from work on weekends: "Because mom worked, we had to stay inside" while other children were allowed to play outside. "We were home by ourselves so we had to stay inside ... always being responsible. Since mom worked, we did housework. Then we'd go to get special food for cleaning the house, but not play." A second example illustrates how quickly her sense of self could shift. She recalled an incident when she visited her mother in the hospital: "I was a chunky girl. Mom had bought me pink hot pants. I thought I was so pretty in them. But Dad was making fun of me, teasing me because I was so chunky ... that I had chunky thighs. I felt hurt because I thought I was so pretty in them." She added, "I was just hurt he didn't think I was pretty or special. ... I was embarrassed I wore that. I thought, 'Oh gosh, take them off.'" Most vivid was the sense that she could think she was "something special," but others could be laughing at her.

Julie's full set of memories revealed four developmental themes:

- My self-image shifts, depending on what others say (a self concept).
- Men are distant and don't understand what I need (a relational pattern).
- Patience and responsibility are important (an adaptive strategy).
- Social situations are threatening (a lesson learned).

We both have noticed that clients find themselves unexpectedly emotional in recalling these stories. They do not anticipate the reappearance of emotions associated with an incident they may not have discussed with anyone since it occurred. For us, listening to these sometimes painful recollections arouses our own emotions, such as compassion, protectiveness, and empathy. We sometimes find ourselves "debriefing" each other following some of the more painfully dramatic stories.

In the initial conjoint therapy session, we summarized the developmental themes to the couple, writing them in two side-by-side lists on a large dry-erase board. Andrew sighed anxiously as he listened to the narrative that identified and illustrated his themes. At times, he appeared uncomfortable as JR read the summary of his memories while SKB wrote the themes on the board. He stole glances at his wife during this presentation, observing her reactions to his stories. Both members of the couple expressed grief and sadness as they thought about his loneliness during childhood and his desperate attempts to connect with others. They were sitting next to each other on a love seat, and at one point, he appeared surprised but pleased as Julie reached out to hold his hand. He also seemed grateful to have his childhood experiences given such attention. His themes now were visible for both of them to see, and were expressed in language he himself had never used in the past. Similarly, as SKB shared Julie's memories and JR wrote the accompanying themes alongside Andrew's, the couple continued to touch each other in comforting ways. We, too, were moved by their growing responsiveness to one another. Andrew moved to sit closer to his wife, put his arm around her, and gave her tissues as she cried from the emotional pain aroused by hearing her own recollections read aloud.

Once the themes were listed side by side, our first question was straightforward: "Do these themes seem familiar to you? Do they really describe what it was like for you to be a child?" Both quickly and emphatically agreed. Andrew expressed amazement, not only that his list captured his experiences, but that Julie's list captured his understanding of her patterns.

Then we asked, "How do you see these themes interacting in your relationship? Which themes interact easily, and which ones tend to create problems for you?" There was a long pause at this point, as the couple took time to compare the themes with their own experiences. All the while, they held hands.

Andrew began the discussion. "I wonder if my low self-worth is a reason I've tried so hard to succeed as a lawyer." Julie agreed, and added, "And by the way, your long hours have been a problem for me as well because your drive to succeed seems to have no limits at times." They exchanged several comments about this theme.

Then they began talking about Andrew's impulsive financial behaviors. Andrew explained why he spends the way he does. "When I spend large amounts of money at one time, I feel good about myself. Like I've made it somehow ... like I'm special." This joint exploration of developmental themes is not always smooth, but the bumps can provide teachable moments for couples to see their themes in action. As Julie shared how various spending sprees have affected her emotionally, Andrew at first was quick to defend and explain. We pointed out these behaviors and asked him to consider what theme was at work. Initially, he tended to focus on her criticism of him. Again, we emphasized, "Which of *your* themes is being activated right now?" "Well, when Julie talks about my poor spending habits, I feel ashamed and bad about myself." "What happens next?" JR asked. "I withdraw. I don't want to hear about it because I don't want to feel bad." This observation was significant for both of them as it helped provide a context for Andrew to think about other strategies he has used to avoid feeling badly about himself. It also helped Julie to better understand of how pervasive his low self-worth had been.

Both Andrew and Julie quickly grasped a central point as they discussed these questions: Their current relationship patterns had developed early in life, long before they had met each another. We find that virtually all couples draw this same conclusion when they see their own themes in written form. At this point, blaming comments lessen as they begin to reflect at a very personal level on what they have brought as individuals to the relationship.

Andrew and Julie generated most of their insights on their own and discussed them together. We offered a few interpretations along the way. For example, when Andrew berated himself for spending large amounts of money to moderate his feelings of ineffectiveness and shame, JR reframed his self-critical thought: "Andrew, could it be that this is not so much a personal failure as an illustration of your need to conform to an important social norm for most men? Many men believe that high occupational achievement should improve self-esteem because it will win admiration and appreciation from others." Similarly, when the couple began criticizing his overuse of benzodiazepines, JR reframed the behavior. "Andrew, could it be that the larger issue is the internal stress that makes you susceptible to overusing anxiety drugs? Are the pills more of a symptom than a treatment?"

Andrew then wanted Julie to understand how afraid he was as a child. He reported that he saw the world as terribly dangerous. We encouraged him to share these remembered fears by giving her some examples. "Talk to her," we said. "Look at her as you share these memories." He was able to describe how unimportant he felt to his parents and how utterly alone he felt most of the time. He appeared vulnerable and childlike as he concluded, "I was scared a lot. I had to protect myself."

In an effort to help him consider how these early experiences and lack of attachment with his parents influenced his marital relationship, we queried, "How do you think this has affected your approach to Julie? Can you tell her?" "I really don't know how to connect with you," he said hesitantly. "I'm afraid that any complaint I have will send you packing. You'll just walk out." "Is that why you withdraw?"

she asked. SKB continued, "What happens, Andrew, when you pull back from her?" "Well, I guess it only increases my shame in the long run. But I don't want to be abandoned and hurt." Julie then acknowledged she had noticed his sensitivity to conflict and criticism. "But the reason I tell you I don't like your isolation and spending is to improve our relationship, not end it." She pointed out the irony. "You say you're afraid I will leave you when I bring up problems, but when you withdraw from me, that's exactly what it feels like to me. You are leaving me."

Julie also was able to deepen her self-understanding. She could acknowledge her self-appointed role as the "responsible parent" in the relationship, her extreme discomfort and anger when his actions were irresponsible, her humiliation from his playboy flirtations and infidelity at work, and her fear that she was not pretty or desirable enough. Furthermore, although she rather expected Andrew to adhere to the masculine norm of ignoring her needs (as modeled by her father), she had found herself talking to him about her desires over and over, like a broken record. But she continued to feel unheard, confirming her belief that men are distant and unreachable.

With these perspectives in place, Andrew and Julie were able to see their relational difficulties in a much larger context. In subsequent sessions, they occasionally returned to their familiar attack-and-defend style. One time, we responded by simply pointing at the board in front of them. "Which theme is being activated at this moment?" Andrew was able to say, "It's my low self-worth again. Whenever I feel bad about myself, I seem to go on the attack." JR asked, "When you are in this self-critical mode, but then criticize Julie, what happens for her?" Andrew paused for a moment, looked at her list of themes, and said, "Maybe I make it harder for her to contribute to the relationship? I know she likes to feel responsible for the practical stuff, and when I criticize her, well … I don't know?" He looked at Julie, who finished the thought: "Then I change what I think about myself," she said pointing at the board. "Instead of feeling productive, I feel stupid." Andrew replied, "Is that why you get angry with me?" "Partly, yes. But when you get down on yourself, you also go off and do things on your own. Like that car you bought with cash we didn't have. That leaves me feeling totally discounted. Then I get down on myself, like I don't matter … and then I just get so angry at you." Andrew was able to see that his behavior had prevented him from hearing Julie's legitimate concerns about their finances as well as contributed to her sense of worthlessness in their marriage.

At times, their work was intensely emotional. They discussed the incident that was still raw for both of them. Just after Julie found out about Andrew's attempt to become sexual with a client, she was enraged and came after him. Andrew had hidden behind a locked bedroom door. "You have no idea how terrified I was," he said. "I thought you might have a weapon." JR interjected, "What did you really want from Julie at that moment?" "I wanted to feel close to her, not fear. I've felt fear all my life. It sucks and I'm tired of it ..." At this, his tearfulness escalated into full body sobs. Julie was deeply moved by his expressions of vulnerability, and said, "I had no idea you feel so strongly about me. Do you really want to be close to me?" Her tone was inviting, not sarcastic. Andrew nodded. SKB asked, "Julie, what do you want him to know?" Without a word she turned to him and put both arms around his neck. He responded with a hug, and the two of them just held each other for several emotional seconds.

Their discussions became more collaborative. In one session, Andrew asked the therapists, "How can I get closer to Julie and still feel safe myself? Whenever I open myself up and try to say what I really want, I get scared and back off." JR responded, "Do you feel like asking her about that?"Andrew turned to Julie with an expectant look. "Are you asking what feels close to me?" He nodded. "Well, if you would tell me once in a while that you appreciate my managing our finances, that would feel good. I think I'd feel closer to you ... like you valued me. You know?" Andrew seemed lost in thought, until JR observed, "It looks like you're thinking hard about this one." "Yes," he said. "I wonder if this works both ways. If I knew that Julie respected my work as an attorney, then I'd feel stronger about it myself, and less likely to attack. Maybe if we could both do this ... we'd be ... what do you call it ... is it supportive?

Throughout, the two of us talked with each other in front of the couple about what we were noticing in the sessions. JR would say, "Supavan, I wonder what you'd think if we went back and asked Andrew more about his comment that he worries about his impact on the children." Or, SKB would say, "John, I'm observing something really interesting about how Andrew and Julie are talking to each other right now. Are you?" In this way, we tried to model communication that was clear, respectful, and facilitative. Our overall role included offering some interpretations, pointing out patterns, and modeling an emotionally safe working relationship.

Outcome

Andrew's individual treatment for personality traits and substance abuse continued 8 hours a day for 12 weeks. The marital work occurred in two blocks of time during those 12 weeks, near the beginning and again near the end of his treatment. The couple's sessions were intense, lasting 18 hours over 3 days. The treatment team recommended that Andrew initiate follow-up marital therapy upon his return home. The couple agreed to do so, and he reported by phone and e-mail over the next 2 years that the marriage had survived with a broader appreciation of their vulnerabilities, and with the use of more effective communication and problem-solving skills. Both believed the future of the marriage was promising and secure.

FINAL COMMENT: THE ROLE OF THE
THERAPEUTIC SHADOW

We end with a critically important point. And it is personal. We certainly
have found that men become deeply engaged in couple's therapy when
they are given the task-oriented approach of identifying developmental
themes from early life. But there is a deeper layer of involvement. We
believe that a "shadowing" process occurred in our work with Andrew
and Julie. They observed our interactions with each other—our cohesion, synchrony, humor, collaboration, mutual respect, management of
divergent views, and regard for boundaries. Our intent was to engage
with them in ways that allowed an awareness of these factors to remain
as an internal and influential presence in their relationship, long after
they left our consulting room. We hoped that our approving and emotionally supportive stance toward their efforts would be revealed in our
verbalized respect for their competence, insight, cooperation, affection,
resilience, and capacity to change.

We expected them to forget some of our comments about specific
points of marital contention, such as their disagreements about finances
or parenting. But we hoped that in the shadows of their memories, they
might remember the experience of being present with us. They may
be unable to describe the subtle features of our conversations, such as
tone, nuance, and prosody. Yet we hoped these less focal factors might
become the most influential part of what remained from working with
us. Neuroscience evidence supports this shadow understanding of therapy, having demonstrated that effective psychotherapeutic relationships
actually change brain structures (Schore, 2003).

Given this view of our potential therapeutic influence, we try to model
effective relational attitudes and skills for couples. We openly treat each
other with warmth and appreciation. We read each other's cues, check in
regularly with what the other is observing, and treat those observations
with respect. In front of the couple, we negotiate the direction our discussion might take. In the long run, we hope these illustrations of a collaborative relationship will be internalized in their own approach to each
other. Long ago, Horwitz (1974) called this process the "internalization
of the therapeutic alliance." Laborsky (1984) illustrates the idea with the
story of two boys who stand at the edge of a swimming pool, wanting to
jump into the water. One easily jumped, but the other couldn't. The first
explained, "'My parents told me it was okay, and I saw others jump in. ...
I can tell myself it will be okay.' ... The second one explained, 'I was told
that, but I can't realize it. So I can't jump'" (Laborsky, 1984, p. 26).

This version of the therapeutic alliance forms the theoretical core
of our work with couples (cf. Allen et al., 1996; Book, 1997; Frieswyk
et al., 1986; Frieswyk, Colson, & Allen, 1984; Laborsky, 1997; Teyber,
2000). Couples examine their own relational difficulties while observing our interactions with each other. Their observation of us silently

encourages them to begin revising their own long-held relational schemas. How does this work? I (SKB) have noticed that John's willingness to be attuned to my efforts in therapy, to listen and support me rather than compete for control, have been helpful in setting a tone for how men respond to their wives. He is patient, affirming, sensitive, and non-judging of me. He openly thinks and explores *with* me. By observing his approach toward me, men experience a gentle challenge to developmental themes that may have been problematic for them, such as "Others are not responsive or available," or "I must always be in control." In a similar vein, I (JR) have found that Supavan's approach to me influences the tone of men's comments to their partners. When she has a perspective different from mine, she does not hesitate to offer it. Her assertiveness is clear, consistent, and very kind. I typically respond with interest and openness. I do not feel upset, offended, or threatened. This nonreactive stance not only is reassuring to the man in the moment (because therapy remains focused on the couple) but also is illustrative of the idea that the kindly expression of alternative views is not inherently threatening. Multiple relational themes can be illustrated in this way.

This conjoint approach to couples therapy does not exclude therapists who work alone with couples. Not at all. Individual therapists can administer the STEM or other early memory assessments in separate meetings with each member of a couple, and then bring them together to examine their developmental themes. Object relations theory still applies. Take Rex and Heather. Rex is authoritarian, demanding, and accusatory, whereas Heather is cautious, cowering, and self-blaming. Both individual therapists and conjoint therapists model relational skills with every comment, gesture, and glance. If a solo male therapist speaks to Heather with respect, kindness and clarity in front of Rex, then Rex has a live demonstration of how he might talk differently to his wife. Or, if an individual female therapist speaks to Rex with directness, self-confidence, and clarity, then Heather can begin imagining how she might speak differently to her husband. In this way, individual therapists also become new "parental" objects who are soothing, containing, and compassionate, thus casting their own therapeutic shadows onto the lives of a couple in the years to come. Couples pay close attention to their therapists, individual or conjoint. In thinking about their own early life relational patterns while observing us, couples can begin cocreating new modes of engaging with each other.

Sid Frieswyk, a clinical psychologist who has worked with couples for more than 45 years, has mentored the development of our understanding of couples counseling. He summed his view of our approach in a personal comment to us that also happens to capture a sense of the exceptional fulfillment this work has for us.

Where to find a better example of a couple working together smoothly and collaboratively than in the discussion of early life memories and their implications? It is this exercise that brings to life a process that changes everyone who joins in. It is a process that may contrast sharply with the dimly remembered engagements with mom and dad from the earliest moments of life. The modeling of parental engagement is what leads to the emergence of a self yearning for and capable of engaging in the intricate intimacies of adult life with a life partner. The power of the current engagement with another couple is that it offers a "new object relationship," a model for intimacy not hitherto experienced. In this way, you all will have done something to be remembered. (S. H. Frieswyk, personal communication, January 31, 2010)

ACKNOWLEDGMENTS

We are deeply grateful to Sid Frieswyk for casting his "therapeutic shadow" on our understanding of early life memories. His enduring presence in our lives has refined our thinking, improved our writing, and immeasurably enriched our lives.

REFERENCES

Addis, M. E., & Mahalik, J. R. (2003). Men, masculinity, and the contexts of help seeking. *American Psychologist, 58*(1), 5–14.

Adler, A. (1937). The significance of early recollections. *International Journal of Individual Psychology, 3,* 283–287.

Adler, A. (1998). Analyzing early memories. In C. Brett (Ed., Trans.), *What life could mean to you.* Center, City, MN: Hazeldon. (Original work published 1931)

Allen, J. G., Coyne, L., Colston, D. B., Horwitz, L., Gabbard, G. O., Frieswyk, S. H., & Newsom, G. E. (1996). Pattern of therapist interventions associated with patient collaboration. *Psychotherapy, 33*(2), 254–261.

Balswick, J. (1988). *The inexpressive male.* Lexington, MA.

Bettner, B. L. (2007). Recreating sibling relationships in marriage. *Journal of Individual Psychology, 63*(3), 339–344.

Book, H. E. (1997). *How to practice brief psychodynamic psychotherapy.* Washington, DC: American Psychological Association.

Bruhn, A. R. (1992a). The early memories procedure: A projective test of autobiographical memory, Part 1. *Journal of Personality Assessment, 58*(1), 1–15.

Bruhn, A. R. (1992b). The early memories procedure: A projective test of autobiographical memory, Part 2. *Journal of Personality Assessment, 58*(2), 326–346.

Christie, A. (1977). *Agatha Christie: An autobiography.* London: Collins.

Clark, A. J. (2004). Editor's note: Early recollections. *Journal of Individual Psychology, 60*(2), 105–106.

Cuervo-Lombard, C., Jovenin, N., Hedelin, G., Rizzo-Peter, L., Conway, M. A., & Danion, J. M. (2007). Autobiographical memory of adolescence and early adulthood events: An investigation in schizophrenia. *Journal of the International Neuropsychological Society, 13*(2), 335–343.

Curran, M., Hazen, N., Jacobvitz, D., & Feldman, A. (2005). Representations of early family relationships predict marital maintenance during the transition to parenthood. *Journal of Family Psychology, 19*(2), 189–197.

Davidow, S., & Bruhn, A. R. (1990). Earliest memories and the dynamics of delinquency: A replication study. *Journal of Personality Assessment, 54*(3–4), 601–616.

Deaner, R. G. Y., & Pechersky, K. (2005). Early recollections: Enhancing case conceptualization for practitioners working with couples. *The Family Journal, 13*(3), 311–315.

Faulkner, W. (1951). *Requiem for a nun*. New York: Random House.

Fowler, J. C., Hilsenroth, M. J., & Handler, L. (2000). Martin Mayman's early memories technique: Bridging the gap between personality assessment and psychotherapy. *Journal of Personality Assessment, 75*(1), 18–32.

Freud, S. (1938). Book I, Psychopathology of everyday life. Childhood and concealing memories. In A. A. Brill (Trans.), *The basic writings of Sigmund Freud* (pp. 62–68). New York: the Modern Library. (Original work published 1901)

Freud, S. (1989). Screen memories. In P. Gay (Trans.), *The Freud reader* (pp. 117–128). New York: Norton. (Original work published 1899)

Frieswyk, S. H., Allen, J. G., Colson, D. B., Coyne, L., Gabbard, G. L., Horwitz, L., & Newsom, G. (1986). Therapeutic alliance: Its place as a process and outcome variable in dynamic psychotherapy research. *Journal of Consulting and Clinical Psychology, 54*, 32–38.

Frieswyk, S. H., Colson, D. B., & Allen, J. G. (1984). Conceptualizing the therapeutic alliance from a psychoanalytic perspective. *Psychotherapy: Theory, Research, and Practice, 21*, 460–464.

Goddard, L., Dritschel, B., & Burton, A. (1996). Role of autobiographical memory in social problem solving and depression. *Journal of Abnormal Psychology, 105*(4), 609–616.

Harris, S. M., & Dertsch, C. A. (2001). "I'm just not like that": Investigating the intergenerational cycle of violence. *The Family Journal, 9*(3), 250–258.

Hawes, C. (2007). Early recollections: A compelling intervention in couples therapy. *The Journal of Individual Psychology, 63*(3), 306–314.

Horwitz, L. (1974). *Clinical prediction in psychotherapy*. New York: Jason Aronson.

Hurst, M. A. (1997). The best fit in counseling men: Are there solutions to treating men as the problem? *Dissertation Abstracts International: Section B: The Sciences and Engineering, 58*(3-B), 1534.

Koch, K., Pauly, K., Kellermann, T., Seiferth, N. Y., Reske, M., Backes, V., Stöcker, T., ... Habel, U. (2007). Gender differences in the cognitive control of emotion: An fMRI study. *Neuropsychologica, 45*(12), 2744–2754.

Krohn, A., & Mayman, M. (1974). Object representations in dreams and projective tests. *Bulletin of the Menninger Clinic, 38*, 445–466.

Laborsky, L. (1984). *Principles of psychoanalytic psychotherapy: A manual for supportive-expressive treatment*. New York: Basic Books.

Laborsky, L. (1997). *How to practice brief, psychodynamic psychotherapy*. Washington, DC: American Psychological Association.

Levant, R. F. (2001). Desperately seeking language: Understanding, assessing, and treating normative male alexithymia. In G. R. Brooks & G. E. Good (Eds.), *The new handbook of psychotherapy and counseling with men: A comprehensive guide to settings, problems, and treatment approaches* (Vol. 1, pp. 424–443). San Francisco, CA: Jossey-Bass.

Loftus, E. F. (1993). The reality of repressed memories. *American Psychologist, 48*, 518–537.

Mahalik, J. R. (2000). Gender role conflict in men as a predictor of self-ratings of behavior on the interpersonal circle. *Journal of Social and Clinical Psychology, 19*, 276–292.

Mahalik, J. R., Locke, B. D., Ludlow, L., Diemer, M., Scott, R. P. J., Gottfried, M., & Freitas, G. (2003). Development of the Conformity to Masculine Norms Inventory. *Psychology of Men and Masculinity, 4*, 325.

Mayman, M. (1968). Early memories and character structure. *Journal of Projective Techniques and Personality Assessment, 32*, 303–316.

Monahan, R. T. (1983). Suicidal children's and adolescents' responses to early memories test. *Journal of Personality Assessment, 47*(3), 258–264.

Parks, E. D., & Balon, R. (1995). Autobiographical memory for childhood events: Patterns of recall in psychiatric patients with a history of alleged trauma. *Psychiatry, 58*(3), 199–208.

Professional Renewal Center. (2008). *Multidisciplinary assessment and treatment for professionals.* Retrieved November 30, 2008, from http://www.prckansas.org/

Rabinowitz, F. E., & Cochran, S. V. (2002). *Deepening psychotherapy with men.* Washington, DC: American Psychological Association.

Robertson, J. M., & Fitzgerald, L. F. (1992). Overcoming the masculine mystique: Preferences for alternative forms of assistance among men who avoid counseling. *Journal of Counseling Psychology, 39*(2), 240–246.

Robertson, J. M., & Khamphakdy-Brown, S. (2007). *Summary of Themes from Early Memories (STEM).* Unpublished manuscript. Available as an e-mail attachment from the authors at jrobertson@prckansas.org.

Rotter, J. B., & Rafferty, J. E. (1950). *Manual: The Rotter Incomplete Sentences Blank.* Cleveland, OH: The Psychological Corporation.

Schore, A. N. (2003). *Affect regulation and the repair of the self.* New York: Norton.

Schore, A. N. (2006, April 30). *Affect regulation and the repair of the self.* Conference presentation handout at the University of Kansas, Lawrence.

Shields, S. (2002). *Speaking from the heart: Gender and the social meaning of emotion.* New York: Cambridge University Press.

Shulman, D. G., & Ferguson, G. R. (1988). Two methods of assessing narcissism: Comparison of the Narcissism-Projective (N-P) and the Narcissistic Personality Inventory (NPI). *Journal of Clinical Psychology, 44*(6), 857–866.

Spiegel, D., Butler, L. D., & McConkey (Eds.). (1997). Repressed Memories, Section II. In L. J. Dickstein, M. B. Riba, & J. M. Oldham, (Eds.), *Review of Psychiatry* (Vol. 16). American Psychiatric Press.

Teyber, E. (2000). *Interpersonal process in psychotherapy: A relational approach* (4th ed.). Stamford, CT: Brooks/Cole.

Thoughts of Eric Hoffer. (1971, April 25). *The New York Times Magazine,* pp. 55, 57.

Tulving, E. (1983). *Elements of episodic memory*. Oxford: Clarendon Press.

Watts, R. E. (1997). Using family-of-origin recollections in premarital and marriage counseling. *Individual Psychology: Journal of Adlerian Theory, Research & Practice, 53*(4), 429–434.

Watts, R. E. (2000). Techniques in marriage and family counseling. In R. E. Watts (Ed.), *The family psychology and counseling series* (Vol. 1, pp. 53–56). Alexandria, VA: American Counseling Association.

Wenzel, A., Jackson, L. C., & Holt, C. S. (2002). Social phobia and the recall of autobiographical memories. *Depression and Anxiety, 15*(4), 186–189.

Williams, J. M. G. (2003). *Autobiographical Memory Test scoring manual.* Unpublished manuscript.

Williams, J. M. G., & Broadbent, K. (1986). Autobiographical memory in suicide attempters. *Journal of Abnormal Psychology, 95,* 144–149.

Wong, Y. J. (2008, August). *Re-envisioning men's emotional lives: An application of social constructionist perspectives*. Symposium presentation at the annual convention of the American Psychological Association, Boston, MA.

Adlerian Couples Therapy
The Case of the Boxer's Daughter and the Momma's Boy

MATT ENGLAR-CARLSON AND JON CARLSON

To our knowledge, this chapter on Adlerian couples therapy with men is the first scholarly work to directly blend Adlerian therapeutic ideas with recent ideas generated from the new psychology of men and masculinity. In developing his theory, Alfred Adler (strongly influenced by his wife Raissa; Balla, 2003) accounted for the influence of gender socialization in looking at the mental health of men and women (Adler, 1992/1927). Whereas Freud initially framed masculinity in psychosexuality and a biologically oriented drive, focusing on the Oedipal complex (for boys this addressed rivalry with the father and the fear of castration), Adler looked at gender development in a more psychologically oriented, subjective psychology created in a sociopolitical context that fully considered the influence of cultural and societal factors (Ansbacher & Ansbacher, 1956). Adlerian theory provides our theoretical context, yet we both adopt a masculine sensitive approach (see Englar-Carlson & Shepard, 2005; Englar-Carlson & Stevens, 2006; Englar-Carlson, Stevens, & Scholz, 2010; Stevens & Englar-Carlson, 2010) in tailoring psychotherapy to consider how gender socialization affects men and women. Because it is beyond the purview of this chapter to review the basics of Adlerian psychology, the interested reader is referred to Carlson and Englar-Carlson's (2008) paper. This chapter examines the application of Adlerian couple's therapy with male clients, looks at the blending of masculine-sensitive psychology with the Adlerian approach, and then presents a case example.

ADLERIAN COUPLES THERAPY

Adlerians put a particular emphasis on marriage and committed relationships. After all, Adler recognized marriage as one of the basic social tasks confronting individuals in life. He suggested that each person has a need for developing a close and intimate relationship with at least one other person (Ansbacher & Ansbacher, 1956). Whereas this can be viewed as an individual need, Adler believed it was also a social and community need, noting, "marriage is a task for two people living and working together as part of humanity and society and thereby connecting the past and future" (Nicoll, 1989, p. 1).

Adlerian couples counseling puts a specific emphasis on meaning for each person, as meaning helps give importance to the experiences in life. One's perspective on meaning is developed early in life, as one's birth order and perception of roles in the family provides the basis for one's psychological orientation to the world. Gender norms and cultural expectations would also strongly influence one's perspective. Adler used the term *private logic* to denote one's individual perception of their world (Carlson & Sperry, 2000), and noted this was the basis for the development of an individual's lifestyle—literally, one's style of dealing with life, what other theories call, personality (Carlson, Watts, & Maniacci, 2006). It is important to note that any marriage or committed relationship signifies the bringing together of two unique lifestyles.

The focus on meaning is important in working with couples (Carlson & Sperry, 1998). Meaning refers to the goals and cognitive expectations one has for the relationship and for one's own place in that relationship. Meaning therefore drives behavior, which, in turn, influences the ways in which the individuals in couple relationships interact with one another (Carlson & Sperry, 2000). Partners come to relationships with their own unique private logic (e.g., ideas conceived in childhood that comprises one's deeply established personal beliefs or constructs) and lifestyle rules. Each attempts to get needs met through one's own lifestyle approaches and rules. In that frame, the Adlerian counselor considers that the couple's behavior, rather than being essentially dysfunctional, may actually be a creative way of negotiating differences and finding solutions to their problems. The counselor attempts to identify and use this creativity to find behavior that leads to a constructive outcome for the couple (Carlson & Sperry, 2000). Thus couples have good intentions in their behavior, and often have relationship skills, yet somehow in the blending together of two people with their own lifestyles and beliefs, they are not getting the desired outcomes. Couples are taught how to make their relationships reciprocal and cooperative instead of destructive. They are able to see positive alternatives to what ordinarily would have been overwhelming challenges (Dinkmeyer, 1993).

Couples counseling proceeds by blending Adlerian ideas about relationships with notions of effective communication. Carlson and Dinkmeyer (2003) described specific behaviors that are observable in couples that have satisfying relationships. Individuals in well-functioning relationships each accept responsibility for their own behavior and for developing their own sense of self-esteem. They encourage, value, and accept one another and work together to make goals for their relationship. Communication is open and honest. Partners listen empathically to the others' feelings and make an effort to understand the dynamics that are impacting their relationship. Conflicts are solved by thoughtfully choosing words and behaviors that support the needs of the relationship rather than the needs of the individuals. Roughly speaking, Adlerian couples counseling follows four stages.

Treatment Process and Strategies

Stage 1: Relationship Building

The first goal is to create hope for the future (Hawes, 2007). Therapy begins with establishing a relationship of empathy and understanding. Couples are helped to identify both internal and external resources that will enable them to become more optimistic about the outcome of counseling. Investigation of the problem often begins prior to counseling, when couples fill out assessment inventories that provide information about their perceptions of the problem, when the problem started, whether there were any events that influenced the development of the problem, medical and social histories, and why the couple initiated counseling at this time (Carlson et al., 2006).

Stage 2: Assessment

Adlerians work to shift the focus from problems to focus on clients' strengths. Clients are asked to consider how their relationships would look if they were happier. Therapist goals include an increase in social interest and community feeling with an emphasis on four primary objectives: (1) decrease symptoms; (2) increase clients' functioning; (3) increase sense of humor; and (4) change clients' perspectives (Carlson et al., 2006, p. 130). This is accomplished by promoting understanding and insight about purposes, goals and behaviors; by enhancing communication, problem-solving, and conflict resolution; and by encouraging commitment to growth and change (Carlson, Sperry, & Lewis, 2005).

The use of a lifestyle assessment and discovery of early recollections can help couples understand how their expectations, behavior, private logic, and *basic mistakes* (mistaken notions and faulty assumptions that become self-defeating aspects of a person's perceptions, attitudes, and beliefs) influenced their original relationship contract and the ways that they interact with one another (Abramson, 2007; Hawes, 2007). Some Adlerians might use a formal instrument like the Life-Style Inventory (Kern, 2002), whereas others might use a simple questions and observation to assess and explore life-style with clients. Abramson (2004) suggested that couples sense that the other has characteristics that will help them attain their goals and live according to the rules of their life-styles. Therefore, the therapist will want to know what the implicit and explicit agreements were regarding the roles each would assume in the couple relationship. Ongoing assessment will help uncover the capability the partners have in working toward a healthy relationship. The therapist explores how well each partner can understand the other's point of view; their ability to accept, appreciate, and respect one another; their acceptance of the fact that not everything is likely to go as they want it; and their ability to remain autonomous while still being part of a union.

Stage 3: Interpretation and Insight

The next stage of Adlerian therapy is creating insight through interpretation. Often the counselor explores how the couple met, their perceptions of their roles in the relationship, and the ways they create conflict in the present. The counselor helps the couple realize how they each attempt to guard their own self-esteem by undermining the other's conditions for self-esteem. Using Adlerian theory, the counselor is often active in providing interpretations and observations to the clients with the intention of identifying the real issues at the core of the conflict. Interpreting clients' basic mistakes and lifestyle rules is often useful. Clients realize that their partner's behavior is not necessarily meant to hurt the other. Instead, the purpose of the behavior is to help the individual establish his or her place in the relationship and to become appreciated and accepted (Abramson, 2007). By gaining insight, couples can view their problems in a more constructive and nonblaming manner.

Stage 4: Reorientation

The final stage of the process is reorientation. In this stage, the focus is on putting insight into action. Clients are encouraged to continue to take risks and make changes in their lives outside of therapy. Clients are reoriented toward having a sense of belonging, engaging in social interest, accepting their own imperfections, and acting on the world with a sense of confidence, humor, and friendliness (Corey, 2009) The reorientation is the process of applying new cognitions and behaviors to the relationship. Adlerians consider themselves to be teachers and guides as well as therapists. They teach clients the skills necessary to have healthy communications and relationships, leading to a happier and more harmonious life together. Counselors guide clients toward a relationship that is based on encouragement, respect for one another, an equality of roles, and an atmosphere of cooperation (Abramson, 2007).

AN ADLERIAN APPROACH TO MASCULINE-SENSITIVE PSYCHOTHERAPY

Masculine-sensitive psychotherapy draws needed attention to the ways that masculinity influences a man's life and the practice of psychotherapy (see Brooks & Good, 2005; Englar-Carlson & Stevens, 2006; Levant & Pollack, 1995; Pollack & Levant, 1998). For us, being masculine-sensitive means tapping into the way that men relate to the world and employing a wide range of strategies and activities that appeal to men and that have been shown to facilitate therapeutic engagement and the development of effective psychotherapy relationships (Englar-Carlson et al., 2010). Many of the guidelines on masculine-sensitive psychotherapy emphasize a clear understanding of how gender influences how men experience the world both intrapersonally and interpersonally. Men's socialization into masculine roles contributes to their gender identity and their ways of thinking, feeling, behaving, presenting problems, and attitudes toward and potential fears about psychotherapy (Englar-Carlson et al., 2010). Many guidelines on therapeutic practice with men emphasize engagement strategies and intervention, but few are firmly grounded in a theoretical model. We believe that the Adlerian model provides a strong theoretical base for masculine-sensitive psychotherapy.

In his original theorizing, Adler was clearly aware of social inequality and gender politics, noting, "All our institutions, our traditional attitudes, our laws, our morals, our customs, give evidence of the fact that they are determined and maintained by privileged males for the glory of male domination" (1992/1927, p. 123). Like feminist scholars (Brown, 2010), Adler early on recognized the impact patriarchy had on men and women, and on their relationships with each other. Further, for men, Adler clearly identified the duality of patriarchy in that it benefited and harmed men. Adler noted the myths of masculine superiority and alleged inferiority of women and advocated a sociocultural stance of understanding gender issues. This is a part of the Adlerian model, in that Adlerians are urged to understand the sociopolitical nature from which one's lifestyle is embedded. Bitter, Robertson, Healey, and Cole (2009) outlined a pro-feminist model of Adlerian therapy whereas slight modifications could be included to add even more of an awareness of gender-related cultural influences. Though much of this model is grounded in integrating feminist models of psychotherapy, most theoretical models of masculine-sensitive therapies are largely influenced by feminist therapies (see Brooks, 2010; Englar-Carlson & Stevens, 2010).

An important step in working with men involves taking the time to learn about masculine culture in general and about the specific worldview of individual male clients in particular (Englar-Carlson et al., 2010). The consideration of gender role socialization and a client's "masculinity" in each step of the psychotherapy process is in line with what Good, Gilbert, and Scher (1990) referred to as *gender aware therapy*. In terms of assessment, Griffith and Powers (2007) emphasized gender guiding lines and role models. Applied specifically to men, gender guiding lines would include an assessment of what is means to be a man, how these notions were developed in relation to one's parents, and also how larger cultural forces and institutions have reinforced these models. Assessment questions (as listed in Bitter et al., 2009) could include:

- What did you notice about your mother/father?
- What was their relationship like?
- Who made decisions in the family?
- Did your parents fight (and how were their fights resolved)?
- What are three adjectives for men/women?

When working with couples, an assessment of both partners provides basis for understanding one's gender identity and how it has been taught, reinforced, and ultimately brought into the current relationship.

Adlerians place a high value on social equality and on the building of egalitarian relationships. Adler (1956, p. 432) noted:

> If each partner is to be more interested in the other partner than in himself, there must be equality. If there is to be so intimate a devotion, neither partner can feel subdued or overshadowed. Equality is only possible if both partners have this attitude. It should be the effort of each to enrich the life of the other. In this way each is safe. Each feels that he is worthwhile; each feels that he is needed.

A core notion is the recognition that each person is unique and has an equal right to be valued and respected, including understanding how our differences are experienced by others (Bitter et al., 2009). This has particular meaning for couple's counseling with men. It is well documented that many men initially experience going to therapy as extremely difficult, as something to avoid at any cost, and usually as the last resort (Rabinowitz & Cochran, 2002). Men often believe that they are coerced into therapy (by a spouse, employer, or the law) and express a great deal of resentment. Englar-Carlson and Shepard (2005) added that many men enter couple's counseling in a one-down position, assuming that their perspectives will not be valued or heard. They assume the counselor will take the side of the other partner. Further, this worry might be heightened because of his concern that counseling endorses feminine-associated behaviors (e.g., sharing of feelings, willingness to self-disclose) over masculine ones and therefore the counselor will ally with the female partner. Adlerians can address this by an activity calling attention to what both partners bring to the session and the relationship. In addition, Bitter et al. (2009) noted the widespread Adlerian use of "tentative guessing" in which the counselor, after careful listening, shares ideas and invites the couple into a "shared consideration of meaning." Offered in a tentative way (e.g., "Could it be ..."), tentative guessing notes the perspectives of each partner and the context in which these perspectives were developed. It suggests that both partners will be engaging in a change process (i.e., not just the male client), which can reduce the anxiety that it is only the male client who needs to change. Yet more important, tentative guessing is a subtle way that the counselor can bring questioning about gender roles and norms into the session so that the couple can begin to engage in perspective taking about the other's gendered experiences of being in the world (Englar-Carlson & Shepard, 2005). The counselor can use gender socialization to logically examine why the couple is having difficulty; in many ways this can be validating. Thus men can ponder their own gender socialization while being introduced to the notion of a "redefinition of masculinity" (Levant, 1997) that most likely is more consistent with their own internalized models of manhood (Smiler, 2004).

Although mystery about and fear of what happens in psychotherapy is potentially present for all clients, it is often a more salient issue for men (Vogel, Wester, & Larson, 2007). As a relatively active approach that emphasizes early assessment and psychoeducation, Adlerian therapists tend to be clear about the different stages and process of being in counseling. As outlined earlier, Adlerian couples counseling roughly follows three stages (following the building of the therapist–couple relationship). Clients are aware of these stages, and the counselor works to actively integrate the couple into the process so that they take insight from the process of assessment and actively integrate that into their lives together through selected activities and interventions. For men, there may be less uncertainty about the counseling process and the expectations of what will be expected of him as a client are clear from the onset.

Finally, and potentially most important, the Adlerian concept of social interest seems particularly relevant for many men and for work with couples. Social interest is the development of feeling of being part of the larger whole, a sense of belonging to and participating for others for the common good (Carlson & Englar-Carlson, 2008). Adlerians view one's social interest as the true measure of mental health, and thus developing social interest becomes a focal point in clinical intervention. For work with couples, this can be developed with each other. Further, many people are good at looking out and providing for their children or other family members, but social interest can be addressed outside of the family within the local and larger community. Ways to tap social interest parallel with male socialization include encouraging men to be involved in their respective communities by "doing" something for others. This can be volunteer work; donations of time, money, or effort; or involvement with youth via coaching or mentoring.

CASE EXAMPLE: THE "BOXER'S DAUGHTER" AND "THE MOMMA'S BOY"

The following case example illustrates a masculine-sensitive application of Adlerian couples therapy.* In particular, this review focuses on how the theoretical underpinnings address gender issues with an emphasis on masculine-sensitive therapy. Jon Carlson is the therapist, and the switch to the first person ("I") reflects his perspective. The couple met with Jon nine times over a 13-month period, and these sessions were part of a taped video that was recorded for training purposes. The long gaps between sessions were related to the couple's own schedule of requesting therapy and the availability of the recording studio. In many ways, the gaps in treatment are not that uncommon in practice, and both authors believe that much can be accomplished when sessions are held far apart. The clients, Carl and Freida, have been married for 6 years. Freida is of Finish background and emigrated from Finland 6 years ago to further her education. She was 28 years old and an only child. She was tall with blue eyes and blond hair. Her father had been a professional boxer but during Freida's childhood he was mainly unemployed while her mother was a teacher and primary breadwinner for the family. Carl was a 40-year-old Caucasian, and the youngest and only male of five children. He was tall, tanned, and handsome. His father was a truck driver and his mother was a maid. His father spent most of his time on the road and away from the family. At the time of our work together, Carl was unemployed and spent much of his time at home. Until recently, he had a high-paying union construction job, but it was lost following a worksite accident that subsequently required two back surgeries. Freida was in the process of completing a master's degree, whereas Carl was a high school graduate with no additional formal education. The couple met through an on-line dating service, and within a year got married. Freida stated they sought couples counseling due to "financial issues resulting from Carl's gambling problem." Carl states that their financial problems were a result of his career ending injury and subsequent unofficial "career" as a gambler.

Since this case study is focused on masculine-sensitive therapy, a deeper appreciation of Carl is warranted. Carl came from a working-class family background. His father, though often absent, reinforced a model of masculinity in which the worker/provider tradition of men (Skovholt, 1990) was valued above contact with family. Like his father, engaging in work helped Carl feel like he had met one of society's criteria for manhood. Earning a good income through his construction job allowed Carl to fulfill his culturally prescribed role as a provider

---

* The sessions reviewed were videotaped. Dialogue reported in this case example is verbatim. Identifying information and demographics have been altered in order to maintain confidentiality.

for Freida (Bernard, 1981; Christiansen & Palkovitz, 2001; Loscocco, 2007). Work gave Carl a sense of purpose and meaning, and served as a central component of his identity as a man and his self-esteem (Axelrod, 2001; Heppner & Heppner, 2001). His physically demanding and dangerous construction job exemplified the notion of "high risk, high reward," in that Carl gained a great deal of status as a "real man," yet the title was a tenuous proposition that was anything but guaranteed (Vandello, Bosson, Cohen, Burnaford, & Weaver, 2008).

Losing his physical health, and subsequently his job, was devastating to Carl and threatened his social-constructed status as a man. His self-esteem and sense of competence plummeted as he vacated his role of family provider and Freida took over. In a series of risky, yet ultimately futile attempts to regain his role as provider, create money for the family, and cope with the emotional pain of his multiple losses (career, health, role in the family), Carl began gambling. Though he had good intentions (in creating money), the outcome of losing the couple's savings only created a deeper sense of shame and worthlessness. As a testament to the tenuous nature of manhood and the notion that "real men are made and not born" (Vandello et al., 2008, p. 1326), Carl had seemingly become unmade, showing that "men who contribute little (or are 'good for nothing') do not even count as men" (Vandello et al., 2008, p. 1327).

Unlike many men, Carl did not seem reticent or reluctant to come to counseling. I assumed the costs of not coming to counseling were so great that he had buried or ignored these fears. Yet I also wondered if Carl had more or less surrendered to Freida, acknowledging that he could no longer control his problems and that Freida had the power in their relationship (Good & Robertson, 2010). Thus my concern was less about his ambivalence to be in counseling and more about the inwardly turned shame he had about being at this point in his life and marriage. When Carl came to counseling, he was at the point where one of the only things he had not lost was Freida, yet he seemed almost resigned to the fact that their relationship was slipping away. He was pretty much out of cards to play, and in many ways it seemed as if couple's counseling was the final desperate hand he had left. He essentially had no face left to save and presented in the first session as a meek man who accepted all the blame. It was clear that if counseling was to be successful, Carl needed to get his mojo back and feel like a capable man again.

Before the first session, Carl and Freida completed precounseling intake forms, which I saw as a positive sign as to their degree of motivation. The forms revealed the differences in education, culture, health, and family constellation. Neither provided early recollections, as they indicated they could not remember their early childhood. However, Freida stated when she was 9 she learned she had a half-brother. She met him on one occasion but was later told he had died.

The First Session

In Adlerian couples therapy, it is important in the first session to outline the process of treatment, assess the dynamics of the relationship, to help the couple understand the possible transgenerational patterns they may be acting out, and to engage the couple through listening and providing each partner with a reason to want to stay engaged in treatment. This was accomplished by helping the couple to understand their relationship issues from a different perspective as well as to understand that there is a "him," a "her," and an "us" in the relationship.

Early questions asked the couple to talk about their parents and their parent's relationship. Freida described her parent's relationship as quite volatile with constant yelling and screaming, whereas Carl saw his parent's relationship as nonexistent. His father was rarely around, and when he was home his parents would fight. Carl would often defend his mother, which led his Dad to call him "the Momma's boy." Each commented that the arguments between their parents were never resolved; rather they were just extended to the next time they would fight and yell about the same things. Both saw their mothers as the decision maker and boss of the family. They both had poor opinions of their fathers, viewing them as imposing physical specimens yet pretty ineffective as parents and marital partners. Carl felt the only contribution his father made was financial.

As the initial issues were presented, it was my impression that they had created a relationship pattern where Freida was a blamer and Carl a victim. Growing up as the youngest in a family of all women I guessed this was a familiar role for Carl. Freida, on the other hand, an only child with a father who was a popular boxer, seemed more ready to attack.

Jon Carlson: What do you want to talk about?
Freida: Finances. It is really a sore subject. He has a gambling problem and doesn't want to admit it and doesn't know how much this really bothers *me*!
Jon Carlson: Is it a current problem?
Freida: Well, he still gambles, but it is not as bad as it was when he lost everything we had.
Jon Carlson: Carl, what is your take on this?
Carl: I admit it is a bad thing. So that is why I don't argue with her when she brings it up. I had a career-ending injury and then two back surgeries and I have not been able to get back on my feet and get a good paying job.
Freida: The worst part was that he lied and wasn't honest. A year ago he lost a great deal of money. This was right around the time my dad died and I was already such a mess. He said he would not do it again, and then he did. We are also having another big problem. I don't talk to his family. He talks to his mother, but I have not talked to any of them for over a year.

Jon Carlson: Wow. In this past year you have had a dad die, financial problems, a cut-off from his family, a career ending injury, and two back surgeries?

This couple has multiple problems. The way they address problems was for Freida to attack and Carl to withdraw and give in. She ends up overfunctioning and he feels disempowered and yet neither seems to have the skills needed to resolve these or other issues. I was not surprised with Carl's retreating reaction, as the loss of his physical ability, job, and savings were all shame-inducing events. Whereas I was curious about his history with shame, I know many men experience threats to one's masculinity through shame. Of course for many men being in counseling itself often implies weakness and a failure to be self-sufficient, thus they come into counseling with shame and fear (Levant, 1997; Park, 2006). What struck me initially about Carl's shame was that it was terribly obvious, and I could understand why Freida would keep attacking him. I knew right away my task would be to encourage the awareness of strengths in Carl (Kiselica & Englar-Carlson, 2010) and to curtail the language that reinforced Carl as not being capable. It was also critical that I provide the couple with feedback about how they cocreate their problems:

Jon Carlson: Where did you learn this pattern? Freida, you are parenting him and seem to be "on" him for all sorts of things that he doesn't do exactly right. Carl, you keep quiet and withdraw, which further irritates Freida. Yet it seems like you are attempting to deescalate the tension.

After assessing for violence, I began to focus on the issue of Carl's competence and work situation:

Jon Carlson (to Freida): Is it possible for you to look at him as a competent person?

Freida: Not since he hurt *me* by gambling and lying. He has not been competent in a long time.

Jon Carlson: Keeping agreements is very important in marriage.

Freida: I think it is less the gambling and more the keeping of agreements that hurts me.

Jon Carlson (to Carl): Is it safe for you to talk to Freida? Is she too critical?

Freida (begins crying): My mom and dad never listened to me and now Carl doesn't listen to me?

Carl: She is always critical. But I don't do much right so I need someone to criticize me?

Jon Carlson: What do you think will happen if both of you keep this up? Freida being critical and Carl not listening and acting like a little boy? It is like Freida has become the foreman and Carl the inept employee? Carl what can you do to make Freida more confident in you? How can you change the pattern? Can you become the competent tradesman you were before the accident?

I got the sense they were another case of the classic "she needs to shut up and he needs to show up" couple. I framed these questions using a work metaphor since I felt that Carl's unemployment was a significant issue for him and the couple. Adlerians view work as one of the core tasks of life, and Carl's unemployment and lack of active pursuit in finding another vocation appeared to be a significant contribution to both Carl and Freida's unhappiness. Further, one of the core challenges for men is often associated with career advancement and identity at midlife (Connell & Messerschmidt, 2005; Heppner & Heppner, 2001). Further, the more a man is concerned with success and work, the more psychological distress that he will experience relative to men less concerned (O'Neil, 2008). Carl had lost his job affecting his identity and self-worth. This also affected his identity as a man. I realized Carl needed to get a sense of himself back to raise his role in the relationship. So I addressed Carl as though he were competent and able to step up. I clearly stated that their relationship was doomed if they were to rigidly remain in their roles of Freida being the only person who had worth and Carl as the one who had nothing. They needed to share the competency and success with each other.

We went on to talk about the way Freida was handling her problems with Carl's family by cutting them out of her life. It was suggested that cutoffs rarely works in families, but as an only child she did not know much about getting along in families. In an attempt to build some competence and self-worth in Carl, I noted how this was an area where Carl could "help her" learn about the acceptance and tolerance needed when you live in a large family. This was purposely phrased as a way to appeal to Carl's sense of altruism as a man as well as step toward rebuilding his own pride in his ability to be of help. The couple left with an understanding that they both had a big role in the current relationship problem. They realized that Carl needed to do more, while Freida needed to let him by doing and saying less.

As the session ended, there was hope in the room. Carl and Freida held hands, they appeared motivated to change and willing to try on new roles, and I had a good feeling that they both had the potential to make this marriage work. After all, up until this point they were both pouring energy into the relationship, it just happened to be misdirected. They both worked hard to change the other person rather than focusing more on oneself.

Session 2

Due to unavailability of the studio and the couple, our next session took place 4 months later. During this long layoff I did have updates from the couple that they were doing OK. My immediate goal in session 2 was to determine what had happened since our first meeting and then to begin working on changing some of the patterns that were identified. They both reported that Carl has been busy applying for jobs, but he had not found one. Freida indicated that she has backed off harassing Carl, but Carl did not completely agree. I saw his disagreement as a good thing, since he was no longer being defenseless in the relationship. I pointed that out to the couple. As we progressed, Freida quickly began to parent and Carl to misbehave.

Freida: I have high expectations for us and he doesn't want to change. His problem is not just gambling, but actually he is doing nothing and I am still working three jobs.
Carl: I have not gambled in months, but she will point this out to me forever.
Jon Carlson: Probably not, because at this rate you will not be together that long.

In this rather blunt confrontation, I tried to help them see the future consequence of their current behavior. My bluntness here is a combination of my own personality of using sarcasm tinged with a bit of humor and my Adlerian training to provide active feedback and observations when they are clear. I also believe that feedback that is short, direct, and to the point appeals to men since there is no confusion about the meaning. My comment here was not mean-spirited nor inappropriate, but rather ironic, challenging, and pointed out the obvious. By this point, I had also assessed the relational style of the couple, but specifically Carl, and I was tailoring my style to theirs. Kiselica (2006) noted the importance of recognizing the relational style of men in contrast to their conception of how therapy should proceed. Further, I was being genuine and real at this moment, and I was treating the couple as real people rather than problems that needed to be solved (Englar-Carlson et al., 2010). Both Carl and Freida looked at me and fully grasped the seriousness of my comment. Both paused, and Carl nodded at me a couple of times. I could see the sadness and desperation in his eyes. After a moment, Freida looked at me and almost pleaded.

Freida: I don't want to but I can't help it. I need to get it off my chest.
Jon Carlson: I guess you are deciding then to have either a nonexistent or miserable relationship?
Freida (long pause and nodding): I think I can stop when we are financially secure.
Jon Carlson: You actually realize that you have a choice about stopping and plan to do it when you are financially secure. Yet when is that? Is anyone really financially secure? You need to work on being emotionally secure now. (*Both nod their heads.*) What can Carl do to show you that he is trustworthy and working on his problem?

This was the crux of the session. I was honest and used irony again to point out the absurdity of their relationship and faulty logic, trying to make it clear that if they maintained their current course of action, the unhappy outcomes were rather well defined. I think Freida picked up on the seriousness of this, and in a measured attempt began to back down from attacking Carl and provide an opening for change. I felt that this was the ideal opportunity for Carl to gain back his legs in the relationship, which is what both Carl and Freida desperately wanted. Also, I think it was important for Carl to have something clear to do that could allow him to show action empathy, which is the ability to take action based on how a person sees things from another's point of view (Levant, 1995). This was an attempt to build Carl's strengths (Kiselica & Englar-Carlson, 2010).

As the session progressed, Freida noted how it was important for her to be able to ask Carl to do things and for him to actually do them. Carl said he wanted to be the man in the house and carry the burden of the family and that in so many ways he needed to feel useful and needed again. It has been noted that for men the ability to feel successful in society often contributes to their sense of masculinity (Cha & Thébaud, 2009; Dyke & Murphy, 2006), and Carl was desperately looking to strengthen that part of his identity. Freida talked about how she did not enjoy being around Carl all that much because he was not comfortable or relaxed and that she felt that Carl was abandoning her. She misses the guy he used to be and she wanted to help get him back. I felt a process comment here was needed, so I asked Carl about what makes it hard to show that vulnerable part of himself to Freida. He talked about how hard it was to access that part of him since he has surrounded that guy with anger. I believed he was afraid of revealing more about his loss of status as a man to Freida and have her point it out. In order to reduce this threat, Carl had surrounded himself with anger, which is a typical response for men when their manhood is threatened (Vandello et al., 2008). I joined with Carl and encouraged him to speak a little bit more.

Carl: The guy is still in there but is having a hard time. I am so mad at times that I get away from you so you don't see me that way. I am afraid if you saw me so weak you would leave me.

Freida (voiced with compassion and caring): You believe that if you lose control you will lose me? Do you really worry about that?

(Carl nods.)

Jon Carlson: This is a real marital mystery. The thing that you are doing to keep from losing Freida is the very thing that is pushing her away. Is she being the kind of partner that you want *now*? A partner who provides understanding without judgment?

Carl: If she can accept me like this then I can be myself and I will have control again.

Later in the session, the couple practiced understanding one another and realized they have been focusing on sending and not on receiving messages with their partner. A key moment of this session occurred when Carl was able to speak about how his unemployment and injury has significantly impacted his view of himself as man. In a sense I believed that both Carl and Freida were aware of this, but this served as the first time they actually communicated about it with each other. It was critical that Freida did not pounce on Carl for his honesty, but rather acknowledged that man was still within Carl. There seemed to be an emotional connection when they realized they both missed the guy Carl used to be.

Session 3

The third session was one month later, and the couple reported that they were having better communication with much less anger. The last session had provided some tangible experiences and ideas that they had been able to build upon. They agreed that taking the time to understand how the other felt had led to solving some of their problems. Freida was not pursuing as much since Carl was listening more attentively. They both felt the "guy Carl used to be" was starting to show up more often. They also felt good about being able to help each other, and the relationship, make improvements. After this update, the focus shifted to the couple's relationship with Carl's family.

Freida: We had a conflict with Carl's family. I tried to get his mom to connect more often and then his sister called and told him he should stop harassing mom. Carl told her to stay out of his business and that if she doesn't he said he would kill her.
Carl: I guess I sort of flipped out and they are now scared of me.
Freida: Now nobody is going to talk for a long time.

I reframed Carl's protection of Freida as an attempt to reach out to Freida and show that he could protect her. Carl was in the process of regaining his sense of being a man, and many acts of aggression in men can be understood as responses to anxiety about living up to standards of masculinity and having to prove oneself (Malamuth, Linz, & Heavey, 1995; Vandello et al., 2008). The intent seemed fine and even understandable, yet his actions and words went overboard and were inappropriate. Both nodded and agreed, and Carl quietly stated, "I messed it up." I could see that being separated from his family pained Carl. I got the sense that Carl could make this better with his family, and I wanted to appeal to the side of him that was capable. I also felt that put Carl in the role of bringing the family closer together could help develop his social interest. I bluntly stated, "Okay Carl, let's make this better?" I attempted to join with him as if we had started a new project. I suggested that Carl needed to make a repair attempt and to state that "he really wants to have better relationships with his entire family and is sorry for his role in messing things up. I am sorry that I get angry and scare people." Carl said he would to this, and that was truly his intention, but he still feels mad because he is 40 years old and they still treat him like the baby.

Freida: They do this because you act like a baby and have temper tantrums.
Carl: I can't control it.

Providing some encouragement and highlighting more of Carl's strengths, I challenged him, indicating that he does a good job of controlling his temper in other settings, he has done a fantastic job recently with Freida, and he can also do it here. A discussion took place in which Carl realized on his own that he needed to practice calming himself, and I suggested he begin learning and practicing meditation. Again, I felt giving Carl something tangible to do would help reinforce the strengths he already had and allow him to feel capable when he faced challenges. Some initial instruction was provided in the session, and Carl and Freida were both responsive to the meditation practice. They both felt a bit calmer. Carl realized in this session that if he wanted to stop being treated like a baby he needed to start acting like an adult.

Session 4

The fourth session took place 2 weeks later. Carl had spoken with his family, and it had gone remarkably well. They were both practicing basic meditation by doing mindful breathing with each other twice a day. The couple was putting into practice what they had learned over the past few months. They seemed more connected and communication had improved. Carl was working at giving Freida feedback when he did not feel understood rather than walking away or stonewalling. They seem to be getting closer together even though many things had not really improved. Carl was still unemployed and they still had limited finances, yet they seemed less consumed by this. During the session they talked about future plans and about the possibility of having children, with Carl as a stay-at-home parent. I got the sense that an aspect of Carl's sense of masculinity had shifted from being consumed by the role of worker and provider (which had been his father) to considered adopting the parental role of being a good father and parent (which has been his mother's role). Like other men with poor relationships with their father, I could see how Carl was bolstered by the fantasy of not repeating the parenting sins of his own father with his own children (Horn Mallers, Englar-Carlson, & Carlson, in press). I also commented during that session how I noticed they were thinking more about who they are as a couple. They were both more positive and seemed to be truly listening to each other. Sometimes just being with a couple and letting them connect is healing.

Session 5

In the fifth session, a few weeks later the couple reported more challenges. However, rather than being as active as before, I actively encouraged the couple to put to use the tools and skills they had learned to confront their concerns. During the session, many of their issues were sorted out and the couple practiced breathing and meditation.

Communication was discussed and the couple was taught to be able to identify four types of communication (requests for action, information, understanding and involvement, and inappropriate interaction). Insight was gained as the couple agreed that Freida often seeks understanding, but that Carl usually provides action. We discussed how that is not an atypical pattern between men and women, that is relatively normal, but nonetheless ineffective communication if one stubbornly refuses to try to provide what the other needs. Carl understood this, noted that it could be really hard, but that he would focus more on giving her the type of communication that she wants.

Carl: This is really difficult. I often feel like I will burst if I don't do something. When another man, even if he is her boss, treats her badly, it is a man's job to stand up for his wife.

Jon Carlson: Even if she asks you not to?

Freida: He is too stressed and is not in control.

Carl: It just seems like I can't help myself and act before I think.

Jon Carlson: This is a great example of what we just talked about. Carl, you seem to be acting impulsively as you responded in a manner that is intended to help, but because it does not consider Freida's needs, it becomes misguided. You need to learn to catch yourself and respond in a way that is helpful to your wife.

My goal here was to provide an in vivo opportunity for Carl to be aware of moments when he refuses to give Freida what she wants. Carl had previously indicated that he wanted to work on this and was also quite good at following up outside of session. In this role, I was acting somewhat like a relationship coach with Carl, because in previous sessions I noticed that he seemed to welcome the feedback. Some men might get defensive or push back, but Carl seemed more genuinely interested in doing this differently.

As the couple struggled with a difficult topic, I then provided an opportunity to reexamine how mindfulness meditation could be helpful to them. Both realized just how "tightly wired" they were. I helped them to see that they are busy trying to control others as a way to reduce stress when they need to control themselves. Carl appreciated knowing that he now had several ways to deal with stressful situations. Using a construction metaphor, I commented how Carl was expanding his toolbox of skills. He has learned to listen, breathe, talk, stay in the room, and other self-control strategies. Continuing with this theme, Freida jokingly said that his only tool prior to counseling was trying to beat up people or gamble when things did not go his way. They both smiled.

Session 6

We met again a month later and there was some mixed news. The good news was that Carl got a steady job for a handyman's service and he was feeling good about this opportunity, but he was suddenly very busy. The downside of this job was that Carl was sliding on keeping many of his agreements with Freida. Transitions are often hard for couples, and in times of stress it is very easy to slide back into old patterns of not being a good partner for Freida.

During this session, the couple recognized a few things. They both seemed to realize that they do have a good relationship, but that they each can be difficult to live with. That was accepted by both in a healthy manner of humorous self-depreciation. Also, the recent transition of Carl going back to work was reframed as a significant test to see if they could stick to their relationship gains. In the process of Carl feeling more like a man again, he was forgetting to maintain some of his aspects of his masculinity. The couple was able to identify some of their familiar patterns that were problematic if allowed to continue. Both agreed to work on their role in addressing the parts of the marriage that made them unhappy.

Session 7

Our seventh session took place 3 weeks later, and it had previously been scheduled as our final session together. As we began, Freida seemed almost panicked and became emotional over feeling unimportant, that things were unfair, and that it was hopeless trying to improve the marriage. Carl seemed mystified by her response, as he thought things were much better between them.

Jon Carlson (to Freida): You seem to be striving so hard to be strong and hard working like your mother and mother-in-law and yet they are both miserable.
Freida: My mother never had time for me. Carl is just like her. He says he cares but she said that to.

This type of dialogue continued as Freida seemed to automatically vent many of her life's frustrations. Neither Carl nor the therapist was able to console her. Toward the end of the session, I commented how it was not uncommon for couples to have a difficult time with closure. In many ways, ending counseling signaled that a couple was on their own and some couples often fear that they will not be able to maintain gains. Freida acknowledged that she had trouble with transitions and really was not over her father's death. She added that she probably came to the United States to get some distance from her mother.

I knew, however, that they were not same couple today as the one I met during our first session. I observed that whereas everything was not perfect in their marriage or their lives, the reality was that it never would be. As a couple, however, they had made significant progress in their ability to weather hard economic times and unemployment, navigate new boundaries and communication with Carl's family, and of course both Carl and Freida had gained new tools in communication, empathy, deepening connection, meditation and relaxation, and honesty in their ability to discuss their concerns. Above all, they were committed to each other and had rebuilt their trust. I suggested that we could schedule a session in month to evaluate their progress and follow up.

Session 8

Our last session together was held about 6 weeks later. For the most part, things were generally improved and they seemed to be making better decisions together. Both apologized for the last session and indicated that they were upset that couples counseling was coming to an end, and they both had a moment of testing their faith in each other. Since that session, however, they had done okay, found some renewed faith in each other and the marriage, and they were hopeful that they were working together on shared goals. The therapist reviewed with the couple some of the topics that were covered in the session.

As we came to an end, both were pleased, surprised, and proud that so much was covered in such a short time period. They also commented on how important it was to keep their agreements and conversations going. Freida indicated that she felt it helped her to have a mediator, but even more she thought that it was important for Carl to have someone who understood what he was going through.

Carl realized that he needed to separate home and work life, react differently to others and to not take Freida's words so personally. Freida realized she needed to be more patient and compassionate. She also realized that she knew all the skills but just needed to use them more often. Finally, they expressed that they would recommend the therapist to other couples in distress but only wished there were more sessions available for them.

CLOSING THOUGHTS

Adlerian couples therapy emphasizes personal responsibility and equality between partners. When this is blended with a masculine-sensitive approach, the outcomes can be beneficial to male and female clients. Masculine sensitive therapy acknowledges the role of gender socialization in constructing our relational patterns, but it also strives to create a therapeutic space in which men's and women's experiences are both acknowledged and validated. Of course, validation is not enough, since many of those experiences contribute to keeping couples fixed in unhealthy patterns of relating. Here the notion of creating reciprocal and cooperative relationships emerges, and the therapist works to assess where a couple is (and where they come from) and provide clear direction in creating meaningful change. The goal is to help the couple see positive alternatives to what ordinarily would have been overwhelming challenges (Dinkmeyer, 1993).

In the case study, Carl and Freida presented as a couple whose fixed patterns of relating to each other had clear origins in their own family constellation. Many of the problems that couples develop in relationships come from the patterns learned (or not learned) in our families of origin. These patterns are transgenerational and passed on almost without conscious awareness from generation to generation. Carl and Freida cared for each other, had good intentions, and some relationship skills, but their behavior was not bringing them closer together. Somehow in the blending together of these two people with their own lifestyles and beliefs, they were not getting the desired outcomes. The result of Carl's recent job loss, physical injury, and failed career as a gambler had created a dynamic in which his low self-esteem made him the perfect victim and fall guy for the relationship. Rather than fearing or avoiding couple's counseling, Carl seemed motivated to engage in counseling since it could be his last ditch effort to save his marriage.

The therapist was not a referee but rather an active participant focused on helping each person to understand his or her own relational patterns and how they play out in their relationship. After careful assessment, the therapist provided active feedback on how the couple preserves their problem together; and through suggestions, directives to change behavior, and skills training, the couple makes progress. A key component of this was reaching out to Carl, not as a failed man but rather as a capable man with the potential of becoming the man he wanted to be. As Carl and Freida learned to better understand each other, and each of them treated Carl as the able person he had been and could be, they engaged in less blaming behavior and experienced more acceptance of responsibility for their role in the problem. The therapist actively modeled the skills that the couple eventually acquired such as listening, attending, emotional regulation, and keeping agreements. The therapist helped the couple to understand that by learning certain skills they could develop the satisfying relationship they both desired. Finally, it was important for the therapist to practice patience by trusting the couple and the process, and not panicking when things were not going well.

Therapy for couples that is focused on the couple, and not the individuals, and remains sensitive to different socialization patterns of men and women can provide an effective and deeper, structural level of treatment. The changes will continue to develop over time. Adlerian therapy provides the seeds for many of the skills needed for men and women to have satisfying relationships.

REFERENCES

Abramson, Z. (2004). *Lomdim Zugiyut* [Learning Couples]. Tel Aviv, Israel: Modan.

Abramson, Z. (2007). Adlerian family and couples therapy. *The Journal of Individual Psychology, 63*(4), 371–387.

Adler, A. (1956). *The individual psychology of Alfred Adler.* New York: Basic Books.

Adler, A. (1958). *What life should mean to you.* New York: Capricorn Books. (Original work published 1931)

Adler, A. (1992/1927). *Understanding human nature.* Oxford, United Kingdom: OneWorld.

Ansbacher, H. L., & Ansbacher, R. R. (Eds.). (1956). *The individual psychology of Alfred Adler.* New York: Harper-Perennial.

Axelrod, S. D. (2001). The vital relationship between work and masculinity: A psychoanalytic perspective. *Psychology of Men & Masculinity, 2,* 117–123.

Balla, M. (2003). Raissa Epstein Adler: Socialist, activist, feminist—1873–1962. In Adlerian Society of the United Kingdom and The Institute for Individual Psychology (Ed.), *Adlerian Yearbook, 2003* (pp. 50–58). Chippenham, Wiltshire, England: Antony Rowe, Ltd.

Bernard, J. (1981). The good-provider role: Its rise and fall. *American Psychologist, 36,* 1–12.

Bitter, J. R., Robertson, P. E., Healey, A. C., & Cole, L. K. (2009). Reclaiming a profeminist orientation in Adlerian therapy. *The Journal of Individual Psychology, 65,* 13–33.

Brooks, G. R., & Good, G. E. (Eds.). (2005). *The new handbook of psychotherapy & counseling with men: A comprehensive guide to settings, problems, & treatment approaches* (Rev. ed.). San Francisco, CA: Jossey-Bass.

Brooks, G. R. (2010). *Beyond the crisis of masculinity:* A transtheoretical model for male-friendly therapy. Washington, DC: APA

Brown, L. S. (2010). *Feminist therapy.* Washington American Psychological Association Books.

Carlson, J., Sperry, L., & Lewis, J. A. (2005). *Family therapy techniques: Integrating and tailoring treatment.* New York: Routledge.

Carlson, J. D., & Dinkmeyer, D. (2003). *TIME for a better marriage.* Atascadero, CA: Impact.

Carlson, J. D., & Englar-Carlson, M. (2008). Adlerian therapy. In J. Frew & M. Spiegler (Eds.), *Contemporary psychotherapies for a diverse world* (pp. 93–140). Boston, MA: Lahaska Press.

Carlson, J. D., & Sperry, L. (1998). Adlerian psychotherapy as a constructivist psychotherapy. In M. Hoyt (Ed.), *The handbook of constructivist therapies: Innovative approaches from leading practitioners* (pp. 62–82). San Francisco, CA: Jossey-Bass.

Carlson, J. D., & Sperry, L. (2000). Adlerian therapy. In F. M. Dattilio & L. J. Bevilacqua (Eds.), *Comparative treatment for relationship dysfunction* (pp. 102–115). New York: Springer.

Carlson, J. D., Watts, R. E., & Maniacci, M. (2006). *Adlerian therapy: Theory and practice.* Washington, DC: American Psychological Association.

Cha, Y., & Thébaud, S. (2009). Labor markets, breadwinning, and beliefs: How economic context shapes men's gender ideology. *Gender & Society, 23*, 215–243.

Christiansen, S., & Palkovitz, R. (2001). Why the "good provider" role still matters: Providing as a form of paternal involvement. *Journal of Family Issues, 22*, 84–106.

Connell, R. W., & Messerschmidt, J. W. (2005). Hegemonic masculinity: Rethinking the concept. *Gender and Society, 19*, 829–859.

Corey, G. (2009). *Theory and practice of counseling and psychotherapy* (8th ed.). Belmont, CA: Thompson Higher Education.

Dinkmeyer, D., Sr. (1993). Marriage therapy through strength assessment. *Individual Psychology: The Journal of Adlerian Theory, Research & Practice, 49*(3/4), 412–418.

Dyke, L. S., & Murphy, S. A. (2006). How we define success: A qualitative study of what matters most to women and men. *Sex Roles, 55*, 357–371.

Englar-Carlson, M., & Shepard, D. S. (2005). Engaging men in couples counseling: Strategies for overcoming ambivalence and inexpressiveness. *The Family Journal, 13*, 383–391.

Englar-Carlson, M., & Stevens, M. (Eds.). (2006). *In the room with men: A casebook of therapeutic change.* Washington, DC: American Psychological Association.

Englar-Carlson, M., & Stevens, M. A., & Scholz, R. (2010). Psychotherapy with men. In J. C. Chrisler & D. R. McCreary (Eds.), *Handbook of gender research in psychology* (Vol. 2, pp. 221–252). New York: Springer.

Good, G. E., Gilbert, L. A., & Scher, M. (1990). Gender aware therapy: A synthesis of feminist therapy and knowledge about gender. *Journal of Counseling and Development, 68*, 376–380.

Good, G. E., & Robertson, J. M. (2010). To accept a pilot? Addressing men's ambivalence and altering their expectancies about therapy. *Psychotherapy: Theory, Research, Practice, & Training, 47*, 306–315.

Griffith, J., & Powers, R. L. (2007). *The lexicon of Adlerian Psychology* (2nd ed.). Port Townsend, WA: Adlerian Psychology Associates.

Hawes, C. (2007). Early recollections: A compelling intervention in couples therapy. *The Journal of Individual Psychology, 63*(3), 306–314.

Heppner, M. J., & Heppner, P. P. (2001). Addressing the implications of male socialization for career counseling. In G. R. Brooks & G. E. Good (Eds.), *The new handbook of psychotherapy and counseling with men* (pp. 369–386). San Francisco, CA: Jossey-Bass.

Horn Mallers, M., Englar-Carlson, M., & Carlson, J. D. (in press). Father–son relationships. In S. Dunham, S. Dermer, & J. Carlson (Eds.), *Poisonous parenting: Toxic relationships between parents and their adult children.* New York: Routledge.

Kern, R. M. (2002). Lifestyle Questionnaire Inventory. In R. Kern & D. Eckstein (Eds.), *Psychological fingerprints* (69–70). Dubuque, IA: Kendall Hunt.

Kiselica, M. S. (2006, August). Contributions and limitations of the deficit model of men. In M. S. Kiselica (Chair), *Toward a positive psychology of boys, men, and masculinity.* Symposium presented at the meeting of the American Psychological Association, New Orleans, LA.

Kiselica, M., & Englar-Carlson, M. (2010). Identifying, affirming, and building upon male strengths: The positive psychology/positive masculinity model of psychotherapy with boys and men. *Psychotherapy: Theory, Research, Practice, & Training, 47*, 276–287.

Levant, R. F. (1995). Toward the reconstruction of masculinity. In R. F. Levant & W. S. Pollack (Eds.), *A new psychology of men* (pp. 229–251). New York: Basic Books.

Levant, R. F. (1997). The masculinity crisis. *Journal of Men's Studies, 5,* 221–231.

Levant, R. F. & Pollack, W. S. (Eds.). (1995). *The new psychology of men.* New York: Basic Books.

Loscocco, K. (2007). Gender patterns in provider role attitudes and behavior. *Journal of Family Issues, 28,* 934–954.

Malamuth, N. M., Linz, D., & Heavey, C. L. (1995). Using the confluence model of sexual aggression to predict men's conflict with women: A 10-year follow-up study. *Journal of Personality and Social Psychology, 69,* 353–369.

Nicoll, W. G. (1989). Adlerian marital therapy: History, theory, and process. In R. Kern, E. C. Hawes, & O. C. Christensen (Eds.), *Couples therapy: An Adlerian perspective* (pp. 1–28). Minneapolis, MN: Education Media Corporation.

O'Neil, J. M. (2008). Summarizing twenty-five years of research on men's gender role conflict using the Gender Role Conflict Scale. *The Counseling Psychologist, 36,* 358–445.

Park, S. (2006). Facing fear without losing face: Working with Asian American men. In M. Englar-Carlson & M. A. Stevens, (Eds.), *In the room with men: A casebook of therapeutic change* (pp. 151–173). Washington, DC: American Psychological Association.

Pollack, W. S., & Levant, R. F. (1998). *New psychotherapy for men.* New York: Wiley.

Rabinowitz, F. E., & Cochran, S. V. (2002). *Deepening psychotherapy with men.* Washington, DC: American Psychological Association.

Skovholt, T. M. (1990). Career themes in counseling and psychotherapy with men. In D. Moore & F. Leafgren (Eds.), *Problem solving strategies and interventions for men in counseling* (pp. 39–53). Alexandria, VA: American Association for Counseling.

Smiler, A. P. (2004). Thirty years after the discovery of gender: Psychological concepts and measures of masculinity. *Sex Roles, 50,* 15–26.

Stevens, M. A., & Englar-Carlson, M. (2010). Counseling men. In J. A. Erickson-Cornish, B. A. Schreier, L. I. Nadkarni, L. H. Metzger, & E. R. Rodolfa (Eds.), *Handbook of multicultural counseling competencies* (pp. 195–230). New York: Wiley.

Vandello, J. A., Bosson, J. K., Cohen, D., Burnaford, R. M., & Weaver, J. R. (2008). Precarious manhood. *Journal of Personality and Social Psychology, 95,* 1325–1339.

Vogel, D. L., Wester, S. R., & Larson, L. M. (2007). Avoidance of counseling: Psychological factors that inhibit seeking help. *Journal of Counseling and Development, 85,* 410–422.

6

Relational Growth in Men Using Imago Relationship Therapy

WADE LUQUET

"My husband does not want to come," Sarah revealed of her husband, Taylor, when she made the appointment. Of course, I had heard that before, as have most couples therapists. The thought has often crossed my mind that if it were not for men, my caseload would be constantly filled. Men do not seem to relish the idea of going to therapy; and who could blame them? The counseling process asks men to step into a world that is typically foreign to them, and one that most have been taught to avoid since childhood. For most men, to deal with feelings and to think deeply about their relationship goes completely against their learned, rational tendencies (Deering & Gannon, 2005).

And yet, these tendencies that might serve them so well in war and at work does not serve them quite as well in the relationship world. Engaging men in psychotherapy is an obstacle that most therapists face when working with couples—one that might be a bit less daunting if approached in a way that works with how men think, and then shows them new pathways of relationship. The theory and techniques of Imago Relationship Therapy (IRT) can give the therapist a way of connecting with men that may prove to be less threatening, more engaging, and allows both partners in the relationship to grow and expand their emotional and cognitive repertoire. This chapter will illustrate the IRT technique of couples dialogue, show how to use the dialogue to increase empathy in men, and how to use that empathy to encourage change through the technique of behavior change request.

BASIC IMAGO THEORY

Imago relationship therapy is based on the premise that we choose partners who possess both positive and negative characteristics of our early childhood caretakers (Hendrix, 1988). An imprinting has occurred that causes us to seek what is familiar to us in another person. We make an unconscious decision to fall in love with that person in an effort to have corrective empathic experiences so we can move past old behavioral patterns that may interfere with our relationships. The problem is that most couples are not aware of this and continue behaviors that cause hurt, rather than healing, in the relationship. This is an unconscious process that when brought into the light for the couple helps them understand how to use their relationship to heal past wounds and move beyond destructive behavior patterns.

IRT employs several exercises and skills that help the couple understand that their relationship has a purpose beyond survival and friendship. Couples are taught a dialogue process that allows them to fully hear each other on a deep level, which often allows them to validate that the other makes sense. They are then able to offer an empathic response to their partner. It is through this validation and empathic response that an understanding takes place that allows for changes in behaviors that will contribute to a healing of past wounds. When couples are able to hear each other at this level and heal past wounds, they are able to live beyond the pain that may have defined their behavior and their relationship. Now less self-absorbed by the pain, they are able to take their relationship into new heights of companionship, and some have said a sense of spirituality within the relationship as they experience the other on a deeper level.

The therapist takes on the role of educator and facilitator of the process. Therapists teach the couple the theory behind Imago, teach the process of couples dialogue, and guide the couple through processes that utilize the dialogue, including reimagining the partner as an ally in healing, as well as reintroducing caring behaviors into everyday behavior. The therapist steps back from the typical role of the transferential object, and instead works with the transference that has already occurred between the couple to facilitate understanding and new behaviors that will allow the couple to take the relationship beyond the stuck patterns they have been experiencing. Many of these ideas are introduced to the couple in the first session.

THE FIRST SESSION DETERMINES
THE COURSE OF THERAPY

Taylor reluctantly came to the therapy session. He was cordial, but seemed a bit nervous as I shook his hand and welcomed him and Sarah. She, on the other hand, seemed relieved to be coming to find help for their marriage, something she had been asking Taylor to do for at least a year. He felt they could do the work on their own and did not need someone telling him how to handle his marriage. She was comfortably dressed in a stylish sweat suit, looking the part of the harried mother of young children—hair pulled back with just a little make-up and just getting off her cell phone with the sitter making sure everything was fine at home.

Taylor was nicely dressed in a pair of neatly pressed khaki pants, a polo shirt, and loafers, giving the impression of a fairly successful man. Taylor's very successful father—a vice president in a large company where he began as a factory worker while in college—trained him early on to dress neatly and carry himself in a professional manner. He and his three brothers used their father as a role model and all have finished college, married well, and found good jobs in professional fields. Taylor holds traditional values about his role in the family as protector and provider, although he does not have a problem with Sarah working part time now that they have young children. Appearances are important to Taylor and he enjoys maintaining his masculine and successful image.

However, on this day, Taylor seemed to have a look of defeat on his face, as if coming to therapy was an admission of failure—a feeling most men work to ward off (Stosny, 2009). It would be important that the tone of the first session be established as one of trust and success rather than failure and blame. Therefore, avoiding the "What's wrong?" and "What brings you here today?" questions would be important not only because of the feelings they evoke, but quite honestly Taylor may not know the answer to those questions or may prefer to keep the answer to himself at this early stage (Moynehan & Adams, 2007). He needed to have some success in answering questions correctly so he would have confidence in the therapy and the therapist.

Instead, the first session begins by asking the most diagnostic of questions in couple's therapy, and one he would more than likely know the answer to. "Can you tell me the story of how you met?" I relaxed as I saw Taylor smile and begin to recall how he met Sarah at work. She had been hired as part of a consulting team on a computer project and he could not take his eyes off of her. He remembered that she was wearing a nice business suit that was tasteful, and showed off her figure and her deep green eyes. He felt as if their connection was almost instant, "We could talk for hours." Sarah remembered that time period in much the same way, "He was like a little puppy dog always wanting to follow me. I wish I had that now." Their answer had provided hope for the therapy and how it would progress. Because they had remembered the meeting fondly and with details, they were likely to want their 15-year marriage to continue and be willing to work toward finding a connection (Buehlman, Gottman, & Fainsilber, 1992). Had their answer been delivered with little energy and detail, it would have been a clear indication that there was a lot of work to do.

While we kept things initially light and the couple was not fully aware that this was part of an assessment, we were also gaining trust with each other so we could get into more difficult subject areas that prompted their visit. To keep Taylor engaged and give hope that he would return to future sessions, it was important that we go with his cognitive learning style for a session or two, while at the same time giving attention to Sarah's desire for connection with her husband. Imago relationship therapy does this by teaching the skill of couples dialogue.

APPEALING TO THE COGNITIVE: INTRODUCING THE AFFECTIVE

Taylor and Sarah had drifted apart. Although they could once talk about everything, they barely spent any time together now. This was mostly due to neglect of the relationship: He became very involved in work, and she became involved in family. There were no known affairs, although Sarah has considered having one as a way just to make a connection with someone. Instead, she just spent time with their kids, a son who is 10 and a daughter who is 8, her mother, and her sisters. Whenever Sarah tried to talk to Taylor, he seemed to minimize what she was saying or offer ways to fix the problem when all she wanted was for someone to listen. He became less of a trusted friend to her and she often felt her feelings were stupid when he would try to offer her solutions. Taylor is a rational thinker who likes things to be fixable and make sense. Sarah, while certainly more than capable of rational thought, is the more emotional partner of the two. By gender, this would be statistically, though not always, true of most couples with males taking on a logical approach to problem solving and females more in tune with their emotion. And yet, their growth in the relationship will not be in helping them do more of what they are good at, but more of what needs to be developed. Taylor will need to hold on to his rational self while developing the capacity for empathy and emotion. Sarah will need to keep her emotions while learning to use logical processes to manage her emotions using self-soothing techniques. In the first session, the couple will be taught a dialogue process that allows them to do just that.

To many, the couples dialogue seems like active listening, and in many ways it is. The major difference is how the couple is taught to think about the dialogue process. In most models that use an active listening technique, the skill is taught as a means of hearing what the other said. Certainly it is important for couples to hear each other and imago therapists use dialogue to facilitate hearing the other. Yet, Imago therapy's takes the skill a bit further by teaching the couple to use their dialogue for personal growth in addition to hearing their partner. The major difference between the usual active listening technique and the imago couples dialogue is how it is framed to the couple and the depth of the resulting conversation. The personal growth comes when listening partners can hold on to their own beliefs while at the same time allowing their speaking partners to have their own way of viewing the situation. This will initially cause a sense of anxiety in the listening partners as they let go of the idea of being right and give in to the idea that there can be more than one way to view a situation. The personal growth in the couples dialogue process occurs as the anxiety lessens and a maturity of attempting to understand the other sets in as a matter of course in the relationship.

Couples dialogue is a three-part process of mirroring what is heard, validation of the other, and offering empathy for what was said. This is not something that will come naturally, but will take time and practice with the counselor acting as a coach during the process. Taylor and Sarah will be given a brief lecture on brain functioning in order to give the couples dialogue a context. This will appeal to Taylor's rational self so he understands why he is participating in an exercise that may feel stiff and rote at first.

The couple will be taught how brain functioning affects their conversations and may keep them from hearing each other completely. We are creatures with a triune brain (McLean, 1964) and a prefrontal cortex that are all fully in play in our conversations (for the complete lecture, see Luquet, 2007). Our brains are divided in three parts, with the reptilian brain reactively taking charge in our arguments. This is the section of the brain located at the base of the skull that is interested in our safety. When it senses danger, it will tell us to fight, run, freeze, hide, or submit—often referred to as the fight-or-flight response. Couples are quickly able to realize that they do these same things in their arguments. Most certainly recognize their fights, but they can also recall times when they left the room, froze and hoped the fight would end, stayed at work or another room, or gave up in frustration as a way of stopping the fight.

Couples are taught about the mammalian brain where we house the ability to form relationships and experience feelings. They learn that their logical processes, Taylor's favorite part of the brain, is the larger portion that surrounds the first two and is known as the cerebral cortex. Because of this layer, we are able to sense time, use tools, do math, and come up with logical solutions. The prefrontal cortex is the moral and judgment center—the part of the brain that keeps us calm and in check. When the prefrontal cortex is working well, the couple is able to respond calmly to each other and listen intentionally rather than reactively from the reptilian brain, which takes over in an argument. All of the parts are important and by understanding how the brain works, Taylor and Sarah may be able to develop an emotional intelligence that will allow them to settle themselves, become less reactive, hear what the other is saying, and respond appropriately (Atkinson, 2005; Goleman, 1996).

Following this brief lecture, couples are given an exercise to help them viscerally understand what they just learned and start the process of learning dialogue. Taylor and Sarah are asked to face each other and have a 3-minute mini-argument or frustration. The following dialogue transpired.

Sarah: You are just too busy. You never seem to have time for me.
Taylor: Well, I have to work. We have a lot of bills to pay and I can't just sit and talk. There is too much to do.
Sarah: But I need to talk to you sometimes. I can't just talk to the kids. I need some adult conversation.
Taylor: You have your mom and sisters. Can't you just talk to them?
Sarah: I didn't marry them. I'm married to you and I need you to listen to me sometimes. I feel like giving up on us sometimes.
Taylor: It's not that bad. You have most of the things you need. I just need to concentrate so we can pay for these things.
Sarah: I have everything but a husband. I really need a husband and a friend.
Taylor: I'm your friend.
Sarah: Not the kind I need.

This short sequence was typical for Taylor and Sarah. Sarah was interested in developing a relationship, whereas Taylor was interested in minimizing the problem and helping Sarah find a solution that did not involve him giving up time or making connections. They were then introduced to the couples dialogue and asked to discuss the same subject. Taylor decided that he would start as the receiver, or listener, of the message and was instructed to find a safe place to calm his reptilian brain so his fight-or-flight response would be less likely to be triggered. Once he had himself safely on a beach in his mind, he was instructed to mirror what Sarah said to him. He was also guided through the validation and empathy process, which required him to put himself in Sarah's position to guess what is going on for her internally. Taylor was also given instructions on how to check if he heard what Sarah was saying and to encourage her to say more. Sarah was instructed to use "I" statements to make her statements less triggering and more likely to be heard.

Sarah: I feel very lonely and ignored. When I try to talk to you, and you offer solutions, it feels like you don't care about what I am feeling.
Taylor: So if I'm getting it, when you try to talk to me and I offer solutions, it feels like I don't care about your feelings. And you feel lonely and ignored. Did I get that?
Sarah: Yes.
Taylor: Is there more?

Sarah: Yes, I just need you to listen to me sometimes. I don't need you to solve the problem. I need you to hear what I am going through.

Taylor: I can do that.

Therapist: Not yet, Taylor. You need to hear her first. Can you mirror what she said?

Taylor: Yes. I hear you saying that you just need me to listen. You need me to hear what is going on for you and you don't need for me to solve your problem. Did I get that?

Sarah: You did.

Taylor: Is there more?

Sarah: Yes. I feel invisible in this relationship. When I don't feel you are hearing me, I feel very alone and sad. It's like I don't matter in this relationship. I want to matter.

Therapist (softly): Stay safe, Taylor. Just mirror back what she said.

Taylor: So if I'm getting it right, you are feeling invisible when I am not hearing you. You feel like you don't matter and you want to matter. Did I get that?

Sarah: Yes.

Therapist: Taylor, can you validate what she said? Does it make sense to you that she feels that way?

Taylor: It does. I suppose when someone feels they are not listened to they feel that they do not matter and that their problems and thoughts are not important.

Therapist: Good. Can you tell her that?

Taylor: I can see that if I ignore you, you would feel invisible and like you did not matter. That makes sense to me.

Therapist: I wonder how that makes her feel?

Taylor: I would guess that would make you sad, lonely, and like you did not matter in the relationship.

Sarah: Yes, you got it.

At this point, Taylor was beginning to experience a small amount of empathy but mostly he was seeing the logic of the couples dialogue process. He can see that it keeps her calmer when he hears her, yet he still has not connected to the process emotionally. It would take a few weeks of practice and daily homework assigned each session for the process to become fluid and less rote. At that point, Taylor would be introduced to processes that deepen the dialogue process and give him the experience of feeling empathic toward Sarah.

Simultaneously, Sarah would also have to make some changes, especially so Taylor would not feel that it was all about him and that he was being picked on—a sure way to have men leave the therapy process. Taylor's concern was that Sarah was too emotional and dramatic about things. And at times, he was right. Many times she was that way because he was not listening and she had to say things louder and more dramatic to get his attention. But sometimes she was making things bigger than they needed to be which overwhelmed Taylor and brought about his flight-and-freeze response. He became flooded by the emotions. Sarah would have to be taught to use the structure of the couples dialogue to keep her emotions at bay so Taylor could hear what she needed to say. When men are feeling less flooded emotionally, they can become more fully involved in the dialogue and be open to change. Part of Sarah's growth will be to become more cognitive as a way to give structure and voice to her emotions. In the early stages, the couples dialogue will help provide the structure for this to occur by slowing her down and allowing her to feel heard.

Taylor: Sometimes I get overwhelmed by your emotions. I don't know what to do, so I just get quiet. It's like I'm trying to wait for the storm to end.

Sarah: So if I'm getting it, you feel overwhelmed by my emotions and you get quiet and hope things will pass. Did I get that? Is there more?

Taylor: Yes, it's just hard for me to hear when things get so intense in your voice. I just shut down. And I'm sure that frustrates you like it overwhelms me.

Sarah: You're saying that it's hard for you to hear me when my voice gets so intense. You shut down and you realize that it frustrates me. Did I get that?

Taylor: Yes.

Sarah: Is there more?

Taylor: I do like how things go when we use the dialogue process. Things don't get so intense, so I feel like I can listen to you. I am hoping that when you find yourself getting loud and emotional that we can stop for a minute and talk in dialogue as we have been trying to do.

Sarah: So you like the dialogue process and you are hoping that we can switch over to the dialogue, especially when I start to get emotional. You'd be more available to listen to me if you did not feel so overwhelmed by my emotions. Did I get that?

Taylor: Yes you did.

Sarah: That makes sense to me. I know how my emotions can get intense, so if I am able to use the dialogue, I can imagine that you would feel safer and more present to hear me.

Taylor: Thank you.

Sarah and Taylor were beginning to understand that they were in a mutual growth process that required both of them to make changes in order for the relationship to succeed and expand to its full potential. In order to fully realize this, they would need to develop a deep empathy for each other. The dialogue has slowed them down so they can hear each other, and now they would be introduced to deep empathy processes.

REIMAGING: INTRODUCING MEN TO EMPATHY

Empathy for others involves two simultaneous processes: cognitive structure and affective surrender (Jordan, 1991). A simple way to think of this is the ability to say, "I can see you feel that way. It's not me, but I can see you feel that way." It is the ability to be able to momentarily feel for the other, and then be able to pull back and recognize that the feeling belongs to the other while still maintaining contact with them. In other words, deeply validating the other's experience while preserving the self. Men are quite good at the cognitive structure part of the process, "It's not me," but have their most difficulty with affective surrender, "I can see you feel that way." Part of this seems to be due to fear that by letting go and feeling for the other they may lose their rational sense of self. It is also true that most men are seldom encouraged to deal with emotions and thus lose the skills needed to cross into emotional territory. This lack of ability has frustrated women for centuries as they look for a mate who can understand and validate their emotions. And like an atrophied muscle, the ability to experience empathy is there, it just needs to be exercised.

Heinz Kohut, developer of self psychology, wrote that empathy is to the psychological life what oxygen is to the physical life (Siegel, 1996). For humans to live without empathy would be to the emotional self what living without oxygen would be to the physical self—we would simply die, or as Kohut (1971) points out for a lack of empathy of others, we would develop narcissistic and self-centered tendencies. Oftentimes marriages regress to a state of little or no empathy between partners, or to what Mason referred to as the "relationship nightmare" (2005, p. 144). Without empathy, couples experience a disconnection that leads to isolation from each other and a self-absorption, and thus, the relationship suffers. In IRT, the relationship is considered primary over the individual. Mason states "the relationship has at least as much power over the individuals as the individuals have over the relationship. IRT suggests that rather than there being individuals having a relationship, the relationship has individuals" (Mason, 2005, p. 139). With IRT, the attempt is made to breathe oxygen back into the relationship by restoring empathy and connection through the dialogue process.

The couples dialogue of IRT offers a safe way for men to experience emotion and regain empathic connection while at the same time providing a cognitive structure that keeps them from losing their rational self. In fact, it is built into the three-part process. Mirroring is a cognitive process where receivers merely say back what they heard to make sure they heard it correctly. Validating is stepping into the other's world momentarily to see if it makes sense to them. And offering empathy is a way of guessing what the other feels. It is simultaneously a cognitive and affective process. For rational thinkers, it puts them into the position to look at emotions. For the emotional partner, the dialogue slows them down and keeps them from becoming reactive by helping them think about what is being said. This process alone will help exercise those less used cognitive and affective structures. However, the process can be deepened.

Imago recognizes that many frustrations in relationships stem from childhood frustrations that have gone unconscious. Some people may not like their partner to be late because when they were a child their parents were late and they were frightened. Some may not like to have their partner ask too many questions because they had a smothering parent and now they feel they need some space. This information oftentimes stays unconscious and partners may not recognize that they trigger these wounds by their behavior. A deepening of the dialogue can help reveal these wounds and at the same time create empathy in the receiving partner.

Taylor and Sarah have now had a few weeks of practicing dialogue. They recognize that the dialogue mostly helps their frustrations, and that it sometimes escalates their frustrations because they are now talking about things they had been avoiding. They have continued with the dialogue because they recognize it as a safe way for them to talk through their frustrations and issues. They feel that they have the basic dialogue process down and are interested in learning more about using it for other frustrations. The therapist will now coach them into a deepening process that will help them tap into the source of their frustrations and, hopefully, help them experience deep empathy. As often happens, the core issue of Sarah feeling ignored has reemerged. Although Taylor has been listening to her more, there are times where she feels ignored and this seems to ignite her anger and sadness.

Sarah: While you have been listening to me more, there are times when I still feel like you want to get away from me.

Taylor: So you acknowledge that I have been listening to you more, but there are times when you can still feel me wanting to get away from you. Did I get that?

Sarah: Yes.

Taylor: Is there more?

Sarah: Yes. When it feels like you want to get away from me, I wonder what is wrong with me. What do I do that makes you feel so repulsed and want to leave so quickly.

Taylor: So when I try to get away quickly, you wonder what is wrong with you and what might make me feel so repulsed and want to leave so quickly. Did I get that?

Sarah: Yes.

Therapist: Sarah, I noticed that the feeling of being ignored and not wanted comes up a lot for you. Does that feeling and what is going on between you and Taylor remind you of anything from your childhood?

Sarah: I think so.

Therapist: Can you talk about it with Taylor? He will make it very safe for you and he will mirror back what you are saying so you feel fully heard. Maybe you can start your sentence by saying, "When I was a little girl ..."

Sarah: When I was a little girl, things were too busy. We had five kids in the family and my parents were both working hard to take care of all of us. We were on our own a lot. I was a kid who had a lot to say. And believe it or not, there was no one to say it to, even with so many kids in the house. We had a short amount of time to get our point across before our parents moved on to the next thing.

Taylor: So if I'm getting it, your parents were so busy taking care of all of you that there was little time for them to listen to you. You said you had a lot to say, and even with all of the kids in the house, it did not seem like you had anyone to talk to. Did I get that?

Sarah: Yes.

Taylor: Is there more?

Sarah: Our family seemed to be on survival mode. What we thought did not seem to be of importance. (*Sarah is now tearful.*) As much as my parents tried, they did not have time to listen to me. I felt so alone and like what I was thinking and feeling did not matter. I really had no one to go to, so I had to talk to my friends.

Taylor (now leaning forward and speaking softly): So I'm hearing you say that you did not feel important. Your parents did not have the time to listen to you because they were so busy. And you were left feeling alone and like you did not matter. You turned to your friends to listen. Did I get that?

Sarah: Yes.

Taylor: Tell me more about that.

Sarah: It was really sad. While it seems like a good thing to be a part of a large, loud, usually fun family, it was really lonely. We had to do what the group wanted to do. I was more a part of a brood rather than an individual with thoughts and feelings. Now I just want someone to see me and not ignore me.

Taylor: So while it would seem to be a good thing to be a part of a large family, it was really sad. You all did things as a brood and you were not able to be seen as an individual. Now you just want someone to see you and not feel ignored.

Therapist: Taylor, does that makes sense to you?

Taylor: It really makes sense to me. And I can see how when I cut you short on our conversations, it would bring that feeling back for you. I can see what makes you want to be heard as an individual.

Therapist: And you imagine that makes her feel ...?

Taylor: I can imagine that when I cut you off, you might feel alone, ignored, and maybe invisible. Did I get that?

Sarah (tearfully): Yes, thank you for hearing me.

Taylor had now heard Sarah in a way she needed to be heard. Rather than fighting back or cutting her off, he had been able to momentarily step into her world and see how his behaviors brought her back into her own pain of childhood. He had experienced true empathy for her and was beginning to flex that long forgotten muscle that would allow him to make empathic contact with his wife. Taylor and Sarah would be shown several other empathy-building skills whose description is beyond the scope of this chapter (see Luquet, 2007, and Hendrix, 2007) including the parent–child dialogue and the holding exercise. These exercises would allow Taylor to understand Sarah's feelings while at the same time preserving his self. As he was able to see that most of the energy behind her frustrations was related to past wounds, he was able to connect to Sarah more while feeling less blamed and less of a need to fix things for her.

TWO STEPS FORWARD, ONE STEP BACK

Now at the stage where Taylor was most open to Sarah's emotional self, he is also most vulnerable to his fear of emotions—hers and his own. A week after this session, Taylor and Sarah found themselves in a huge argument that left them both feeling scared, vulnerable, and angry again. He was not so sure he wanted to be so vulnerable with Sarah at this point. After all, his brothers and his father were not this involved with their wives' vulnerabilities and feelings. They had all been taught to get over things quickly and figure out a solution. The dialogue process seemed quite slow to Taylor and, quite frankly, much of it felt unnecessary. His reaction left Sarah scared that things would return to the way they were just when she was beginning to trust him again. She wondered if things could ever get better between them.

What Taylor was experiencing was typical in IRT. This way of hearing each other is new for many couples, especially for men. Taylor had been taught to hold his feelings in and deal with things rationally. To live in his male-dominant family, he created an adaptation and learned to suppress feelings and accentuate rational thinking. Listening to Sarah's feelings was a threat to that adaptation and it was causing anxiety. The therapist listened attentively to Taylor using the dialogue process. Taylor was able to calm down a bit as the therapist listened. It is certainly understandable that this process moved slower; after all, at work he makes immediate decisions and he is a good problem solver.

Oftentimes, men want to run their personal lives like they run their work lives, and in reality, it just does not translate. The therapist spent some time talking to Taylor about his anxiety and how dealing with a relationship partner is much different than dealing with work situations. He was reminded that what he and Sarah were doing before learning this process was not working for them either.

Therapist: Taylor, I can see how this is difficult and frustrating for you to do because it seems so inefficient.

Taylor: Yes, I can get to the point so much faster with my usual way of doing things.

Therapist: I can see how it would seem that problems are solved faster the way you typically do things. Let's think about whether that is a hundred percent true. Did the problems come up again?

Taylor: They did seem to come up over and over again. They never seem to go away.

Therapist: So, maybe it just seemed to solve the problem faster. Maybe it just postponed the problem?

Taylor: Maybe.

Therapist: Tell me about how this goes against the messages you got growing up in your family about taking care of emotions.

Taylor: We were told to keep things bottled up. Emotions only got in the way of reason, so we just did not deal with it.

Therapist: So you were taught to keep things bottled up and not deal in emotions but more in reason. Did I get that?

Taylor: That's right.

Therapist: So would it be fair to say that the dialogue is going against the messages you received and may be causing you some anxiety because you were taught to bottle up emotions?

Taylor: I think so. That makes sense.

Therapist: Tell me more about that.

Taylor continued to talk about what it would be like to go against the messages he learned as a child growing up, and came to his own conclusion, through dialogue with the therapist and Sarah, that what he was learning was probably better than the way he typically handled things in the past. Taylor also was assured that his anxiety would return and he would want to go back to fixing things many times. It is natural to go back to what he was used to doing, and there will be many times when fixing a problem is appropriate, such as how they are going to pay a bill or how they are going to get their kids to several different events on the same day. However, if he stays attentive and he sees an emotion behind what Sarah is saying, that would be a good time to enter into the dialogue. There was also a conversation about how his marriage and that of his parents and brothers would now be different from each other, and that he and Sarah needed to work together to maintain their connection even under the pressure of his family that may notice and not approve of his spending the time to listening to his wife. While this was a tough time for the two of them, they were able to regroup and continue with the processes.

All of this insight and connection Taylor and Sarah have been developing over the past 5 weeks or so, while important, is not enough. Now that they have skills for connection and empathy, Taylor and Sarah need to make some behavior changes that will prevent a rewounding and give them the opportunity for personal growth. Imago relationship therapy does this through a process called the behavior change request.

RESTRUCTURING FRUSTRATIONS: "FIXING" THE REAL PROBLEM AS A PATHWAY FOR PERSONAL GROWTH IN MEN

Taylor was always good at coming up with solutions to Sarah's problems. Now the dialogue had shifted his usual way of dealing with Sarah and he has learned to listen to her regarding what she needs to feel connected and heard by him. This alone would begin to heal her frustrations that began in childhood and are triggered by similar behaviors exhibited by Taylor. Yet in times past when she took the next step and requested behavior change, he felt coerced into making changes. As a result, the changes seldom lasted for more than a few weeks. Now that he had an empathic connection to Sarah and could see the pain his behaviors caused her, he seemed more willing and open to hearing what she needed. At this point, if Sarah were to come at him strongly with her frustrations, he might revert back to his old behaviors as he had in the past. She needed a safe way to approach Taylor about changes she needed from him that would give her what she needs and simultaneously bring about lasting change in him while maintaining the connection they have developed through the dialogue.

Behavior change in Imago Relationship Therapy starts with the premise that a frustration is a desire stated negatively. The reptilian brain has a difficult time hearing a frustration and often interprets the expression of one as a threat. Thus, the brain will do what it is designed to do when it feels threatened and go into a fight-or-flight mode. To soften the start-up (Gottman, 2000) of the request for behavior change, couples are instructed to change the frustration to a desire. For example, "I hate when you are late" becomes "My desire is that you arrive on time." "I hate when you ignore me" becomes "I would like for you to take what I am saying seriously." In this format, frustrations are easier to hear by the receiver who can more readily respond to the request. However, a desire does not give enough information for the receiver to perform the change in a way that might be healing to the sender. The desire will have to be taken one more step into a positive, measureable, doable, and time-limited behavior change request.

Behavior change requests (BCRs) are a structured means of giving instruction to the receiving partner on exactly how to perform a behavior change that might bring about a difference in behavior that meets the need of the sender, and at the same time is sustainable and growth-producing for the person making the change. It is important that the requested change be a stretch into new behavior but not an impossible task. To ask a person to do something they have never done to perform a new behavior every time or 7 days a week is a setup for failure and more frustration. To make the request for 3 days this week or once this week for 20 minutes may be more doable and meets the criteria of time limited and measurable. The idea of the BCR is to phrase the request in a way that can be heard and acted upon. Once acted upon, the person who receives the behavior change has a need met and the person performing the change enters into a new behavior that begins to slowly exercise the parts of him- or herself that have atrophied due to nonuse. Repeated use of the requested behavior will exercise the unused attribute and the task will become easier to perform and a more natural part of the personality. As is said in imago relationship therapy, "Your partner has the blueprint for your growth."

To illustrate this with Taylor and Sarah, we would go back to an earlier dialogue when he talked to her about how he feels overwhelmed by her emotions and hoped that they could talk about heated issues in dialogue. Taylor had a desire to talk in dialogue; however, it was not formalized as a request for change. It would be important for Sarah to learn how to control her emotional tone so she can be heard by Taylor. They were guided into a behavior change request a week after he spoke to her about how he feels overwhelmed by her emotions. They were given a short lecture about frustrations being desires stated negatively, and that it would be important to put their frustrations into desires if they want to be heard by the other. Taylor was able to say to Sarah that his desire would be that she talk to him in a calm manner in dialogue so that he could better hear her. She was able to mirror his desire back and understand that intense emotions overwhelms him and he reacts by getting quiet and avoiding contact with her. At this point, the therapist helped Taylor craft several requests for behavior changes that would help him stay in the conversation with her while at the same time asking her to make a substantial change in the way she expresses herself that will bring about a personal change if done over a period of time. The behavior change request would be positive, measureable, and doable.

Taylor: When we need to talk about something important, I would like for you to come to me as calmly as you can and say, " I need to talk to you and I would like for you to hear me in dialogue." I'd like for you to do this twice this week.

Sarah: So if I need to talk to you about something, twice this week you would like for me to come to you as calmly as I can and say that I'd like to talk to you in dialogue. Did I get that?

Taylor: Yes.

Sarah: Is there more?

Taylor: Twice this month if you find yourself angry or agitated, I would like for you to go into another room for at least ten seconds and breath to calm down as much as you can before coming to me and requesting a dialogue.

Sarah: So if I find myself angry and emotional, you would like for me
to calm myself down in another room for at least ten seconds
before coming to you to talk in dialogue. And you would like
for me to do that at least twice this month. Did I get that?

Taylor: You did.

Therapist: And Taylor, you're saying that when Sarah does these requests,
you will make yourself available to hear her. Is that right?

Taylor: That's right. I'll be able to listen.

These requests will not be easy for Sarah. She is being asked to
contain her emotions so that Taylor is not triggered and goes into
withdrawal and avoidance. It's not that she will ignore her feelings,
but rather she will contain them so they are not so overwhelming for
Taylor. Her growth here is to add some structure to her emotions so
that they can be better understood by a more compassionate and connected Taylor.

Of course, Sarah will also have some request of Taylor. Oftentimes
the couples requests will seem like the opposite of each other. Where
Taylor asks for less emotional conversations, Sarah is likely to ask Taylor
to validate her emotions. But that is exactly the point. Partners do not
have what the other needs. Rather, what the partner needs is what the
other most needs to grow into. Behavior change requests promote collaborative self-development that allows each partner to grow into areas
where they may have a deficit. Not surprisingly, Sarah's request would
ask Taylor to stretch into dealing with her emotional self and need to
be recognized.

Therapist: Sarah, it seems that Taylor is understanding what you were
trying to tell him about feeling ignored and unimportant in
your family and how that recreates itself in your frustrations
now.

Sarah: Yes, he does.

Therapist: Maybe this is a good time to present him with a behavior
change request like you learned a few weeks ago. I'm wondering if you could ask him if you could present him with
a request. And maybe you can give him several requests so
he has some choice about what he might be willing to do for
you.

Sarah: Taylor, I'd like to make a behavior change request. I'm wondering
if you could make yourself safe and available to hear me.

Taylor: I can. I can hear you now.

Sarah: This is about my not feeling heard by you and feeling ignored.
My desire is to feel heard and not feel ignored. So what would
help with that is three times this week when you come home
from work I would like you to put your things down, come
over and give me a hug for fifteen seconds, and let me know
you are available to listen. I would like for you to give me

fifteen minutes of sustained attention and listen to me in dialogue.

Therapist: Can you tell him what sustained means to you?

Sarah: Sustained means looking me in the eyes and no computer, TV, or mail to distract you.

Taylor: So if I'm getting this, you would like for me to give you a hug for fifteen seconds when I get home from work and listen to you three times this week for fifteen minutes using dialogue giving you sustained attention meaning no TV, computer, or mail to distract myself, and looking you in the eyes. Did I get that?

Sarah: Yes, you did.

Taylor: Is there more?

Sarah: Yes, once this month, I would like for you to approach me and ask me what I would like to do for fun this week and you get a babysitter and we go out and do just what I want to do.

Taylor (laughing): Oh, man! You mean I have to get the sitter? And you might take me to a chick flick?

Therapist: Alright, Taylor. Now stick to the mirroring. No one said this would be easy.

Taylor: All right, so you said once this month, you would like for me to ask you what you would like to do this week, get a sitter, and we do exactly what you want to do. Did I get that?

Sarah (giggling): You did. I can't wait to think something up.

Taylor: Is there more?

Sarah: My desire is to have the things I do noticed. My request would be that twice during the week you approach me and tell me you noticed something that I've done around the house. I'd love for you to say something like, "I noticed that you put a new flower arrangement in the living room" or "I've noticed that you've gotten through that stack of bills you were wanting to get through."

Taylor: So you would like for me to notice some things you have done around the house and let you know that I have noticed by telling you. You would like for me to say things like, "I noticed that you've done something different in the living room" or "I noticed that you got through the bills you were working on." You'd like for me to do this twice this week.

Therapist: Good. Now Taylor, you don't have to do any of these things. They are just requests. But I'm wondering if there is any one thing she has asked for that you could agree to do this week?

Taylor: Yes, I think I can do the first one and listen to her three times this week for fifteen minutes using dialogue. I will have to be less distracted, but I think I can do that for you.

Sarah: Thank you.

Therapist: Sarah, can you finish these sentences? By doing that, you will begin to heal my childhood wound of …

Sarah: By doing that, you will begin to heal my childhood wound of ... um ... not being important and feeling invisible in my family.
Therapist: And it will make me feel ...
Sarah: It will make me feel more connected, important, and like I matter.
Taylor: That makes sense to me.

Taylor now had several behaviors he could choose from Sarah's requests that would challenge him, and at the same time meet some of her needs. While they seem like reasonable requests, they would not be easy for Taylor because they would be new or underused behaviors. He will have to stretch his personality to complete the behaviors, but as he does, the behaviors will become more a part of his repertoire and they will become easier and more fluid. It is unlikely that either of them will be able to complete the request perfectly, but they should be able to make enough changes to lessen the frustrations of the other and encourage growth in themselves. It is important to note that they are each responsible for their own behavior and their behavior changes, and the BCR list will provide a map for optimum growth and healing.

HELPING MEN STAY CONNECTED

Taylor had come a long way in 8 weeks, and Sarah was feeling more comfortable and safe in their relationship. They were noticeably more playful, affectionate, and connected. And yet, it is far too early to consider their work a success because, after all, it had only been 2 months, and a few inconsiderate behaviors could bring them right back to where they started. It would be important for the two of them to stay connected by maintaining their behaviors and to also recognize that they will have some setbacks.

A real gift any therapist can give to their client is to emphasize that progress is not linear, but rather a series of steps forward and backward. Although things may go well for a while, they can expect that there will be times when one will not live up to the expectation of the other and hurt feelings will come back. This was stressed with Taylor and Sarah, and they were taught that they have the tools to get themselves back on track toward the progress they have made in therapy. Imago therapy employs the analogy that couples dialogue is like a canoe and the couple is in the canoe paddling together. If they find themselves facing a large wave, they should do what any good canoeist would do and head directly into the wave. If they find that they have fallen out of the canoe, they need to crawl back in and continue facing the waves using dialogue. Creating safety and using dialogue will have to become a way of life for Taylor and Sarah when they face frustrations, which they inevitably will.

For these new skills and the new ways they have learned to deal with each other to become permanent, they will have to become a habit. And habit comes from repetition. Repetition in this case comes from homework and a follow-up plan. Each week, Taylor and Sarah had been given homework to do between sessions including practicing dialogue, showing care for each other, visualizing the future of their relationship, some written homework regarding their childhood and how they chose each other, and having fun and belly laughs. They were now spending more time together and were used to the idea that relationships are work. As the therapy winds down, they now need to be presented with a follow-up plan that will keep them in the habit of using the skills they have learned so they can stay connected and continue on their marriage journey. Taylor and Sarah were presented with a plan during their last session. They were given a handout of a suggested week-by-week program to keep them using the imago processes they had learned (see Luquet, 2007). The program called for them to utilize the dialogue on a regular basis, to continue to reimage each other as an ally rather than an enemy, and to participate in activities that promote fun and laughter between them. They were reminded that their relationship was a journey and that they could expect ups and downs, and they should always return to the dialogue they had learned when they experienced frustration. They were told about a book by Harville Henrdrix and Helen Hunt titled *The Couples Companion: Meditations and Exercises for Getting the Love You Want* (1994) that had a series of 365 daily meditations and short exercises that they should consider using to keep their relationship intentional and moving forward. Many couples have found this book to be a very useful tool in helping them maintain the progress they made in the therapy sessions.

Taylor and Sarah also made a 3-month follow-up appointment and committed to do so for a year. It is important for couples to know that like teeth and the dentist, relationships also need follow-up to make sure things are on track. Just knowing that they were going to come back to see the therapist gave them the incentive to keep working, and comfort in knowing that they will be able to talk about any problems they may be having with the process or in the relationship.

ADVICE FOR FEMALE THERAPISTS WORKING WITH MEN

Certainly most male therapist have received an initial phone call from a distraught wife stating that they think their husbands would relate better to a male. And while this may or may not be true, the most important trait of any therapist is to be open and relatable. In the now classic research by Lambert (1992), he found that the factors that influence the outcome of therapy has little to do with the model used. His decades of research indicates the factors and their corresponding contribution to successful psychotherapy outcome include the following:

Client factors (40%)—Social supports, personal strengths, talents, resources
Relationship factors (30%)—Empathy, acceptance, warmth of the therapist
Expectation factors (15%)—Expectation and hope for change
Model/technique factors (15%)—Theoretical model and technique employed by the therapist

For the female therapist, and any therapist for that matter, empathy, acceptance, and warmth are important to make a connection with a male client. This does not mean being overly mushy and sweet—men would see through that—but knowing how men connect. Using some friendly, appropriate humor and a little bit of praise for what they do for their family goes a long way in connecting to men who often have an "atta boy" or praise deficit. While it may be discovered that they are, in fact, not doing enough in the relationship, it is best approached by acknowledging what they have done well, then slipping in how they can expand their behaviors to make things even better—a softened start-up, if you will. Keep in mind that when men say they are doing their best, they truly believe that they are doing everything they can in the relationship. Acknowledge that first and then explore ways in which men can learn what many missed in their socialization process—how to relate to others in an empathic and connecting manner. The skills taught in imago relationship therapy can provide the tools for men to learn these behaviors in a structured and safe manner.

If a male client becomes testy or confrontational with the therapist, it is best to stay with the process and respond in dialogue. A few rounds of mirroring and validation of their points can be disarming if male clients feel threatened. Once they feel heard and understood, male clients will usually calm down and work with the therapist again. Being heard is soothing to the threatened brain, and given enough safe responses from a spouse or a therapist will calm the clients to the point that they learn the therapist has their best interest in mind, and you are not something to defend against. Also, if these clients can experience the dialogue process with the therapist successfully, they may be more likely to use it in situations with their partner. When the client develops trust in the therapist, their hope and expectations will rise, and now 45% of the outcome factors are positively directed. Add this to a good therapeutic model that fits the therapist and the clients situation, and the possibility of a positive outcome are very good according to the Lambert research.

Men treating men also have an advantage in that the male client seldom worries about being "feminized" by the therapy. There is a basic unspoken understanding between men that we will not force you to do anything in therapy that may be considered effeminate. However, it is often a fear of men in couples therapy that the female therapist and their spouse will join together to reshape them to become a "girlfriend" in the marriage. While it would be wise for men to take on some of the qualities of a good girlfriend—listening, being available, kind words, and attentiveness—it is not necessary for men to lose all aspects of their masculinity. In fact, most women would say that they would not want their male partners to lose the qualities of decisiveness, strength, and self-assuredness. It is important that men are able to keep these desirable qualities while at the same time developing the others. If a man senses that the two women in the room are ganging up on him, he may become defensive and retreat (Wexler, 2009). All couples therapists, regardless of gender, must keep in mind that the object of introducing men to empathy and feelings is not to make them more like women but rather to make them into better men. Empathy and feelings are not "feminine"; they are human qualities, regardless of gender. Having access to empathy and feelings makes anyone a better person.

FINAL THOUGHTS

It is difficult for many men to become engaged in processes that go against their learned rational tendencies. Many men harbor within themselves what Alfred Adler called "masculine protest" or "the tendency for a person to display an exaggerated 'masculine' striving for power to avoid 'feminine' traits" (Nelson, 1991, p. 490). For men to submit themselves to couples therapy is a stretch that some are not able to make with their partner. Those that do take the chance need the opportunity to stretch without being broken. To accomplish this, it is best to go with men's thinking and acting tendencies while introducing the emotional aspect so necessary in healthy relationships. As men often enter therapy to rid themselves of a specific problem rather than personal growth, introducing emotion is a delicate task. Plus, any type of therapy that involves men getting in touch with emotions goes against culturally prescribed behaviors and attitudes about what it means to be masculine (McKelley, 2007).

Imago relationship therapy offers a systematic approach to helping couples develop a safe connection through a clear communication process and an understanding of how relationships can be used for personal growth. With the therapist acting as an educator and facilitator, the couple learns new skills and information that allows them to use their relationship for emotional understanding of the other. It is a therapeutic approach that works with men because it is based on logical concepts that introduce emotional experiences. Those men who tend to look at things more rationally are able to understand that the brain needs to be calmed down to lessen anxiety and fear. They understand that when there is less anxiety, there is less need to defend the self, which leads to the possibility of understanding the other's point of view. This now allows them to be open to the possibility of emotion in the other, which may allow them to experience their own emotions as they experience empathy. And when empathy develops for the other, men are better able to grasp the concept of a behavior change request as a measurable and doable behavior change that may lead to a different and more desirable behavior. Most important, they now understand the reason for the change and feel less coerced.

And what would be the most desirable outcome in Imago Relationship Therapy with men? Certainly couples understanding and responding to the needs of their partner would be the stated goal of the work. But how great would it be if these same men and their partners raised their own sons without masculine protest? How would things change if these transformed men let their sons know that it is good, and indeed healthy, for them to experience emotions and show empathy toward others? Helping couples to expand the emotional experiences of their marriages has a larger reach than the two people in the relationship. Children are watching carefully and learning about relationships from their parents. Helping couples learn relationship skills through couples therapy may have a greater consequence than helping couples continue their marriage. It may be that couples like Taylor and Sarah parent their children differently, and these young men and women will grow up with more empathy and compassion for each other with less resistance to seeking help when they need it for their relationships.

REFERENCES

Atkinson, B. J. (2005). *Emotional intelligence in couples therapy*. New York: W.W. Norton.

Buehlman, K. T., Gottman, J. M., & Fainsilber, L. (1992). How a couple views their past, predicts their future: Predicting divorce from an oral history interview. *Journal of Family Psychology, 5*(3–4), 295–318.

Deering, C. G., & Gannon, E. J. (2005). Gender and psychotherapy with traditional men. *American Journal of Psychotherapy, 59*(4), 351–360.

Goleman, D. (1996). *Emotional intelligence: Why it can matter more than IQ*. New York: Bantam Books.

Gottman, J. M. (2000). *The seven principles for making marriage work*. New York: Three Rivers Press.

Hendrix, H. (2007). *Getting the love you want: A guide for couples*. New York: Henry Holt.

Hendrix, H., & Hunt, H. (1994). *The couples companion meditations and exercises for getting the love you want*. New York: Pocket Books.

Jordan, J. (1991). *Women's growth in connection: Writings from the Stone Center*. New York: Guilford.

Kohut, H. (1971). *The analysis of the self: A systematic analysis of the treatment of narcissistic personality disorders*. New York: International Universities Press.

Lambert, M. J. (1992). Implications of outcome research for psychotherapy integration. In J. C. Norcross & M. R. Goldfried (Eds.), *Handbook of psychotherapy integration* (pp. 94–129). New York: Basic Books.

Luquet, W. (2007). *Short-term couples therapy: The Imago model in action*. New York: Routledge.

Mason, R. (2005). Imago, relationships, and empathy. In H. Hendrix, H. LaKelly Hunt, M. T. Hannah, & W. Luquet, (Eds.), *Imago relationship therapy: Perspectives on theory*. New York: Routledge.

McKelley, R. A. (2007). Men's resistance to seeking help: Using individual psychology to understand counseling-reluctant men. *The Journal of Individual Psychology, 63*(1), 48–58.

McLean, P. (1964). Man and his animal brains. *Modern Medicine*, February 3.

Moynehan, J., & Adams, J. (2007). What's the problem? A look at men in marital therapy. *The American Journal of Family Therapy, 35*, 41–51.

Nelson, M. O. (1991). Another look at masculine protest. *Individual Psychology, 47*(4), 490–497.

Siegel, A. M. (1996). *Heinz Kohut and the psychology of self*. New York: Routledge.

Stosny, S. (2009, March 1). Case: Male-friendly couples counseling: Finding love beyond words. *Psychotherapy Networker, 33*(2).

Wexler, D. B. (2009). *Men in therapy: New approaches for effective treatment*. New York: W. W. Norton.

Finding the Words

Working with Men in Emotionally Focused Therapy (EFT) for Couples

PAUL S. GREENMAN, GEORGE FALLER,
AND SUSAN M. JOHNSON

Gender differences have long been the subject of investigation and debate, both inside and outside the scientific community. Research over the last 40 years has clearly demonstrated that aside from the indisputable physiological differences between men and women, there are also definitive emotional, behavioral, and interpersonal ones (e.g., Bergman, 1995; Brown & Gilligan, 1992; Huyck, 1977, 1991), particularly in the realm of heterosexual couple relationships (e.g., Baucom, McFarland, & Christensen, 2010; Gabriel, Beach, & Bodenmann, 2010; Gottman, 1994; Gottman & Silver, 1994; Wexler, 2009). Although the relative contributions of biological and sociological factors to such differences remain somewhat controversial, there seems to be consensus in the psychological literature that men and women do indeed differ, among other things, in their experience and expression of emotion (Levant et al., 2006; Pollack, 2006). This can have a profound impact on couple relationships and on the outcomes of the psychotherapies designed to improve and enhance them (Wexler, 2009).

EFT FOR COUPLES: A MALE-SENSITIVE APPROACH

Although clients' gender does not appear to affect psychotherapy outcomes (Clarkin & Levy, 2003), there is evidence in the individual psychotherapy literature that some psychotherapists work more effectively with men, some work more effectively with women, and some about equally as effectively with people of both genders (Owen, Wong, & Rodolfa, 2009). Findings such as these have led some clinicians (e.g., Brooks, 2010; Rabinowitz & Cochran, 2008; Rochlen, 2005; Wexler, 2009) to emphasize the importance of taking gender differences into account when conducting psychotherapy, particularly when doing so with men in either an individual or a couple context (Knudson-Martin, 2008). The rationale behind the development of male-sensitive approaches is that men generally have a harder time engaging in the activities germane to psychotherapy (e.g., identifying and discussing feelings, considering the intra- and interpersonal impact of one's own behavior and that of others, showing vulnerability, asking for help) than do women, for a host of reasons related to both biology and socialization (Wexler, 2009).

Fortunately for clinicians who treat couples, men and women are nonetheless from the same planet. Fundamental needs for safety, security, and closeness that are common to all people underlie the socioemotional differences delineated in the psychological literature (Bowlby, 1988; Mikulincer & Shaver, 2007). One of the principal aims of emotionally focused therapy (EFT) for couples (S. Johnson, 2008; S. M. Johnson, 2004; S. M. Johnson & Greenberg, 1985) is therefore to capitalize on the commonalities in men and women's relational experiences, borne out of these universal needs, in order to help them overcome the conflicts and disconnection that are often exacerbated by gender differences in the experience, regulation, and expression of emotion. A key strength of EFT is the therapist's use of the strong emotions that people typically experience in couple relationships as the primary instrument of change (S. M. Johnson, 2004). Instead of trying to minimize, bypass, or otherwise quell emotions, clinicians who practice EFT normalize and validate the fear, sadness, and loneliness that men and women experience when they face major challenges in their relationships, and they encourage the integration of these core emotions into couples' interactions in order to structure new ways of responding and communicating between partners (S. M. Johnson, 2004; S. M. Johnson & Greenman, 2006). Core emotion is distilled and expanded and shaped into new emotional signals that then evoke new responses to and from one's partner.

One could make the case that EFT for couples as it is currently practiced and taught is already a male-sensitive approach to couples therapy because of the extraordinary emphasis that EFT therapists place on these universal human needs for safety, closeness, and comfort, needs that are just as salient among men as among women. In fact research suggests that EFT is a successful intervention with men who are described as "inexpressive" by their partners (S. M. Johnson & Talitman, 1996). General clinical experience is that men respond well to the clear and empirically validated model of love relationships offered by EFT and to the collaborative and supportive nature of EFT interventions. These factors are linked to the popular EFT interventions and educational programs (S. Johnson 2009; S. M. Johnson & Rheem, 2004) implemented in recent years with men in traditional "macho" professions, such as army vets, firefighters, and first responders. However, it is essential that a therapist create and maintain a climate conducive to men's expression of vulnerability and need, which is a crucial ingredient of success according to the results of process research on EFT (Bradley & Furrow, 2007; S. M. Johnson & Talitman, 1996). Men and women also display distinct behaviors and physiological reactions in their couple relationships (Gottman, 1994; Gottman & Silver, 1994); EFT therapists must be aware of these in order to foster the kind of in-session self-disclosure and heightened emotional experiencing that leads to a lasting emotional bond between couples.

OVERVIEW OF CHAPTER

The primary goal of this chapter is to provide a guide for practitioners on how to work successfully with men using EFT for couples. Given the delicate task of encouraging men to recognize and voice their vulnerabilities and softer emotions to their partners in front of a complete stranger (i.e., the therapist), which is essential to positive outcomes in EFT, we will illustrate how the creation of a safe, supportive environment in therapy and the use of specific emotionally focused interventions can encourage men to recognize, deepen, label, and express the wide range of emotions and fundamental needs that arise in their intimate relationships, and how this contributes to increased closeness and relationship satisfaction for both partners.

A brief overview of EFT for couples will lead into the presentation of background information on the types of challenges that EFT therapists may face when working with men, including manifestations of masculine gender role stress (MGRS; Jakupcak, Osborne, Michael, Cook, & McFall, 2006; Moore & Stuart, 2004; Saurer & Eisler, 1990) and normative male alexithymia (Levant et al., 2006), a propensity for emotional shutdown and withdrawal in stressful situations (Gottman, 1994; Gottman & Silver, 1994), a heavy emphasis among men on performance and achieving positive results in their close relationships (McKelley & Rochlen, 2010; Wexler, 2009), and a tendency to focus more exclusively than women do on sex and sexuality when discussing their relationships (S. Johnson, 2008). Afterward we will discuss specific ways in which EFT therapists can address these challenges, using a detailed case illustration. We will conclude with comments on ethnic diversity and the role of the therapist's gender in EFT.

EMOTIONALLY FOCUSED THERAPY (EFT) FOR COUPLES

EFT: An Experiential and Systemic Therapy

EFT for couples is an experiential and systemic intervention. EFT practitioners actively collaborate with clients to help them establish new meanings for their relational experiences (S. M. Johnson & Greenman, 2006). This reflects the experiential–humanistic roots of EFT. The therapist's conceptualization and presentation in EFT of couples' problems as the result of rigid, self-reinforcing interaction patterns triggered by context cues and specific partner behaviors are systemic in origin. The following is a condensed overview of EFT; detailed descriptions of the stages and steps of EFT are available elsewhere (Bradley & Johnson, 2005; S. M. Johnson, 2004; S. M. Johnson & Greenman, 2006).

There are three stages to EFT: negative cycle de-escalation (Stage I), restructuring interactions and key bonding responses (Stage II), and consolidation/integration (Stage III; Bradley & Johnson, 2005; S. M. Johnson, 2004). The therapist follows a specific set of steps within each stage of EFT "in order to help couples recognize and combat their negative interaction cycles and establish a secure emotional connection" (Greenman, Young, & Johnson, 2009, p. 150). EFT therapists work hard to encourage, support, and actively direct partners' interactions as both people in the couple become more aware of their own and their partners' vulnerabilities. The key is to be able to recognize and respond to each other's expressed needs for closeness and affection in ways that lead to the formation of a secure attachment bond.

Empirical Support for EFT

Studies of the efficacy of EFT for couples have generated impressive results. A meta-analysis of outcome studies conducted by S. M. Johnson, Hunsley, Greenberg, and Schindler (1999) demonstrated that in EFT, 70% to 73% of couples recovered from relationship distress and 86% to 90% of distressed couples exhibited significant increases in relationship satisfaction. The effects of therapy tend to be stable at follow-up even for couples at high risk for relapse and those whose distress is complicated by traumatic emotional injuries (Cloutier, Manion, Gordon Walker, & Johnson, 2002; Halchuk, Makinen & Johnson, 2010). There is also evidence of EFT's effectiveness with couples in which partners suffer from posttraumatic stress disorder (PTSD; MacIntosh & Johnson, 2008) and depression (Dessaulles, Johnson, & Denton, 2003). EFT is used with couples facing chronic physical illness (Kowal, Johnson, & Lee, 2003), addictions, and a variety of mental health and adjustment issues (S. M. Johnson & Bradley, in press)

CHALLENGES WHEN WORKING WITH MEN IN EFT FOR COUPLES

As previously mentioned, the behaviors and emotions that men and women manifest in their couple relationships do indeed differ, despite common underlying emotional needs. For this reason, it is important for therapists who practice EFT to be aware of the emotional and behavioral variables specific to men that are particularly relevant to couple relationships and to the EFT undertaking. Please note that this is not an exhaustive list; the challenges presented here are only those that have received attention in the scientific and clinical literature.

Masculine Gender Role Stress and Normative Male Alexithymia

There is empirical support for the construct known as masculine gender role stress (MGRS) and its impact on men's feelings and behaviors in intimate relationships. MGRS is the "conflict or stress [that men] experience ... in trying to adhere to dysfunctional gender role expectations" (Moore & Stuart, 2004, p. 132). According to the theory behind MGRS, young boys are socialized to follow a "boy code" (Pollack, 2006), which stipulates that they must display strength, independence, and boldness; develop problem-solving skills; achieve high social status; and curb the experience and expression of feelings of affection, need, and vulnerability (Wexler, 2009). According to Pollack (2006), the boy code "shames boys toward extremes of self-containment, toughness, and separation. ... It shames boys away from their emotional vulnerability and basic need for human connection, just when they need it most" (p. 190). Wexler (2009) suggests that the boy code morphs into the "guy code" as young men get older, with all of the same restrictions on the experience and display of emotions and vulnerabilities. It is especially difficult to adhere to these perceived gender norms when men are confronted with situations in which they might feel vulnerable, sad, or otherwise in need, and these are the very experiences that people tend to have in the context of their intimate relationships (Johnson, 2008). This helps explain the feelings of often intense stress and pressure that men report feeling in their relationships when problems arise.

The results of a study conducted by Moore and Stuart (2004) suggest that men who experience high levels of MGRS are prone to display angry, aggressive responses and to make attributions of negative intent to interlocutors when they are exposed to conflict in intimate relationships. This is consistent with the emotional reactions observed in men in laboratory settings during conflicts with their intimate partners (Gottman, 1994;

Gottman & Silver, 1994), described in more detail later. Couple therapists practicing EFT must therefore be acutely aware of the possibility that the interpersonal discord that men experience in their couple relationships, along with the tasks that constitute EFT for couples, can be a source of tension and discomfort when they run counter to the guy code.

One manifestation of the boy/guy code in men's lives and relationships has been referred to in the scientific literature as "normative male alexithymia" (Levant et al., 2006). Levant and colleagues claim that when young boys are socialized to adhere to traditional male gender norms that encourage the restriction of emotional expression, they have difficulty developing an awareness of their emotions and needs, and even more difficulty finding words to express them (Levant et al., 2006). This hardship identifying and labeling emotional experiences appears to be widespread among men, and it can contribute to the strain they experience when attempting to negotiate the terrain of interpersonal relationships. Levant and colleagues (2006) write that in the current day and age, "Men are often expected to take on a greater share of nurturing activities with their children, and the demands of two-career families often call for improved communication skills. Men need the ability to listen actively, express emotional empathy, and discuss their own feelings. Because the male role socialization process limits development of these abilities, many men are ill-prepared for these roles" (p. 213). This lack of preparation can create strain in couple relationships, to which men's reflex is often to shut down and withdraw despite the strong but nebulous feelings that they experience inside.

Shutdown and Withdrawal

Indeed, stonewalling and withdrawal during marital conflict are typical responses in men whose relationships are likely headed for divorce (Gottman, 1994; Gottman & Silver, 1994). However, the lack of emotional responding that their partners observe on the surface does not adequately reflect the physiological arousal and distress that many men experience during conflicts with their intimate partners. Gottman found that during the hundreds of conflictual marital exchanges that he recorded, men's blood pressure and heart rate tended to reach much higher levels than their wives' did, and they remained so long after the wives' blood pressure and heart rate decreased to normal levels (Gottman, 1994; Gottman & Silver, 1994). Gottman explains that to cope with this stress, men tend to subsequently attempt to escape from the tension-inducing situation by stonewalling, or withdrawing emotionally (and sometimes physically by leaving the room or the house) and suppressing their emotional experience. Research on emotion (Gross, 2001) suggests that this suppression tends paradoxically to increase arousal in both the suppressor and interactional partners. Withdrawal thus appears to be a key mechanism by which men attempt to reduce physiological tension and negative emotion that arises during relationship conflicts.

Withdrawal in attachment relationships tends then to fuel the fire of distress and conflict. In response to their partners' withdrawal, women tend to become more anxious, abandoned, and angry, and to feel more dismissed and alone than when the conflictual exchange began (S. Johnson, 2008). Couple therapists often hear men's reports of feeling overwhelmed or numb during difficult exchanges with their wives, followed by an effort to calm themselves by distancing or numbing out (S.M. Johnson, 2004). Therapists practicing EFT need to understand that often the stonewalling that they observe in their male clients does not reflect disinterest in the relationship or in the therapeutic process. It is, rather, an attempt to manage intense feelings of rejection or abandonment and the helplessness they evoke. These emotionally inexpressive men are often invested in their relationships and highly distressed when they perceive their relationships to be going awry, especially if it appears to them that their relationship problems are due to their own failings or inadequacies.

Performance Orientation

Men, especially those who adhere to traditional gender roles, tend to be oriented toward problem solving and performance in many aspects of their lives, including their relationships (Wexler, 2009). For this reason, it is often extremely difficult for them to accept chronic problems that arise repeatedly in their couple relationships, because they perceive such issues to reflect their inability to be capable husbands or lovers. This affects their sense of self-efficacy and self-worth (Wexler, 2009), which likely contributes to ongoing physiological manifestations of distress.

This performance orientation appears to be important when tackling the delicate matter of convincing men to seek out and stay in any kind of psychological treatment. For example, the results of a recent study of a national sample of adult men in the United States reveal that men who conform to traditional gender norms appear to view psychological interventions labeled "executive coaching" more favorably than identical interventions referred to as "therapy" (McKelley & Rochlen, 2010). Wexler (2009) suggests that clinicians emphasize the practical aspects of their interventions, regardless of their theoretical orientation. In line with these recommendations, it is important for therapists conducting EFT to speak specifically about the manner in which the intervention helps develop concrete abilities (e.g., comforting, reassuring, asking for support) that will improve the quality of the relationship and help both partners to get more of the closeness and security that they want.

Focus on Sexuality

Although safety and closeness are universal desires in intimate relationships for both men and women, men tend to ask for sex more frequently than they do for affection and nonsexual touching. S. Johnson (2008) suggests that this has to do with a "funnel[ing] of ... attachment needs for physical and emotional connection into the bedroom" (p. 192), which, again, appears to be related to traditional male gender restrictions on the clear recognition and expression of physical needs *and* emotional needs. Once again, EFT therapists need to be attuned to the possibility that their male clients' seemingly exclusive focus on sexual problems in the relationship might actually represent their best attempt at establishing any kind of meaningful connection with their partners.

EFT: SUGGESTIONS FOR WORKING WITH MEN

Therapists who practice EFT are well equipped to address a number of these challenges because of the emphasis in EFT on creating a supportive environment and the therapists' systematic ability to regulate, order, and clarify key emotional responses that are the music of the dance between partners. The attachment framework set out in EFT offers clients a systematic guide to the processes of connection and disconnection.

The very first step of EFT entails creating, from the initial moment of contact, a safe and supportive environment in which each partner feels comfortable enough to explore his or her difficult feelings and to be attentive to those of the other. Throughout the intervention, therapists take care to validate each partner's experience, while simultaneously helping them understand how their typical ways of coping with difficult situations and the strong emotions that accompany them (e.g., adopting a stonewalling, defensive stance, or becoming aggressive and critical) feed negative cycles and exacerbate hurt and attachment anxieties.

At first the nature of EFT can be intimidating for men, given its integration of emotional experience into every aspect of the intervention. For this reason, it is vital that EFT therapists pay attention to the psychotherapeutic process, that is, the manner in which they perform their interventions, and the impact that these have on their male clients.

Addressing MGRS and Normative Male Alexithymia

In work with men, it is imperative that EFT therapists foster a safe environment by explicitly validating many of the elements discussed in this chapter, including the fact that many men are socialized to restrict their emotional experiences and that talking about or otherwise exhibiting vulnerability run counter to much that men have learned about being male. It is also helpful to reflect the ways in which a focus on practicality and finding solutions to problems has, in many contexts, been effective and necessary. By slowing down the process and asking clients to focus on their feelings and sensations in the moment, EFT therapists help men (and women, for that matter) build a more extensive vocabulary for describing the emotions they are experiencing and using these as a guide for constructive action.

In addition to the therapist's support and validation, an excellent antidote to the stress that working with emotion might cause is directing a man's attention to his wife's expressions, both verbal and nonverbal, of approval as he takes the risk of exposing himself more fully to her. Therapists carefully structure these interactions and help partners to respond in this manner, creating a new corrective emotional experience for each pa rtner and framing both partners' inner emotions as workable and understandable rather then overwhelming and chaotic.

Overcoming Shutdown and Withdrawal

At the end of Stage I of EFT for couples, partners recognize that their typical ways of managing the hurt, fear, sadness, loneliness, and frustration that emerge when they feel disconnected from their partners, which often include stonewalling or blaming, are actually causing many of the problems they wish to avoid. This is cycle de-escalation (S. M. Johnson, 2004). As described by Greenman and colleagues (2009), Stage II of EFT involves changing the music of this dance by supporting one partner at a time to deepen his or her primary emotions, attachment longings, and sense of self in the relationship, and to express these to the other partner. Therapists help the other partner hear, receive, and integrate this information, which is often hard to take in because it is so new. Finally, the therapist attends to the specific wants and needs that emerge and assists in their expression. During Stage II, the therapist choreographs the couple's interactions ("enactments") with an emphasis on asking them to express directly to each other their primary emotions (e.g., sadness and fear when uncertain of the other's love) and needs for closeness. The goal is to help the withdrawn partner gradually become emotionally engaged in the relationship and the pursuing partner to become less hostile and critical.

Stage II of EFT is where men learn to expand and find words for their deeper emotional experiences in an effort to actively reengage with their partners. Therapists encourage them to put their longstanding concerns, needs, and feelings into words, and to ask their spouses to respond to them. A critical element here is the therapist's support of the female partner to process her husband's new way of expanding his experience and interacting with her, and to adopt an understanding and compassionate stance (Bradley & Furrow, 2007). Thus, therapist communications of understanding, attention, and caring to both partners are essential if men are going to take the risk of making themselves vulnerable to their wives, and if wives are going to receive and respond favorably to it. If the intervention proceeds according to plan, withdrawer reengagement occurs at the end of Stage II, and the male partner is no longer shut down emotionally (S. M. Johnson, 2004). A withdrawer can then:

- Recognize his part in the negative cycle and how he impacts his partner, as in "I do shut down and shut you out."
- Access, order, and express the deeper attachment fears underlying withdrawal or attacking behaviors, as in "I thought I was just angry but now I know I am drowning here. Alone in a silent still world."
- Assert attachment needs in a way that helps partners to respond positively, as in "I do want to be close. I need you to give me a chance here. I will make mistakes but I need your support and reassurance."

Integrating a Performance Orientation Into the Dance

In our experience, as with other habitual responses, it is best to expand on clients' tendency to want to achieve and perform rather than try to eradicate it. When working with men who adopt traditional gender roles, it can be helpful to direct their attention to the manner in which their direct communications of sadness, fear, or needs for closeness draw their partners closer to them. Although EFT for couples is not a didactic, skill-building therapy per se, therapists can nonetheless frame this as the "development of effective communication skills" and point out to their male clients that when they take the risk of expressing their needs and vulnerabilities, their partner feels better, and they end up getting the closeness that they want. When therapists discuss EFT with their male clients, it helps if they emphasize the fact that they will be acquiring tools to help them perform more effectively in their relationship, including learning how to identify and act on their own and their partner's emotions in order to increase affection and closeness. The understanding that most female partners desire the other's emotional presence and support above all and that this is often the solution that makes a difference is also a revelation for male partners.

Addressing Sexuality

In EFT for couples, therapists construe sexuality as an important part of the attachment dance. Indeed for many men the only place they are touched or held or allow themselves to express need is in bed. Therapists help partners, both men and women, recognize and accentuate the ways in which sexuality helps them connect with their partner. EFT therapists emphasize the role of sex in maintaining a secure attachment bond, along with the role of a safe, loving relationship in enhancing sexual pleasure (S. Johnson, 2008). In work with men, this often involves helping them expand their awareness of and vocabulary for their own attachment needs for closeness, safety, and comfort, and encouraging them to ask for these things directly and unequivocally from their wives in and out of the bedroom. EFT clinicians also support wives to hear and understand that when their husbands ask for sex, they are often seeking something more complex and interpersonal than orgasm, which often involves a longing for emotional closeness and connection.

CASE STUDY: JOHN AND MARY

The following case study illustrates the challenges inherent in working with men in EFT for couples, along with the suggestions discussed.

Background

John and Mary have been married for 9 years and have two children, John Jr. (7 years old) and Megan (age 5). John is a lieutenant in the New York City Fire Department and Mary is a nurse at a local hospital. Both sought marriage counseling because of increased fighting and threats of separation. As the following excerpts illustrate, they displayed a pursue–withdraw pattern in which John defends himself and stonewalls, and Mary tends to criticize and display frustration toward John.

Stage I

Session 1

Therapist: So what does a fight look like between you two?
Mary: I try to talk to him and he just walks away. It drives me nuts, so I follow him. I can't believe he is so disrespectful.
John: What is the point of talking when she is in one of her mean, nasty places? I try to avoid fighting, but she won't quit until it gets ugly. (*Containment, restriction of emotional experience typical of traditional male gender role.*)
Mary: That's always his answer: avoid talking about anything (*voice getting louder*). I can't take it anymore! It's like I am living alone. We are strangers. I do not know what happened to him.
Therapist: So you are getting angry now just thinking about not being able to get John to respond?
Mary: Wouldn't you? What's the point of being together if we never talk?
Therapist: Right. So you keep trying to get him to talk, even when he does not want to. And the more he tries to get away the angrier you get. It's pretty normal for someone to get angry if they want to talk and they don't get a chance. (*Validation of client experience.*)
Mary: Exactly. He knows just how to make me furious and push my buttons.
Therapist: So John, what is happening to you now as Mary talks about your relationship? (*Emphasis on John's experience in the moment—help finding words to describe his feelings.*)

John: It's so frustrating. She makes a big deal out of everything. She likes to fight. I just want some peace (*sighing and leaning back into his chair*). I'm tired of her attitude all the time. I wish she could be more secure and just leave me alone. She is such a high-maintenance drama queen.

Therapist: It's very frustrating and it seems all the fighting drains your energy. (*Responding to the sighing, directing John's attention to his own feelings and naming them.*) You hope if you just avoid the conversation then maybe there will be no fight. Am I getting it right, John? (*Checking in with John, maintaining therapeutic alliance.*)

John: Yes. I'm glad it makes sense to you. She just doesn't get it.

Therapist: What is it she doesn't get?

John: How not talking can be a good thing. She thinks something is wrong with me. It's not my fault; she gives me no other choice. Every time I try to work it out it only turns into a bigger fight. It's so annoying; I wish she could talk to someone besides me to blow off steam.

Therapist: When Mary comes to you to talk, you say to yourself "oh no, here comes another fight" and you try to stop it by getting away. Am I right John, you often feel stuck in a corner with the only options being to exit or stay and fight back? (*Linking feelings to specific behaviors in the relationship.*)

John: It's not easy. But yeah that's what it's like. I tune her out and go into my little cave and wait for her to blow away. I usually go to the garage and work on a project. I try to make the most use of my time. There is no point in talking.

Therapist: I can tell both of you are frustrated and annoyed. Mary you try to talk to John to fix some problems and he does not seem to be interested or have the time. John you want to get along with Mary and not fight but she keeps bringing up issues to fight over. No wonder there is so much tension and distance between the two of you. It seems to me that the two of you have fallen into a cycle where both of you are trying to survive but end up reacting in the worst way possible for each other. (*Framing of the cycle as the couple's common enemy.*)

Mary: I'm not sure I understand. I can't see how trying to talk to him to save our marriage is reacting in the wrong way.

Therapist: Both of you are trying your best. It is hard to see the bigger picture when your needs are not being met. (*Validation.*) Mary when you reach out to John in the hopes of fixing the relationship, he is not available. What is that like for you when John walks out?

Mary: Terrible. It seems he just doesn't care anymore. I get so angry because he doesn't want to try.

Therapist: And John what is like for you to hear Mary tell you that you don't try?

John: I hear it all the time. I'm sick of listening to her.

Therapist: It is often difficult for partners to see the merry-go-round when they are caught in this negative dance. You both let me know if I am getting your cycle right. Mary you try to reach out to John in the hope he will respond and connect with you. You are cautious because you are expecting him to not want to talk. John, when she initiates a conversation, you get defensive because past experiences tell you this is dangerous ground. So you try to not fight and attempt to protect the relationship by giving it some breathing space. Mary, you see his leaving as him not caring and you get angry. You follow him and try to let him know how hurt you are. John, her anger only reinforces your feelings about not wanting to talk, of being blamed, and you shut down further. Mary, you see him detach and you turn up the heat. Both of you get stuck in this place where you feel alone and blame the other person as the bad guy. (*Representation of the cycle and of each partner's role in it.*)

John: I never looked at it like that but it seems logical. I'm not trying to hurt her feelings; I just don't have the energy to keep fighting. I don't know why she wants to be around me if all we do is fight. I wish we could get along better.

Mary: It's hard to understand how his not talking is an attempt to protect our relationship. It seems like an excuse to me. But I do agree that if his withdrawal is so bad for me then the reverse must be true that my anger is difficult on him. I guess I know that but it's hard to stop.

Therapist: Of course it is. You want a response but somehow you keep missing each other and ending up far away from each other. Let's try to find a way to bridge the gap.

The therapist is laying the groundwork for the partners in this couple to unite against their negative cycle. It is essential that they grasp that when they are caught in the cycle and feeling disconnected, this is when they need each other the most. Unfortunately, this is also when they are most likely to be emotionally unavailable. Each partner must recognize his or her role in creating and maintaining the cycle.

In our experience, the explicitly nonpathologizing stance that therapists take in EFT appeals to men because it validates their experiences and the value of shutting down. At the same time, therapists encourage them to accept responsibility for the unintended effects on their partner. It is imperative to normalize the walls that protect them if we hope to help men become more flexible emotionally. Men who can barely recognize emotions usually welcome the opportunity to discuss the armor that protects them. By validating the need to protect oneself during stressful times, therapists provide men with a language to start sharing the perceived need for protection. Framing men as resilient instead of broken makes it safer for them to risk. Otherwise, the therapist might get caught in the cycle and begin banging futilely upon the male with-drawer's walls, reinforcing his resistance. To make matters worse, the absence of such validation might also intensify the male withdrawer's underlying fears of emotional inadequacy.

It is important to note that one notable exception to emotional constriction in men is anger. Anger that results in abusive behavior is a contraindication for EFT. This issue is discussed in more detail in the EFT literature (S. M. Johnson, 2004). Many men have no dif-ficulty expressing their anger, which can be very beneficial when it aids in survival and the overcoming of obstacles. Regrettably, when anger is the only emotion that sees the light of day, its effects on a relationship can be devastating. EFT therapists must therefore nor-malize and validate the usefulness of anger and tie it back into the couple's interactional cycle, all the while expanding clients' emo-tional repertoire.

Stage II

In Stage II the therapist collaborates with the partners to create a positive cycle of reaching and responding that fosters a positive cycle of secure bonding. In a typical pursue–withdraw couple, the therapist encourages the withdrawn male to begin to reengage first (S. M. Johnson, 2004), by accessing and sharing deeper emotions and needs. The therapist helps clients acknowledge and process their anxieties about being flooded or exposed and validates that they feel safer in the cognitive realm. As the therapist directs the couple's attention to their direct moment-to-moment perceptions, bodily experience of different emotions (e.g., tightness in the stomach or chest) and attachment meanings, the couple can begin to put words to their deeper experience. This is a watershed moment because men are experiencing significant emotions in real time and finding satisfying and positive ways to deal with them.

Session 6

In Session 6 John attempts to reengage with his feelings and his part-ner. He is able to state that when he feels hopeless and sees himself as a failure, he senses that his options are to numb out or to get angry. Either response reinforces Mary's underlying fear of being unloved and unlovable, and amplifies her criticism. To change the cycle it is neces-sary to help John reengage emotionally and Mary to soften. A softening happens when the blaming spouse is able to risk asking clearly and con-gruently for attachment needs to be met from a position of vulnerability instead of anger.

Therapist: You report having a great week together. What is working so well?

John: I'm not sure but there is less tension and it's easier to talk.

Mary: I agree. We are both trying and spending more time together. I am less critical and he is sticking around. There is definitely less fighting, but he still doesn't open up to me. It's like I now get teased with little openings, which is better than nothing, but I'm left hungry for more.

John: You are always hungry for more (*angry tone*). It's never enough for you. I don't know why I bother. Go fill yourself up somewhere else. This restaurant is closed!

Mary: I don't know why *I* bother (*angry and defensive*). Am I supposed to be happy with crumbs? It shouldn't be that difficult to talk to me. You don't talk much to anyone.

(John shakes his head and looks up at the ceiling.)

Therapist: You both are getting caught in the cycle again and I want to slow it down a little. John, I noticed when Mary said she shouldn't be happy with crumbs, you shook your head and looked up at the ceiling. What is happening? (*Directs John's attention to his emotional experience.*)

John: I'm not sure. Nothing really. Same old crap from her. Just trying to tune her out.

Therapist: So help me out here. I am not sure I understand that part of you that is unsure. When Mary isn't happy with you, what happens?

John: I get frustrated because here we go again. (*Labeling affect.*) The peace only lasts so long.

Therapist: So when you hear her talking about being unhappy, a part of you says the peace is over. What is that like for you? (*Deepening emotional experience.*)

John: It sucks. It is annoying (*angry tone*). I'm sick of her being unhappy about everything.

Therapist: Right, so when she is unhappy that feels annoying. When you say it sucks, help me understand what that means for you.

John: I don't feel anything. I just know it is unfair.

Therapist: So when your wife tells you she is unhappy with you that causes a "sucky" feeling that also seems unfair. This seems like a pretty difficult place to be in. As we talk about it now do you feel anything in your body?

John: Not really. (*Normative male alexithymia. John shrugs his shoulders*).

Therapist: I notice, John, you shrugged your shoulders. Do you feel tightness in your shoulders or chest?

John: I guess my chest feels tight. Like some kind of pressure.

Therapist: So when your wife talks about feeling unhappy, that makes you feel pressure in your chest and that feeling sucks and feels unfair. Things were going well and then boom, it went south in a flash.

John: Yup (*looking down at the floor*).

Therapist: So as you talk about these feelings John, you look at the floor. What is that about?

John: I don't know, I guess I just want that pressure to go away.

Therapist: When Mary continues to talk and is displeased and you feel the pressure and it will not go away, that must be a tough place for you to be.

John: I'm stuck with nowhere to go. I don't know why it bothers me so much.

Therapist: You are doing a great job, John, describing your experience (*slowly*). Right now, as you describe feeling stuck with nowhere to go, what is that like?

John: I don't know. When I am stuck I feel hopeless and helpless, and I don't like that feeling.

Therapist: Right, so when you are stuck you feel hopeless. That crappy feeling is your body telling you that Mary is disappointed. There seems to be no escape from letting her down. Almost like you have no choice but to just bear all of that pressure and responsibility. Your feelings seem right on John. You are stuck to bear the weight with no relief. That must be a real difficult place. Am I getting it right?

John: I never really think of it that way but it seems to fit. (*Looking at the floor.*)

Therapist: Again John as you talk about these normal feelings you look to the floor. (*Normalizing, validating emotion, and pointing out to John his typical ways of trying to cope with them.*) Help me understand. Is that what is happening?

John: It seems I shouldn't be that bothered by her unhappiness. It's like I own her stuff. It's all pretty pathetic, this cycle stuff. I don't like talking about it.

Therapist: So as you talk about feeling hopeless when Mary is disappointed with you, part of you agrees and another part feels it is pathetic to feel this way. Is that right John?

John: Yeah. I don't like those feelings and I feel I shouldn't have them.

Therapist: Like you should be stronger and be able to not allow Mary to impact you as much?

Mary: Impact him; I have no impact on him. He is like a rock. I get more attention from the mailman (*voice getting angrier*).

Therapist: It is difficult for you Mary to believe that underneath the rock is a man who feels stuck and hopeless. Typically, all you see and hear is nothing so what you are hearing now is hard to take in. (*Helping Mary process new information about John.*) That makes sense, how could it be otherwise (*validation of Mary*)? As much as you want him to express emotions, when he finally does it is nearly impossible to receive because it is so foreign. Your body can't trust it. Am I getting it right?

Mary: Yes! I heard him saying the words, but it is hard to believe that's really him, kind of like he is saying what you want him to say. I just don't see myself having such an impact.

Therapist: That's why your cycle is so resilient. When one person risks to change it always makes sense why their partner can't receive it and effectively blows up the risk. The tough part of missing each other like that is that it only reinforces the distance between you two. So when John talks about feeling hopeless and is afraid he can't get it right with you, Mary (*John nods in agreement here*), and when he shares those feelings, you don't believe them. Then this only strengthens John's fear that he will never get it right. Then when John feels hopeless like he can't get it right, he withdraws even further, reinforcing your fears that you can't get any attention and that he doesn't care. At this point you're back on the merry-go-round, both trying to survive and each not being there for the other.

John: So how do we get off? (*He expresses his desire for solution, skills, instructions.*)

Therapist: You are figuring out a way off right now by both working together. As John you continue to reengage with your experience and Mary you continue to express what is underneath your anger, you are developing the ability to see each other differently and to react to each other differently.

Slowly helping men realize that their emotions are an integral part of their being is essential to getting them to confront the blocks to their emotional connections with others. As men learn to trust and experience their emotions, they come to understand that ignoring them is costly and irrational. Therapists must often slow down and reflect the process that is unfolding in front of them in order to help clients reengage emotionally, as the therapist in this excerpt did. The therapist is an active, moment-by-moment coregulator and coprocessor of emotions who assists clients in finding the words to match their experience. Empathy and validation of their experiences are critical for success in helping men unpack and divulge their feelings. EFT therapists use empathic conjectures to create more breathing space for clients to integrate and acknowledge their total experience. The client is the final authority on whether the therapist's words fit.

Session 14

In this final excerpt, the male client continues to struggle with his vulnerabilities until the therapist facilitates a communication of these to his wife.

Therapist: So, John, you continue to make progress staying present and talking to Mary about your experience instead of shutting down. How are you able to do this?

John: I guess I understand that although tuning her out may work in the short term it makes matters worse for both of us. I also think Mary is making it easier by trying to be gentler instead of attacking. That certainly helps (*laughing*).

Mary: I'm glad we're both trying. It is nice to reconnect (*smiling*).

Therapist: It is great to see you both smiling and having fun with each other. Are there times when you still miss each other?

Mary: We did yesterday (*raising her voice*) when I tried to talk about the kids struggling with school. He didn't want to talk and we got into a fight.

Therapist: What is it, Mary, that you were trying to get from John?

Mary: I need more help. The kids are not doing well and I do not know what to do!

John: I don't know what to do either (*putting his hands up in the air*).

Therapist: So what is happening to you John as Mary talks about needing help?

John: I get frustrated (*squeezing his hands together*). I don't know what to do.

Therapist: You feel Mary is asking you for answers and you do not have them? Even now you are squeezing your hands in frustration. (*Reflection, deepening of emotional experience.*)

John: Right. If I got answers I will give them. I resent being put into a position where there is nothing I can do.

Therapist: What is it like for you to not have answers?

John: I go back to that place of feeling stuck, useless, hopeless (*rubbing his chest*).

Therapist: So it's that sucky feeling of letting Mary down (*slow voice*). (*Integration of material from previous sessions.*) Is that tightness in your chest returning?

John: Yes, it's back. I hate this feeling and I resent being put in this position. (*Using anger to exit the more vulnerable feelings.*)

Therapist: It is frustrating to go to this place where you have no answers and are so powerless to not disappoint Mary. You don't know how to make it better. Does it feel like you are failing her?

John: Of course (*angry tone*). I should be able to give her what she needs. It sucks to always let her down and come up short. I feel like a loser (*looking down at the floor*).

Therapist: So underneath the tuning Mary out is this part of you that feels like a loser. That must feel real bad. It makes sense to me why you would not want to stay in this place. It must be awful to feel like you are failing. Can you help me understand what that is like for you?

John: Pathetic and wimpy (*shaking his head*). I pride myself on being strong and having answers. If I don't have the solutions then I am no good.

Therapist: I think I'm getting it. So when you go to that sucky place where you have no answers, underneath you feel like a loser and that you are no good. (*Therapist feels and reflects John's shame.*) Am I getting it right?

John: I don't know why she would want to be with me (*putting his head into his hands*). I don't want to be with myself when I feel so weak and incompetent.

Therapist: Right. So this is a really uncomfortable place for you. Like there is something wrong with you, and if Mary sees it what do you think will happen?

John: She wouldn't want to be around me. I would have no purpose. (*John accesses attachment panic—fears of rejection, loss, and abandonment.*)

Mary: I don't think you're failing John. I know how hard you try.

Therapist: Hold on a minute, Mary. John you are taking a big risk right now. You are letting Mary into that dark place where you feel so much pressure. You feel hopeless, weak, and defective. You never show anyone this side of you. I'm amazed at your courage. What do you think it would be like to turn and tell Mary that underneath the shutting down are these feelings of being broken and being uncomfortable? (*The therapist sets up an enactment—he does not use the label "fear" because firefighters are so conditioned to reject this concept.*) That Mary will not want you?

John: I don't know. It's real hard. I think she knows it (*again looking at the floor*).

Therapist: Of course it is difficult. You are doing a great job, John. Mary never sees this side of you. Can you tell her about feeling defective and weak?

John: I wish I had the answers (*shifting gaze from Mary to floor*). When I don't know how to fix a problem I start to feel inept and I know you don't want to be around a loser. No one does! I don't want to be around myself. So I leave and try to find something to accomplish. I'm sorry to let you down.

Mary: You definitely are not a loser (*she reaches over and rubs his hand*).

Therapist: So what is happening to you Mary?

Mary: I feel sad when he feels broken. I never knew he felt that way. I always thought there was something wrong with me, like he didn't want to be around me. I really appreciate him letting me in (*John reaches over and gives Mary a hug*).

Therapist: That's awesome you two. You are getting it right, finding each other. Great work!

In this session John continued to identify and express his attachment fears and concerns, which Mary validated and then thanked him for sharing with her. For many men, a fear of failing and being unworthy of their partner's love underlies their anger and avoidance. The therapist's job is to bring these softer feelings to the surface and to help the partner embrace them along with the needs implicit in them. In the next session John is able to ask directly for Mary's reassurance and tell her that he needs to feel important to her. He also asserts himself by asking her to slow down her critical responses so that he can learn to come close and share with her. She is then able to become more open and responsive to him and share her own vulnerabilities and needs.

Both partners learn to shape a safe-haven bond where both can be different (part of being securely attached is that differences and separateness are not perceived as threats) and also connected.

CULTURAL CONSIDERATIONS

The process of EFT focuses on universal anxieties and ways to cope with these anxieties and universal needs. These universals apply across gender and across cultures. For an extensive discussion of EFT and questions related to cultural diversity, please see Greenman, Young, and Johnson's (2009) chapter on EFT with intercultural couples. In it, the authors discuss the importance of attending to the ways in which cultural differences concerning the experience and expression of emotion can lead to confusion in couple relationships. They emphasize the salience across cultures of basic needs for security, support, and emotional closeness but caution therapists that people's preferred method for meeting attachment needs can differ along cultural lines. For this reason, therapists who practice EFT would do well to ask specific questions about how clients from cultures other the therapist's own identify and express strong feelings related to relationships.

THERAPIST'S GENDER

Clinical experience suggests that men who participate in couples therapy with a female therapist might be more wary at first. They are often concerned that the therapist will side with the female partner. For this reason, it is essential that female therapists practicing EFT (or any other couple therapy) attend to the therapeutic alliance with the male partner at all times, particularly when broaching issues that are likely to cause discomfort or distress (that is, female therapists must remain attuned to signs of withdrawal from the process or other markers of a rupture in the alliance, and attend to them with exploration of what is occurring in the moment for the male partner, followed with empathy and validation). However, it is important to note that a strong therapeutic alliance with both partners, regardless of the therapist's gender, is the cornerstone of EFT for couples. It is the first and most important step in the intervention, and it is the therapist's responsibility to ensure the quality of his or her bond with both clients from the moment of first contact until termination.

SUMMARY AND CONCLUSION

Men are faced with a number of unique challenges in relationships, especially when they are socialized to adhere to traditional gender norms that restrict their experience and expression of emotions. Their attempts to achieve stability and connection with their partners are at times ineffective because these attempts do not always reflect the depth of their caring and concern for those they love. Provided that therapists are aware of and attuned to men's sensitivity and potential discomfort with strong emotion, provided that they provide a safe, nurturing environment in which men can explore their experiences in detail, EFT for couples can help men learn to identify, describe, and integrate their emotional experiences into their relationships in order to create lasting, loving bonds with their intimate partners.

REFERENCES

Baucom, B. R., McFarland, P. T., & Christensen, A. (2010). Gender, topic, and time in observed demand–withdraw interaction in cross- and same-sex couples. *Journal of Family Psychology, 24*, 233–242.

Bergman, S. J. (1995). Men's psychological development: A relational perspective. In R.F. Levant & W.S. Pollack (Eds.), *A new psychology of men* (pp. 68–90). New York: Basic Books.

Bowlby, J. (1969). *Attachment and Loss: Volume 1: Attachment.* New York: Basic Books.

Bowlby, J. (1988). *A secure base.* London: Routledge.

Bradley, B., & Furrow, J. (2007). Inside blamer softening: Maps and missteps. *Journal of Systemic Therapies, 26*, 25–43.

Bradley, B., & Johnson, S. M. (2005). An integrative contemporary approach. In M. Harway (Ed.), *Handbook of couples therapy* (pp. 179–193). Hoboken, NJ: Wiley.

Brooks, G. R. (2010). *Beyond the crisis of masculinity: A transtheoretical model male-friendly therapy.* Washington, DC: American Psychological Association.

Brown, L. M., & Gilligan, C. (1992). *Meeting at the crossroads: Women's psychology and girls' development.* Cambridge, MA: Harvard University Press.

Clarkin, J. F., & Levy, K. N. (2003). Influence of client variables on psychotherapy. In M. Lambert (Ed.), *Bergin and Garfield's handbook of psychotherapy and behavior change* (5th ed.). New York: Wiley.

Cloutier, P. F. Manion, I .G., Gordon Walker, J., & Johnson, S. M. (2002). Emotionally focused interventions for couples with chronically ill children: A 2-year follow-up. *Journal of Marital and Family Therapy, 28*, 391–398.

Denton, W. H., & Burwell, S. R. (2006). Systemic couple intervention for depression in women. *Journal of Systemic Therapies, 25*, 43–57.

Dessaulles, A., Johnson, S. M., & Denton, W. H. (2003). Emotion-focused therapy for couples in the treatment of depression: A pilot study. *American Journal of Family Therapy, 31*, 345–353.

Gabriel, B., Beach, S. R. H., & Bodenmann, G. (2010). Depression, marital satisfaction, and communication in couples: Investigating gender differences.
Behavior Therapy, 41, 306–316.

Gottman, J. M. (1994). *What predicts divorce? The relationship between marital processes and marital outcomes.* Hillsdale, NJ: Lawrence Erlbaum Associates.

Gottman, J. M., & Silver, N. (1994). *Why marriages succeed or fail … and how you
can make yours last.* New York: Simon & Schuster.

Greenman, P. S., Young, M. Y., & Johnson, S. M. (2009). Emotionally focused couple therapy with intercultural couples. In M. Rastogi & V. Thomas (Eds.),
Multicultural couple therapy (pp. 143–165). London: Sage.

Gross, J. (2001) Emotional regulation in adulthood. *Current Directions in
Psychological Science, 10,* 214–219.

Halchuk, R. E., Makinen, J., & Johnson, S. M. (2010). Resolving attachment injuries in couples using Emotionally Focused Therapy: A three-year follow-up.
Journal of Couple & Relationship Therapy, 9, 31–47.

Huyck, M. H. (1977). Sex, gender, and aging. *Humanitas, 13,* 83–97.

Huyck, M. H. (1991). Predicates of personal control among middle-aged and
young-old men and women in middle America. *International Journal of
Aging & Human Development, 32,* 261–275.

Jakupcak, M., Osborne, T. L., Michael, S., Cook, J. W., & McFall, M. (2006).
Implications of masculine gender role stress in male veterans with posttraumatic stress disorder. *Psychology of Men & Masculinity, 7,* 203–211.

Johnson, S. (2008). *Hold me tight: Seven conversations for a lifetime of love.* New
York: Little, Brown & Co.

Johnson, S. (2009) *The Hold Me Tight program: Conversations for connection.
Facilitator's guide.* Ottawa, Canada: International Center for Excellence in
Emotionally Focused Therapy.

Johnson, S. M. (2004). *The practice of emotionally focused couple therapy: Creating
connection* (2nd ed.). New York: Brunner-Routledge.

Johnson, S. M., & Bradley, B. (in press). Emotionally focused couples therapy.
In J. Bray & M. Stanton (Eds.), *Handbook of family psychology.* New York:
Blackwell Publishing.

Johnson, S. M., & Greenberg, L. S. (1985). Differential effects of experiential
and problem-solving interventions in resolving marital conflict. *Journal of
Consulting and Clinical Psychology, 53,* 175–184.

Johnson, S. M., & Greenman, P. S. (2006). The path to a secure bond: Emotionally
focused couple therapy. *Journal of Clinical Psychology: In Session, 62,*
597–609.

Johnson, S. M., Hunsley, J., Greenberg, L., & Schindler, D. (1999). Emotionally
focused couples therapy: Status and challenges. *Clinical Psychology: Science
and Practice, 6,* 67–79.

Johnson, S. M., & Rheem, K. D. (2006). *Becoming a couple again: Creating connection; A group for post-deployed military couples.* Bethesda, MD: Strong Bonds,
Strong Couples, LLC.

Johnson, S. M., & Talitman, E. (1996). Predictors of success in emotionally focused
marital therapy. *Journal of Marital and Family Therapy, 23,*135–152.

Knudson-Martin, C. (2008). Gender issues in couple therapy. In A. Gurman (Ed.),
Clinical handbook of couple therapy (pp. 641–661). New York: Guilford Press.

Kowal, J., Johnson, S. M., & Lee, A. (2003). Chronic illness in couples: A case for emotionally focused therapy. *Journal of Marital and Family Therapy, 29,* 299–310.

Levant, R. F., Good, G. E., Cook, S. W., O'Neil, J. M., Smalley, K. B., Owen, K., & Richmond, K. (2006). The Normative Male Alexithymia Scale: Measurement of a gender-linked syndrome. *Psychology of Men & Masculinity, 7,* 212–224.

MacIntosh, H. B., & Johnson, S. M. (2008). Emotionally focused therapy for couples and childhood sexual abuse survivors. *Journal of Marital and Family Therapy, 34,* 298–315.

McKelley, R. A., & Rochlen, A. B. (2010). Conformity to masculine norms and preferences for therapy or executive coaching. *Psychology of Men & Masculinity, 11,* 1–14.

Mikulincer, M., & Shaver, P. R. (2007). *Attachment in adulthood: Structure, dynamics, and change.* New York: Guilford Press.

Moore, T. M., & Stuart, G. L. (2004). Effects of masculine gender role stress on men's cognitive, affective, physiological, and aggressive responses to intimate conflict situations. *Psychology of Men & Masculinity, 5,* 132–142.

Owen, J., Wong, Y. J., & Rodolfa, E. (2009). Empirical search for psychotherapists' gender competence in psychotherapy. *Psychotherapy Theory, Research, Practice, & Training, 46,* 448–458.

Pollack, W.S. (2006). The "war" for boys: Hearing "real boys'" voices, healing their pain. *Professional Psychology: Research and Practice, 37,* 190–195.

Rabinowitz, F. E., & Cochran, S. V. (2008). Men and therapy: A case of masked depression. *Clinical Case Studies, 7,* 575–591.

Rochlen, A. B. (2005). Men in (and out of) therapy: Central concepts, emerging directions, and remaining challenges. *Journal of Clinical Psychology, 61,* 627–631.

Saurer, M. K., & Eisler, R. M. (1990). The role of masculine gender role stress in expressivity and social support network factors. *Sex Roles, 23,* 261–271.

Wexler, D. B. (2009). *Men in therapy.* New York: W.W. Norton.

8

Integrative Behavioral Couple Therapy
A Male-Sensitive Perspective

BRIAN BAUCOM

The rich and multilayered tapestry of partners' individual and relational histories create dilemmas for many couples presenting for therapy. Complimentary differences between partners that served as initial sources of attraction frequently become sources of distress, frustration, and isolation over time; likewise time magnifies and exaggerates early conflictual differences. A great many couples make countless efforts to solve their conflicts through behavioral change prior to entering therapy, and most have experienced the incredible frustration of realizing that their attempts to solve their problems have either not worked to their satisfaction or have ironically intensified the very problem they were attempting to resolve. Acceptance presents couples with an alternative stance to use in solving long-standing disagreements and a method for reducing distress associated with differences that are irresolvable through behavioral change. Integrative behavioral couple therapy (IBCT; Jacobson & Christensen, 1996) is an empirically validated (Christensen et al., 2004; Jacobson, Christensen, Prince, Cordova, & Eldridge, 2000), behaviorally based therapy that builds on this notion by cultivating and using acceptance in combination with behavioral techniques to help partners assume more collaborative stances that promote reconciliation and intimacy, and that can be used to address challenges frequently encountered by men during couples therapy.

IBCT views relationship distress as primarily being the result of the polarization of differences between partners (Jacobson & Christensen, 1996). Partners inevitably enter into relationships with numerous individual differences, such as different models for how relationships work, preferences of closeness and independence, and desires for stability and change; some of these differences are sources of pleasure and desire, whereas others create friction from the outset of the relationship. The actual differences between partners are important, but the ways that the couple handles both types of differences are given primary importance in IBCT. Polarization occurs when attempts to resolve conflict-producing differences cause the sources of the difference to become more extreme. This process very commonly plays out either as negative escalation or as a version of the demand–withdraw interaction pattern. Negative escalation refers to exchanges of increasingly negative, hostile, or critical comments and behaviors. The demand–withdraw interaction pattern (Christensen, 1987) occurs when one partner, the demander, frequently nags, complains, or criticizes the other in an attempt to create change in the relationship and the other partner, the withdrawer, avoids interactions, quickly terminates interactions, or is unresponsive during interactions in an attempt to resist making changes. Demands are typically voiced as requests for specific behavior change; however, there is also commonly an unspoken and unmet underlying emotional need, such as for increased emotional closeness, that is the true motivation for the request. When one partner demands that an emotional need be met through specific behavior change, it sets the stage for the couple to engage in a power struggle over whether the specific behavioral change will be made rather than how to meet the underlying emotional need. This process results in both partners becoming more extreme in their positions over time, more isolated from one another, and less able to compromise on a solution. Interrupting and reversing the polarization process is a major focus of IBCT. These goals are accomplished by assisting the couple in recognizing the polarization process, using acceptance-based interventions to reduce emotional reactivity; promote the sharing of and response to unmet emotional needs; and creating realistic, authentic, and enduring behavioral and emotional changes for both partners.

One challenge in working with men in behaviorally based couple therapies in general is that there is a well-documented gender difference in the way that the polarization process manifests through demand–withdraw behavior in heterosexual couples. Though both men and women demand more and withdraw less when discussing areas of dissatisfaction they have identified relative to talking about areas of dissatisfaction identified by their partners, women generally demand more than men and men withdraw more than women (e.g., Christensen, 1987). This gender difference in demanding and withdrawing behaviors is amplified when couples discuss areas of dissatisfaction in the relationship identified by women; here, women tend to take on a demanding role and men tend to take on a withdrawing role (e.g., Christensen & Heavey, 1990). The complication this tendency creates for couples therapists is that women initiate couples therapy more often than men (Doss, Atkins, & Christensen, 2003) and tend to identify more areas of dissatisfaction in the relationship than men (Heyman, Hunt-Martorano, Malik, & Slep, 2009). Therefore the early stages of therapy are likely to be dominated by issues identified by women. This constellation of factors primes the couples therapist to engage in the same demand–withdraw pattern with the man as his female partner may be engaging in at home, especially if behavioral change interventions are used early. IBCT suggests that beginning with acceptance-based interventions is one method for reducing this possibility and helping partners shift into a less polarized stance from the initial session.

For example, imagine a couple that presents for therapy because of ill-defined communication problems and a lack of intimacy between the two partners that has developed over many years of marriage. If the husband in this couple typically withdraws when the wife raises concerns about the relationship, she may react to his withdrawal by blaming him for her distress and placing the responsibility for improving their relationship on his ability to be less withdrawn and more engaged (Davey, Fincham, Beach, & Brody, 2001). If the therapist were to begin with behavioral exchange to increase intimacy or by teaching the couple communication skills designed to help the husband be more expressive of his own thoughts and feelings, two things will likely happen. One, he may experience himself as the identified patient in the therapy, feel that he must change in order for the situation to improve, and react negatively to the pressure associated with being responsible for repairing the relationship by withdrawing further. Two, doing so may reinforce the idea that communication is only effective when it results in concrete action to "fix" the source of a problem. The issue here is that not all problems are solvable through behavioral change but rather require expression of and response to conflict-related emotions. An alternative acceptance-based approach that would be less likely to reenact the demand–withdraw cycle is to first identify the interaction patterns in which the couple typically engages by describing the behavioral sequences but making no attempt to change either partner's behavior. Acceptance is fostered by describing the behavioral patterns as they occur without assigning blame to either partner. Once the patterns are identified, an IBCT therapist would then work with both partners to identify and to share the emotional vulnerabilities that get triggered during conflict using soft, nonblaming language. By reframing conflict as sequences triggered by emotional vulnerabilities, responsibility for improving the relationship is redistributed between both partners and includes both self- and partner-initiated possibilities for change.

The purpose of this chapter is to give the reader a basic familiarity with the major tenants and intervention strategies of IBCT, to discuss how they can be used to help couples shift out of a strong demand–withdraw pattern with a particular focus on working with withdrawing men, and to discuss how IBCT can be used to sensitively address men's needs in couples therapy. It is not intended to provide a thorough discussion of conducting IBCT. Readers interested in more detailed information about IBCT theory and techniques may find it helpful to consult Christensen, Wheeler, and Jacobson (2008) or Dimidjian, Martel, and Christensen (2008). This chapter begins with an overview of the development of IBCT along both theoretical and empirical lines. The major techniques of IBCT, including assessment, acceptance-based interventions, and change-based interventions, are then illustrated in a case example that involves common challenges experienced by men in couples therapy including engaging in a strong demand–withdraw interaction pattern. The chapter concludes with discussions of how standard techniques of IBCT may be modified to be consistent with differing cultural norms and of gender-related issues to be mindful of when conducting IBCT.

It is important to note that this chapter primarily discusses male issues in the context of heterosexual couples because the majority of the basic and applied research on which IBCT is based has been conducted with heterosexual couples. Though there has yet to be an empirical test of IBCT in gay male couples, anecdotal evidence suggests that IBCT can be used to address similar relationship dynamics regardless of the gender composition of the couple. Additionally, emerging research (Baucom, McFarland, & Christensen, 2010; Peplau & Fingerhut, 2007) suggests that men in gay male couples experience similar relationship dynamics to those described in heterosexual couples in this chapter and that those relationship dynamics are related to relationship distress in similar ways for gay and heterosexual men.

HISTORICAL AND THEORETICAL DEVELOPMENT OF IBCT

IBCT grew out of the behavioral marital therapy (BMT; Jacobson & Margolin, 1979) tradition. Empirical evaluation and theoretical refinement of BMT have been major areas of effort over the past 30 years; IBCT represents the most recent development in this line of evolution. BMT's view of and approach to treating relationship dissatisfaction and BMT's limitations are important foundations for clarifying the need for and the development of IBCT. BMT views the ratio of positive to negative reinforcers in a couple and the perceived benefits and costs of alternative relationships as the primary determinants of relationship satisfaction. A wealth of research supports this model in documenting more frequent and intense negative interactions and lower levels of positive interactions in distressed and divorcing couples relative to satisfied couples (see Weiss & Heyman, 1997, for a review). The major focus of BMT interventions are therefore to assist couples in reducing negative interactions while also making possible and encouraging increased positive interactions.

BMT uses rule-governed change strategies to help partners deliberately change their behaviors. Partners collaborate with their therapist to create rules for altering behavior that are practiced in therapy and then enacted outside of sessions. Two broad categories of rule-governed interventions are used in BMT. The first of these is behavior exchange (BE), which refers to directive techniques for increasing positive interaction. "Love" days (Weiss, 1975) are one example of BE. On a love day, one partner agrees to do more activities than usual that the other has rated as being pleasurable. BE is most successfully used to create positive change in areas that are not sources of distress between partners. Though BE may diminish conflict indirectly by reducing opportunities for disagreement, it is not intended as a strategy for directly resolving entrenched conflict. Communication and problem skills training (CPT) is used to provide couples with a set of skills to work through conflict and disagreement. BMT uses didactic instruction, modeling, and monitored rehearsal to teach couples two forms of CPT, communication training (CT) and problem-solving training (PST), which are described in the section on change focused strategies below.

Of all the couples therapies that have been tested in randomized clinical trials, BMT enjoys the most empirical support and has long been established as an empirically supported treatment for relationship distress (e.g., Baucom, Shoham, Mueser, Daiuto, & Stickle, 1998; Shadish & Baldwin, 2005). Despite the wealth of studies documenting BMT's effectiveness, a relatively large percentage of couples either do not show significant improvements at treatment termination or lose treatment gains following treatment termination. Of all couples who begin BMT, about half show significant increases at termination (Jacobson et al., 1984) and about two-thirds of the half of couples that improve during treatment maintain those gains for 2 years (Jacobson, Schmaling, & Holtzworth-Munroe, 1987). This pattern of results led researchers and therapists to ask two important questions. First, who are the couples that benefit from BMT? Analysis of empirical outcomes revealed that spouses who responded positively to BMT were more committed, emotionally engaged, and egalitarian; shared similar definitions of an ideal relationship; and were younger than spouses who failed to benefit from BMT (Jacobson, Follette, & Pagel, 1986). Jacobson and Christensen (1996) interpreted the combination of these factors to indicate that couples who have greater ability and desire to change are more likely to benefit from BMT than those who do not. Second, how can BMT be made more effective for couples who are not good candidates for traditional BMT?

IBCT (Jacobson & Christensen, 1996) was developed as one answer to this second question. IBCT is based on a fundamentally different model of relationship distress than BMT's in an attempt to address the difficulties experienced by couples presenting for therapy that do not have the ability or willingness to deliberately change all of the conflict-producing aspects of their relationship. Both IBCT and BMT view conflict as normative and inevitable for couples. The two approaches diverge in the extent to which each assumes conflict to be the main cause of enduring distress. BMT views enduring distress to be the result of conflict-producing deficits in skills acquisition or implementation and skills provision as the primary mechanism of change in couple therapy. IBCT views skills deficits as a contributor to dissatisfaction but places much greater emphasis on the origins of conflict, such as individual differences between and vulnerabilities of partners. For example, though men and women are equally likely to use problem-focused coping strategies, men are much less likely to use emotion-focused coping strategies relative to women (e.g., Howerton & Van Gundy, 2009). This gender difference may translate into men being able to acquire and implement both problem-solving and communication training skills effectively but being less likely to use communication skills to share emotion. Part of the hesitancy to use communication skills to share emotion may be related to men's tendency to define the self as agentic, autonomous, and instrumentally oriented (Twenge, 1989). If communication skills encourage egodystonic behavior for men, they may be less likely to use the skills to express emotion unless expressing emotion can be reframed in an egosyntonic manner. IBCT suggests that both partners' understanding of the emotional vulnerabilities that contribute to a husband's hesitancy to use communication skills to express emotion may lead to decreases in conflict and increases in intimacy as large, if not larger, than those that would be created by generally using communication skills more frequently.

IBCT additionally suggests that rule-governed behavior change cannot be used to resolve all relationship problems, particularly those associated with long-standing individual differences between partners. In cases where one partner is not willing or able to make a requested change, acceptance-based interventions can be used to help partners become less reactive to individual differences and thereby reduce the impact the individual differences have on relationship satisfaction.

Early in relationships, complimentary differences between partners are often exciting and create attraction. With the passage of time, the benefits of these differences frequently fade away and result in these differences becoming less attractive and tolerable. Conflictual differences that tap into partners' emotional vulnerabilities are commonly threats to relationship satisfaction from the earliest stages of a relationship. The strong emotions associated with vulnerabilities put many partners at risk for using coercive strategies such as nagging, criticism, and angry withdrawal to try to create change in their relationships. These attempts are often unsuccessful and likely to produce reactance with both partners increasing the extremity of their positions and feeling greater distance from one another over time. This polarization process makes compromise and resolution ever more difficult and unlikely. Parallel changes also commonly occur in attributions for differences. Partners often come to vilify one another, viewing each other in uncompassionate ways, and understanding their differences as failings in the other. IBCT views relationship distress not only as a product of differences between partners but also the ways that partners react to and understand their differences.

ADDRESSING DEMAND–WITHDRAW BEHAVIOR USING IBCT

The demand–withdraw interaction pattern is very commonly seen in treatment-seeking couples and is a challenging form of polarization to successfully interrupt and restructure. Though demand–withdraw behavior can take any number of different forms, the most common presentation is female demand–male withdraw. Demand–withdraw behavior looks different in each couple but the function remains the same. The male withdrawer's behavior serves to maintain the status quo. This function is achieved by changing the subject, shifting all responsibility for actions and behaviors onto external, uncontrollable factors; giving one-word answers to open-ended questions; and using sarcasm in place of expressing his true thoughts as well as numerous other possibilities. Other subtle nonverbal behaviors, such as physically turning the head or body away from the partner, refusing to make eye contact, initiating or maintaining a closed body posture, and preventing or ending touch, are all indicators of withdrawal and are common during therapy sessions. One important thing to bear in mind is that in-session withdrawing behavior may look quite different from out-of-session withdrawing behavior. The task demands of attending a therapy session usually prevent some of the more extreme versions of withdrawal such as refusing to talk about a problem area at all, physically leaving the room, or beginning an alternative activity, such as reading or checking e-mail. Women's demanding behavior also takes both overt and subtle forms. Some demands will be very clearly stated as such; however, historical context is also an important determinant of when a request for change can be considered a demand. If the request has been repeatedly made in a similar form or fashion, then the request can be considered to be a demand. This guideline holds true even when the demand is made using positive or endearing language. Cross-cultural research has shown that women in highly patriarchal cultures demand using less direct and more positively valenced methods such as flattery and flirtation but that the functional outcome is similar in that men typically respond with resistance to the request (Rehman & Holtzworth-Munroe, 2006).

Part of the difficulty in working on a demand–withdraw pattern comes from the multiple factors understood to be involved in the occurrence of demand–withdraw behavior. Due to space limitations, a limited number of these factors are discussed next. Please refer to Eldridge and Baucom (in press) for additional coverage of empirical studies of demand-withdraw behavior.

One important set of correlates of demand–withdraw behavior is socioculturally influenced personality variables that tend to differ between men and women. The different socialization experiences of boys and girls are linked to differences in the degree to which men and women prioritize and pursue relationally oriented and individually oriented goals. By and large, men are socialized to develop a stronger sense of self-reliance and a greater orientation toward taking tangible action to solve problems, whereas women are socialized to place a great deal of importance on relationships and to be more expressive about feelings related to problems (Davies & Lindsay, 2001). One example of how socialization experiences contribute to demand–withdraw behavior is seen in differences in desired closeness and independence within relationships. Women typically desire more closeness in relationships than men, and men typically desire more independence than women (Christensen, 1987). Differences in desired level of closeness within the marital relationship are strongly related to the occurrence of demand–withdraw behavior with the demander desiring greater closeness than the withdrawer and the withdrawer desiring greater independence than the demander (Christensen & Shenk, 1991).

Another important aspect of personality that contributes to demand–withdraw behavior is each partner's level of emotional reaction to conflict. A number of studies have shown that higher levels of emotional arousal experienced during conflict are related to more frequent and intense demand–withdraw behavior (e.g., Baucom 2010). Both partners tend to show elevated levels of emotional responding when engaging in demand–withdraw behavior, but contrary to prior thought (Gottman & Levenson, 1988), it appears that demanders may experience more arousal during conflict than withdrawers (Baucom, 2010). Though much work and thought has been devoted to understanding how emotional arousal is generally related to demand–withdraw behavior, recent research suggests that the conflict-related emotional arousal is associated with different emotions for demanders and withdrawers. Demanders tend to report feeling anger and frustration, while withdrawers tend to report feeling anxious and fearful (Baucom, 2010). Thus in seeking to help a couple disengage from a strong female demand–male withdraw pattern by reducing emotional reactance to conflict (one of the primary goals of IBCT's acceptance-based interventions), it is important to consider that potentially different emotional experiences of the same conflict are further contributing to the tendency to engage in polarizing behavioral patterns.

CLINICAL CASE EXAMPLE: RICK AND SHAUNA

The following section illustrates how IBCT can be used to help a couple that is stuck in a strongly polarized female demand–male withdraw pattern shift out of this cycle with a particular emphasis on working with the withdrawing male partner. It is important to bear in mind that though this section focuses on working with the male withdrawer, demand–withdraw should still be thought of as a dyadic phenomenon fueled by both partners' contributions to the cycle. Rick and Shauna are a couple that presented for IBCT identifying lack of trust as the major source of distress in their marriage. When Rick and Shauna began therapy, they were both middle-aged and had been married to each other for 5 years. Rick was Persian, and Shauna was Jewish. This was the first marriage for both partners. Both Rick and Shauna previously had long-term romantic relationships that had ended unexpectedly and traumatically. In Rick's most significant prior relationship, he had become engaged to a woman when he was in his early 20s only to discover that she was also involved in a physically intimate relationship with his older brother. The infidelity wasn't revealed until the couple had begun making plans for their wedding, and Rick felt a tremendous amount of shame, rejection, and betrayal in explaining to his family why the wedding was being called off. In Shauna's most significant prior relationship, she had unintentionally gotten pregnant by a boyfriend of a couple months after a night of heavy drinking when she was in her late teens. She decided to get an abortion and decided not to tell her boyfriend. She was unable to live with the secret and quickly ended the relationship without much explanation.

During their early therapy sessions, Rick was frequently subdued, spoke quietly, and often paused for long periods of time before responding to questions from Shauna or from the therapist. His answers were typically very concrete and brief. He frequently appeared uncomfortable and anxious during sessions and expressed much of his emotion nonverbally by shifting positions in his chair, cleaning his glasses, and refusing to make eye contact with Shauna. In contrast, Shauna was often very animated during sessions. She spoke with her hands, talked rapidly, and had exaggerated facial expressions. She used lots of metaphors and commonly interrupted and preempted Rick. Their early sessions typically involved a lot of talk from Shauna and very little from Rick. In the following excerpts, identifying details have been altered to protect the anonymity of the couple.

Sequencing and Phases of Intervention in IBCT

The general format of IBCT is to begin with a three-session assessment phase where couples complete a conjoint intake session and two individual assessment sessions. These assessment sessions are then followed by a feedback session. Though a distinction is made between this assessment phase and the subsequent active treatment phase, the main goal of the assessment phase, development of the formulation, can be considered an intervention in its own right. The assessment phase is followed by the active treatment phase, which typically begins with and emphasizes acceptance-based interventions, as seen in Rick and Shauna's treatment. The termination phase focuses on helping the couple to consolidate their ability to recognize activation of each spouse's vulnerabilities and to use acquired techniques to interrupt their polarization process.

Assessment

The main goal of the assessment phase is to develop a case conceptualization, referred to as the formulation, and a treatment plan in collaboration with the couple. The primary means of developing a case conceptualization in IBCT is to use a functional analysis of behavior. In IBCT, functional analysis is used to identify core vulnerabilities that are activated across conflict areas and the broad patterns of behavior that the couple engages in during conflict. Though specific sequences of events are often helpful in understanding broader behavioral patterns and core themes, less emphasis is placed on individual, molecular behaviors in favor of attending to what these behaviors represent and how they are involved in the couple's polarization process.

Assessment is accomplished over the course of three sessions. The first session is a conjoint session with both spouses present and the following two sessions are individual sessions. These three assessment sessions are then followed by a feedback session where the formulation and treatment plan are presented to the couple.

Rick and Shauna's therapist, who was a man, began the first conjoint assessment session by collecting enough information about the couple's presenting problems to begin understanding areas of particular conflict and frequent behavioral patterns during conflict. Shauna had recently discovered that Rick had taken out several credit cards in her name without telling her that he was doing so by forging her signature on the applications. She made this discovery when a past due bill was sent to their home and she contacted the credit card company to find out what was going on. When she confronted Rick, he confessed that he had applied for the credit cards and also revealed to her that he had done so because they were in a large amount of financial debt that she also did not know about. His business had been struggling and, prior to applying for the credit cards, he had taken out a second mortgage on their house when his business stopped being profitable. The decline of his business and having a second mortgage in his name left him without adequate credit to apply for a credit card so he had forged her signature on the credit card applications to try to buy himself time to dig out of the financial hole without having to tell Shauna about what was happening.

As Rick and Shauna told the details of their presenting problems, their behavioral tendencies during conflict began to emerge. Shauna was very expressive about the intense betrayal, anger, and sadness that she felt toward Rick, whereas Rick included frequent rational justifications for his decisions and expressed relatively little affect or emotion. Additionally, Rick did not answer many of the questions that Shauna angrily asked him about why he made these decisions. Once the therapist recognized this behavioral sequence as a form of demand–withdraw behavior, he intervened in a way designed to interrupt the cycle while also validating both partners' emotional needs without validating the consequent behavior:

Therapist: I'm going to interrupt you both for a minute here. I've noticed a couple of times during this first session that Shauna, when you are angry and ask Rick a question about why he decided to take out the second mortgage and the credit cards and to not tell you about what was going on financially, Rick, you seem to have trouble making eye contact with Shauna and knowing how to answer her questions. I know that I'm just meeting you both for the first time today and am still getting to know you both, but Rick, I wonder if her questions bring up some feelings of shame or vulnerability for you.

(Long pause.)

Rick: Yeah, I guess so. At least a little bit. I mean, I don't feel scared or anything, but it does remind me of how badly I screwed things up.

Therapist: I think that your feeling that way is a really important part of what I'm seeing here in our first session and why the two of you feel so stuck. We'll spend much more time talking about this cycle, but I also want to make sure that we are able to talk about a couple of other areas of your relationship today.

The remainder of the initial conjoint session was spent gathering information about the developmental history of the relationship, including what had initially attracted Rick and Shauna to each other. Doing so helps the therapist to further develop initial hypotheses about the roots of the polarization process as well as to remind the couple of the positive aspects of behavior or personality that later come to be experienced as undesirable.

Following their conjoint assessment session, the therapist met separately with each spouse. These individual assessment sessions were used to gather more information about the presenting problems and to discuss the partner's family of origin and previous romantic relationship experiences. Because the therapist had seen Rick assume a strong withdrawing role during the initial conjoint session, he planned to use Rick's individual session to introduce the idea of functional analysis of behavior (i.e., antecedents lead to behaviors which in turn lead to consequences) without Shauna's presence. The reason that the therapist wanted to introduce this idea during Rick's individual session is that partners who are quick to blame the other for causing or maintaining problems often use functional analysis to show their partners are at fault for the couple's problems. Rick had not been blaming of Shauna at all during the conjoint session; rather, he had spent most of the time defending himself. Introducing functional analysis during individual assessment sessions can also help develop and strengthen the therapeutic alliance with partners who tend to intellectualize and to quickly assume a problem-solving stance, as is frequently the case for agentic men. The therapist presented the idea of functional analysis to Rick as something that would be a core part of the therapy.

Therapist: One of the things that happens for many couples is that there tend to be themes that play out in their arguments time and again in many different places where there is conflict. One of the core components of this therapy is recognizing these themes and understanding why they are happening. It has been my experience that it is really important to understand why the themes in your relationship get activated as they do before trying to change the way that the two of you interact so that we can know what it is that needs to be addressed. The first step in this process is figuring out what the themes are and what it looks like when they get activated for the two of you. One tool for doing this is to think about things in three different steps: where the conflict starts, how you both respond, and what happens as a result. I'd like to spend a little time today thinking back to our conjoint session and getting your thoughts about what happened when we were talking about the debt in each of those three phases.

This technique was intended both to introduce the idea of functional analysis to Rick when he would be more likely to be able to hear it given the reduced emotionality of the individual session and to give the therapist access to Rick's thoughts so that he would have a better sense of what happened internally for Rick when the couple got into a demand–withdraw cycle. IBCT maintains that the therapist's responsibility is to the couple, so anything discussed during the individual sessions is assumed to be fair game to raise in subsequent conjoint sessions unless a spouse specifically requests that the therapist not reveal a particular piece of information in a conjoint session. In this case, an IBCT therapist will work with the partner to reveal the information to the partner himself or herself but will not continue therapy with knowledge of crucial information that is relevant to the couples therapy that is not shared by both partners for an extended time. If a request is made to not disclose information shared during an individual session that is not relevant to the couples therapy, an IBCT therapist would honor this request. For example, an IBCT therapist would not continue therapy with knowledge of an undisclosed, ongoing affair in the current relationship but would continue therapy with undisclosed knowledge that one partner's parent had had an affair. This perspective requires the therapist to discuss how confidentiality applies in individual sessions. In Rick and Shauna's case, this arrangement allowed the therapist to use information gathered during Rick's individual assessment session to empathically join with Rick when he was withdrawing during subsequent conjoint sessions by suggesting that Rick may be thinking or feeling some of the things that came to light during the functional analysis conducted during Rick's individual session.

The therapist synthesized all of the information into the case conceptualization, or formulation, which was presented to and discussed with Rick and Shauna in the feedback session.

Therapist: I see you both as having complimentary emotional vulnerabilities that get triggered in a very strong way when you talk about your financial situation and what led up to it. Shauna, you've had repeated experiences of betrayal and abandonment, both from your family and from some of your earlier romantic relationships. I think that these experiences may have contributed to a feeling that you can only count on yourself for happiness and success. When you two started your relationship, Rick was very committed from your first date. I think that this sense of commitment might have allowed you to feel safe and to trust and depend on Rick.

Rick, when you were fired from the job that you had had for 15 years, a job that you really liked and took pride in doing well, you told me that that was incredibly humiliating and that it had been very hard to share those feelings with Shauna. You've also told me that being a financial provider for your family is a really important part of your sense of what it is to be a good husband and that being financially successful has been important to you for a very long time.

When Rick started his career as a consultant, the two of you had significantly less time together and seemed to have felt distanced from each other as a result. Rick, it sounds like you were really worried about the success of your new career and had difficulty not getting stuck in that worry when you and Shauna were able to spend time together. When your consulting business didn't go well, you panicked and took out a second mortgage so that you could buy some time and not have to tell Shauna about what had happened.

Does that sound pretty accurate to the two of you so far?

Shauna: Yeah. But you're leaving important parts out. I felt so betrayed by what Rick did. How could he not tell me what was happening?

Therapist: I know that this was devastating for you. For both of you. And that's the other part of how I see this affecting your relationship and what I really think is at the core of the lack of trust that you both feel right now. Rick, I think that you were worried that Shauna would tell you that you were a failure if she found out what was happening.

Rick: Maybe. I mean, I really just needed some more time so that I could get some more clients and pay off the credit cards. I didn't think that she'd ever need to know.

Therapist: I really hear that it's hard to acknowledge that it felt so bad when you were in such major financial debt. I think that it feels that way to both of you. Shauna, when you found out that Rick had kept this secret from you, I think that it may have triggered your fear of abandonment. I wonder if some of the recent shifts that you've described about wanting Rick to come to you for your advice about his business could be a way for you to feel more in control and less exposed.

Shauna: Well, I don't know. It definitely scared me when I found out what happened. I mean, if that's possible, what else is he hiding from me? Know what I mean?

Therapist: I know that it brings up those kinds of questions for you. And here's the thing that is so striking to me. Based on what I know about the two of you so far, it looks to me like when these vulnerabilities get triggered, you each tend to take on a role that feels like it is going to undo some of the bad feeling. Rick, what I've seen you do most is withdraw. When Shauna gets angry at you or really wants you to tell her why you did what you did, you seem to pull back and kind of wait out her anger. And Shauna, what I've seen you do most is get really angry at Rick. The thing that is so striking though is that it looks to me like you both are doing some of these things coming from a place of feeling unsafe, attacked, or vulnerable but that feeling isn't being expressed to each other at all so all that you've each got to go off is the behavior that you each see the other doing. Rick, I would imagine that you're really often thinking, "Why is she still so angry at me? Doesn't she know that I didn't do this on purpose?"

Rick: Yep.

Therapist: And Shauna, I imagine that you keep thinking something like, "Why can't he just tell me why he did it so that I can understand and make sure that it never happens again?"

Shauna: That's true.

The remainder of the feedback session was spent discussing how the couple understood this process and beginning to unpack the emotional vulnerabilities of each partner.

There are several aspects of the way that the therapist worked with Rick and Shauna that exemplify how some of the general strategies of IBCT can be applied to conduct male sensitive couple therapy. One of the most important of these is the way that the therapist began with and maintained a nonjudgmental, descriptive, dyadic formulation throughout the feedback session. This type of formulation reframes the couple's distress as being an understandable consequence of both partners' behaviors without blaming either one for being the root cause of the problem. Framing the couple's distress in this way was important for both partners. For Rick, it allowed him to participate in the discussion without having to assume or deny responsibility. Participating in the discussion in this way allowed Rick to be more open and responsive to what both the therapist and Shauna were saying as well as more disclosing about his own emotional experience than he was typically able to be at home with Shauna.

Acceptance-Based Strategies

Presenting the formulation to Rick and Shauna in the feedback session laid the groundwork for the acceptance-based interventions that their therapist started with in the intervention phase. This groundwork is a crucial prerequisite for using acceptance-based interventions because it clearly places the distress that both partners are feeling within a dyadic conceptualization. Rick, as is common of many men, understood his distress as an individual phenomenon related to an individually solvable situation. He could at least temporarily resolve the anxiety associated with his new career by getting money from another source, a second mortgage. In Rick's mind, it was more his inability to provide than his decision to not talk with Shauna about the situation that was causing the two of them distress. Women tend to use relationship-schematic processing, or understanding relationship conflict to be the product of a transaction between partners, more often than do men (Sullivan & Baucom, 2005). Using a functional analysis of behavior to propose the formulation helps both partners understand their distress as a result of their interactions around and reactions to sources of conflict. Doing so also allows the therapist to model empathic understanding of both partners' experience of the conflict. This modeling sets the stage for the intimacy-enhancing techniques that the therapist used early on with the couple.

The major treatment goal of IBCT is to help couples reshape the natural contingencies of their relationships by becoming more understanding and accepting of each other. Once understanding and acceptance is enhanced, it can be leveraged to help partners work together to make desired changes. Acceptance itself can be considered an affective-cognitive change that frequently leads to additional spontaneous changes in behavior. It also may allow for deliberate change to be created in areas that were previously too polarized for collaboration on preferable alternatives. For this reason, IBCT also includes deliberate changes strategies.

IBCT acceptance-based interventions fall into two categories: intimacy enhancing techniques and tolerance building techniques. Intimacy enhancing techniques include empathic joining and unified detachment. These techniques seek to help couples turn their problems into vehicles for increased intimacy. Tolerance-building techniques, such as pointing out the positive aspects of negative behavior, enacting negative behaviors in the therapy session, faking negative behaviors outside of the session and self-care (Jacobson & Christensen, 1996), are used to lessen the impact of conflict on both partners.

The goal of empathic joining is to create an emotional connection between partners, especially when they are feeling most vulnerable while discussing long-standing conflicts, by eliciting and heightening emotional disclosure between partners. An empathic reaction is most likely to occur when one partner discloses deeply felt thoughts and emotions that pull the other into an emotional resonance. Most often this empathic reaction is triggered by "soft" disclosures that include expression of vulnerable feelings and that avoid accusation. Feelings such as Rick's fear of rejection and Shauna's fear of abandonment would be examples. Couples in distress frequently present the self as strong, tough, and able to attack and defend with "hard" disclosures that include blame, contempt, and hostility. Because they are attacking, these expressions usually create separation rather than closeness. Therefore, to achieve empathic joining, an IBCT therapist must often transform hard disclosures into softer ones.

Soft disclosures can be promoted by reframing interactions using themes from the formulation. It is not uncommon for some couples to have difficulty making soft disclosures. Acknowledging the vulnerable emotions underneath hard expression can feel exposing to couples. In other couples, the rigidity that typically accompanies an extreme polarization process leaves partners so entrenched in their own positions that it is difficult for them to consider alternative explanations for their behavior. In these instances, therapists can encourage empathic joining by suggesting the possibility of similar vulnerabilities in both partners.

A typical example of how soft disclosures can be used to elicit vulnerable disclosures is seen in the following example from Rick and Shauna's case. When Rick and Shauna engaged in their demand–withdraw pattern, Rick would frequently suggest that Shauna was overreacting and that her criticisms of him didn't make sense, and he was very reluctant to share any of his own feelings about the issue at hand. The therapist was able to slow down the cycle of negative and hurtful comments by exploring if Rick was having feelings that were difficult to share with Shauna and was focusing on her behavior as a way to take the focus off himself.

Shauna: I just don't understand why he would want to hurt me like that and not tell me what was going on with our money.

Rick: That's a stupid thing to say. I wasn't trying to hurt you and you know that. Plus, I mean, any normal person knows that sometimes business investments go bad and you have to do whatever you have to do to make it through those times.

Shauna: What? How can you say that my feelings are stupid? I don't have to explain to you why I feel that way and we're not talking about everyone here. We're talking about me. What's wrong with you? You are an ass. Why did I ever marry you?

Therapist: Whoa, whoa. I'm going to interrupt you both. It looks to me like you two are in that demand–withdraw pattern that we've talked about so much, and I would guess that you're both feeling angry, alone, and hurt right now. I want to take a step back to look at what just happened. Rick, when Shauna said that she didn't understand and asked why you would hurt her that way, I wonder if that triggered some of those shameful feelings that we've talked about being a part of your cycle.

Rick: No, not really. It really just pissed me off. I mean, how can she think that I would want to hurt her? I love her and am trying to do my best for us.

Therapist: Say more.

Rick: Well, I try really hard at my job because it's important to me that she have good things and that we be able to do whatever we want to do. And it is really hard for me when I try so hard and she just doesn't see it. What else could I do? I'm already putting in every free hour that I can. I can't make more clients come to me.

Therapist: It sounds like when she asked why you would hurt her like that, you felt really misunderstood and not gotten.

Rick: Yeah, not at all.

Therapist: Can you turn to her and tell her about that feeling? The not-feeling-understood part.

Examining their demand–withdraw pattern in this way helped both Rick and Shauna acknowledge that their behaviors were not attempts to shut out or to control the other per se but rather were ways that each had used in other areas of their lives to feel less anxious. The soft disclosures encouraged by the therapist also allowed Rick and Shauna to connect with each other in expressing and responding to each other's vulnerable emotions. For example, the therapist suggested at one point that Rick may be experiencing shame, which was a very isolating emotion for him. Rick had difficulty directly acknowledging that he was experiencing shame but was able to describe how he felt misunderstood and unappreciated. The therapist knew that Rick viewed his ability to

provide financially as a major way that he contributed to the relationship, so when Rick framed his response in those terms, the therapist
both validated Rick's experience and used it as a vehicle to encourage further soft disclosure. In doing so, the therapist effectively used
empathic joining in a male-sensitive fashion by using important aspects
of Rick's definition of being a good husband to encourage vulnerable
disclosure and response.

Empathy is also promoted by reducing the aversive emotional arousal
that both partners typically feel during conflict. One way that an IBCT
therapist can achieve this goal is by having spouses talk directly to the therapist rather than to each other when they are not able to express their
thoughts using soft disclosures. Without the provocative reactions of
their partner, each member of the couple may be able to disclose feelings
and thoughts to the therapist that are less inflammatory than they might
express to each other.

Another intervention technique for reducing emotional reactivity is
unified detachment. The goal of unified detachment is very similar to
that of empathic joining—to allow couples to talk about their problems without using blaming and attacking hard expressions. The difference between empathic joining and unified detachment is that whereas
empathic joining heightens emotions, unified detachment is used to
contain and to reduce the emotion associated with conflict by engaging
in intellectual analysis. When unified detachment is successful, couples
are able to recognize their relationship themes as they happen and to
see how isolated events are connected by way of this theme.

There are a number of techniques that an IBCT therapist can use
to promote unified detachment. One is to discuss the sequence of
events surrounding a recent incident and to reframe the events using
the themes and patterns from the formulation. Another unified detachment strategy is to use humorous names for the roles that each partner
plays in the couple's overarching pattern. Another unified detachment
technique is to have partners talk about the problem as an "it." Bringing
a fourth chair into the room to represent the problem can help couples
see their interaction patterns as something external to both of them and
generate additional perspective for the couple. A final unified detachment technique is to instruct the couple to imagine that the therapist
is present when they have a disagreement outside the therapy sessions.
Both of these final two strategies are designed to keep disagreements
from escalating emotionally, even when the therapist is not physically
present.

Although unified detachment and empathic joining are conceptually
distinct, they are often used together in the same session, and there
are no concrete rules for when to heighten and when to dampen emotion. The course of therapy should be guided by the functional value of
the interventions for each problem for each couple. For example, there
were some areas of conflict related to trust that were highly emotionally
evocative for Rick and Shauna early in therapy where the combination

of unified detachment and empathic joining was most effective. One example of this was who would be responsible for making the monthly second mortgage payment. Shauna's sense of betrayal and Rick's fear of rejection were elicited so automatically and strongly during discussions of this topic that there was little opportunity for both spouses to have a different emotional experience of one another while entrenched in their usual positions in the conflict. To help the partners shift out of these positions, the therapist engaged Rick and Shauna in a detailed analytic examination of what had happened the previous month when the mortgage was due and an analysis of how each had behaviorally responded to the other's actions. After slowing down the usual escalation of the conflict with this detailed analysis, both partners were less emotionally aroused and were able to transition into empathic joining with a discussion of some of the emotions that each had experienced during the previous month and during the unified detachment exercise.

While IBCT views increasing empathy between partners as a primary mechanism of change, it is also important to acknowledge that it is not possible to foster empathy for all sources of conflict. It is recommended that empathic joining or unified detachment be attempted before deciding that increased acceptance is not possible. When it becomes clear that intimacy-enhancing techniques are not effective, tolerance-building strategies can be used to minimize the negative impact of problems and the amount of time needed to rebound after a destructive interaction.

IBCT incorporates four tolerance-building techniques. The first technique, pointing out the positive aspects of negative behaviors, involves making use of a functional understanding of problematic behaviors to explain (or to remind partners) how some aspect of negative behaviors serves an adaptive purpose for the relationship while still acknowledging that there are negative aspects of the behavior. It is important that there be a genuinely positive aspect to the negative behavior; this strategy should not be used when if it feels forced or seems disingenuous. Practicing negative behaviors, the second technique, during therapy sessions is a strategy used to desensitize partners to behaviors that do not have positive aspects and to discuss the role of the behavior in the polarization process. Faking negative behaviors at home involves instructing partners to pretend to engage in a problematic behavior at a time when they are not already feeling pulled to do so and are not feeling intense emotion. This technique provides an opportunity to gain additional insight into the impact of their behavior on the partner and may reduce the emotional reactivity of both partners to the behavior. A final tolerance-building technique, self-care, can be used to lessen the frustration associated with problematic behaviors by exploring alternative methods for meeting partners' needs. At least partially meeting otherwise unfulfilled needs may make partners more tolerant of and less reactive to distressing behaviors. This technique also reminds partners that they do not have to solely rely on one another to meet all of their needs, which may in and of itself reduce the amount of emotional pressure that each places on the other.

One example of a tolerance-building technique that was helpful for Rick and Shauna was to encourage Rick to engage in greater self-care. Before Rick had started his consulting business, he used to find a lot of pleasure and relaxation in woodworking. He had given up woodworking altogether when he had begun spending more time working at his consulting business, feeling that he already had so little time to spend with Shauna that he couldn't spend time on his woodworking hobby. The couple's financial problems also complicated the situation. Rick had begun accumulating the tools he needed to accomplish more complicated projects but still lacked some of the tools that he would have liked to have had and also preferred to work with expensive woods. In exploring the possible value of returning to woodworking, the therapist first had to address the elements that had led Rick to stop initially. Rick had not felt that he had a choice about whether to spend time on a hobby of his own when he was already spending some much time at work. This sense of obligation had led Rick to feel required to spend time with Shauna. As a result, he was more emotionally reactive than he would have otherwise been. This rule was created without any discussion and was self-enforced. Shauna was completely unaware of this rule and was supportive of Rick taking some time for himself, even though it meant that they would have less time together. Rick and Shauna were also able to come up with a creative solution to the financial aspect of his woodworking by finding a woodworking class at a local community college that gave Rick access to all of the tools that he needed.

CHANGE-FOCUSED STRATEGIES

IBCT also incorporates behavior exchange (BE) and communication (CT) and problem-solving training (PST) developed as part of BMT. A thorough description of these change-focused strategies is beyond the scope of this chapter. Please refer to Epstein and Baucom (2002) for additional discussion of BE, CT, and PST.

In brief, BE refers to interventions aiming at directly increasing positive interactions for the couple by helping partners commit to deliberately engaging in behaviors that would be pleasing for one of the partners. As described at the outset of the chapter, BE is used to increase the frequency of nonconflictual, positive interactions between partners, whereas CT and PST are used for resolving conflict. CT focuses on describing sequences and contexts of events, expressing thoughts and feelings about the self, conveying understanding of content, and providing emotional support. CT skills are intended to be broadly applied to routine interactions as well as volatile and emotional disagreements. CT skills are generally divided into two categories: one set for the speaker and one set for the listener. Skills for the speaker include speaking subjectively, sharing your own thoughts and feelings, being as specific as possible, and speaking in relatively short segments; skills for the listener include demonstrating understanding verbally through paraphrasing and summary as well as nonverbally through tone of voice, facial expressions, and body posture (Epstein & Baucom, 2002). The skills taught in PST are much more narrowly focused on creating solutions for specific problems. Many variations and permutations of PST exist; most of these share the common steps of defining the problem to be discussed, brainstorming possible solutions without evaluation, weighing the pros and cons of each possible solution, selecting a solution, agreeing on a plan for implementing the solution, and setting a timeframe for evaluating the effectiveness of the solution.

Two principles govern the use of change-focused interventions in IBCT. First, IBCT implements behavior change strategies using contingency-shaped change for maintaining and generalizing behavior change. Contingency-shaped behavior strategies use natural consequences to reinforce behavior change by shifting the context of interactions. One example of creating contingency-shaped change is to help partners increase empathy for one another. The closeness that is experienced while being empathic is positively reinforcing for partners and will help solidify the behavioral and contextual changes that made the empathic connection possible. For example, if Rick shares that he is terrified about not being able to provide financially for Shauna and that being a reliable financial provider is an important part of his definition of being a good husband, he will be much more likely to continue sharing vulnerable emotions if Shauna is able to respond by genuinely understanding his anxiety and validating the reality of his feelings even if she feels differently about the amount of time that he works. Another important aspect of contingency-shaped change is that it generally feels more genuine to couples than rule-governed change. This increased authenticity makes change more meaningful since it is clear that changes are being initiated by partners instead of by adherence to a set of rules.

A second guiding principle of using change-focused strategies in IBCT is that a functional analysis is used to guide the delivery of these interventions. Only skills that are helpful for a particularly problematic pattern are taught in IBCT. For example, a couple may really struggle with defining the problem to be solved when engaging in problem-solving conversations. An IBCT therapist would use the principles of problem definition from PST but would not also guide the couple through the other steps of PST if they were already able to effectively create and implement a solution once the problem had been defined. In doing so, the IBCT therapist is maintaining an emphasis on contingency-shaped change. The positive experience of successfully resolving a problem using skills the couple naturally possesses is more likely to reinforce a change in problem-defining skills than is going through the remainder of the PST guidelines.

For example, Rick and Shauna viewed the issue of their credit card and mortgage debt very differently. Rick was very focused on the practical aspect of paying down the debt, whereas Shauna, though concerned with the practical implications of their debt, was more focused on the fact that Rick had not told her about the debt. In working with the couple to create a solution to their financial problems, the therapist first had to help the partners see that they were focused on different aspects of the same problem by saying, "I get the sense that even though you are both talking about your debt, you are referring to different pieces of the problem. One of the things that is really important for couples to do when they are trying to solve a problem is to make sure that both people agree on what it is that they are trying to solve. I'd like for us to make sure that you both agree on what it is that you're trying to solve here before we move on to figuring out how to solve it."

CONSIDERATION OF CULTURAL DIVERSITY IN USING IBCT

It is vital to be sensitive to cultural norms and values when working from an IBCT perspective. Individual cultural experiences and beliefs often play a crucial role in shaping what it means to be a partner, a husband, or a wife as well as the range of acceptable behaviors in which each can engage. One area that requires particular attention and thought is the model of power distribution and sharing that is presented to a couple. Given the emphasis on both partner's sharing vulnerabilities, it would be easy to assume that IBCT takes a progressive sociopolitical view on romantic relationships and considers egalitarian relationships to be ideal. In fact, IBCT is based on a functionalist understanding of relationships and does not view any particular model of power sharing in relationships to be ideal. The ideal relationship is the one that works for both partners, regardless of what that translates into in terms of power sharing. Consistent with this notion, research has shown that IBCT is an effective treatment for a diverse range of individuals and couples. Ethnic minority couples were found to respond to both IBCT and Traditional Behavioral Couple Therapy (TBCT) in a similar manner as Caucasians in a large-scale randomized clinical trial (Yi, George, Atkins, & Christensen, 2004).

CONSIDERATION OF THERAPIST'S GENDER

As was noted at the outset of this chapter, it is important to be mindful of the potential for recreating a polarized dynamic in the therapy room that mirrors the polarization process in the couple. Awareness of this possibility may be particularly helpful for female therapists. Men are particularly sensitive and resistant to being influenced by women when women use highly competent styles of communication (see Carli, 2006, for a review). This tendency creates a dilemma for female therapists, particularly those with a more directive style. On the one hand, a highly conflictual couple may need the therapist to display her expertise in order to feel contained and safe; the couple may also pull for the therapist to be more directive to keep conflict from rapidly escalating. On the other hand, a highly withdrawn male may react to these displays of competence and influence by withdrawing further. A solution to the dilemma comes from findings demonstrating that men's resistance can be reduced by warmth and communality, or a shared sense of purpose and understanding (e.g., Carli, 2001). These findings suggest that it may be particularly important for female therapists to develop a strong therapeutic alliance with withdrawn men before attempting to help them shift into being more active. One way to foster warmth and communality with highly withdrawn men during the early stages of therapy is to be very upfront about the primary goal of the assessment phase, developing an understanding of the couple's polarization process as a dyadic phenomenon, and the importance of doing this before making any attempts to change it. For example, a therapist might say something like, "I want to make sure that I have a clear understanding of both of your perspectives on what it is that's bringing you into therapy. I've found that it is crucial that we all share the same sense of what we're working on and what we're working toward before we start thinking about what you'd like to be different and any possibilities for making those changes. Today's main goal is for me to learn about what it is like for you to be in your relationship so I want to ask you to really focus on your experience of your relationship."

SUMMARY OF ISSUES RAISED IN THE CHAPTER

Polarization is assumed to be the primary determinant of relationship distress in IBCT. One very common form of polarization is the demand–withdraw interaction pattern. This pattern frequently involves male withdrawal during issues where women are requesting change in the relationship. Polarizing behaviors are often related to unexpressed vulnerabilities that may be influenced by differential socialization experiences of men and women, and to strong emotional reactivity to conflict. IBCT includes acceptance-based strategies that can be used to help men shift out of a rigid tendency to withdraw when their wives make requests for change and to promote increased closeness and intimacy between partners. When men experience less pressure to change, it often allows them to make subsequent behavioral changes that are experienced as more natural, are more enduring, and are more consistent with self-concept than are those created with deliberate change-focused interventions. In instances where it is not possible to foster empathy between partners, tolerance-building techniques can be used to reduce the destructive impacts of conflict on both partners. After using tolerance-building interventions, it may be possible to return to intimacy-enhancement strategies and to use them more effectively now that the couple has developed a more collaborative stance. Finally, change-focused techniques can be flexibly used to provide a more structured approach for introducing acceptance-based ideas, to intervene in instances of skills deficits or when these interventions are specifically requested.

As a final note on Rick and Shauna, they completed a full course of therapy over approximately 6 months. At termination, as well as 2 years later, they both reported levels of relationship satisfaction in the non-distressed range and engaged in substantially lower levels of demand–withdraw behavior. The decrease in demand–withdraw behavior was particularly notably when discussing areas of change identified by Shauna.

REFERENCES

Baucom, B. (2010). Power and arousal: New methods for assessing couples. In K. Hahlweg, M. Grawe-Gerber, & D. H. Baucom (Eds.), *Enhancing couples: The shape of couple therapy to come* (pp. 171–184). Cambridge, MA: Hogrefe.

Baucom, B., McFarland, P., & Christensen, A. (2010). Gender, topic, and time in observed demand/withdraw interaction in cross- and same-sex couples. *Journal of Family Psychology, 24,* 233–242.

Baucom, D. H., Shoham, V., Mueser, K. T., Daiuto, A. D., & Stickle, T. R. (1998). Empirically supported couples and family therapies for adult problems. *Journal of Consulting and Clinical Psychology, 66,* 53–88.

Carli, L. (2001). Gender and social influence. *Journal of Social Issues, 57,* 725–741.

Carli, L. (2006). Gender issues in workplace groups: Effects of gender and communication style on social influence. In M. Barrett & M.J. Davidson (Eds.), *Gender and communication at work* (pp. 69–83). Burlington, VT: Ashgate.

Christensen, A. (1987). Detection of conflict patterns in couples. In K. Hahlweg & M. J. Goldstein (Eds.), *Understanding major mental disorders: The contribution of family interaction research* (pp. 250–265). New York: Family Process Press.

Christensen, A., Atkins, D. S., Berns, S., Wheeler, J., Baucom, D. H., & Simpson, L. E. (2004). Traditional versus integrative behavioral couple therapy for significantly and chronically distressed married couples. *Journal of Consulting and Clinical Psychology, 72,* 176–191.

Christensen, A., & Heavey, C. L. (1990). Gender and social structure in the demand/withdraw pattern of marital conflict. *Journal of Personality and Social Psychology, 59,* 73–81.

Christensen, A., & Shenk, J. L. (1991). Communication, conflict, and psychological distance in nondistressed, clinic, and divorcing couples. *Journal of consulting and clinical psychology, 59*(3), 458–463.

Christensen, A., Wheeler, J. G., & Jacobson, N. S. (2008). Couple distress. In D. H. Barlow (Ed.), *Clinical handbook of psychological disorders* (4th ed., pp. 662–689). New York: Guilford.

Davey, A., Fincham, F., Beach, S., & Brody, G. (2001). Attributions in marriage: Examining the entailment model in dyadic context. *Journal of Family Psychology*, 15, 721–734.

Davies, P., & Lindsay, L. (2001). Does gender moderate the effects of marital conflict on children? In J. Grych & F. Fincham (Eds.), *Interpersonal conflict and child development* (pp. 64–97). New York: Cambridge University Press.

Dimidjian, S., Martel, C., & Christensen, A. (2008). Integrative behavioral couple therapy. In A. Gurman (Ed.), *Clinical handbook of couple therapy* (4th ed., pp. 73–106). New York: Guilford.

Doss, B. D., Atkins, D. C., & Christensen, A. (2003). Who's dragging their feet? Husbands and wives seeking marital therapy. *Journal of Marital and Family Therapy*, 29, 165–177.

Eldridge, K., & Baucom, B. (in press). Couples and consequences of the demand–withdraw interaction pattern. In P. Noller & G. Karantzas (Eds.), *Positive pathways for couples and families: Meeting the challenges of relationships*. New York: Wiley-Blackwell.

Epstein, N., & Baucom, D.H. (2002). *Enhanced cognitive-behavioral therapy for couples: A contextual approach*. Washington, DC: American Psychological Association.

Gottman, J. M., & Levenson, R. W. (1988). *The social psychophysiology of marriage*. Clevedon, UK: Multilingual Matters.

Heyman, R. E., Hunt-Martorano, A. N., Malik, J., & Slep, A. M. S. (2009). Desired change in couples: Gender differences and effects on communication. *Journal of Family Psychology*, 23(4), 474–484.

Howerton, A., & Van Gundy, K. (2009). Sex Differences in Coping Styles and Implications for Depressed Mood. *International Journal of Stress Management*, 16, 333–350.

Jacobson, N. S., Christensen, A., Prince, S. E., Cordova, J., & Eldridge, K. (2000). Integrative behavioral couple therapy: An acceptance-based, promising new treatment for couple discord. *Journal of Consulting and Clinical Psychology*, 68(2), 351–355.

Jacobson, N. S., Follette, W. C., & Pagel, M. (1986). Predicting who will benefit from behavioral marital therapy. *Journal of Consulting and Clinical Psychology*, 54(4), 518–522.

Jacobson, N. S., Follette, W., Revensdorf, D., Baucom, B., Hahlweg, K., & Margolin, G. (1984). Variability in outcome and clinical significance of behavioral marital therapy: A reanalysis of outcome data. *Journal of Consulting and Clinical Psychology*, 52, 497–504.

Jacobson, N. S. & Christensen, A. (1996). *Acceptance and change in couple therapy: A therapist's guide to transforming relationships*. New York: Norton.

Jacobson, N. S., & Margolin, G. (1979). *Marital therapy: Strategies based on social learning and behavior exchange principles*. New York: Brunner/Mazel.

Jacobson, N. S., Schmaling, K. B., & Holtzworth-Munroe, A. (1987). Component analysis of behavioral marital therapy: 2-year follow-up and prediction of relapse. *Journal of Marital and Family Therapy*, 13, 187–195.

Peplau, L. A., & Fingerhut, A. W. (2007). The close relationships of lesbians and gay men. *Annual Review of Psychology, 58,* 405–424.

Rehman, U., & Holtzworth-Munroe, A. (2006). A cross-cultural analysis of the demand-withdraw marital interaction: Observing couples from a developing country. *Journal of Consulting and Clinical Psychology, 74,* 755–766.

Shadish, W., & Baldwin, S. (2005). Effects of behavioral marital therapy: A meta-analysis of randomized controlled trials. *Journal of Consulting and Clinical Psychology, 73,* 6–14.

Sullivan, L., & Baucom, D. (2005). Observational coding of relationship-schematic processing. *Journal of Marital and Family Therapy, 31,* 31–43.

Twenge, J. (1989). Changes in masculine and feminine traits over time: A meta-analysis. *Sex Roles, 36,* 305–325.

Weiss, R. L. (1975). Contracts, cognition, and change: A behavioral approach to marriage therapy. *The Counseling Psychologist, 5,* 15–26.

Weiss, R. L., & Heyman, R. E. (1997). *A clinical-research overview of couples interactions.* Hoboken, NJ: John Wiley & Sons.

Yi, J., George, B., Atkins, D., & Christensen, A. (2004). *Ethnic minorities in couple therapy: How do they fare?* Unpublished manuscript.

9

The Gottman Method
Theory and Case Study

KARL BERGENSTAL

Men are frequently more difficult than women to engage in psychotherapy. Therefore, when conducting couples therapy, special sensitivity to men's reactions and tendencies is warranted to improve the success of the treatment. John Gottman has conducted 35 years of research on couples and has constructed a comprehensive theory regarding what influences and enhances a couple's stability and satisfaction. This chapter will present Gottman's research, theory, and therapeutic approach while emphasizing his insights regarding men's issues and couples counseling.

This chapter will begin with Gottman's research on prediction of divorce. It will then present his Sound Relationship House, a model of relationship functioning and dynamics, which is based upon his research. Next, Gottman's therapeutic approach, which is an outgrowth of this research and theory, is presented. Because I believe that attachment styles are almost always a prominent issue in all relationships, I show how men's usual and particular bonding needs can be supported in the Gottman couple approach. Finally, a case example is presented to illustrate how I utilized Gottman's approach with a couple in my private practice. Throughout the chapter the information and approaches that are particularly relevant and unique to men are emphasized. Finally, the therapeutic approaches recommended in this chapter are expected to work as well with a female or male therapist. Although it may go without saying, names and some history in the case example have been altered to preserve confidentiality.

PREDICTION OF DIVORCE

Gottman became famous for his claim that he could predict with over 90% accuracy which couples he studied would eventually divorce (Gottman & Levenson, 1992). The following are his main summarized research findings on the causes of marital dissatisfaction and dissolution in contrast to stability and happiness.

Ratio of Positivity to Negativity

Stable, happy couples show a ratio of 5:1 positivity to negativity during conflict (observed as they discussed an area of disagreement), whereas couples headed for divorce had a corresponding ratio of 0.8:1. In non-conflict situations, the ratio of positivity to negativity for happy couples is 20:1 (e.g., humor, affection, smiling, and interest vs. anger, fear, and sadness). Thus, we ought not declare war on negativity but make sure that it is adequately balanced with positivity.

Four Horsemen

Not all negativity is alike. Anger, for instance, can be used to enhance proactive change. However, the following "four horsemen of the Apocalypse" were found to be corrosive.

Criticism—Global description of a flaw in the partner's personal-ity; for example, statements that begin with "you always" or "you never," or name calling or diagnosing to imply the partner has a character flaw. The antidote to criticism is to learn to complain well, that is, about specific issues (e.g., "You didn't make the bed as you said you would," instead of "You never follow through on your promises"). Women tend to complain more than men.

Defensiveness—Counterattacking or whining (innocent victim stance). The antidote to defensiveness is to accept some responsi-bility for at least a small part of the problem.

Contempt (sometimes accompanied by belligerence)—To put the partner down, make him or her feel inferior, or to put yourself on a higher moral plane. The mindset is to look for flaws and mis-takes. A husband's contempt predicts a wife's illness (Gottman, 1994a). Contempt is the single best predictor of divorce; it is the "sulfuric acid of love." All couples exhibit the presence of some aspect of the four horsemen, but in happy marriages the amount of contempt is essentially zero. Gottman recommends that thera-pists label contempt as psychological abuse and unacceptable. The antidote of contempt is changing from a mindset of fault finding to creating a culture of appreciation.

Stonewalling—The listener withdraws while staying in the room, as seen in looking away and crossing arms, as opposed to giving clues of tracking, such as head nodding. Eighty-five percent of stonewallers are men. A main reason men engage in stonewalling is to reduce high levels of psychophysiological hyperarousal, which they find highly aversive. Thus, men avoid the conversation to avoid a fight (them blowing up). The antidote for stonewalling is self-soothing (learning to relax and take time outs from the conflict). During timeouts men tend to rehearse thoughts of righteous indignation and retaliation, and thus need to learn to focus on calming thoughts.

Persuasion styles

Couple happiness does not occur only in validating couples (partners who first listen calmly then try to gently persuade each other). Volatile or passionate couples (partners who immediately and forcefully express their point of view) and avoidant couples (partners who are hesitant to disagree or persuade each other) can also show high levels of stability and happiness. It is the mismatches in these three styles that predict divorce (Gottman, 1994b). Mismatches are treated much like other perpetual issues (see later) and the goal is acceptance and sensitivity to persuasion style differences.

THE SOUND RELATIONSHIP HOUSE (SRH)

Figure 9.1 is a visual depiction of the Sound Relationship House (SRH; modified from Gottman & Gottman, 2005), which is Gottman's theory of how relationships work based on his research. The first level of the SRH is love maps, which involves partners knowing each other and periodically updating this information. The amount of cognitive room (knowledge; e.g., recall of how they met, knowing partner's worries, life dreams, best friends) that men devote to their partner (actively cultivate) was found to predict marital satisfaction within the first year of marriage (Gottman, 1999). To strengthen love maps, Gottman recommends asking open-ended questions on a daily basis, such as at dinner, and having daily stress-reducing conversations in which the spouses take turns sharing the stressors of the day with the listening spouse engaging in active listening, as opposed to challenging or advice giving.

The second level of the SRH is the fondness and admiration system, which is the antidote for contempt. Frequent and spontaneous expressions of affection and appreciation are recommended.

The third level, turning toward versus turning away, involves small, everyday responses to the spouse's direct but frequently subtle bids for

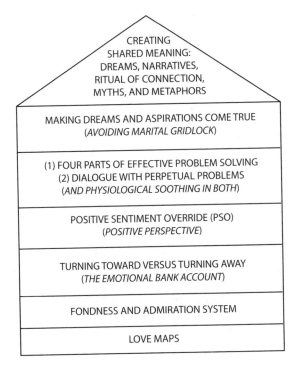

Figure 9.1   The Sound Relationship House (SRH).

attention, affection, or support. Turning toward builds an emotional bank account, a reservoir of goodwill.

These first three levels of the SRH combine to form the basis of friendship in the marriage, the presence of positive affect in nonconflict situations. They also provide the ingredients for the fourth level, which Weiss (1980) coined as positive sentiment override (PSO). PSO forms the basis of successful repair attempts that de-escalate negative affect during conflict situations. Gottman found that couples who were successful in their repair attempts were 83% likely to be stable and happy 8 years later, even if they scored high on the four horsemen. The ability to repair and de-escalate forms the basis for physiological soothing, which is essential to regulate conflict in the next level.

The fifth level is conflict regulation. Note that Gottman uses the term *regulation* as opposed to *resolution*, as Gottman and Levenson (1999) found that 69% of the conflicts discussed by couples are perpetual, in that they continue to occur because they are rooted in differences in personality or needs that are fundamental to their core definition of self (Gottman, 1999). Thus, what matters is not solving these problems but being able to create a dialogue about the perpetual problems with positive affect and communication of acceptance of the partner and even amusement at the recognition that "there we go again."

Problem-solving techniques (the five social skills listed later) are taught to achieve full resolution or compromise of the 31% of problems that are solvable, and regulation is taught (with some degree of compromise) for the 69% of problems that are perpetual.

The sixth level of the SRH is making dreams and aspirations come true (avoiding marital gridlock). Gridlock occurs when a discussion of a perpetual problem keeps cycling back repeatedly over the same ground, usually with much frustration and even rejection. Gottman views gridlock as usually caused by a failure to understand the symbolic conflict or hidden dream underneath the conflict. To discuss the hidden dreams, couples are coached to interview each other to help discover the meaning of the issues that are usually rooted in childhood experiences. By better understanding their partner, they are more apt to be sympathetic to their partner's perspective and more willing to find a way of helping them to achieve their deeper needs.

The top, seventh level of the SRH (creating shared meanings) involves the couple bonding on a deep level to create a new family culture, with rituals, narratives, and patterns of behavior that integrate and honor both of their personalities and values.

The seven levels of the SRH are interconnected because the top level of dreams and narratives of the individuals and couples cycle back to the first level, the foundation of knowing each other. See the upcoming case example, which illustrates how assessment of Gottman's SRH levels enhances treatment planning.

THERAPEUTIC APPROACH

Gottman's four main goals and therapeutic emphases of couple's therapy are as follows:

1. Move from gridlock to dialogue—Most couples come to therapy gridlocked on one or more perpetual issues. Gottman attempts to work with one of these issues within the first or second session to give the couple relief and hope. He utilizes the technique "dreams within conflict" to address the perpetual issue. This intervention is more likely to be successful if the friendship in the marriage is in reasonable shape and the couple can engage without flooding and without the use of the four horsemen. The intervention entails having one partner become the speaker, with the objective to describe what the issue means to him or her, describing beliefs, history, symbolic underpinnings, why it is important to him or her, and what the hopes are for an outcome. The listener's goal is just to hear the partner's side, not judge it, by asking clarifying and facilitating questions, such as "tell me the story of that." The couple then switches

roles. The initial goal is not to try to persuade the partner or to solve the problem, but to just discuss and better understand it. "The bottom line of life's dreams is this: You don't want to have the kind of marriage in which you win and are influential in the marriage but wind up crushing your partner's dream" (Gottman, 1999, p. 249). The next step in the dreams-within-conflict intervention is to find some way to honor one another's dreams. At the lowest level, honoring can mean interest, respect, or words of encouragement. At the higher levels, there is a joining in the partner's dreams and teamwork. Using the exercise of compromise (described below) may be appropriate. The whole process may take years, so the therapist is just starting the couple in a new trajectory.

2. Successful processing of a fight—The first processing of a fight is done in sessions where the therapist helps the members of the couple understand how they got into the muddle and what is the meaning of the issue to them, and to move from an adversarial mode to an admitting or collaborative mode (Wile, 1993). The therapist then recommends using the same processing techniques at home.

3. Establishing five social skills—These include:

    A. Labeling the four horsemen and replacing them with antidotes.

    B. Practicing softened start-up—Gottman points out that women are more likely to start conversations about problems than men are, hence the common demand–withdrawal or attack–defend or pursuer–distancer dynamic between men and women. Gottman reports that "discussions invariably end on the same note they begin" (Gottman & Silver, 1999, p. 161). Thus, women are taught to pick a calm time, complain not blame, use "I" messages expressing their feelings and needs ("you" messages are more apt to create defensiveness). It should be noted that nonresponsiveness of men in nonconflict situations ("turning against") predicted harsh startup in women.

    C. Developing a mechanism for men to accept influence and act nondefensively—Although men's willingness to be influenced and openness to compromise is found in general to predict marital happiness and stability (Gottman, 1979), this dynamic was seen as especially influential in violent marriages (Jacobson & Gottman, 1998). In the latter study, women rejecting influence predicted nothing, but men rejecting influence predicted violence.

    When softened start-up and accepting influence are combined, a synergistic "double-play combination" is created in what Gottman calls "emotionally intelligent marriages" (Gottman & Gottman, 2005, p. 31).

    D. Practicing repair, de-escalation, and physiological soothing of self and other—When negative affect arises, first and foremost it is imperative that the couple watch for flooding, the state of diffuse physiological arousal (DPA) that occurs when a person's pulse exceeds about one hundred beats per minute, which then induces the fight-or-flight response with release of the hormones adrenaline and cortisol. During this state of DPA, cognitive focus is narrowed and effective reception of information and influence and problem-solving are greatly reduced. Couples need to learn to monitor negative affect and de-escalate tension before flooding occurs, via repair attempts (i.e., acknowledgment of tension, apology for offensive statements, empathetic statements, etc.). If flooding has occurred, timeouts should be taken and honored by either partner as a helpful and caring measure. Couples should learn to self-soothe with various relaxation techniques (breathing, muscle relaxation, pleasant imagery). Preferably, they should also agree on a time that they can continue their discussion.

Gottman (1999) found that men became emotionally flooded by lower levels of negative affective behavior than is the case for females. He believes this flooding is a major cause of male withdrawal and eventual stonewalling. (See the case example for illustration.)

E. Seeking compromise—Gottman first advises striving for an attitude of compromise (following the Aikido principle that "to yield is to win"; Gottman & Silver, 1999). Once this attitude has been achieved, the couple then draws concentric circles on a piece of paper. In the inner circle the partners list aspects of the problems they cannot give in on. In the outer circle they list aspects that they can compromise about. They then share their information with their partner looking for common basis of agreement.

4. Building friendship as the base for effective repair—Couples are encouraged to daily practice the following: develop love maps by thinking of great open-ended questions that might be asked over dinner and that will allow them to learn about their partner; be responsive to the bids for acknowledgment or validation of their partner; find creative ways to show respect, admiration, and affection. Using daily stress-reducing conversations with partners using active listening and avoiding advice or criticism will help the partners process daily tension and help make the relationship a "port in the storm."

INTEGRATING THE GOTTMAN METHOD WITH OTHER APPROACHES

The third edition of the *Clinical Handbook of Couple Therapy* (Gurman & Jacobson, 2002) categorizes Gottman's approach as psychoeducational and preventative, which accurately describes Gottman's style of intervention. His approach is more educational than most other couples therapies. However, other approaches are highly compatible with his approach and they complement each other. For instance, Gottman at times recommends behavioral exchange (BE) emphasized by the cognitive-behavioral approach (Baucom & Epstein, 1990). (BE asks the partners to list and then perform behaviors that would make their partner happy and then try to notice when the other is also performing their list.) Gottman also recommends Wile's (1999) technique of speaking the leading edge thoughts for a couple member. (This technique involves the therapist making speculations about what a partner might be thinking or feeling to dramatize each partner's experience). Gottman's approach to "perpetual problems" is quite similar to "acceptance" espoused by integrated behavioral couple therapy (Jacobson & Christensen, 1996). (Acceptance, and then tolerance, that all couples have some unsolvable problems can lead to collaboration by the partners to make necessary and helpful shifts in expectations and compromises to improve the quality of the relationship.)

Additionally, and quite important, the Gottman method has been found to be quite compatible with and complementary to emotionally focused therapy (Johnson, 2004, this volume), which is based on attachment theory. Being an attachment theorist, I find that a perpetual issue for most couples is their bonding style. Although all people (both genders and mammals for that matter) have a lifelong need for a secure base for comfort and understanding as well as a healthy ability to separate from that base, I find that men more than women are more comfortable in their attachment cycle with autonomy and solitude than with intimacy and closeness. Applying the Gottman techniques of social skills and regulation of perpetual issues is quite helpful to men in dealing with their attachment needs. (See case example for illustration.)

CASE EXAMPLE

Joan and John were in their mid-40s, with two teenagers approaching their college years and under mounting financial stress. Joan initiated couples therapy because John was frequently loud, defensive, and belittling with his words; in the distant past he had also been physically violent with pushing. John's belligerence, name calling and demeaning putdowns were escalating since he had been laid off 8 months before. Although Joan understood that John was depressed because of their reversal of roles, as she was now the breadwinner and he was unable to provide for his family, she also admitted that at times she was insensitive toward him with her poorly worded or poorly timed complaints about his housekeeping. John, on the other hand, was initially unable to accept any responsibility for the decline in their marriage, as he viewed his anger at Joan as justifiable under his occupational circumstances and in response to her demands.

He presented as defensive, agitated and justifying his blowups due to her provocations saying, "She just attacks me out of the blue." It became apparent early in the sessions that John became easily reactive to minor slights and most efforts by Joan to influence him to change.

An initial history revealed that Joan grew up in an abusive and neglectful household from which she eventually fled in her teenage years, forcing her to take charge of her life, fend for herself, and vow to never be controlled or mistreated again. She would retreat and withdraw if conflicts became intense. Similarly, John was raised by a very domineering, authoritarian, and verbally abusive father. He learned to cope by staying vigilant and acting out, such as having frequent fights in school.

In deciding where to begin intervention, I assessed, via the SRH model (see earlier), that the couple had a fairly good friendship base (levels one through three), as they enjoyed their time together and were considerate and attentive when they were not in conflict, their sex life remained satisfactory, and they had warm memories of when they first fell in love (many couples "rewrite history" as their current dissatisfactions tend to cause negative distortion of historical recall of the relationship). Also, although they each rated their current satisfaction in the relationship as 4 to 5 (out of a possible 10), both rated their commitment to the marriage as 8 to 9. Overall, I rated them as having good positive sentiment override. Conflict regulation was obviously poor due to presence of the four horsemen, and I suspected flooding was likely a problem for John. I surmised that their abuse histories were likely contributing to perpetual underlying and currently gridlocked conflict about control and safety. I was unsure at this point regarding their attachment styles and bonding cycle. The seventh level regarding the establishment of meaningful rituals and mutually satisfactory family culture was also unclear to me at this point, but this issue could wait to be considered.

After I met with Joan and John individually to rule out domestic violence, my first challenge in using a male-sensitive perspective in the conjoint treatment was how to engage a man who was depressed, psychologically brittle, and defensive. I also needed to deal immediately with John's contempt responses toward Joan, since, as Gottman has noted, contempt is toxic to a relationship and if not dramatically reduced, treatment would likely fail (Gottman, 1994a, 1999). Consistent with the Gottman method, I use three interventions when dealing with men who are highly reactive and also appear vulnerable to experiencing shame and flooding: (1) build rapport with empathic listening; (2) use humor to reduce defensiveness; (3) provide psychoeducation on the nature of men's physiological responses to relationship conflict.

Therefore, I began relatively early in the first session by commiserating with John about the difficult circumstances he was in and did my best to build rapport with him by allowing him to vent about his financial, occupation, and self-esteem challenges. However, although I reassured him that frustration and anger in his situation would be understandable, I informed him about the difference between anger and abuse, including how contempt was so harmful to a marriage, the "sulfuric acid of love." To lighten the conversation and lessen his defensiveness, I told him about the Monty Python skit, "The Argument Clinic," in which a man pays to have an argument and enters room A, whereupon a well-dressed man at a desk immediately launches into a verbal attack of invective insults and putdowns, such as "You no good intruder. What gives a person like you the mistaken confidence that you are good enough to speak with me?" When the customer protests that he didn't think this qualified as an actual argument, the man politely responds, "Oh, I'm sorry. This is abuse; arguments are in room A-1 down the hall." Fortunately, John understood the point I was making about criticism and contempt.

In the first session, I also began brief exploration and explanation of flooding, and the need to be calm if John and Joan were to adequately process information during a discussion or disagreement. The notion that there was a biological process that influenced John's problematic behavior was especially reassuring to John as well as to Joan; not only did it reduce his shame, but it sent the message that couples counseling was a place where he would learn new information. I have found in general that letting men know therapy is a learning experience facilitates their engagement with treatment and disarms their fear that my primary interest would be in analyzing their emotional life. After hearing my explanation about flooding, John and Joan both committed themselves to monitoring their tension levels and taking timeouts if either person was nearing a 7 level on a 1 to 10 scale of arousal.

I began the second session with John and Joan by reviewing their week and exploring how they did with their goals of affect monitoring and control. They were pleased that there were fewer blowups, but that they did not know when to take timeouts. I more fully explained the concept of DPA and flooding, and I explained that, typically, men were more quickly reactive and took more time to come down from flooding. I asked if they would be willing to wear pulse oximeters to better become aware of their physiology, particularly in reaction to their interaction patterns. Pulse oximeters are inexpensive sensors that are easy for clients to use at home and give visual readouts of their pulse rate as well as beeping sounds when the rate climbs to a rapid speed. Because the concept of flooding is such an integral part of the Gottman method, we routinely use the devices, but therapists of any orientation might find them useful as part of a program of relaxation training. This is especially so with men, who may relate to using "tools" and pragmatic interventions. John was fascinated with the idea, coming from a technical background, and Joan was willing to try anything if it would help. I also sensed that John felt less ashamed of his tendency to become flooded in conflict when he learned that men's tendency to become highly aroused with stress hormones when in a fight was a common finding in the research literature.

Later in that session, Joan and John got into a small argument, initiated by Joan's complaint that John was not doing enough to find a job. John's oximeter started to beep almost continuously, meaning his pulse had elevated to higher than one hundred beats per minute. I intervened and taught relaxation techniques: breathing, muscle relaxation, and imagery. I also reviewed with them one of the rules of timeouts: By showing a timeout signal, either partner could put a hold on the conversation until they both agreed it was safe to continue.

Over the course of the next few weeks, John and Joan became quite accomplished at preventing the beeping of the monitors and they became more attuned with their own and their partner's levels of arousal. I could see John's face beam as he described a conversation where the oximeter never beeped. This feeling of mastery and control over his body gave John, as it does with many of my male clients, confidence, pride, and a strengthening of his commitment to therapy. In the next three sessions John also became more understanding of the need and right that Joan had to raise requests and complaints in the marriage. I explained that complaints were necessary to express wishes and make the relationship as satisfying as possible (i.e., no one is a mind reader regarding what the spouse is needing), and that direct but tactful requests were most effective. I worked with John to help him see that being defensive stopped communication. He was able to learn the antidote for defensiveness: looking to take some responsibility for at least a part of her complaint.

It was also at this point that I tried to get John to see the wisdom of accepting influence from Joan. As is typical for many men when I explain this concept, John balked at the notion. "Does that mean I have to say yes to everything she wants?" he said with alarm. Joan laughed, adding, "Yes it does, dear." But John was truly concerned; he feared I was asking him to surrender his power as a man. The Gottman method uses the term *accepting influence* to minimize defensiveness, but some men do have an immediate negative reaction. What I do in these situations is make clear that his wife had to make a change as well. John would accept her influence but Joan would use a soft startup (i.e., demands would be phrased as requests, and spoken without insistence and harsh tonal quality). Creating this quid pro quo put John at ease and also clarified that I was not suggesting he give in to her every demand. When I make the case to men for accepting influence, I often add a bit of praise, noting that I thought John had the emotional intelligence to pull off this change in the relationship. For male partners, ensuring that the balance of power in the relationship remains equal, plus appealing to their strengths, enables them to experiment with accepting influence at home. The actual reduction in conflict they experience usually removes any last concern that their masculinity is being compromised.

After Joan and John were able to communicate with less volatility, we began work on their perpetual issue of control and safety. I had each of them, with my assistance, interview the other regarding their backgrounds and experience with control as they grew up, and what they had needed and wished for as a natural adaptive outgrowth of their upbringing. When they better understood the other's deep needs and tendencies about controlling their situation and managing conflict, they became more accepting of the other's coping/personality tendencies. Their statements such as "there we go again," said with a sense of humor, was a clear sign that they were honoring their partner's perspective and had progressed from gridlock to dialogue on this ongoing issue.

Despite their progress, John remained frequently frustrated that Joan "never stayed in the conversation" long enough to gain a sense of closure or resolution. Joan was worn out by John's intense style of confrontation and she quickly felt overwhelmed and wanted to terminate the discussions. Thus, they had developed a typical attack–defend or demand–withdrawal pattern. We explored their long-term and persistent persuasion styles and they acknowledged their engrained differences: John was a member of the debate team in high school and he was naturally drawn to enjoying lively exchanges of differing points of views. Joan, on the other hand, had always had a tendency to avoid confrontations and arguments; she enjoyed confluence and bonding with others by finding commonalities in their beliefs. With discussion they came to see that their volatile/passionate and avoidant persuasion styles were another perpetual issue about which they also needed to dialogue on an ongoing basis. They came to understand that accepting and honoring their differences (not forcing change) was the only healthy approach to the issue. They both made a concerted effort to compromise, with Joan attempting to make a good faith effort to tolerate more intense and prolonged discussions, and John attempting to tone down his expressiveness and argumentativeness and to allow Joan to take timeouts when she felt flooded.

In the last stage of therapy, I wanted to strengthen their underlying friendship. Now that they had learned to have less stressful conversations, I encouraged Joan to allow John to discuss his loss of the breadwinner role and resultant crises of identity. I have found it critical that men who have lost self-respect—or perceive that they have lost it in the eyes of their spouse—can feel safe to express their associated feelings. Earlier in treatment, this would have been impossible because of the level of volatility, the presence of the four horsemen, and John's tendency to become flooded.

It was also in this final stage of therapy that the perpetual issue regarding their attachment styles became apparent. John made it clear that while he wanted constructive, resolvable conversations about their roles and responsibilities, it made him feel very vulnerable to engage in intimate conversations about their feelings and needs for each other. Joan, on the other hand, had difficulty feeling secure and safe in the relationship if she did not have these close explorations together on a regular basis. Using Gottman's dreams within technique, they gained insight and more acceptance regarding the origin and differences in their bonding styles. Also, having Joan apply a soft, nonharsh startup regarding her needs for closeness, while honoring and being mindful of John's sensitivity in this area, helped facilitate more comfortable closeness for both of them.

With less intense communication and some progress on key perpetual issues, including their report that they were able to process a fight at home on their own, we all now thought their main goals had been achieved, so we focused on the termination process. We reviewed the various levels of the SRH and found that each level was fairly sound. I complimented them on their friendship, calmer conflict regulation, and better acceptance of their perpetual issues. Before they stopped, I emphasized the value of the stress-reducing conversations to allow John to find a port in the storm of his career/identity crisis. Joan also found ways to reflect appreciation for his efforts in their home, and he showed more gratitude for her hard work in the workplace. Finally, to address level seven of the SRH, I had them write and share their life's mission statement and discuss how they could make each other's dreams become reality.

SUMMARY

Gottman's research on couples has yielded helpful information that is specific to men's responses in couple relationships. These data on men, especially when utilized within the context of Gottman's theoretical model of how relationships work (Sound Relationship House), has been shown in a case example to be particularly relevant and helpful in making men feel more understood and improving the outcome of their couples therapy.

REFERENCES

Baucom, D. H., & Epstein, N. (1990). *Cognitive-behavioral marital therapy.* New York: Brunner/Mazel.

Gottman, J. M. (1979). *Marital interaction; Experimental investigations.* New York: Academic Press.

Gottman, J. M. (1994a). *What predicts divorce?* Hillsdale, NJ: Lawrence Erlbaum.

Gottman, J. M. (1994b). *Why marriages succeed or fail.* New York: Simon & Schuster.

Gottman, J. M. (1999). *The marriage clinic.* New York: Norton.

Gottman, J. M., & Gottman, J. S. (2005). *Gottman method couples therapy: Manual for advanced study.* Seattle, WA: Gottman Institute.

Gottman, J. M., & Levenson, R. W. (1992). Marital processes predictive of later dissolution: Behavior, psychology, and health. *Journal of Personality and Social Psychology, 63,* 221–233.

Gottman, J. M., & Levenson, R. W. (1999). Rebound from marital conflict and divorce prediction. *Family Process, 38,* 287–292.

Gottman, J. M., & Silver, N. (1999). *The seven principles for making marriage work.* New York: Three Rivers Press.

Gurman, A. S., & Jacobson, N. S. (2002). *Clinical handbook of couple therapy.* New York: The Guilford Press.

Jacobson, N. S., & Christensen, A. (1996). *Integrative couple therapy: Promoting acceptance and change.* New York: Norton.

Jacobson, N. S., & Gottman, J. M. (1998). *When men batter women.* New York: Simon & Schuster.

Johnson, S. M. (2004). *The practice of emotionally focused couple therapy.* New York: Brunner-Routledge.

Weiss, R. L. (1980). Strategic behavioral marital therapy: Toward a model for assessment and intervention. In J. P. Vincent (Ed.), *Advances in family intervention, assessment and theory* (Vol. 1, pp. 279–271). Greenwich, CT: JAI Press.

Wile, D. B. (1993). *After the fight: Using your disagreements to build a stronger relationship.* New York: Guilford Press.

Wile, D. B. (1999). Collaborative couple-therapy. In J. Donovan (Ed.), *Short-term couple therapy.* New York: Guilford Press.

10

The PAIRS Program

Engaging Men Through a Unique Psychoeducational Approach

LORI H. GORDON AND ELLEN PURCELL

Unlike other chapters in this book, PAIRS (Practical Application of Intimate Relationship Skills), the program described in this chapter, is not intended as counseling or psychotherapy but rather as a psychoeducational intervention. Its approach is one that seems to be less threatening than psychotherapy to men who are in relationships needing mending. Many of the exercises or concepts presented can be adapted into more traditional approaches to couples counseling. We have also found that professionals, once trained in PAIRS, have the ability to understand relationships from a fresh perspective. When providing assistance to couples, they easily become aware of relationship competencies that are missing and can begin introducing PAIRS tools and concepts to fill the void. In the office, this skills-based treatment process is called Office PAIRS. The therapist can offer the tools and concepts that fit as opportunities arise. PAIRS-trained professionals often prefer that couples experience a PAIRS class prior to engaging in significant relationship work in the office. After a PAIRS class experience, the therapist can more easily guide the couple in the use of the skills they have learned for continuing healing, growth, and relationship repair.

PAIRS was the outgrowth of the first author's interest in relationships and an invitation early in her professional career to develop a graduate-level course for counselors. The feedback from the counseling students about their personal relationship transformations was so remarkable that she created PAIRS from that class and brought it to her Family Relations Institute. It has continued to grow since that time and has enrolled tens of thousands of participants worldwide and thousands of instructors globally.

Even though the PAIRS program is titled "education," clinical experience and research findings (Daire, 2009; DeMaria, 1998; Durana, 1994) indicate that it is therapeutic. Because the workshop is not based on providing a mental health diagnosis and does not present itself as counseling, many men feel comfortable attending the workshops dubbed "relationship education." Attending PAIRS does not threaten participants' career advancement even in the military and does not bring into question participants' emotional stability. Because the workshops are offered in a classroom setting and built around humorous experiential exercises, they seem to be a more effective and less threatening way to involve men in learning how to improve their relationships.

PAIRS is an educational experience that is designed to teach attitudes, emotional understandings, and behaviors that nurture and sustain healthy relationships. Participation in the workshop develops emotional literacy, enhances empathy, teaches a language about intimacy, and allows participants to balance their thoughts and feelings about intimacy. This approach to relationship education includes relatable metaphors; jargon-free, nonblaming logic and humor; and teaches participants the difference between what they have learned about love in contrast to work. One of the important ideas, communicated early in the program, is that the two most fulfilling areas in life are love and work (Fromm, 1956), and that while we spend years preparing to be competent at work, most of us have not been taught systematically about sustaining love. Therefore, the workshop focuses on teaching skills that diminish reluctance to commit to marriage and a relationship, typical male fears. The opening workshop of a PAIRS relationship education program provides relief to those fears and instills hope. Important ingredients to successfully engaging male participants in the workshop include:

1. A nonblaming, nonjudgmental logic—Trainers communicate to participants that their difficulties in relationships are not their fault. We didn't learn it because it wasn't taught. Participants are told that they can learn it here.
2. Specific relationship awareness—Fromm (1956) writes about the two primary areas of fulfillment in life as work and love. However, the traits we learn to be successful at work during our school years (being emotionally guarded, competitive, aloof, etc.) are often the opposite of what is necessary for fulfillment in love (confiding, appreciation, cooperation, empathy, and affection). This is

especially so for traditional male careers, such as police, military, attorneys, computer programmers, and so on.

3. Humor—Especially humor that is illustrative of some aspect of relationships. For example:

> A couple who had saved their funds for a special transatlantic airline flight together, and excitedly boarded a beautiful new plane, took their plush beautiful new leather seats, and as the plane rose into the air, heard a voice over the loudspeaker saying, "Congratulations on being on the first totally automated flight. This unique flight is state of the art technology. It is an aviation first! This plane is being flown by automatic pilot, automatic copilot, automatic navigator! Your flight is being monitored by ground control. You have a choice of first run movies at your seat and gourmet menus prepared in advance by excellent chefs that will be presented shortly. We want you to sit back and relax, and know that on this miracle of technology, this aviation first, that nothing can go wrong ... go wrong ... go wrong ... go wrong ..."

Many couples fantasize that when they choose to marry, the relationship somehow goes on autopilot and nothing will go wrong. The reality, of course, is different. This kind of humor helps to diffuse the distress many couples feel about having difficulties in their own marriages. It also helps them become more open to learning new relationship skills.

4. The logic of emotion—In workshops we use simple, jargon-free language of pleasure and pain, happiness and unhappiness. We provide an explanation of behavior that is nonstigmatizing and is not based on a psychiatric diagnosis. It is a relief to men that they can begin to understand themselves and their partner in ways they had not before, leading to more perceptive and empathic interactions. Partners often remarkably quickly become better friends and even best friends.

5. Experiential exercises—Throughout the workshop, we engage participants in a variety of experiential exercises that behaviorally reinforce the information that has been presented. These exercises lead to a lessening of anxiety as participants learn quickly what they need to do to manage their relationships and to apply their lessons to themselves and their partners. We have found, for example, that the exercises help men learn how to strengthen their capacity for relatedness, empathy, and emotional connection. These exercises and their related concepts provide a new language, using terms such as the *Relationship Roadmap*, the *Dialogue Guide*, the *Daily Temperature Reading* and *Love Knots* described later. These and other terms, such as the *Emotional Jug, Dirty Fighting, Letting Go of Grudges, Doghouse Release, Emptying the Jug,* and *Emotional Allergy Infinity Loop* are described in extended sessions of the classes, and in the first author's book, *Passage To*

Intimacy (Gordon, 1993). They provide a tool kit (often described as a treasure chest) of clear, understandable terms and a variety of experiences that can be applied in almost all couple situations.

6. Perception of gender differences—In some PAIRS trainings, men and women are separated into men's and women's groups. The men seem to particularly enjoy these groups as the frank statements men make to each other in men-only groups normalizes many of their feelings. Both genders seem to be enlightened by the group conversations and the subsequent couples discussions that result. Men respond to the logic, the metaphors, the behavioral exercises and the humor that are introduced in the groups. Consequently, men often are the most active in urging that sessions continue.

AN OPENING WORKSHOP

The first meeting of a PAIRS workshop is particularly challenging for the trainer to engage participants and manage participants' anxieties, their lack of trust, and discomfort in being present. It is essential that the trainer be at ease in order to put the participants at ease. (The opening workshop is usually 3 hours.) Most participants are referred by therapists, pastors, or friends; or self-referred as a result of reading an article. Most have no idea what the workshop will entail. Twenty to thirty participants are seated in a classroom, many appearing somewhat anxious and waiting for the class to begin.

A typical couple that we will refer to throughout this chapter are John and Mary, a couple in their late 30s who have been married for 15 years. John is tall, with straight brown hair in a crew cut, recently retired from the military. He is dressed very carefully, looking somewhat stern. Mary has long brown hair, is also medium height and slender, and appears anxious. They have two sons, Evan 13 and Joshua 10. This couple was referred by Mary's physician, regarding Mary's recurring painful stomachaches, which he thought might be related to her stressful marriage.

The trainer enters and opens with a humorous story designed to set participants at ease. John then raises his hand and curtly states, "I don't believe in this touchy-feely stuff. I don't want to be here. I'm only here because of Mary." The trainer nods, tells him that she appreciates him telling her, and assures him that he doesn't have to do anything except be there. Because the trainer was sensitive to the male participant's discomfort with the very idea of a marriage workshop, she was able to help him let go of his guardedness. Part of the trainer's sensitivity was to the male participant's anxiety that he would be pressured to display emotions, in his mind, a setup for potential failure and humiliation.

Participants are next introduced to a critical belief about relationships, which is that most of us hope that nothing will go wrong when we begin our lives with our partner. But we shortly discover that there are disappointments in our most cherished relationships. For example, we may have expectations of the people we are closest to that they may not know about, and often we ourselves do not realize, until we feel disappointment. We have beliefs particular to our closest relationships; these are called Love Knots. Love Knots are beliefs such as

- "If you love and care about me you would know what I want and you would do it."
- "You would talk to me. You would listen to me. You would not interrupt me. You would remember my birthday, our anniversary. And if you don't, it doesn't mean you don't know. Of course you know. It means you don't care. So when I decide that you don't care about my feelings, I wonder why should I care about yours. So when you tell me what you want, I won't be very interested."

And the relationship goes downhill from there. At this point there are some smiles of recognition, but participants are still a bit wary. John nods his head slightly. Mary smiles nervously, but says nothing. They are both still sitting stiffly, not touching.

The trainer continues to give other examples of these knots including

- "If I try to tell you how I feel, you interrupt... or criticize or judge or..."
- "If you are unhappy, I should be able to fix it." (That one is very specific to men.)
- "If I ask you how you feel, you may think I'm intruding, so I don't ask. If I don't ask, you think I'm not interested, so you don't confide."

Confiding in relationships is the heart of what emotional closeness is about and being able to share feelings, thoughts, wants, likes and dislikes are essential to what we call bonding.

Bonding is a need not unlike the basic human needs of air, water, shelter, and food except that bonding is the only need that as adults we can't fill for ourselves (as the trainer describes this, she is drawing the Relationship Road Map, Figure 10.1).

Bonding includes emotional openness and physical closeness, ranging from the closeness of affection to that of sensuality and sex. Although we have long known that infants need bonding, we have only more recently discovered that aging seniors need people to be interested in them, to visit them, to be affectionate to them. We have come to realize that this need for bonding goes on throughout life. The ability to fulfill this need with the person we are closest to gives rise to feelings of desire, pleasure, and love. And the inability gives rise to feelings of distrust, distress, and can even cause disease. Note that there are many diseases related to unhappiness, such as depression, despair, addictions, alcohol,

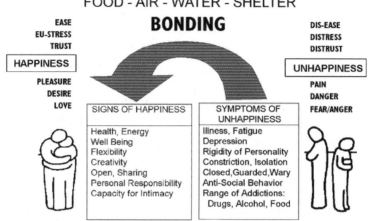

Figure 10.1   Relationship road map.

drugs, even violence. The trainer points out this logic illustrated with the structure of the relationship road map. The fact that we have begun the workshop with psychoeducation, presenting intellectually compelling ideas and research, means we are staying within the male partner's comfort zone. We are able to engage him, without threatening him by asking him prematurely to engage in a bonding exercise. True to form, at this point, John looks thoughtful and starts writing a few notes; Mary looks a little surprised that he is doing that and appears interested in what he might be writing.

STRESS STYLES OF COMMUNICATION

Stress responses occur when we are under stress or anticipate that we will be upset, which affects our behavior. Using the stress response circle (a pie-shaped diagram, divided into three parts labeled Self, Other, and Issue), the trainer explains that we display a variety of responses. An example of the first response is a woman who is worried that her partner won't like what she's thinking or feeling, so she appeases or placates. She doesn't want to upset her partner. She doesn't express her feelings so she denies her self. On the chart, the trainer puts an X over the word *Self.* Or a person may believe his partner is going to blame him, so he blames first. He might say, "It's all your fault." By doing so he cancels out her feelings and belief. On the chart, the trainer puts an X over the word *Other*. The third response is that one person decides that he doesn't want to deal with feelings at all—they are too messy and unpredictable. This is called the computer response, or the super reasonable, and it involves quoting authority, law, rules, regulations, and ignoring emotions. On the chart, the trainer Xs out both *Self* and *Other*. The fourth and last response is that given a problem or anticipating stress, we may say to ourselves: "I don't know what to do, so I will pretend that there is no problem. What problem?" This style is called the distractor or irrelevant. When we respond this way, we ignore self, other, and the issue. On the chart, the trainer crosses out all three. At this point, John has a thoughtful smile, and Mary is nodding her head, concealing some enthusiasm at recognizing their styles. They seem to both relax a bit in their chairs.

The trainer now indicates that the class will conduct an exercise, since most of us don't learn from long lectures. (This involves role-playing the four stress responses, all of which have accompanying body stances.) The trainer asks the group to stand up to participate in the first exercise. There is a demonstration by the trainer and an assistant, or an experienced participant, of the placating body posture, which has one hand over the heart pleading as there is often heartache, and the person is down on one knee. The group is instructed to take that posture and simultaneously say placating statements, such as "I'm sorry ... it's all my fault ... I really don't know anything ... I never do anything right," holding this posture as instructed for about 15 seconds, and checking in with themselves about how familiar this posture is and how their body feels. John reluctantly joins the exercise. He seems to have difficulty getting down on his knee and looks decidedly uncomfortable. Mary quickly gets down on one knee, joins immediately, possibly realizing that this is her common stress style. The trainer notes that this stress style may well be the source of a variety of chronic ailments, such as sleep or digestive problems.

The next stress style, which is blaming, is demonstrated. Each person rigidly stands straight up, left hand on the hip, right hand pointing out, and simultaneously says blaming comments like "It's all your fault ... you never do anything right ... what's wrong with you!" "You're just like your mother!" John points, and stands straight, but doesn't say the phrases. He has a broad smile as he watches others do this. Some become aware that this a well-known posture for them. Many share a good laugh over this insight as the rest of the group also laughs somewhat embarrassedly. Mary does not join in the laughter but looks tearful and takes out a tissue.

This exercise continues through the third posture, the computer or super reasonable (a rigid military stance), where the trainer reminds them "Love is an emotion, a feeling. When we tune out feelings, we may also tune out love." John stands stiffly and says nothing, as does Mary.

Finally, they role-play the fourth body posture, the distractor. John watches the group, smiling again, and Mary actually does the distractor style and is smiling, too. The trainer, partner, or an experienced group member first demonstrates each stress style. Three elements to this exercise gradually facilitate the male partner's involvement in the workshop: (a) there is a specific action he can perform, which not only connects with the male's preference for doing but also gets him (and his partner) out of their chairs, releasing any nervous energy that might have been accumulating while they were just sitting and listening; (b) there is a quality of play to the exercise, which also helps to loosen tension; (c) when participants do posture exercises, they have a visceral experience. Something is actually happening, an internal physical and emotional sensation, that cannot be denied. Thus, John begins to appreciate that the workshop may actually impact him; he has moved from "I am willing to give this a try for my wife's sake" to "I'm starting to enjoy this myself."

The trainer invites the group to sit down and to suggest a problem that might be role-played in front of the group. John, now engaged and wanting the workshop to help his relationship, volunteers the argument he and Nancy have been having over her parents' upcoming visit. The trainer and an assistant then role-play spontaneously using a shifting variety of the four stances to deal with this problem, using the styles that have just been modeled. John and Mary and most group members often spontaneously laugh as they watch. We end the role-play by hugging each other and the group applauds.

The trainer instructs the participants to divide into groups of four, without their partners, to (a) think of a problem situation, (b) select the role or person each will play or represent, and (c) privately decide which stress style each one will start with. John stands alone as everyone else moves into groups. This is an awkward moment for him, so the trainer immediately encourages a few people to join him. In group experiences like this one, it is critical that the trainer recognizes that some participants—often the male partner—will not easily connect with others and need help joining a group. In that moment for John, he was beginning to feel shame, and the trainer's quick response prevented him from further emotional discomfort. Mary has easily found a group to work with, and is smiling and chatting with those in her group.

When each group has decided on a problem situation, a role, and stress styles to start with, the exercise starts. There is enormous activity as each group simultaneously begins practicing. John seems to take on a stress style and hesitatingly participates using the words but not the body postures. Mary is laughing in her group and seems to be having fun with the exercise. After about 2 minutes, the exercise is called to a stop and group members are asked to stay in the position they are in. They are asked to reflect on how that position feels for them, identifying how familiar or unfamiliar it seems. They are instructed to continue with the problem in their group but each is to choose another stress style to use. Stress styles are simultaneously pointed out on the board or on a poster (numbers 1 to 4), and participants are instructed to start. This process is repeated four times so that each group member has the opportunity to try each of the four styles in trying to solve the problem they are dealing with in their pretend family or workgroup of four. Some groups laugh heartily, others look slightly confused and just stand there, as does John. Mary clearly has enjoyed this process.

At the end of this role-play exercise, the groups of four are instructed to sit down with their group and discuss with one another what this exercise has felt like for them. They are asked to consider which styles or situations were familiar or unfamiliar, and to identify when they have experienced them. The discussions are animated and continue for about 10 minutes. John appears to get involved in the discussion with his group, as does Mary in her group. This exercise not only produces laughter and thoughtfulness, but increases connection and ease in the workshop. This is often in contrast to how participants feel about their partner at the beginning of the workshop.

After a break the couples come back together with their partner to start the next exercise. John and Mary seem noticeably more relaxed. John is turning to the person next to him, smiling and chatting. The trainer instructs the couples to place their chairs back to back about a foot apart. In this position, they are instructed to begin to talk with each other about what they are realizing. John and Mary try to talk but clearly are not hearing each other. The trainer instructs them to close their eyes for a moment, and monitor whether they are feeling heard and understood, and how they are feeling about themselves and their relationship to each other. Typically, they cannot hear each other in these back-to-back positions. They are asked to realize how often this happens, such as when they talk from separate rooms or are occupied with other things. Most participants smilingly acknowledge that they have not been heard or understood. At the trainer's next instruction, the group is told for one member of the couple to stand up and the other to sit down at their partner's feet. Mary stands up, and John sits on the floor at her feet, and they continue discussing what they are realizing. When the trainer asks them to close their eyes, report how they feel in that position, and how they feel about themselves and their relationship, John says he feels like a child at her feet, doesn't like it at all, and resents her standing over him. Mary says she feels disconnected from him, lonely, and doesn't like being up there alone. The trainer then instructs them to reverse their positions. When they do this, Mary acknowledges that she feels intimidated by his standing over her and says that he thinks he is superior to her. John retorts that someone has to make decisions. The last step in the exercise is for each of the couples to sit and face each other with eye contact, possibly holding hands or knee to knee, and continue talking about what they are beginning to realize. John now says he realizes that his style could be called super reasonable, and although it is logical, he can see how it distanced him from Mary. He comments that his father behaved that way toward his mother. Mary confides that she hardly ever felt heard or listened to and she believed that he rarely understood her feelings.

The perceptions experienced by the participants can be powerful. John and Mary both tapped into some strong emotions, as well as insights into their own contribution to relationship difficulties. Therefore, following this last position, the trainer leads the group in processing their experience. It is clear to most that the final position (face to face, called the leveling position) feels the best. The trainer explains that this fifth position is one where we can express our thinking or feeling without placating, blaming, being super reasonable, or irrelevant, and can listen to understand each other. In this position we have the best possibility of solving whatever problems are there (including even reaching out for help). John is taking more notes, and Mary does the same.

DAILY TEMPERATURE READING

The next exercise in the first workshop is the Daily Temperature Reading (DTR, described on wallet cards which are handed out; Figure 10.2), which has five parts (or steps) for the couple to practice in the leveling position. The first part, which the trainer demonstrates, is appreciations, such as "I really appreciate your calling me when you were going to be late yesterday." The class is instructed to share an appreciation with each other taking turns doing the appreciating and being the listener. The trainer tells participants that the listener's only job is to understand and perhaps appreciate the appreciation. Mary appreciates that John is attending this workshop with her. John hesitates, and then says he appreciates that she welcomes him whenever he comes home.

The next step of the DTR is new information, to keep the other one up to date. The trainer demonstrates, by saying "New information is that I have to work late this week, or the car is making a funny sound." The trainer then instructs the class to practice this. Mary tells John

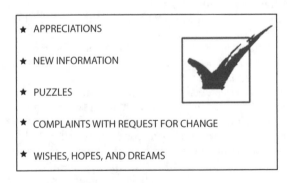

★ APPRECIATIONS

★ NEW INFORMATION

★ PUZZLES

★ COMPLAINTS WITH REQUEST FOR CHANGE

★ WISHES, HOPES, AND DREAMS

Figure 10.2   Daily temperature reading.

"My old classmate Gloria called today and we're meeting for lunch on Wednesday." John reports that he is flying to Boston on Thursday for his job.

The third step—puzzles (which means a question)—helps to avoid mind reading by providing an opportunity to check out something that is not clear and which might lend itself to making assumptions. The therapist demonstrates, saying, "I noticed you were very quiet last night, and I wondered if you were upset about something." The trainer also demonstrates that a response could be "No, actually, I was fine. I had a sinus headache all day and wasn't feeling well." John asks the puzzle: "I noticed the grocery bill was very high this month, and I don't understand why." The fourth step is described as complaint with request for change whose description and role-playing is temporarily postponed to a later workshop, when there will be a more complete exercise for complaints.

The last step is wishes, hopes, and dreams. The trainer demonstrates by saying "I hope we can have a quiet weekend at home this weekend." John says "I have a dream that when we retire we can live in North Carolina." Mary says that she would like to go to dinner and see a new movie this weekend. The trainer emphasizes the importance of keeping hopes and dreams alive in relationships, even while day-to-day challenges may take attention from positive thoughts of things we hope for. The group is instructed to offer some appropriate physical touch at the end of the exercise, perhaps a hug. As they complete the exercise, John reaches out and takes Mary's hand, looks directly at her with a tentative smile. Mary wipes her eyes with a tissue and seems tearful to see him responding.

THE DIALOGUE GUIDE

The next exercise is a guided exercise in confiding about a complaint and learning the process of listening with empathy. The Dialogue Guide (Figure 10.3) is described as a way to initially process the complaint with request for change portion of the Daily Temperature Reading, because complaints are hard to listen to and even often to give.

To introduce the Dialogue Guide, the trainer points to a chart and describes how couples can use this to present a complaint with a request for change. It is not enough to complain; we need to know what we are asking for. The guide includes a number of sentence stems, radiating out the circle like spokes of a wheel.

The trainer demonstrates how this works, with the listener repeating back each sentence stem to be sure that it was heard accurately. The trainer instructs the class to pick a complaint that identifies a specific behavior (rather than a feeling). The trainer indicates that, after each stem sentence, the listener is to say back what was heard and to try to say it with empathy, not like a robot. The speaker is to go all the way

Figure 10.3   Dialogue Guide.

around the sentence stem circle clockwise and finish with "I hope ..." stopping after each sentence for the listener to say what was heard. The trainer emphasizes that the part of the listener is equally important to that of the speaker in dealing with a complaint, and participants learn that the process is called empathic listening. By breaking down a problem into small manageable parts there is a greater chance of success than some overwhelming, overarching, vague complaint. The trainer now asks the class to decide who will be the speaker and who will be the listener, and to practice.

Standing by Mary, the speaker, the trainer hears her say, "I notice you don't like my driving." The trainer tells her that is a feeling or thought rather than a specific behavior. She revises her statement to "I notice ... that often when I drive the car, you give me directions and advice on my driving."

John and Mary's Dialogue Guide sounds like:

Mary: I notice ... that often when I drive the car, you give me directions
    and advice on my driving. (*John repeats what was heard after
    each stem.*)
      I assume ... this means that you don't think I know how
    to drive.
      I wonder ... how you think I've been driving for years on
    my own when you aren't in the car.
      I suspect ... that you are a very competitive driver who
    wants to take the absolute fastest route.

(On the other hand) I believe for me ... that I like to relax when I am driving, and I don't even care if I arrive at our destination 5 to 10 minutes later than if I'd rushed and changed lanes.

I resent ... that your tone feels like you are talking down to me like a child.

I am puzzled ... why there is so much urgency about getting places so fast when we aren't late.

I am hurt ... that you don't see how upset I am when you talk to me this way.

(John looks surprised by what he's hearing, and frowns slightly, but repeats the sentence slowly.)

I regret ... that this causes tension and stress when we are together in the car.

I'm afraid ... that this will make me not want to have you in the car with me when I drive.

I am frustrated ... that you haven't picked up earlier that this bothers me.

I behave by ... getting very quiet and withdrawn for some time afterwards.

I am happier ... when we can relax and have fun when we're driving together.

(Mary hesitates and looks a bit worried before asking for what she wants. She expresses her want with difficulty.)

I want ... to ask that unless there is a danger you are warning me about, that you not tell me at all how to drive.

I expect ... that it will be difficult for you to do.

I appreciate ... that you are a careful and excellent driver yourself.

I realize ... that we have different styles of driving, and you believe you are trying to be helpful.

I hope ... you can relax and sit back and just enjoy the ride, and we can have conversation and enjoy being in the car together.

After they complete this exercise, John inquires: "Why does this exercise have to be so long?" The trainer responds, "The sentence stems provide an opportunity to offer thoughts and feelings he may not even have known his partner had, and the partner may not have realized." A group member asks: "What if the behavior doesn't change?" The trainer suggests that participants can start using the Dialogue Guide again to point that out, and to start by saying "I notice ..." Sometimes using this stem alone serves as a reminder and requires no follow through. If that is not helpful, then another, more involved PAIRS skill that is taught in a later workshop—the Fair Fight for Change—is appropriate. Many problems and misperceptions can be avoided by bringing them up in the daily temperature reading or in the dialogue guide. We teach that "Love is a feeling. Marriage is a contract. A relationship is work. The question is, can you work out a contract you're both happy with?"

Mary offers, "This exercise gave me the words to say what I felt." From across the room, a man raises his hand and says quietly, "Me, too." It is clear that participants feel hopeful about their relationship as a result of their work so far. Both Mary and John agree that this process has helped them deal with something that has come up for them often in the past. Mary is grateful that she now knows a way to ask for change. John says, sounding somewhat pleased, "I think we may have just resolved something we haven't been able to resolve in our entire marriage."

At the close of the workshop, the trainer asks the group to move their chairs into a circle and request any comments about what they are realizing. One man volunteered "I learned more today than in ten years of psychoanalysis." John, holding his wife's hand, said, "This is the first time I ever felt fully heard."

DISCUSSION

The introduction of bonding as a biologically based need in the very first class is a surprise to some men who believe that, as a man, they should be sexual people and should want sex, but the notion that they should want cuddling, affection, confiding, touch separate from sex is a contradiction of everything they had thought of as masculinity. To learn in this first class that this is a legitimate need that goes on throughout life from infancy to aging, and that this is a need to fill with a significant other in an ongoing way is a surprise to many. It is also for many a contradiction of what they had learned about appropriate behaviors at work and their years of training for their careers that never included any instruction about the qualities that nurture intimacy in their close relationships. To include in the first class an educational experience that encompasses humor, laughter, joy, insight, understanding, and a deepening connection with their significant other, gives men the hope that they are able to learn a new way of being that strengthens and restores or renews feelings of love.

Anecdotally, there has been extensive feedback that PAIRS relationship education programs have been equally meaningful across a wide variety of cultures including England, France, Taiwan, the Soviet Union, South America, South Africa, Israel, Australia, China, and Japan. Such feedback is illustrated in this correspondence from Stefan Neszpor, MD, a PAIRS instructor from Australia, who wrote:

> In a sense, PAIRS helps to create a metaphoric sacred space for the couple where they can begin to understand and comprehend the notion of intimacy. They begin to appreciate a greater diversity in each other's

personality and resourcefulness, while also broadening their understanding of themselves. PAIRS provides the process to help develop, within a loving relationship, the sacred crucible of intimacy. (S. Neszpor, 1997, personal communication)

Additionally, PAIRS consistently receives feedback from instructors around the world about cultures as diverse as Caucasian, Black, Hispanic, Asian, American Indian, Creole, Eastern European, and Middle Eastern who have all responded enthusiastically to their PAIRS classes.

After experiencing PAIRS, men become far more willing to participate in individual or couples counseling, especially about specific issues that have arisen for them during the class. It is particularly useful if the counselor who treats them has experienced PAIRS language and concepts, and can refer to them or use them in counseling.

We have also found that some single, separated, or divorced men have chosen to take PAIRS on their own wanting to know what will help a relationship work out or understand what destroyed a past relationship. Anecdotally, we have found that simply doing the DTR with their children and former spouse on weekly family visits restored some marriages. We have also seen divorced couples who chose to attend PAIRS as individuals who restored their marriages when they discovered what had gone wrong and learned how to change it. For those for whom the marriage could not be restored (e.g., committed to someone else, could not forgive what had gone wrong, etc.), participating in PAIRS allowed the couple to become less bitter and cooperate as friends.

Although it is beyond the scope of the chapter to discuss the remaining classes of the PAIRS workshops, the interested reader is referred to Lori Gordon's books, including *Passage To Intimacy* (1993), and *Love Knots* (1990).

SUMMARY OF ISSUES RAISED IN THE CHAPTER

This chapter expands knowledge and understanding about a logical educational process for sustaining or restoring fulfilling couple relationships. It normalizes for many men an awareness of the lifelong need for emotional and physical intimacy. It provides a new language that is simple to understand and use. It allows the couple to share a common language of relationship that can be an efficient shorthand to communicate. It teaches emotional literacy and empathy. It provides a clear roadmap of how to reconnect when relationships have become distanced. Men relate to the logic of learning skills that allow them to feel masterful in this complex area of emotions and expression of feelings—an area where women are often far more skilled. PAIRS shows how to develop the necessary skills to actualize normal human needs. This training helps expand the notion of what it is to be a man, to connect to a more complete range of feelings, beliefs, and behaviors. It

provides experientially in the very first class, the enjoyment and experience of being emotionally open in a way that results in men feeling
closer to their partner. The training provides immediate problem-solving skills that men enjoy.

Men relate especially to the presentation of the concept of the logic of
emotion—that we move toward what is a pleasure and move away from
what is painful. They also appreciate that a way to experience pleasure
is through bonding by having emotional openness and physical closeness
with their loved one. The PAIRS tools and language provide a practical, logical sequence of skills and a toolkit (again, a relatable, masculine
comfort term) to choose from in various stressful situations that allow
men to achieve that goal of bonding. The skills are time limited. In class
time, practice time is limited to the agenda for the class. Couples are
advised when applying the tools in actual situations with one's spouse
that a time is mutually agreed upon in advance. For example, the daily
temperature reading is often agreed upon with a limit of 20 to 30 minutes, while the dialogue guide is often requested of one's spouse in the
range of 60 minutes so that the intention is that discussion will not go
on forever into the night. Control is kept in the conversation through
the structure of the tools and the permission for a specific timeframe.
Also, most tools require empathic listening or mirroring what they have
heard, yet the tools finish with a hug and no requirement to fix the
problem or agree with what has been said. This approach typically feels
more comfortable and diminishes the flooding and feelings of being
emotionally overwhelmed that many men can experience when talking
with their partners about feelings. By putting a logical structure to the
tools, there can be a sense of control and greater ease. Repeated suc-
cesses connecting this way with their partner can support the feeling of
mastery of what had previously been, for most men, unchartered territory of vulnerability and emotional openness together.

REFERENCES

Daire, A. (2009). *Results of highly distressed marriages participating in 9-18 hour PAIRS workshops.* Unpublished research study prepared for PAIRS Foundation. University of Central Florida, FL.

DeMaria, R. (1998). *Satisfaction of married couples who participated in a marriage enrichment program: PAIRS.* Unpublished doctoral dissertation, Bryn Mawr College, Bryn Mawr, PA.

Durana, C. (1998). Enhancing marital intimacy through psychoeducation: The PAIRS program. *The Family Journal, 5*(3), 204–215.

Framo, J. (1965). *Intensive family therapy.* New York: Harper & Row.

Fromm, E. (1956). *The art of loving.* New York: Harper & Row.

Gordon, L. (1990). *Love knots: How to untangle everyday frustrations and argu-ments.* New York: Dell.

Gordon, L. (1993). *Passage to intimacy.* New York: Simon & Schuster.

Special Populations and Issues

11

Male-Affirmative Couple Sex Therapy

BARRY MCCARTHY AND ALISA A. BREETZ

Sex therapy is best conceptualized as a subspecialty of couple therapy. As is typical for couple therapy, the majority of clinicians conducting sex therapy are female. In addition, it is typically the woman who initiates couple therapy because she is disappointed in the man and the marriage, and hopes that therapy can resolve the problems. If sex therapy is initiated because of a female sexual problem (female inhibited desire or nonorgasmic response), the man is generally a willing participant. However, if therapy is initiated to address a male sexual problem (especially inhibited desire, erectile dysfunction, or ejaculatory inhibition), the man is often a very reluctant client. In such cases, he often avoids therapy. A little known fact is that when couples totally stop being sexual it is almost always the man's decision (McCarthy & Metz, 2008). He has lost his comfort and confidence sexually. Sex is now a source of frustration and embarrassment rather than desire, pleasure, and satisfaction. His decision is typically made unilaterally and conveyed nonverbally. In fact, often the man blames the woman rather than being honest with himself and his partner. The woman often feels confused, not sure whether to blame him, herself, or the relationship.

Given the unique feelings of shame that many men feel about their sexual difficulties, as well as common tendencies to avoid therapy, we present in this chapter a male-affirmative approach to sex therapy. Male-affirmative couple sex therapy proposes a gender sensitive, prosex, and pro-relationship approach focused on acceptance of the inherent variable nature of sexual functioning and the need to integrate intimacy and eroticism to develop a couple sexual style that enhances relationship functioning. Although we present a case example that explores the issue of couple sex therapy for male hypoactive sexual desire disorder, or HSDD (better described as inhibited sexual desire), it is important to note at the outset that a male-affirmative model can be adopted when treating any sexual issue. In this chapter, we use the narrative of this particular case to model how a male-affirmative therapist can work with and speak to a male partner from an empathic stance.

MALE HYPOACTIVE SEXUAL DESIRE DISORDER (HSDD)

The great majority of both professional and lay public literature on HSDD focuses on the common problem of female HSDD. However, male HSDD is a very real problem, involving both primary and secondary manifestations. By far the most common pattern is secondary HSDD, often caused by sexual dysfunction, especially erectile dysfunction (ED) and ejaculatory inhibition (EI). In essence, the man has lost confidence with erections, intercourse, and orgasm. He has fallen into the cycle of anticipatory anxiety, viewing intercourse as a pass–fail performance test, and feeling increasing frustration and embarrassment leading to sexual avoidance. He feels, "I don't want to start something sexually that I can't finish." He not only stops intercourse sex but any kind of sensual or sexual touching. By age 65, approximately one-third of couples have ceased sexual activity, and by age 74 the percentage rises to two-thirds (Lindau et al., 2007). This is an unfortunate and unnecessary loss for the man, woman, and couple.

Perhaps as many as 10% of men experience primary HSDD (McCarthy & McDonald, 2009a). In essence, the man is not comfortable with and does not value intimate, interactive couple sexuality. The most common cause of primary HSDD is a sexual secret. The most common sexual secrets (by order of frequency) are

1. A variant arousal pattern (benign paraphilia)
2. Greater comfort with masturbatory sex (often with Internet porn) than couple sex
3. A history of sexual trauma that has not been dealt with
4. Conflicts over sexual orientation

Often these men blame the partner for the desire problem. A key assessment question to ask in addressing issues of sexual desire during an individual sexual history session is, "In a typical month how many orgasms do you have by any means?" Often the clinician will find a major imbalance, where a man might have 0 to 1 orgasms in partner sex, but 20 to 25 orgasms in masturbation. Typically, his partner is unaware of his hidden sexual life. Leading a "double life" is quite stressful. Usually it will lead to the painful revelation that the man has a major sexual secret that subverts intimate couple sexuality, although this revelation may not occur for years to come. The man is shocked when it does occur and tries desperately to win his partner back.

TRADITIONAL MALE SEXUAL SOCIALIZATION

The great majority of males learn to be orgasmic between ages 10 and 16, usually with masturbation, although some with nocturnal emissions. Being orgasmic with partner sex usually occurs between ages 15 and 20, sometimes during intercourse but often with erotic, nonintercourse sex (manual, oral, or rubbing stimulation). The great majority of young males find that desire, erection, and orgasm are easy, highly predictable, and totally under their control. The most important factor for adolescent and young adult males is that sexual response is autonomous; he can experience desire, arousal, and orgasm and need nothing from his partner. As he ages and becomes involved in more serious relationships, maintaining this criteria of autonomous sexuality and perfect intercourse performance is self-defeating but difficult to change. The traditional image of male sexuality is reinforced in R-rated movies as well as porn videos; he is always turned on, ready to have "sex with any woman, anytime, and in any situation." The learning that "real sex" is about autonomy, control, and perfect performance is ultimately self-defeating for the man, woman, and couple.

Primary Prevention of Sexual Desire Problems

Whereas the traditional approach to sexuality focused on arousal and orgasm, the new mantra for healthy sexuality is to focus on desire, pleasure, and satisfaction (Foley, Kope, & Sugrue, 2011). Early in a relationship, most men experience romantic love/passionate sex/idealization. These are very special feelings—the stuff of a good movie, novel, or love song. Unfortunately, this relationship phase usually lasts between 6 months and 2 years. The function of romantic love/passionate sex is to give the man the courage to be involved in a relationship.

When the relationship becomes a serious, ongoing one or a marital commitment, the task for the couple is to develop a sexual style that integrates intimacy and eroticism (McCarthy & McCarthy, 2009). The sooner the man learns to view the woman as his intimate and erotic friend and to value interactive couple sex, the better.

The first key to primary prevention of male desire problems, therefore, is to maintain a cycle of positive anticipation, pleasure-oriented sexuality, and a regular rhythm of sexual connection. The focus of healthy male sexuality is primarily touch oriented (rather than visual stimuli) and interactive (rather than autonomous).

The great majority of work on treating inhibited sexual desire has focused on women. Advances in the treatment of female desire disorders can, however, inform our work with men. The breakthrough concept in treating inhibited female sexual desire is that of "responsive desire" (Basson, 2007). Rather than hoping for a spontaneous sexual charge, the woman is open to touch (both giving and receiving) as well as emotional needs for connection. As receptivity and responsivity increase, then she is aware of sexual desire. In addition, she feels she has choices of how to proceed: (a) sex play to intercourse; (b) enjoy the sensual connection; (c) do one-way or mutual erotic, nonintercourse sex; (d) functional but less involving intercourse; (e) take a rain check. The sense of choice or alternative scenarios breaks the "intercourse or nothing" power struggle.

The concept of responsive sexual desire is very applicable and helpful for men after age 50 (and even earlier). Rather than wait for the cue of a spontaneous erection or an erotic fantasy, receptivity to sensual and playful touch can elicit male sexual desire. Perhaps the greatest aphrodisiac is an involved, aroused partner. Especially as men age, a major psychosexual skill is learning to "piggyback" his arousal on her arousal. Couples who maintain a healthy sexuality in their 50s, 60s, 70s, and 80s report sexuality feels more genuine and human. They need each other sexually in a way they didn't in their 20s and 30s.

The second key to maintaining sexual desire and function with the aging of the man and the maturing of the relationship is to adopt the good-enough sex model (Metz & McCarthy, 2007). Far too many men cling to the traditional model that real sex should be equated with high eroticism, high frequency, and most of all constant control and perfect intercourse performance. Men who accept this model of sexuality are often the ones who stop being sexual in their 50s and 60s because they cannot maintain the unrealistic performance demands of autonomous erections and perfect intercourse. The truth is that a man's penis is not a machine but an integral, positive part of a complex human being. His penis wilts under perfectionistic performance demands.

Rather than clinging to the perfect intercourse performance model, the "wise" man and couple embrace a variable, flexible model of sexual pleasure and function. The focus is on comfort, pleasure, arousal, and erotic flow to intercourse. When sex does not flow to intercourse, the man (without apologizing or panicking) can comfortably transition to either an erotic, nonintercourse scenario or a cuddly, sensual scenario. Perhaps 85% of sexual encounters will flow to intercourse rather than the traditional pass–fail intercourse test, with the demand that every sexual encounter end in intercourse. At times, the sexual encounter might be more pleasurable and satisfying for the woman, and he can accept this as a normal part of couple flexibility and variability. We urge the man and couple to adopt the good-enough sex model as first class and a wise choice (Metz & McCarthy, 2010). Clinging to the traditional perfect sex performance model results in sexual avoidance and a nonsexual relationship.

The Psychobiosocial Versus Biomedical Model of Male Sexual Dysfunction

The introduction of Viagra (Goldstein et al., 1998) revolutionized professional and public perceptions of male sexual dysfunction generally and erectile dysfunction specifically. The promise (promoted by the marketing ads) was with the "little blue pill" the man would return to totally predictable, autonomous erections of his youth. The woman's only role was to urge her man to consult his physician for the pill and be awed by the result.

Viagra (as well as Cialis and Levitra) serves to enhance vascular efficacy as well as to have a placebo effect. However, it does not return the man to totally predictable erections and intercourse. The best estimate is that 65% to 85% of encounters result in erections sufficient for intercourse. This is a reasonable outcome but not what the man was led to expect and not in keeping with the traditional male sex performance model. In reality, the dropout rate for pro-erection medications is extremely high, 40% to 80%, resulting in a demoralization and nonsexual relationship (McCarthy & Fucito, 2005).

The psychobiosocial model focuses on a comprehensive assessment of psychological, biological or medical, and relational or social factors that promote and subvert sexual function. In terms of desire and function, a positive psychological factor is viewing the development and maintenance of healthy sexuality as a positive challenge. Biologically or medically a positive factor is emphasizing good health habits and using all his resources to deal with illness and side effects of medications. Relationally, an important factor is to view the woman as his intimate, erotic friend. These models reflect very different ways to understand, assess, treat, and design a relapse prevention program for male and couple sexuality (McCarthy & McDonald, 2009b).

A CASE STUDY OF ASSESSMENT AND TREATMENT: MICHAEL AND ZITA

This case study focuses on primary HSDD, the less common form of male sexual desire dysfunction. However, as previously noted, the treatment model is quite similar to dealing with secondary inhibited desire and other sexual problems in a male-affirmative couple sex therapy approach. Therapeutically, the key to this approach is to address male sexual problems in an empathic, respectful manner so that the feelings of shame most men feel about sexual problems is not triggered. Rather, the man becomes aware that this is a common sexual problem, which can be addressed and is changeable. The couple can develop a new, more resilient male and couple sexual style that integrates intimacy, pleasuring, eroticism, and satisfaction.

As usually occurs, the initial phone call was made by the female partner, 39-year-old Zita. She had been married to 53-year-old Michael for 3 years. This was Zita's first marriage and Michael's second. The referral to Dr. McCarthy had come from Zita's individual therapist who thought Michael was depressed and needed individual therapy (Zita's therapist had not met Michael but had been hearing about him during the 6 months of therapy with Zita). During the 10-minute initial phone call, Zita said Michael was a very reluctant client and she had issued an ultimatum that if he didn't reverse the nonsexual state of their marriage she would leave him. Under this duress, he agreed to accompany her to an initial therapy session. Not an ideal way to begin couple therapy.

I (Dr. McCarthy) described to Zita the four-session assessment model I usually recommend: an initial couple session; individual psychological, relational, and sexual history sessions for each partner; and a couple feedback session to develop a treatment plan (McCarthy & Thestrup, 2008). In clinical practice, I try not to be rigid, and certainly not coercive, but many men and couples do appreciate having a structure to the initial therapeutic experience. Zita accepted this recommendation and the structure appealed to Michael.

The initial couple session was very tense and awkward. Michael was a silent, embarrassed client, whereas Zita was very verbal and activated. My first concern was to not reinforce the couple therapy stereotype, prevalent in sitcoms and the media, of the woman in distress controlling the session with her complaints while the man is passive, resentful, and wants to escape the aversive milieu.

One way to refocus the session was to ask Michael about his hopes and intentions before this marriage. He'd hoped for a satisfying, stable marriage that included being sexual. He saw Zita as a strong contrast to his ex-wife. Michael said he found Zita very attractive. Her love for him and pro-sexual approach had been like a breath of fresh air after his divorce. Michael said he still loved her and found her attractive, and did not understand how and why she had become so critical of him and so sexually demanding. Rather than allow a blame–counterblame dynamic to dominate our first session, I turned to Zita and asked her hopes and intentions when she began the relationship with Michael. Zita visibly brightened and recounted how she'd been highly enthusiastic about leaving war-torn Yugoslavia where she had been brutally raped by Serbian soldiers, resulting in the loss of her ability to have children. She saw herself as pro-marriage and pro-sexual and found in Michael a man demoralized by a bitter divorce. Michael had been able to successfully continue in his career as an accountant, but emotionally, relationally, and sexually he was highly dysfunctional.

They recounted their wedding ceremony in Ashville, North Carolina, surrounded by natural beauty and the goodwill of a nondenominational minister, the photographer, and limo driver. Their honeymoon was at the famous Biltmore Hotel. It was a very romantic and sexual weekend.

But the mood turned as Zita recalled their return to Washington, DC, and her growing fear that Michael had pulled a "bait and switch." I interrupted again and asked if she believed the change in sexual desire was intentional. My question resulted in a poignant pause, with Zita's eyes filling with tears as she looked at Michael. He emphatically shook his head saying yes there was a change, but that it was not planned or intentional.

It was apparent in the initial couple session that Zita and Michael were caught in a cycle of hurt and demoralization. They were unclear of what had caused the desire problem and sexual avoidance, and how to address it. In reviewing what they had tried thus far (so past mistakes were not repeated), Michael reported that he had consulted his internist who had prescribed Viagra and later a testosterone gel. He had also consulted a psychiatrist who prescribed antidepressant medication, but Michael was not able to tolerate the side effects. As a couple, they had consulted a pastoral counselor and attended a weekend Christian retreat. As previously mentioned, Zita was seeing an individual therapist. Release of information forms were signed so I could have the benefit of previous clinicians' perspectives on Michael, Zita, and their marital and sexual problems. Rather than waiting for a written report, which was unlikely to come, I called the clinicians the next week and spoke by phone.

At the end of the session, I usually lend the couple a short chapter on desire problems, ask them to read it together, and then discuss both the content and its emotional meaning for them (McCarthy & McCarthy, 2003). Reading itself does not cure people, but it does have two main functions that are particularly valuable for men. First, reading leads to destigmatization of the sexual problem (for example, by teaching that the majority of men do not find Viagra to be a miracle drug) and explains that the most common time for a nonsexual marriage is the early years of the marriage.

Second, it provides empirical evidence of treatment efficacy. Males typically respect a knowledge-based, empirical approach, and learning that sexual dysfunction and couple sex therapy for HSDD has been studied and validated sets positive, realistic expectations for change. Michael was surprised to learn that when couples totally stop being sexual it is usually the man's choice. This made him feel less stigmatized and isolated. Even more important was Michael's learning that this was a changeable problem if the couple worked together as an intimate team. Michael thought of himself as a rational problem solver, but he had felt totally alone and hopeless in dealing with sexual problems, especially in confronting issues of a secret sexual life and sexual desire. This experience is not rare. My estimate is that 80% or 85% of people have sensitive or secret material they have not shared with the spouse (McCarthy, 2002). This is much more likely to be disclosed in an individual session where the spouse is not present.

If the clinician wants a clear picture of each person's psychological, relational, and sexual history, an individual history session is crucial. The session begins with the clinician saying:

> I want to understand your personal strengths and vulnerabilities both before you met and in this relationship. I want you to be as honest and

forthcoming as possible. At the end, I will ask whether there is anything that is sensitive or secret. I will not share that without your permission, but I need to know all I can in order to help you to address these difficult emotional and sexual problems.

Typically, I begin the individual history chronologically by asking how the client learned about sexuality, which allows us to explore formal education, religious background, and family-of-origin learnings, especially parents as a marital and sexual model, as well as influences of peers, culture, and values. I want to explore psychological, as well as relational and sexual learnings in childhood and adolescence, both positive and problematic. I want to not only establish whether something happened but the person's attitudes and feelings at the time and in retrospect. Once I establish how old the person was when he left home I ask the open-ended question, "As you think about your childhood and adolescence, what was the most negative, confusing, guilt inducing, or traumatic thing that happened to you?" This same question is asked at the end of the history about the person's entire life. The question of guilt-inducing, abusive, or traumatic sexual experiences is particularly important for males, who tend to minimize or deny sexual or other types of neglect or abuse.

It is also crucial to carefully assess young adult and adult relational and sexual experiences, again exploring attitudes and feelings at the time and in retrospect. A good open-ended question is to ask, "As you look back on your dating and sexual relationships, which were the most positive relationships and what were the most positive learnings?" The same format can then be used to explore the most negative relationships and learnings, including sexually transmitted infections, unwanted pregnancies, being sexually humiliated or rejected, and so forth. A particularly valuable question is to inquire what was happening psychologically, relationally, and sexually 6 months before meeting the spouse. Was this a positive choice relationship, a rebound relationship, or one made in desperation?

In the case of Zita and Michael, there were a number of significant experiences and themes. Zita's history contained turmoil, abuse, and trauma, but she saw herself as a resilient survivor who emphasized the role of love and sex in providing life meaning. Michael's sexual life story was more traditional and less dramatic but clearly demonstrated his psychological and sexual vulnerabilities. He grew up in an intact but very conflictual and nonloving family. His mother said she did not love his father but married because she was pregnant and stayed with him out of duty to Michael and his three siblings (Michael had an older sister and brother, and a younger brother). One of the hidden family truths was that the mother slept in the upstairs bedroom and the father slept in the basement where there was a stash of sex magazines and videos. Michael's brothers and sister married early because of unplanned pregnancies. Michael was determined this would not happen to him. He described himself as a socially shy adolescent who focused on academics and sports. This was true but the real issue was that he compulsively masturbated to a narrow fetish theme of women's large, formed buttocks. Michael's sexual fetish pattern involved exclusively looking at and touching this body part rather than interactive couple sexuality. This fetish arousal pattern was highly secretive, erotic, and shameful; he shared it with no one. Michael established a high frequency of masturbating exclusively to the fetish theme at least daily and often two to three times a day. Like many men with a secret sexual life, Michael used sex as a way to deal with a range of negative experiences and emotions (loneliness, boredom, and frustration), to go to sleep, to wake in the morning, and to deal with anxiety.

Michael was a 29 year-old virgin when he met his first wife, Sunchu, who was from Thailand and in the United States on a work visa. They met at work; she was very impressed by Michael's work ethic. He was a very focused, successful young professional. Many relationships start as work friendships, which can be a very good way to begin. Unfortunately, for Michael it accentuated the split between his professional self-confidence and his shame over a secret sex life. Sunchu fell in love with him, and her enthusiasm for the relationship and sexual touching was very exciting for Michael. Before marriage, Michael and Sunchu never engaged in intercourse. Her preferred sexual scenario was receiving oral stimulation, and Michael surprised himself by enjoying cunnilingus and her arousal. While orally stimulating her, he would manually stimulate himself to orgasm. This erotic scenario was functional in their relationship.

Sunchu assumed that Michael was conservatively religious and that was why they did not have intercourse, and he willingly reinforced this misperception. Michael experienced high anxiety at their wedding night but was amazed that with her sexual enthusiasm and guidance; intercourse sex went well for the first 5 weeks. Two things occurred that broke the positive cycle. First, Michael began to stroke her buttocks as part of their sex play, and Sunchu made a cutting remark that she wanted a "bush man" not a "butt man." Michael felt humiliated, totally avoided any buttock contact, and regressed to his traditional fetish masturbatory pattern. Second, she became pregnant, an outcome both were very enthusiastic about. She was uncomfortable with intercourse during the pregnancy, and Michael was glad to return to their erotic scenario of cunnilingus and self-stimulation. Neither expected that avoidance would take over and that they would not return to intercourse during this marriage.

They were cooperative, involved parents and life proceeded with an erotic, nonintercourse marriage. In a typical month, they would have partner sex 2 to 3 times, and Michael would masturbate using the fetish 15 to 20 times a month. He was satisfied with life, work, marriage, and family, and was very proud of having a better career and financial success than anyone in his family.

This pattern was broken after 8 years of marriage when Sunchu discovered his use of a large buttock site on the Internet. She was very judgmental, calling him a pervert. The next 2 years were extremely painful with both partners consulting individual and couple therapists and Michael taking antidepressant medication. Sunchu began an affair, partly because she wanted a second child. The divorce process was extremely bitter and painful, but Michael was able to focus on being a cooperative parent and walling off her personal and sexual criticism. As a divorced, 39-year-old man Michael continued to excel at work, be a good father, and even a helpful friend with Sunchu's son from her second marriage.

During the next 11 years, Michael's major sexual outlet was masturbation, although he would go to strip clubs and pay to engage in buttock stimulation, at times to orgasm. Michael balanced work, parenting, and sports. He had every intention of staying single until he met Zita, who had a low-paying administrative position for a firm Michael's company did business with.

A prime attraction to Zita was her neediness and vulnerability. Zita was the first woman he ever introduced his daughter to as well as his "para-" son. Even his ex-wife liked Zita. A big issue, however, was Zita's immigration status. When he married Zita, she was given the coveted green card, which solved a major problem for her and ensured her sense of security. Again, the theme for Michael was the split between his life as a caring, responsible parent and professional with his secret, shameful sexual life. Michael did not share this sensitive information and dilemma with Zita.

At first, their sex life was positive. She was very responsive to receiving oral stimulation as well as open to buttock stimulation. Although she found it unusual that Michael would use self-stimulation before intercourse, Zita was sexually responsive with both erotic and intercourse stimulation, which enhanced Michael's sexual responsivity. This was Michael's best experience with partner sex. For Zita, it was acceptable partner sex, but she was sure it would improve over time.

The incident that destabilized their sexual relationship occurred 3 weeks before the wedding. While Michael was giving oral stimulation and touching her buttocks with one hand and his penis with the other hand, Zita switched positions to do simultaneous oral stimulation. Michael felt sexually intimidated and self-conscious. Like perhaps 15% to 25% of men, Michael was not comfortable receiving oral stimulation; it was a turn-off rather than a turn-on. He tried to compensate by returning to their typical erotic scenario, but she reacted negatively. It was a hurtful, confusing, alienating experience that they did not process in a helpful manner. That was their last sexual encounter before the wedding.

Zita was looking forward to sex on their honeymoon, but Michael experienced a high degree of performance anxiety. When she initiated sex, he tried to reintroduce their old erotic scenario, but Zita said now that we're married let's make "wild, passionate love." This totally destabilized Michael, and he was in full panic mode. He lost his erection and desperately tried to get it back by rubbing her buttocks while doing self-stimulation. Zita experienced Michael as pathetic and obsessed, and she felt terribly hurt and rejected. The worst time to talk about sexual issues is after a negative sexual interaction, nude, lying in bed. Each partner feels very vulnerable and can say and do destructive things. Unfortunately, that's exactly what happened between Zita and Michael. Between tears and anger, Zita said this was the worst night of her life, even worse than being raped during the war. She called Michael a pervert and said she hated him. Michael blamed everything on Zita, saying she was a fat pig who manipulated him into marrying her for the green card. Even 3 years later, both partners felt incredibility violated by the destructive fight that evening.

Over the next 3 years Michael and Zita intermittently tried to address the nonsexual state of their marriage with increasing frustration and alienation. Michael felt blamed and attacked by Zita. He reluctantly consulted his internist, then a urologist, and then an endocrinologist. He also went to a pastoral counselor, a Christian sex counselor, and a religious weekend marital enhancement retreat. Michael felt that the retreat was the only helpful intervention. The retreat stressed love, commitment, and honoring the sanctity of marriage. Michael was very fearful that Zita would repeat the pattern of his first marriage and leave him for another man.

When individually asked about marital and sexual goals, they were complementary not adversarial. Michael emphasized his desire for a loving, committed marriage where he hoped that sex could be revitalized. Zita emphasized a satisfying sexuality where she felt Michael had a genuine desire for her sexually. Zita did want a secure marriage but was increasingly adamant that she would not tolerate a nonsexual marriage.

Each spouse wanted to "red flag" sensitive or secret material. Michael did not want to disclose the history, function, and meaning of his fetish arousal nor what an anxious intercourse performer he was. Zita was willing to discuss everything except how strongly she wanted the marriage to work and how hopeless she felt. I asked each person whether there was a positive reason to maintain the secret, and like the vast majority of individuals, neither Michael nor Zita had a positive reason. I then asked each of them about the negative motivation for maintaining the secret. For Michael, it was shame and the fear that Zita would be repulsed and leave him. For Zita, it was the belief that unless Michael saw her as strong and threatening, he would not change. Negative motivation almost never promotes healthy behavior. With gentle lobbying, each agreed to share the sensitive or secret material at the couple feedback session. As previously mentioned, the best estimate is that 80% to 85% of partners have sensitive or secret material they are afraid to share with the partner. The great majority give permission to share this in a therapeutic manner at the couple feedback session.

Couple Feedback Session

The couple feedback session is the core intervention in this therapy model and serves to bridge the assessment/intervention phase. Typically, this is a 90-minute session with three elements:

1. Describe a new, genuine individual and couple narrative with strengths and vulnerabilities—Focusing on the development of a coherent, comprehensive narrative about psychological, relational, and sexual strength is an important feature of a male-sensitive approach, as it helps to set the stage for the man to address the secret fetish arousal without it completely overshadowing other positive aspects of the individual and relationship. In the case of Michael, throughout his life he had accepted a contingent view of himself and his sexual self-esteem. At 53, it was not too late to accept who he was as a sexual man and to commit to freeing himself from the "poison" of the fetish.
2. Establish a therapeutic plan and agreement, the most common being a 6-month, good-faith effort to establish a healthy couple sexual style. As previously noted, many males avoid therapy to address sexual issues. While part of this avoidance is often linked to feelings of shame, male clients may also have doubts about the efficacy or uncertainty about the process of treatment. The 6-month therapeutic plan allows both individuals to establish positive, realistic expectations regarding the psychological, relational, and sexual effort that will be required. Such a plan may also put many men at ease by responding to their desire for structure and a plan of action. In the case of Michael and Zita, the development of a plan helped Michael to enlist Zita as his intimate, erotic ally in integrating sexuality into his life and marriage, and committed both partners to work toward change.
3. Half of therapy occurs at their home rather than in the therapy session so the exercises facilitate the couple developing a new sexual style. Psychosexual skill exercises utilizing the format of read, talk, and do, provide the man with "tools" to help develop sexual comfort and skill. Such an approach may also appeal to their comfort with being pragmatic. This is especially true when dealing with shame-laden material that may otherwise be avoided in less structured formats that may not provide a framework for how to begin to address such sensitive topics.

In addition to these three elements, a core, overarching feature of successful couple sex therapy, particularly in interactions with men, is to be empathic and respectful rather than blaming or shaming. In this case, I empathically supported Michael's disclosure of his "shameful secret arousal" by remarking that it took courage to disclose this and that the fetish must have made him feel lonely and isolated. Michael's secret sexual life had never been shared with anyone. The fetish was highly erotic, shameful, and secret. These factors are a poisonous combination. I assured Michael this material would be processed in a supportive manner, but needed to be dealt with rather than allowed to again recede into the shadows.

The therapist is very active during the couple feedback session. The emphasis is on developing a genuine narrative that incorporates the person's psychological, relational, and sexual strengths as well as vulnerabilities. In this case, I started with Michael's strengths, which were multiple: He was a well-intentioned, highly functional man who very much loved Zita and wanted a satisfying, stable marriage; he'd always been sexually interested and regularly experienced desire, arousal, and orgasm; he admired Zita's psychological resiliency and her pro-relationship, pro-sexual values; he was now ready to address difficult emotional and sexual issues. Michael brought major vulnerabilities to this marriage: Chief among these was the highly erotic, highly secret and shameful fetish involving large buttocks; high anxiety about rejection and abandonment; a history of a split between confidence with masturbation and lack of confidence in intimate, interactive couple sex; being an anxious sexual performer with Zita, especially regarding intercourse; and fear of Zita's reaction to these sensitive and secret disclosures.

In this part of the feedback session, I am looking directly at Michael and speaking directly to him. It is crucial that the feedback be genuine and specific, especially about Michael learning to be honest and clear about sexual scenarios and techniques rather than hiding and feeling shameful. Especially important is to reinforce the cognition that Michael deserves sexual intimacy, pleasure, and satisfaction in his life with Zita.

Michael was asked if the narrative was on track and whether he wanted to add or edit anything. Michael replied it was right on and he now felt a greater understanding of himself and his sexual dilemmas. I was pleased with Michael's reaction. Although he was very anxious, he did not feel shamed. I then turned to Zita and gave her the opportunity to clarify information and perceptions. I did not ask "How do you feel about this?" because I wanted her to focus on Michael's sexual story, new information, and to process this with moderate emotion (not the extremes of dramatic attacks or denial). The major issue that Zita needed to clarify was whether this was the full story or "another shoe would drop." Michael assured Zita this was the genuine story; there were no other secrets. The therapist being both inquisitive and respectful about the reality of Michael's secret sexual life provided a good model of processing for Michael (as well as Zita). Rather than feeling shameful, Michael could look at the pattern of his secret sexual life and understand how psychologically expensive and draining it had been for him. Rather than a compartmentalized factor, it had controlled his sexual self and his approach to couple sex.

Using the same format for Zita's narrative, it was revealed that the most important issue for Zita were fears of being duped by Michael and an uncertainly about whether he could commit to establishing a genuine sexual connection. Michael acknowledged her dilemma and assured Zita that he was committed to a best faith effort to establish a new couple sexual style.

This set the stage for the agreement to commit to a 6-month effort to creating a new, intimate, interactive couple sexual style that integrated intimacy and eroticism. It was clear to both Michael and Zita that they would have to understand, process, and accept each other as their individual and couple stories evolved. Even more important was their commitment to reengage in terms of intimacy, pleasuring, and eroticism.

While a large portion of the therapeutic change occurs in the therapist's office, perhaps even more occurs in the home, particularly while engaging in psychosexual skill exercises. The first assigned exercise to Michael and Zita was to develop a "trust position." The exercise was done in the nude in the privacy of their home where they could share emotional and physical feelings of security and trust. The position they created was Zita nestled in Michael's arms where they verbally acknowledged the good feelings of being together as an intimate team. The trust position served them well throughout the psychosexual skill experiences as well as outside of them. Whether feeling anxious, having a negative sexual experience, or feeling discouraged, they could use the trust position as a "port in the storm," and experience the comfort and support of being there for each other.

Following the four-session assessment process, couple sex therapy began on a weekly basis. The format (although flexible) began with a fine-grain analysis of the cognitions, behaviors, and feelings (both positive and negative) generated by the psychosexual exercise experiences and discussions during the last week, a continual examination of individual, and couple strengths and vulnerabilities, exploration of the roles and meanings of their new couple sexual style (the bulk of the session), and discussion of how to implement the next assigned homework exercise.

With Zita's permission, I again contacted her individual therapist to share with the clinician the treatment plan and to urge her to take a new perspective on Zita's role as an affirmative partner in the marriage. The therapist, who practiced in psychodynamic and feminist traditions, had previously focused on the theme of why Zita was allowing herself to be revictimized in this marriage. I hoped to encourage an openness to seeing couple sex therapy as a process to heal the hurt and alienation, and as an opportunity to promote healthy intimacy and sexuality for both partners. It helped the individual therapist to conceptualize Michael's problem as sexual shame and avoidance rather than depression and mistreatment of Zita. This approach was helpful in Zita's individual treatment as well as in reducing her threats of abandoning Michael and the marriage. In both media depictions and the therapy field there is a tendency toward male bashing within couple treatment, which is to the detriment of the man, woman, couple, and sexuality. I was determined that my work with Michael and Zita not become a forum for male bashing of Michael.

Maintaining an empathic, respectful approach with Michael was necessary but would not be sufficient to make significant changes. In terms of psychoeducation, it was helpful for Michael to gain an understanding that his erotic maps and his brain neural pathways were very narrow and that shame and self-blame only exacerbated the problem. In trying to create a new intimate, comfortable, pleasurable, and erotic sexual response pattern for Michael and a comfortable, functional couple sexual style required conscious, intentional work. Michael was hopeful this would be a worthwhile investment. The big question for Michael (and Zita) was what role the buttock fetish would play in this new personal and couple sexuality. For most men and couples, it is not possible to successfully integrate a controlling fetish pattern into their couple sexual style (McCarthy & Cintron, 2005). The fetish is too narrow and controlling, involving a rigid erotic pattern that does not integrate into intimate couple sexuality. Zita's willingness to try to incorporate buttock stimulation was seen by Michael as emotionally generous. The reality was any integration would need to involve touching and flexibility because she did not have the large buttocks of his erotic fetish.

In terms of psychosexual skill exercises, I discussed the comfort exercise of experimenting with touching inside and outside the bedroom, clothed and nude, verbal and nonverbal, mutual and taking turns. Within this framework, Michael and Zita were encouraged to experiment with whether it was possible to incorporate buttock stimulation into their touching repertoire. They were urged to do this at least three times to see how it felt to each of them in terms of comfort, pleasure, and eroticism. Zita reported that buttock stimulation was comfortable, and when she was already feeling responsive, it was moderately pleasurable, but she did not find it erotic. However, if Michael found it erotic, then she now felt open to it. Michael found the experiences awkward, neither pleasurable nor erotic. This surprised, disappointed, and frustrated him. Michael's fear was that his ex-wife was right—he was a "sexual loser." He also feared that without the fetish he would never be able to have an orgasm and that eventually Zita would leave him. This is a typical fear of men who have a secret sexual life, that without the fetish they cannot be sexually functional.

Zita's observation that Michael was more comfortable and responsive when he was the giving partner was very important to him and to later treatment interventions. I asked Michael whether he thought Zita valued the comfort and trust experiences. He was so self-conscious and performance oriented that he confessed he really didn't know. Zita assured Michael that she valued the intimacy and pleasuring they were now experiencing. She reinforced that the most important thing for her was the feeling that Michael desired her and wanted to share pleasure and eroticism with her. Perhaps because she stated it so clearly and positively in the therapy session, or perhaps because Michael was now ready to hear it, this time Zita's message got through. With my support of his expressing his intentions and feelings, Michael responded that he did desire Zita both emotionally and sexually, and wanted to be involved and present in their sensual and sexual encounters. Michael's desire was to give Zita pleasure and enjoy her erotic response. Yet, Michael feared he would not be able to discover or share his own pleasure and eroticism.

This is a very common dilemma with men who have a variant arousal pattern and who compulsively masturbate to narrow erotic stimuli. They are fearful they will have no capacity for intimate couple sexuality, which involves sharing pleasure and eroticism. After the woman deals with her feelings of resentment and betrayal over his secret sex life, she can be a powerful intimate and erotic ally. Typically, the woman is much more optimistic about pleasure and sexuality than the man.

Both the professional and public literature emphasizes a history of childhood sexual abuse or trauma as the leading cause of male desire problems. Although that is certainly an issue that needs to be carefully assessed clinically, to assume that it is the problem is not just a mistake but can result in iatrogenic damage. In fact, there is a growing literature that for men the factor of neglect, especially emotionally, can be an important causal factor. In Michael's situation, there were a number of contributing factors to his fetish arousal and psychosexual skill deficits. The key factor in Michael's understanding and change process was not to anticipate a final pass–fail sex performance test but to slowly and carefully confront inhibitions and build a new sensual and sexual repertoire emphasizing comfort, pleasure, arousal, and erotic flow naturally culminating in orgasm during couple sex.

An individualized psychosexual skill exercise was to have Michael stimulate himself to orgasm while Zita held him, talked to him, and stroked his chest. Michael found this an involved, pleasurable experience and was easily orgasmic. Seeing that Michael could be sexually interested and functional with her involvement rather than needing to retreat to his closed off secret world was reassuring for Zita, but she continued to be puzzled by his not valuing interactive sex.

During the next month, the psychosexual skill exercises emphasized self-entrancement arousal and increasing Michael's comfort in developing receptivity and responsivity to Zita's touch. In the therapy sessions, I emphasized that 53 was not too late to learn to enjoy sexual touch and that Michael needed to be aware of both his turn-ons and turn-offs. He found this a daunting task, so we broke it into smaller steps. Michael was encouraged to write one turn-off and give the paper to Zita, who then would verbally agree to refrain from that sexual technique. His major turn-off was simultaneous oral-genital stimulation. Not only did Zita commit to not engage in it, but she told Michael it wasn't a positive technique for her either. I made it clear to Michael that being able to say no to sex was natural and healthy, and did not make him less of a man. In fact, you cannot really say yes to sex unless you can first say no. Michael's next assignment was to identify up to three additional turn-offs he wanted to veto and to see whether Zita could accept the veto without feeling hurt or rejected. Michael could not approach Zita as his intimate, erotic friend when he was afraid of her or when he felt so guilty about the past that he couldn't create a new couple sexual style. In fact, there was only one other technique that Michael wanted to veto—anal sex.

Asking for nonfetish turn-ons was even more of a therapeutic challenge for Michael. Zita was more of a verbal interaction person than a writer, and she agreed to talk to Michael at home in their trust position about her favorite erotic scenarios and techniques. Michael had choices: He could accept these requests, modify them, or say it would not be erotic for him (and therefore them as a couple). Zita made it clear that playful sex and erotic, non-intercourse sex were the most important scenarios for her. This information reduced Michael's anticipatory and performance anxiety. In response, Michael made two requests that Zita was surprised by but open to. First was to accept him using self-stimulation in addition to her stimulation to enhance arousal and erotic flow. Second, for her to initiate intercourse and guide intromission so he reduced "spectatoring."

Both because of scheduling issues and therapeutic strategy, sessions were reduced to every other week. However, Michael and Zita were encouraged to keep the time for themselves: to do a psychosexual skill exercise, go out to breakfast, take a walk, have a discussion about the past, or discuss future hopes and plans. A major theme for Michael was to end the split between his professional competence and rational problem solving and his secret sexual life. Zita came to understand and accept Michael's complexity. A very helpful intervention was his accompanying Zita to her individual therapy session and sitting in for the first half of the session. Zita's individual therapist shared with her how helpful it was to meet Michael. He was no longer a stereotype of a secretive male but a real, complex human being.

A major challenge in therapy with Zita and Michael was their different needs and approaches to therapy goals. Zita was more comfortable with the therapeutic milieu of support and exploration. Her prime need was to feel emotionally and sexually validated in the marriage. Once the secrecy and avoidance of couple sex was confronted, the change in Zita's cognitions and mood were remarkable.

Michael's approach to treatment was in stark contrast to Zita's. He accepted the importance of sharing information and creating a genuine intimate connection, but as a goal-oriented problem solver he felt stymied. Michael was grateful that Zita recommitted to him and the marriage, but he was dissatisfied with therapy progress. He was frustrated by his low sexual desire and ejaculatory inhibition, especially during intercourse. Zita strongly valued therapeutic processing, while Michael most valued specific psychosexual change exercises.

Rather than being adversarial, these perspectives were viewed as complementary. Especially important was Michael's request that Zita be an active participant in and problem solve with him about increasing arousal, erotic flow, and orgasm. The analogy that Michael found very helpful was when he went canoeing he'd learned to go with the flow of the river rather than try to paddle upstream. Michael could learn to go with the erotic flow, and identify and utilize orgasm triggers. The psychosexual skill exercise that was most valuable for Michael involved transitioning to intercourse at high levels of arousal, using multiple stimulation during intercourse, and having the freedom to use orgasm triggers during intercourse. These are key strategies in overcoming EI. The combination of psychoeducation; permission to confront inhibitions; turning to Zita as his intimate, erotic friend; and adopting the good-enough sex model rather than demanding perfect intercourse performance allowed Michael to accept himself sexually and value couple sexuality.

Relapse prevention is an integral component of sex therapy. Although not a perfect couple or perfect sexually, Michael and Zita had made significant emotional and sexual gains. The last two regularly scheduled sessions focused on individualizing a relapse prevention plan (Metz & McCarthy, 2004). For Zita, the most important issue was ensuring they would remain emotionally and sexually connected. They agreed that if 2 weeks went by without a pleasuring, erotic, or intercourse interaction that Zita would initiate the third week. If that did not occur, Michael would initiate the fourth week. If they went a month without a sensual or sexual encounter, Zita would call for a "booster session." This system kept them accountable so they would not slip into an avoidance cycle. Michael's fear was that he would regress to the EI pattern. To counter that, it was decided that if they had three encounters where he did not ejaculate, on the fourth encounter they would engage in an extensive pleasuring and eroticism experience that would include Michael pleasuring himself to orgasm while Zita was holding him and providing multiple stimulation, especially testicle stimulation.

Zita continued to worry that Michael would regress to his secret world of masturbating to fetish images of large buttocks on the Internet. Michael assured her he was committed to staying away from the "poison" of the secret sexual world that had so dominated his life. Michael agreed he would masturbate only when he felt sexual desire and Zita was not interested in being sexual. He would use erotic fantasy material, not Internet sites. Most important, he would deal directly with negative emotions, not use masturbation to "self-medicate." To reinforce transparency and accountability, Michael agreed to initiate a monthly check-in to disclose if there was any secret sex activity, or if he felt vulnerable to a mood, site, or situation. Michael realized that the core issue in relapse was secrecy, and he was committed to sharing his emotional and sexual life with Zita.

Michael and Zita agreed to 6-month, follow-up sessions for the next 2 years. The message is not to treat the marriage or couple sexuality with benign neglect. They would check in as well as set a new couple goal for the next 6 months.

SUMMARY

Male-affirmative couple sex therapy challenges common damaging stereotypes about men and sex. Most important is the unrealistic expectation that male sexuality is simple, with easy desire and arousal and total control and predictability. Under this commonly accepted sexual model, intercourse becomes a pass–fail test. The tyranny of such an approach increases the likelihood of men experiencing feelings of shame and disempowerment when they believe they have failed. Such feeling can prevent a male client from seeking treatment in the first place or can undermine the effectiveness of couple treatment if both partners are not fully committed. As modeled in this chapter, a male-sensitive approach to couple treatment provides important psychoeducation in that the clinician confronts the implications of a performance-focused sexual model head on and instead advocates for the variable, flexible good-enough sex model as a healthier approach to couple sexuality.

As described in this chapter, the male-sensitive therapist takes an empathic, respectful, and encouraging stance so as not to trigger feeling of shame. Treatment is also structured in a way that may appeal to males' desire for organization and action by providing the clients with a clear plan for treatment and outlining psychoeducational exercises that can act as tools and improve self-efficacy.

Rather than attempting to be neutral and value-free, the male-affirmative couple therapist takes a pro-sex and pro-relationship stance. The clinician values the man, woman, couple, and sexuality in their relationship. The message to the man and couple is to express sexuality so it plays a healthy role in the man's and couple's life, without becoming the sole focus of the couple relationship. The therapist encourages the integration of intimacy and eroticism, and advocates for the integrity of the man's "sexual voice" (autonomy), while balancing that with being an intimate team. This is a powerful, affirming message for the male as well as for the couple.

REFERENCES

Basson, R. (2007). Sexual desire/arousal disorders in women. In S. Leiblum (Ed.), *Principles and practice of sex therapy* (4th ed., pp. 25–53). New York: Guilford.

Foley, S., Kope, S., & Sugrue, D. (2011). *Sex matters for women* (2nd ed.). New York: Guilford.

Goldstein, I., Lue, T., Padma-Nathan, H., Rosen, R., Steers, W., & Wicker, P. (1998). Oral sildenafil in the treatment of erectile dysfunction. *New England Journal of Medicine, 338,* 1397–1401.

Lindau, S., Schumm, P., Laumann, E., Levinson, W., O'Muircheartaigh, C., & Waite, L. (2007). A study of sexuality and health among older adults in the United States. *New England Journal of Medicine, 257*(8), 762–774.

McCarthy, B. (2002). Sexual secrets, trauma, and dysfunction. *Journal of Sex and Marital Therapy, 28*, 353–359.

McCarthy, B., & Cintron, J. (2005). Sexual heroin: Variant arousal patterns are an obstacle to intimacy. *Psychotherapy Networker, 29*(6), 77–83.

McCarthy, B., & Fucito, L. (2005). Integrating medication, realistic expectations, and therapeutic expectations into treatment of male sexual dysfunction. *Journal of Sex and Marital Therapy, 31*, 319–328.

McCarthy, B., & McCarthy, E. (2003). *Rekindling desire*. New York: Brunner/ Routledge.

McCarthy, B., & McCarthy, E. (2009). *Discovering your couple sexual style*. New York: Routledge.

McCarthy, B., & McDonald, D. (2009a). Assessment, treatment, and relapse prevention: Male hypoactive sexual desire disorder. *Journal of Sex and Marital Therapy, 35*(1), 58–67.

McCarthy, B., & McDonald, D. (2009b). Psychobiosocial versus biomedical model of treatment: Semantics or substance? *Sexual and Relationship Therapy, 24*(1), 30–37.

McCarthy, B., & Metz, M. (2008). *Men's sexual health*. New York: Routledge.

McCarthy, B., & Thestrup, M. (2008). Couple therapy and the treatment of sexual dysfunction. In A. Gurman (Ed.), *Clinical handbook of couple therapy* (4th ed., pp. 591–617). New York: Guilford.

Metz, M., & McCarthy, B. (2004). *Coping with erectile dysfunction*. Oakland, CA: New Harbinger.

Metz, M., & McCarthy, B. (2007). The "Good-Enough Sex" model for couple sexual satisfaction. *Sexual and Relationship Therapy, 22*(3), 351–362.

Metz, M. & McCarthy, B. (2010). *Enduring desire*. New York: Routledge

12

Male-Sensitive Couples Therapy With Unfaithful Men

STEVEN M. KADIN AND DON-DAVID LUSTERMAN

INTRODUCTION

Wife: How could you do this to me, to us, to our family? You betrayed
our vows, my trust … and for what, that stupid bimbo? What
were you thinking? Why did you do this, and what will stop
you from doing it again?

Husband: Listen, I'm sorry. I can't really tell you exactly what happened.
But it's over. Can't we just move on? (*He looks miserably at his
wife, then therapist, then down at the floor.*)

How many couples therapists are faced with this dilemma of a betrayed
spouse or a suspecting one concerning infidelity? It is an emotionally
charged situation for everyone involved, including the couples therapist. For many therapists, infidelity is a topic they feel ill equipped to
handle but one of the most frequent presenting situations for couples
(Pelusco, 2008; Pittman, 1989). Glass and Wright (1992) found that
approximately 25% of all couples entering couples therapy report infidelity as the presenting problem and another 30% reveal an infidelity in
the marriage. There is a spectrum of statistics concerning the frequency

of infidelity. It is estimated that somewhere between 10% and 40% of all married couples report an infidelity at some point in the life of their marriage (Blow & Hartnett, 2005; Glass & Wright, 1992; Greeley, 1991). Atkins, Baucom, and Jacobson (2001) report that 1 in every 2.7 couples or some 20 million has experienced infidelity in the life of their relationship. In contrast, Smith (1993) reports that 15% of couples had sexual relations with a person other than their spouse (21% men, 12% women). Although more women are committing infidelity as increasing numbers of women enter the workplace and the barriers to divorce and separation have lessened, the majority of cases of infidelity involve men who are unfaithful to a partner or spouse with whom they have an explicit or implicit expectation to remain faithful. It is estimated that over the course of a marriage up to 44% of men commit infidelity versus only 25% of women (Glass &Wright, 1992). This figure of male infidelity may be inflated due to a higher incidence of extramarital sex by men with prostitutes (Lusterman 2005a).

The emphasis in this chapter is on the effective treatment of men in dealing with the intense and complex issue of infidelity. This is not to say that men should be given more focus than women or that men are more important than women in this process. However, women tend to be more comfortable, in general, participating in talk therapy. Men tend to enter therapy either because they are coerced or feel that they don't have any other practical options. They will participate half-heartedly and drop out of psychotherapy; in particular, they drop out of couples therapy more quickly and frequently than women (Brooks, 2010).

Even though men are increasingly utilizing psychotherapy, therapists still contend with male resistance to this form of professional help. In part this is certainly influenced by male socialization of behavior and attitudes, such as stoicism, rugged individualism, and repression or denial of emotional vulnerability. It could also be argued, though, that the reason men have problems in therapy are because couples therapy tends to favor female avenues of relating and conceptualizing, and that we have been negligent in creating more male-friendly intervention models (Brooks, 2010). Working in male-sensitive ways when infidelity is involved is typically complex and emotionally challenging for the therapist. It requires intentionality, flexibility, and authenticity on the part of the practitioner as well as a firm awareness of the therapist's own judgments, personal history, and values concerning the experiences of infidelity.

The two authors, in sum, have close to 80 years of collective experience working with men, couples, and infidelity from which we draw. In this chapter, we examine through case studies the major issues in working with men involved with infidelity, and offer ways of working effectively with these men in a combination of individual and couples treatment.

INFIDELITY DEFINED

What is considered an infidelity? In most committed couple relationships, there is an implicit and oftentimes explicit expectation of both sexual and emotional loyalty and monogamy (Allen et al., 2005; Weeks, Gambescia & Jenkins, 2003).

Infidelity is defined as the breaking of trust, a betrayal of the marital contract. Infidelity occurs when one partner in a relationship continues to believe that the agreement to be faithful is still in force, while the other partner is secretly violating it (Lusterman, 1989). Although extramarital sexual involvement occurs in many infidelities, it is *not* the defining factor. An infidelity can take the form of extramarital sex, an emotional connection that is beyond a friendship, an online relationship, or extensive pornographic activities, among others. In essence, issues of faithfulness, exclusion, deception, and betrayal are at the heart of all infidelities. If there is an extramarital sexual involvement that is known and sanctioned by the couple, there is no infidelity. Lusterman (1989; reiterated by Zur, 2009) notes that if there is no deceit or secrecy, there can be no infidelity.

Typology of Affairs

Every infidelity episode is a complex and unique progression of events that defy simplistic categorizations, generalizations, and standardized treatment formulas. These events serve different purposes, have varied configurations and patterns, affect the individuals involved in various ways, and unfold in varied time frames. Still, it may be useful to describe the differing typologies of affairs.

Glass (2003) describes three types of infidelities: the emotional affair, the sexual affair, and the mixed affair. It is interesting that men and women tend to be most hurt when their partner engages in the type of infidelity they themselves are more prone to. That is, men tend to be more worried that their partner is involved in a sexual infidelity, and women tend to be more anxious that their partner is involved in an emotional or romantic affair.

Brown (2001) classifies several types of affairs including: (a) the intimacy avoidance affair in which one or both parties are frightened of real intimacy and utilize the affair as a barrier to regulate emotional distance; (b) the conflict avoidance affair, which occurs when partners avoid conflict at the expense of not meeting their own emotional needs, and go elsewhere to fulfill those needs; (c) the exit affair, which occurs when an individual decides consciously or unconsciously to end the marriage and devises a backup affair to facilitate exiting the marriage; and (d) the compulsive sexual affair, in which men, more often than women, compulsively utilize sex repeatedly to numb inner pain, shame, or high-anxiety states. For these individuals, a sexual addictive process gains control of them.

Lusterman (2005b) describes *Don Juanism*, also described as philandering or womanizing. In these cases the individual, again mostly men, find that the thrill of the chase and sexual conquest fulfills his narcissistic needs. As opposed to sexual addicts who feel a sense of shame in their compulsions and deficiencies, philanderers feel no guilt or shame about their behavior, and are blissfully unaware of their deficiencies or the impact their behavior has on others, typically objectifying women and the thrill of the chase and conquest. This is, for the most part, planned behavior—the compulsive search for a woman to "find, bed, and forget." In these cases, the focus of treatment is not on deficits of the marriage, but addressing the issues deep within the individual, often involving early family dysfunction or trauma, and whether he is ready to face these patterns of behavior.

Example of Don Juanism

Daniel was a short, well-built man in his late 40s. He was a successful software engineer who was brought into therapy by his wife, Jan, who in a very agitated state complained that all Daniel did was "play with his goddamned computers and his goddamned whores for 20 years." She complained that he ignored her and had constant liaisons with other women, not being able to encounter a woman without attempting to charm her. At first, Daniel would just smile and deny her claims, saying that she was making too big a deal of his encounters, that they didn't mean anything. The next session, Jan came in, enraged. She provided evidence of his philandering, throwing a sheaf of papers at Daniel: Computer printouts that she found on his computer showing a series of women, dates, and locations. He then admitted that he had a series of brief affairs but they were meaningless to him, and he begged her to not end the marriage. Eventually Jan relented a bit and told Daniel that he had a year of his own treatment to figure out "what the hell was the matter with you, but no straying or I'm outta here." There was the risk at this point that Daniel would become defensive and drop out of treatment, but it also gave him the opportunity to confront and begin to change his own long-standing beliefs and behaviors rather than deflect the responsibility for these behaviors onto the relationship.

Lusterman (1989) describes a number of other types of affairs. An *exploratory affair* is one in which one of the partners is deciding whether they want to stay in the marriage and are testing out what it might be like to be with someone else. This is more deliberate than the *accidental affair* when a partner seems to "fall into" the affair without intent or awareness that something is wrong in the marriage. A *retaliatory affair* occurs when one partner has an affair to payback or punish the other for a perceived betrayal or injustice. Many women have retaliatory affairs when they discover their partner's infidelity. For men, however, this sense of injustice may focus on the experience of financial betrayal.

Example of a Retaliatory Affair

Alan was a hard-working probation officer married to Dawn, a stay-at-home mom caring for their two children. Dawn liked to treat herself and her kids the way she did when she was single and working. She began to get behind in paying the family bills and began to utilize a number of credit cards that she opened. In time, her debt, as well as her guilt and shame, grew. The more anxious she became, the more difficult it became for her to reveal her dark secret. When Alan began to get harassing phone calls at work from collection agencies, he confronted her, and the story spilled out. He felt achingly betrayed by the length and extent of her behaviors and the fact that she hadn't come to him when they could have managed this crisis together. It was shortly after this that Alan went on classmates.com and "by chance" reconnected with an old girlfriend whom he arranged to meet and with whom he began an affair.

PHASES OF TREATMENT OF INFIDELITY

Treatment of infidelity can be as varied as the types of affairs that couples become involved in. Nevertheless, the typical arc of events for couples engaged in affairs entail the drama of secrecy, then discovery, often traumatic, followed by treatment. The initial phase of treatment generally centers on the discovery of the affair. This is usually a devastating experience for the discoverer. This phase of treatment must address the sequelae of posttraumatic stress reaction with the characteristics of numbness, flashbacks, irritability or outbursts of anger, and hyperalertness (Glass, 2003; Lusterman, 1998). It is understood that the discovery of infidelity, or even prediscovery, often appears to present as psychopathology when in fact, it is most likely a normal response to a shocking and traumatic experience. It is important to take a detailed history and to normalize the oftentimes dramatic and confusing sets of emotions and behaviors that accompany discovery or suspicions of infidelity.

The second phase of treatment focuses on an examination of predisposing factors or what made the marriage "affair ready." This may involve an exploration of the factors that created the necessary distance for the affair to occur.

The third phase, rapprochement, involves the improvement of the couple's self-disclosure and problem-solving skills. The couple can now more clearly determine whether they can develop a more satisfying marriage or consider the possibility of a good divorce (Ahrons, 1994). It is important to have the flexibility to return to the first phase of treatment of management of the trauma if or when the discoverer is triggered by events or behaviors that increase suspicions or emotional charge.

Snyder, Baucom, and Gordon (2007) describe a similar integrative approach that (a) recognizes the traumatic impact of an affair, (b) builds relationship skills crucial to managing the initial trauma and builds effective decision making, (c) promotes partners' greater understanding of factors within and outside themselves that increased their vulnerability to an affair, and (d) addresses emotional, cognitive, and behavioral processes essential to forgiveness and moving on, either together or separately.

Treatments of men who are involved in repetitive, pursuant affairs utilize much different treatment models. Initial stages of treatment with a womanizing man involve working with the wife. The goal of this first stage is to empower the woman to the point of her being able say to the man, "You will not be in my life until you get individual treatment to admit that you have a problem that precedes our relationship. We have a problem, but you have an ancient deficit. You need to begin to accept who you are." If the man is able to hear this and take action on it in order to save his marriage by entering a course of individual treatment, there is a chance that the couple can work things through and remain together. These cases, though, have a lower success rate than the primarily relationship-deficit affairs (Lusterman, 2005a). In this chapter, we focus on describing treatment for the majority of men committing infidelity who experience "falling into" an infidelity in which these affairs are not sought out they simply occur, rather than those who engage in active pursuit behaviors.

COUPLES IN DIFFERENT FAMILY LIFE STAGES

Couples in different stages of the family life cycle will have other issues that come to the forefront of treatment. When there are children in the home, often couples are pulled apart by the demands on their time, energy, and financial resources. Many men find they are torn between a desire to feel more alive in a loving, emotionally and physically available relationship and loyalty to their spouse and children.

As an example:

Lamar and Serena, a couple in their mid-40s with two children, ages 13 and 10, entered treatment after Serena discovered that Lamar had been having an affair with a family friend over a 2-year period. When she discovered the affair, she asked Lamar to move out. As is the case for the majority of couples in this stage of the life cycle, both were working full time, Lamar as a contractor and Serena as a legal secretary. They were engaged in a sort of tag team, dividing up the responsibilities of household tasks and childcare. What free time they did have went almost exclusively toward family activities. The marital relationship got short shrift and as a result created emotional distance between them.

In meeting individually with the therapist, Lamar expressed his struggle between loving his wife and children and being "in love" with his affairee, Janet. He missed his children terribly and didn't want to alienate his family to the point of losing contact or the respect and admiration of his children. Over several sessions, he began to identify the tremendous primal draw of being a good father to his children. Lamar was so mesmerized by the openness that he experienced with Janet that he did not think through the tremendous consequences to his children and his relationship with them. The shift for Lamar came with the conversations highlighting his deep love for his children and a powerful yearning to be there for them in ways that he lacked in his own relationship with his emotionally absent father. He owed it to his children to explore a new way of being with their mother. He decided to break off contact with Janet and commit to the long painful struggle of possible reconciliation with Serena.

GENDER CONSIDERATIONS IN WORKING WITH UNFAITHFUL MEN

Although there may be certain innate advantages male therapists have in working with unfaithful men, female clinicians can be equally effective in working with these men. A few caveats follow. To connect with the male client and gain his trust, the female therapist must authentically access male parts of herself and personal experiences in common with the unfaithful male. Some traditionally male values and interests that the female therapist may access in herself and use to join with the unfaithful male client include career achievement/ competition, saving/investing, and leading/managing people. Female therapists could possibly discuss the challenge of running a small business, the financial anxiety of paying for their children's education, problem-solving sudoku or crossword puzzles, strategizing how to deal with difficult teens/neighbors/employees, competing in the marketplace or other activities, making the mortgage payment, or saving for retirement. Sharing sports stories and metaphors can also work if the female therapist is a genuine sports enthusiast. She should avoid offering too much guidance or competing with the male client by acting "manly." Since these men are already flooded by spousal expressions of pain, hurt, anger, and other unpleasant feelings, the female therapist must be careful not to evoke their experience with their wives and exacerbate their emotional overload. If her communication is too emotional, the male client might associate the female therapist with his partner, get frightened and withdraw, or stonewall her, possibly leaving therapy (Gottman, 1999). It is preferable that she use a cognitive problem-solving style comfortable with most men, at least in the beginning stages of working with the unfaithful male client. Rather than begin with an exploration of feelings, it would be advisable to establish relational trust before delving deeper.

Example of Gender Sensitivity in the Authors' Collaboration

It is interesting that there was a somewhat parallel process going on with the two authors writing this chapter: one an older, more experienced writer, the other a younger newcomer to the writing world. A perceived hierarchy existed between these two writers as often exists in the relationship between the therapist and a male client. SK came in experiencing a high level of anxiety because it was not his area of expertise—an experience many men have entering therapy. How defensive must SK be? Did he have to look as if he knew what he was doing, assuming competence? Did we have to establish a pecking order or a competition to see who was going to be top dog? D-DL instead took on the role of being reassuring enough and creating enough safety for SK to lower his anxiety and to begin to take risks with greater levels of transparency. D-DL was able to move between the language of the practitioner and the language of the experienced writer in the field. This was done not by teaching, but by modeling and being. We then began to discover a common set of experiences, and to develop common language and metaphors to use with each other. We had to find our other common areas through which we could begin to connect and socialize, such as our shared interest in music and performing. We also shared the struggles of "fitting in as a man." Many men who become family therapy practitioners tend to have some gender-atypical qualities. These are not negative qualities but often make them somewhat less comfortable with more gender-stereotyped men. Since the therapist's use of self is an important element in psychotherapeutic success, we feel that it is important to examine some of the attendant issues. Just as happens in working with male clients, as we worked together, we changed together.

It is essential to be aware that, with most men, that instinctual feeling of defending themselves versus domination or shame is omnipresent. The challenge in doing therapy with men is to shift from a competitive hierarchical paradigm to a collaborative one that says, "I will work together with you, we will change together, I will be open and honest with you, and if I hear bullshit, I will call you on it." This is the process that the authors went through to develop a solid working relationship just as we work with these men to help them through this process.

CASE STUDY: JAMES AND RUTH

James and Ruth were a couple in their early 50s who had been married for 28 years. James was a successful executive who was well known in his community as a powerful but generous benefactor. They had two grown children, Jill, 27, and George, 23, who were both out of the house. James saw himself as a kind and generous person to everyone around him: his wife and children as well as employees in his company. He was particularly generous to Cheryl, a young, beautiful, 21-year-old woman who began as a line staff at his company. He began to spend time with her as a "mentor" and gave her both emotional as well as financial support through college and an MBA program. This relationship was increasingly threatening and enraging for Ruth who felt that "something was going on" with James and Cheryl. James, feeling that he was being persecuted by his wife's "pathological jealousy" for his kind acts toward others, insisted that Ruth go to see a psychologist. The psychologist met individually with Ruth on two occasions and then met with Ruth and James, who was more than willing to meet with the psychologist to make sure she got all the "facts" straight.

The psychologist assessed that there seemed to be a discrepancy between how James perceived his marital relationship and how he was actually behaving toward Ruth, which was in an arrogant and dismissive way. She also saw how Ruth would swallow her anger and feelings of being discounted when she communicated with James. James's characterization of Ruth being paranoid and him being a victim were not adding up for her. The psychologist assessed this as more of a relationship problem and told the couple that her treating Ruth individually would not really accomplish the goals that they sought. She told them that her expertise was not in couples therapy. (This is something that many therapists are unwilling to admit. Thankfully, this therapist had the integrity to act on her scope of practice.) The psychologist suggested a referral to someone who had an expertise in relationship-oriented work. James, not really trusting the judgment and impartiality of this female therapist, requested a male psychologist with some "credentials."

James then called the author, who was known to have expertise in the area of marital infidelity. A phone interview ensued for 15 to 20 minutes to decide whether this was an appropriate case for couples therapy. Although the author's typical practice is to see the couple together in the beginning stages of treatment, the description that James gave over the phone suggested that it might be more helpful to invite him in individually for the initial meeting to see about the "goodness of fit." This was particularly important for James in that he said he wanted to find someone who was competent and could get the job done, qualities that he sought in his successful work dealings. Could this therapist not only talk the talk but walk the walk?

Joining Through a Show of Competency

In this first session it was essential to begin the joining (or "seducing") process with James. James checked out both the competence of the therapist as well as the therapist's view of his competence. In an initial encounter, the majority of men, especially men who are used to the competitive world of business, engage in a sort of dance to determine the pecking order. In this initial meeting, the therapist joined in the dance while avoiding a power struggle with James, offering the client something challenging and useful to him. (Men are used to living in this world of competition and that's the dance that occurs in this meeting with the therapist.) The therapist acknowledged James's business acumen and success in his work world, then expressed that for James to seek relationship consultation entailed risking some vulnerability and trust in the world of the therapist's own expertise. "You know the rules of the game in your work world. That's what has led to your success in that world. I admire that you are willing to take the risk of entering a world in which the rules are less clear to you. I understand the rules in this world which has made me a success at what I do."

Like so many men in long-term relationships, James wanted peace. He wanted his wife to appreciate his efforts to provide for his family and see him as a nice guy, a benign figure in her life. He also wanted to be seen as competent by both his wife as well as the therapist. He was worried that he might lose his marriage. He still felt a strong attachment to his wife although he was not able to articulate this. He was a man who saw himself as a good guy and whose wife didn't understand his positive intent toward Cheryl. He felt that he got more admiration and positive feedback from his employees and colleagues at the company than he got at home from his wife and children.

When asked about the history of his marriage, James said that they used to be friends and that he missed this. He complained a fair amount about Ruth, expressing that he really couldn't see what his wife was getting so upset about. He stated the common complaint that many men come in with who are in long-term relationships: that he loved his wife, but did not feel "in love" with her. Their lovemaking had dropped off. There was no spark between them, except for the spark of Ruth's apparent growing rage over his ambiguous relationship with Cheryl. He admitted that he had close feelings toward Cheryl, in that he felt her appreciation for his help and she seemed to light up when he spent time with her.

Assessing a Relationship Deficit

Assessment begins in the initial phone call. In meeting individually with James, an assessment of the typology and nature of the extra marital involvement was explored. It was determined in his meeting that James had a sufficient level of commitment to his primary relationship, did not possess a history of repeated affairs, and did not have any obvious psychopathology. Treatment considerations are different if the male in question is a womanizer, that is, having had a number of extra marital affairs over time. The assumption in this case is that James has had a fundamental commitment to Ruth and his marriage. He "fell" into the relationship with Cheryl. This is indicative of a deficit in the relationship, and treatment centers on working with James and collectively with Ruth to ameliorate those relationship deficits. (Womanizing, on the other hand, indicates more of a characterological deficit within the man. See "Typology of Affairs" section.)

Getting Buy-In to "Fix the Problem"

It was essential in this first meeting to reframe the task and set the parameters of the work. James's situation was reframed in a paradigm that would make sense to him. Wouldn't it be better for James if he could feel that kind of appreciation and warmth from his wife? Something in the "mechanics" of his relationship with Ruth was not working. Would he like to figure out how to "fix" this problem? There was something in what had been happening in his relationship with Cheryl that made him feel more like a man. Would he like to feel this way with his wife? To address these issues, it became apparent that Ruth must be involved in the process. The parameters of the work were explained to James.

Privacy Versus No-Secrecy Policy

There is a crucial difference between the concepts of secrecy and privacy. Secrecy is most of the time a destructive and distancing factor in intimate relationships. The definition of an affair is a relationship in which one of the partners is involved either emotionally, physically, or both, with another person, and it is kept secret from their partner. It is important not to duplicate this in the couples work. If an individual is going to have a private session, the other partner will always be informed of this. To work with a partner who is reluctant or anxious to admit to their spouse—or sometimes even to themselves—the extent of their secret relationship(s), it is often necessary to meet several times in individual sessions to prepare that person, especially men, to be able to talk openly and honestly to their spouses about their affair, as well as to establish the level of patience required to heal the devastating consequences of the betrayal. While meeting individually with the man, the *content* of these individual meetings must be kept private but not the fact that the meetings are taking place. This privacy rule differs from the conventional wisdom of a no-secrets policy in working with couples. A trusting relationship between the therapist and unfaithful male client must be established over time to help men such as James make sense of their own thoughts and feelings as well as helping them to learn a strategy for articulating those thoughts and feelings in an honest and constructive manner to their spouse. If they are required to reveal thoughts, feelings, and details of the affair prematurely, the guilt, shame, and anxiety that they may be experiencing and their inability to articulate these thoughts and feelings in a safe environment will likely lead to a negative therapeutic outcome. James was reassured that even if or when Ruth was involved in the work, the content of these individual sessions would be kept confidential. James felt comfortable with this and it was explained that the therapist would meet individually with Ruth and then meet together with the couple.

In meeting individually with Ruth, the same rules concerning secrecy versus privacy were explained. Right away, Ruth wanted to know if James was having an affair with Cheryl. It is never the therapist's job to speak for the other spouse, especially when there are dangerous secrets involved. What the therapist can do in this situation is to help Ruth ask her own questions such as: Is he coming home late quite often? Is he not where he says he is? This is a more generic and just way of helping the couple begin to interact with one another in a constructive way as well as avoiding the specter of triangulation that a clinician can so easily fall into in situations such as this. The task is to have each partner feel that the therapist is not colluding in the dance of secrecy that has been going on in the life of this couple.

Modeling Gender-Flexible Behavior

The third meeting was with the couple. Androgyny is a key quality for couples therapists to evince to clients, especially in working with the very emotionally charged atmosphere of infidelity. The therapist must demonstrate bilingual gender skills, bridging separate gender worlds, and speaking both the language of men as well as women. This helps in the joining process with clients as well as translating spouses' hurts, hopes, and preferred strategies to each other. It may also help with modeling how these two can talk to each other despite the emotionally charged environment. The therapist in this situation will want to take a collaborative stance, inviting the couple to take ownership of the process. "I want you guys to help me. What do each of you see as the immediate problem or situation, and what would you like to accomplish?"

* * *

James started out, repeating, "We were good friends. Now I don't get much of anything from her but demands and grief. She doesn't appreciate me like most of the other people in my life do." He wants to feel that appreciation again from Ruth. This astonishes Ruth. She states, "If you gave as much to me as you give to people in your workplace, especially Cheryl, I would be in a much better frame of mind to give you more of that appreciation. It's incredibly painful for me to see you giving so much elsewhere and so little to me and the children."

At this point it is essential to speak James's language to him. The therapist utilized the metaphors, language, and schematics that were meaningful to James. James saw this as a type of mechanical problem to be solved. James was encouraged to let the therapist know that if the therapist's personal style offended him to let him know or if he was mystified, he should let him know. The therapist framed this as a matter of equity in relationship. Is the relationship balanced in terms of what each person is giving? James is asked how he is picturing this. Is this making sense to him? As therapists, we model for our clients a way of interacting, of being in the world. In this case, the therapist needed to proceed carefully with James. James saw himself as both successful and a sincerely nice guy. He did not want to be told what to do by the therapist. It had to fit for him, to make sense within his worldview. At this point, he saw his wife as withholding from him for no legitimate reason. He wanted from Ruth the level of adoration he felt from Cheryl but couldn't really see what he could do differently with her than what he was doing. In the past, the times that Ruth did bring her hurt and disappointment up to James, he felt narcissistically wounded, which would push him toward increased contact with Cheryl. He just couldn't get why his wife didn't see him as Cheryl did: a kind and generous person with positive intent. He had minimal awareness of the emotional impact that his continued behavior was having on Ruth. He actually didn't see how his relationship with Cheryl could be construed as secret and a hurtful betrayal to Ruth. She reacted as a person who has experienced a type of posttraumatic stress disorder (PTSD) over an extended period: pulling away to protect herself or emotionally reacting to triggers reminding her of this "betrayal" by acting out "hot rage" or suspiciously questioning his whereabouts. James could only see a distant shrewish woman. What had happened to his wife?

Lowering the Male Client's Anxiety

To help James see his part in the relationship dance, the first step was to get him to buy in to the process of a combination of individual and couples work. The majority of men coming into therapy where infidelity is the presenting or emerging theme experience a high degree of anxiety that is either overt or covert. Many men are not even aware of how anxious they actually are. They are afraid that they will be criticized or judged by their wives as well as the therapist. In a man's worldview, his woman has the power to give him masculinity or strip it away. Ruth was still very important as well as terrifying to James. So, in this stage of treatment the therapist must be careful to take steps to lower the anxiety to a level in which James could take the risks necessary to (a) admit what was going on to himself, and (b) be able to express this to his spouse in a way that would be transformative for their relationship. If one thinks of anxiety on a 10-point scale, where 1 is complete peace and serenity and 10 is absolute panic, the therapist's aim is to bring these men down to about a 5 level. The utilization of James's language, metaphors, being concrete, and the use of humor were all ways of lowering anxiety for James.

Use of Humor

For many men, humor is a particularly effective vehicle for connecting, building trust, and lowering anxiety. In individual meetings, one can begin with the humor that many men use with one another: a type of sarcastic, biting humor. The therapist must be willing to meet the man at this level. Then, over time, the therapist can model moving from a dark hurtful humor to more of a playful and facilitative humor—to be able to be funny without hurting anyone. This kind of humor can then be utilized in conjoint sessions as an invitation to his spouse to be more of an equal playmate—to share in the human comedy, the theater of the absurd.

As an example, in the early stages of their conjoint work, James and Ruth, at times, would escalate into yelling fights that left both of them hurt, frustrated, and exhausted. They were instructed then to call for timeouts before these discussions escalated to the point of toxic interaction. The therapist asked them to come up with a timeout signal that they could agree on. James, with a grin, suggested, "Let's use a KTO (Kadin time out) rather than a TKO (technical knock out)." We all had a good laugh. The therapist highlighted James's ability to lighten the mood with his playful humor that was inclusive of Ruth. They left the office feeling lighter and friendlier with each other.

Preparing the Male Client for Conjoint Work

It was important to help James shift to a more receptive and effective position before continuing conjoint therapy. The recommendation was made to meet with James alone for several meetings before seeing the couple again. Most women will be able to tolerate this if they feel that the therapist will help their spouses to get it in some way and that they are generally apprised of progress.

Like so many traditional men, James saw psychotherapy as touchy-feely bs, a soft science. In meeting with him it was crucial to begin to ease his mistrust of the therapy process. He was told to let the therapist know if it felt like too much "feminist crap." In this meeting, it was important to find a way to resonate with his hopes as well as fears and at the same time help expand his frame of reference beyond his view of self as just a helpful friend to Cheryl. It was important for James to recognize and articulate that he was more than just friends with Cheryl (Glass, 2003). James was a man who took pride in utilizing his logical mind to accumulate the facts to successfully solve problems. In exploring his relationship with Cheryl, it was proposed that he make a list of ten of his friends on the computer. Would he do the same thing for these friends? Would he have the same level of feeling for them? Would he get from them what he was getting from his relationship with Cheryl? In exploring this in a concrete, systematic and rational manner that was within his frame of reference and comfort zone, James began to accept that his feelings for Cheryl and what he was getting from the relationship in terms of his own gratification gave him a sense of intimacy and reward that he was not getting anywhere else in his life, including his marriage. What began as an office relationship and mentoring process at some point crossed a boundary. For instance, he stopped inviting Ruth to office parties and other functions where he could focus more exclusively on his time with Cheryl. He was yearning more and more for Cheryl's company and gratification, and subsequently keeping this a secret from Ruth.

Addressing the Power Differential

James's lack of awareness of the power differential in the relationship was something to which many therapists can relate. When there is a power differential that is not recognized or acknowledged, it may appear that the individual in the less powered position is getting the same level and type of gratification from the relationship as the powered person is. This male privilege, which is enjoyed by many successful men, was something to which James was completely oblivious. He couldn't understand his part in why Ruth did not have the same admiration for him that Cheryl had. On some level, James knew that he wanted more than what he was getting from this relationship with Cheryl. He couldn't really identify it and certainly couldn't articulate these yearnings. It was determined that this was not an exit affair, where James wanted out of his marriage and was using his relationship with Cheryl as a vehicle to transition out of the marriage. He was able to identify that he valued his shared history with Ruth, their time together with their children, and the vision of growing old together. In this case, James, like many men in long-term marriages, gradually shut down emotionally. A woman like Cheryl then comes along and spices up their lives, bringing them out of depression and boredom into a positive, stimulating feeling state. He began to feel things that had been dormant for a long time. When the unfaithful male experiences this awakening, after a period, he begins to miss his wife and children; he starts missing his vision of family that was so dear to him, what he had been working to protect and preserve. In the beginning stages of a relationship where there is a power differential, men such as James will not experience the anxiety of letting down their romantic interest. It is not an equal relationship. As such, the power differential tends to minimize the risk of being criticized or judged by their romantic interest but also preempts the possibility of developing a multidimensional partnership, which most men (and most adults) want to experience.

When men think of infidelity, they think in terms of the level of sexual involvement. They are typically more honest about their physical involvement because that is where their overt focus tends to be. But men tend to be less clear about their level of emotional attachment. In addition, each gender projects on to the other their own emphasis—women tending to be more fearful of their partner's emotional involvement, men worried about their partner's sexual involvement. Although the relationship with Cheryl had progressed over time to intimate embraces and long lingering kisses, James had never actually had sexual intercourse with Cheryl, so he didn't really understand the level of hurt and betrayal his wife was expressing to him. This was an opportunity to explore with James the typology of affairs described by Glass (2003). Was this a physical affair, an emotional one, or mixed? It is simplistic to define infidelity merely as having sex outside of a committed relationship. There is a spectrum of thoughts, feelings, and behaviors involved in infidelity that can be subtle and complex. The underlying issue here is secrecy and violation of the basic trust. Over time, James was able to buy into this broadened definition of infidelity, and, given this widened view, could begin to understand Ruth's hurt and anger in this context.

For a man like James, therapy entailed a parallel process of helping him learn how to regain the mutual trust that had been eroded in his relationship with his wife and getting him to trust the therapist and therapy process. The therapist modeled interpersonal risk taking, at times sharing what the therapist experienced in the moment and utilizing personal metaphors that fit the client's internal landscape. The therapist must be willing to access and share emotional parts of themselves that speak to the male client. As an example, the therapist and James shared a love of playing music. Sharing on this level first made the work more collaborative, like figuring out a problem together. Music metaphors ensued. For instance, the idea of two people learning to play together involved cooperation not competition. Also, one had to agree on a key to play in and a common beat. By utilizing this shared experience, James and the therapist began to forge a relationship that consisted of common language and experience. This had the effect of lowering James's anxiety and mistrust in the session as well as beginning to see the therapist as an ally in his quest to regain his wife and family.

Developing Recognition and Expression of Feelings

Eventually, the therapist began to challenge James to shift what he was experiencing from a thinking state to the recognition and expression of feelings. This mirrors working with women when they are flooded with affect and the shift is to build a cognitive framework for understanding and managing their feelings. When most men are asked what they are feeling they have difficulty identifying feeling states, what Levant (2003) describes as male alexithymia. They may tell you a thought, that is, "I'm feeling that my wife doesn't understand me." It is more efficacious to ask concrete questions, such as "What are you experiencing in your body right now?" Connecting bodily sensations with feeling states allows men to identify feelings and build an emotional vocabulary to share in eventual dialogue with their partners. For example, James, in an individual session, commented that he was sick and tired of Ruth and the kids giving him the cold shoulder. When James was asked to describe what he was experiencing in his body, he reported feeling a burning in his stomach, heaviness in his chest, and a lump in his throat, which he was told correlated with the physical constellation of sadness.

James began to identify and understand that he had felt for a time an infatuation with Cheryl that went beyond friendship to romantic feelings. But, like coming down from a drug-induced high, he also began to identify an emptiness inside. As well he identified his yearning to feel valued by Ruth, and his anger, resentment, and finally hurt that, for whatever reason, she was withholding this from him. He began to more clearly identify some vague feelings of remorse for withdrawing into his relationship with work and Cheryl.

Once James was able to build up his emotional vocabulary, he needed to practice articulating these thoughts and feelings in a constructive way to Ruth. The therapist directed James in role-plays with an empty chair, which eventually reduced his anxiety and built his feelings of mastery and competence in approaching his wife in a different and more satisfying manner. Being able to practice talking the language of feelings was something new to James. The metaphor was used that the effective expression of feelings was the key that unlocked her heart and the barriers that led to the sense of emotional distance in his marriage. At first James didn't understand how talking about his feelings and listening to Ruth talk about hers was going to solve any problems between them. James, like so many men of action, wanted a plan for fixing the problem. He was very successful in the business world solving problems. It was a leap for him to realize that in intimate relationships hearing and being heard could become a solution in and of itself.

Shifting Blame to Empathy

In a total of six subsequent individual sessions, James's understanding of the impact on Ruth of his relationship with Cheryl was embellished. Once he was able to accept his feelings and behaviors towards Cheryl as a working definition of infidelity, then he needed to be confronted with the hurt and betrayal Ruth experienced over a 6-year period. He needed to move from an angry, defensive stance in which he was blaming and pathologizing her ("pathological jealousy") to an empathic stance. He was given the task of reading up on the subject to enhance his understanding of what Ruth had been experiencing and the range of reactions that he might expect from someone who was experiencing PTSD. (As well, James, like many men in his situation, had to let go of the very powerful feelings he had toward Cheryl. While he was learning to understand and validate Ruth's experience, he also had to make sense of his own trauma of coming to terms grieving the loss of his dreams regarding Cheryl and finding ways of openly and honestly articulating this experience to Ruth.) James was told that the more quickly he was able to research this, the more he could save in therapy costs. This was an effective strategy for James in that he came back with a much more thorough context for understanding what people went through when they feel the basic trust in a relationship is ruptured. The range of Ruth's reactions was also role-played. This was difficult for James because he wanted to argue back with Ruth. James was accustomed to being in charge and wanted to man up. In this case, it was reframed that he could be in charge of effectively managing his own emotions and manning up would be to hang in there with Ruth and validate her experience as she unloaded a lot of pent up hurt and rage. James was also prepared in expecting many questions from Ruth on the nature and details of his relationship with Cheryl. James, like so many men in conversations with their spouses, either would withdraw from contact when vulnerable feelings were being expressed or become defensive and argumentative about whose "reality" was correct. Now that James had developed more of an emotional vocabulary he was coached on sharing his "emotional truth." This was a reality that only he was an expert on and could not be challenged as to its rightness.

* * *

At this point both James and the therapist agreed that it was time to invite Ruth into a conjoint session. This was an opportunity to integrate the gains from the individual work with James into the conjoint work with the couple. Ruth wanted desperately to be heard. In this session, it was reframed that the slew of Ruth's questions was an attempt at getting validation and to utilize this information to begin to trust her instincts again. Again, appealing to James' rational, logical paradigm, he was told, "If you keep things from your wife, then you perpetuate the secrecy that caused distance in the first place. Many men state that they don't want to tell their partners the details of the infidelity because it would hurt them more. This is a classic male perspective: they are responsible for providing the umbrella of security around their family, and therefore can't say any truth that would be upsetting to their spouse. Of course, some of this is self-protection as well in that the man does not want the blowback of strong emotions coming at them from their spouse. These "protection rackets" are ultimately not helpful to the couple. The man must be educated by both the therapist and spouse that giving the details of the affair, in most cases, will help the wife regain the accuracy of her antennae and to trust her instincts again.

* * *

The therapist sat near James and coached him in empathic interviewing (Lusterman, 1998). In subsequent sessions, he helped James listen to what Ruth said without interruption or defensiveness, to acknowledge what she said without having to agree with her, and to validate her feelings. James was able at this time to acknowledge that to Ruth he was having an affair. The therapist rewarded James by saying how smart he was in coming to that conclusion. The couple agreed that they wanted to begin to have an honest dialogue with one another. Did they want to divorce or really try to make the relationship work? They didn't want to lie or deceive each other anymore. They agreed that neither of them wanted to go back to the way it was. In order for this to happen, though, Ruth needed James to be as honest as he could possibly be about his feelings for Cheryl.

Ruth confronted James in the couples session. To her he had violated their marital contract. He was not only cheating on her, he was cheating her out of his interest and his warmth. She told him she wanted to feel respected and loved. With the therapist's coaching, he was able to admit to her how much he was getting from his relationship with Cheryl. This was a very difficult process for James. His default instinct was once again for him to protect and defend. Again, using a language and style that James could relate to, he was challenged—"Don't be a wuss, put everything on the table." This admission was crucial for Ruth in that it was a validation of what she had been feeling for many years. In addition, James was asked to make a commitment to Ruth that he would cut off all contact with Cheryl, which he was reluctantly willing to do.

Telling Truth

Telling hard truths begins to help in the regaining of basic trust in the relationship. Ruth demanded to know the details of the progression of the relationship with Cheryl. How long did the affair last? How did it start? How often did they meet? Who else knew? The more Ruth insisted on the details of the relationship, the more James resisted, feeling that it would just punish and retraumatize her by giving her these details. In meeting individually with James, he was educated on the consequences of the outcome by disclosing the details of his affair. His retort was that it was over and that he didn't want to dwell in the past. Withholding this information from his wife because he thought it would protect her from further pain actually perpetuated the problem. He was withholding information and lying, which led to the affair in the first place. He was challenged to tell her as much as she was asking for. He left the session contemplating this intervention. In the following couples session, James presented a detailed timeline he wrote up on the computer. It spanned the whole length of the office floor. Even though it was painful for Ruth, she was able to let James know that she really felt heard by him and appreciated his honesty.

Turning Points in the Couples Therapy

The couple continued to meet for several more joint sessions. A transformative moment in the change process occurred during one of these conjoint sessions. Ruth was particularly barbed in her comments to James about his lack of caring for her. At one point in the session, James cried out, "I do really care for you. I've really changed. Can't you see how much I've done? Are we working on a better marriage or a divorce?" At this point, he had broken down in tears while saying this. Ruth was stunned into silence. She had never seen him cry. In those few moments, he was able to take all of his armor down. This was a real turning point in the therapy and a cathexis of all of James's work to be present in a vulnerable, honest, and loving way with Ruth.

Ruth, in seeing and *feeling* a difference in James's level of emotional honesty, was beginning to trust her emotional instincts more and slowly beginning to build a new foundation for basic trust with James. Once she found her voice again, she was able to respond to James with a loving smile and a tender touch. This emotional opening up for James was foreign and left him feeling vulnerable to an attack on his manhood. Not only wasn't he attacked, he discovered, but he was actually rewarded for taking this risk with his partner. The therapist was able to comment on his courage in taking this kind of risk, a mature man engaging in a mature love. Ruth, with coaching, was able to let James know that she found his level of emotional honesty and vulnerability very "manly" and ultimately arousing for her. James was both stunned and reassured by this information.

This transformative moment allowed James and Ruth to begin to engage in discussions about how the marriage became "affair ready," and steps they could take to prevent that amount of emotional distance reoccurring in their marriage. This was by no means a smooth transition, and there were several more crises in which Ruth was triggered by suspicions that James was in contact with Cheryl again. James at this point had both the cognitive framework and the expressive tools to effectively address Ruth's anxieties. In one session, they were given the task of writing down in the present moment what they were thinking, being as honest as possible. This was a bit more structured and safer exercise for James to participate in. James was beginning to accept that while both he and Ruth had limitations, that they could trust and respect each other, warts and all. James began to experience not the "same-old, same-old" drudgery of confined, safe interactions that were boring and stultifying, but more of a sense of adventure and novelty in his marriage. In addition, it slowly dawned on James through the therapy process that by being open and honest, and giving to his wife, he was able to receive the love and respect that he so craved in falling into his relationship with Cheryl.

CONCLUSION

Working with men who are involved with infidelity requires skill, sensitivity, and flexibility on the therapist's part. Therapists need to trust their instincts, both in the use of models of change and manner of intervention. This oftentimes requires practitioners to utilize their flexibility in moving between individual and couples treatment. As discussed, in these cases the therapist must speak the language of both male and female—a sort of bi-gender speak. Most men, when they feel anxious about their transgressions, feel guilt or fear, and are ill equipped to effectively respond to their partner's hurt, confusion, and anger. The couples therapist then models how a man can talk to a woman in a way that the wife can be heard and validated. The ability to be able to interact with men in a nonblaming and nonjudgmental manner is crucial to this work. Once these men learn to listen and be heard, their marital relationships become more open, spacious, and compassionate. In successful therapy, these men learn that they can allow themselves to experience vulnerability with their mates and still be "man enough." This allows them to develop the capacity to enjoy a sense of novelty and adventure within their marriages rather than seeking out or falling into these experiences outside of the marital covenant.

REFERENCES

Ahrons, C. (1994). *The good divorce: Keeping your family together when your marriage falls apart.* New York: HarperCollins.

Allen, E. S., Atkins, D. C., Baucom, D. H., Snyder, D. K., Gordon, K., & Glass, S. P. (2005). Intrapersonal, interpersonal, and contextual factors in engaging in and responding to extramarital involvement. *Clinical Psychology: Science and Practice, 12*(2), 101–130.

Atkins, D. C., Baucom, D. H., & Jacobson, N. S. (2001). Understanding infidelity: Correlates in a national random sample. *Journal of Family Psychology, 15*(4), 735–749.

Blow, A., & Hartnett, K. (2005). Infidelity in committed relationships II: A substantive review. *Journal of Marital and Family Therapy, 31*(2), 217–234.

Brooks, G. (2010). *Beyond the crisis of masculinity: A transgenerational model for male-friendly therapy.* Washington, DC: American Psychological Association.

Brown, E. M. (2001). *Patterns of infidelity and their treatment* (2nd ed.). Philadelphia, PA: Brunner-Routledge.

Glass, S. (2003). *Not "just friends": Rebuilding trust and recovering your sanity after infidelity.* New York: Simon & Schuster.

Glass, S., & Wright, T. L. (1992). Justifications for extramarital involvement: The association between attitudes, behaviors, and gender. *Journal of Sex Research, 29*(3), 361–387.

Gottman, J. (1999). *The seven principles of making marriage work.* New York: Crown.

Greeley, A. (1991). *Faithful attraction: Discovering intimacy love and fidelity in American marriage.* New York: Tom Doherty Associates.

Levant, R. H. (2003). Treating male alexithymia. In T. J. Goodrich & L. B. Silverstein (Eds.), *Feminist family therapy: Empowerment in social context* (pp. 177–188). Washington, DC: American Psychological Association.

Lusterman, D. D. (1989, May/June). Marriage at the turning point. *Family Therapy Networker, 13,* 44–51.

Lusterman, D. D. (1998). *Infidelity: A survival guide*. Oakland, CA: New Harbinger.

Lusterman, D. D. (2005a). Infidelity: theory and treatment. In M. Harway (Ed.), *Handbook of couples therapy* (pp. 337–351). Hoboken, NJ: Wiley & Sons.

Lusterman, D. D. (2005b). Repetitive infidelity, womanizing and Don Juanism. In R. Levant & G. Brooks (Eds.), *Men and sex: New psychological perspectives* (pp. 164–181). New York: John Wiley and Sons.

Pelusco P. (2008). Understanding infidelity: Pitfalls and lessons for couples counselors. *The Family Journal, 16*(4), 324–327.

Pittman, F. (1989). *Private lies: Intimacy and the betrayal of intimacy*. New York: Norton.

Smith, T. (1993). *American sexual behavior* (Version 1.2). Chicago: National Opinion Research Center, University of Chicago.

Snyder, D. K., Baucom, D. H., & Gordon, K. C. (2007). *Getting past the affair: A program to help you cope, heal, and move on—together or apart*. New York: Guilford Press.

Weeks, G. R., Gambescia, N., & Jenkins, R. E. (2003). *Treating infidelity: Therapeutic dilemmas and effective strategies*. New York: Norton.

Zur, O. (2009). *Infidelity and affairs: Facts & myths and what works*. Retrieved from http://zurinstitute.com/infidelity.html

13

Brothers of Color in Couples Therapy

Managing the Rainfall and Storms of Discrimination and Racism for Latino and African American Men

JOSEPH M. CERVANTES

The multicultural literature and the emerging guidelines that were eventually written in the early 1990s (American Psychological Association, 1993), followed by subsequent changes (American Psychological Association, 2003), paved the way for a more integrated approach to counseling and psychotherapy for distinct ethnic and racial communities. A significant aspect of the writing over the last 25 years has focused primarily on psychological intervention for individuals as opposed to couples and family therapy. As a result, there continue to be limited conceptual and theoretical models that integrate issues associated with socioeconomic status, impact of ethnic minority membership, residing in violent neighborhoods, and the role of poverty associated with psychological intervention for families (D. W. Sue & Sue, 2003; S. Sue, Zane, Hall & Berger, 2009). The linkage between these important dimensions for communities of color and their integration in meaningful psychological care remains conceptually absent (Ridley, 1995). These findings extend to the life-span experiences of racism and men of color, and how they are disclosed in therapy.

This chapter addresses the issue of couples therapy for Latino and African American men and the consideration of discrimination and racism as a significant backdrop toward effective management of therapeutic success. The economic and sociopolitical complexities of these communities of men are intertwined with psychological nuances, expectations, and daily tragedy, to an extent that has not been well recognized in the literature (Marsiglia & Kulis, 2009). It would challenge even experienced professionals to appreciate the layers of discriminatory practices and related life experiences of these men—a multitude of experiences that have made relationships and family systems difficult to treat competently (Minuchin, Calapinto, & Minuchin, 2007; Pinderhughes, 1989).

The organization of this chapter will begin with an overview of Latino and African American men and some of the primary psychological issues they may bring to couples therapy. The role of discrimination, oppression, and racism will be the backdrop and core dynamic that will characterize the prominent theme of this writing. A review of microaggressions, namely, the daily assaults that typically happen with communities of color, will be discussed. Two case studies, one Latino couple and the second an African American couple, are presented followed by relevant commentary of the clinical material. A central aspect of this writing will focus on strategies that support effective counseling practice with men of color and foster the continued development of multicultural competencies (Cornish, Schreier, Nadkarni, Metzger, & Rodolfa, 2010; D. W. Sue, Arredondo, & McDavis, 1992). Concluding remarks about being a brother or sister of color conclude the chapter.

Throughout this writing, the term *Latino* refers specifically to those men who are either Mexican or Mexican American although the term is typically understood to be more comprehensive (Comas-Diaz, 2001). The terms *Black* and *African American* will be used interchangeably and specifically to men who are ethnically or racially designated as African American and have been born in the United States. In addition, the therapeutic intervention "couples therapy or couples counseling" and "marital therapy" will be used interchangeably without reference to a specific theoretical persuasion or the expected and formalized relationship that assumes that a couple has entered into a legal, marital contract. This chapter will refer specifically to heterosexual couples, as this is the base of experience for the present writer.

MEN OF COLOR: LATINOS AND AFRICAN AMERICANS

Latino (Brown) and African American (Black) men have historically not been given widespread attention in the professional literature on counseling (Casas, Turner, & Ruiz de Esparza, 2001; Mirande, 1997; Parham, 1989; Velasquez & Burton, 2004). Numerous stereotypes have abounded regarding their masculine identities and behavior toward women and families (Billingsley, 1992; Cervantes, 2005; Connor & White, 2006; Franklin, 2004). Characteristically, negative stereotypes have been the prominent dimension, with an emphasis on alarmist behaviors. Some of these alarmist behaviors ascribed to Brown and Black men have included hypersexualized behavior, disloyalty to family, aggressive and violent activity, and nonmotivation to participate in psychotherapy. Researchers and writers in the area of psychological intervention have not been invested in these distinct clinical populations; the lack of attention has contributed to the gap in the literature and perhaps indirectly reinforced the described negative images of these male populations.

Latino males do not constitute a homogeneous nor culturally generic group (Casas, Turner, & Ruis de Esparza, 2001; Cervantes, 2005; Mirande, 1997). Obvious differences include sociocultural variations among Latin American countries relative to specific customs, values, and traditions (Torres, Solberg, & Carlstrom, 2002). For purposes of this current chapter, Mexican and Mexican American men in general are the focus of attention (noting that this group have their own regional and linguistic differences). Major strengths of this Latino group include a strong, family-focused system, typically patriarchal, and often an involved extended family system that may also impact interpersonal relationships and behaviors (Cervantes & Sweatt, 2004; Falicov, 1998; Santiago-Rivera, Arredondo, & Gallardo-Cooper, 2002). Other aspects related specifically to what is expected of a man include a strong value placed on *una persona que cumple con su palabra* (a person of his word); personal and collective pride in the accomplishments of one's family; and expectations of bravery and tolerance (Mirande, 1997). This latter characteristic is described in common, linguistic phrases such as *no te dejes* (don't let anyone take anything from you), *no te rajes* (don't back down), and *tener huevos* (show what kind of man you are). In addition, the value of being *una persona decente* (respectable person) or *bien educado* (socially/interpersonably appropriate) are aspects of this manhood code (Gutman, 2007). As a result, being a Mexican or Mexican American man is contextualized within an expectation of responsibility, self-reliance, and at least an external showing of ethical character. The gene pool of this population includes the racial grouping of Spaniard, Indian, and African roots, all of which contribute to the unique cultural values and beliefs that that are reflected in the varied definitions of manhood and masculine identity (Cervantes, 2010).

African American men have similar yet distinct characteristics but are described as being hypersexual, prone toward abandonment of partners and children, unmotivated to attain financial stability, and irresponsible and prone to violence (Connor & White, 2006; White & Cones, 1999). Current writers have served to erase these negative stereotypes and provide a more accurate understanding of Black manhood (Billingsley, 1992;

Connor & White, 2006; Franklin, 2010). In particular, some of these strengths recognized with African American males have included firm kinship ties, strong work orientation, adaptability of roles, high achievement orientation, and strong religious and spiritual investments (Caldwell & White, 2001; Parham, White, & Ajamu, 2000). What is also accurate for Black men has been the lack of role modeling relative to committed and engaged partner relationship; this lack of role modeling has made it difficult for Black men to have day to day experiences of positive and sustained emotional intimacy and connection (Conner & White, 2006). The presence of historical racism, generations of poverty and low socioeconomic status, and being raised in a "village of caretakers," including grandmother, aunts, uncles, and cousins, have often been characteristic child-rearing experiences for African American males (Franklin, 2004, 2010).

Latino and African American men have a history of negative stereotypes contributing to the lack of interest in the professional literature and limited consideration of their involvement in psychological treatment. A salient aspect of these men's lives remains particularly similar, namely experiences of discrimination, oppression, and racism, which have also been a connecting link for these male populations of color in their selection of partners, level of coping, and partner relationships (Organista, Marin, & Chun, 2010). A brief overview of these concepts is summarized in Table 13.1.

MICROAGGRESSIONS AND MACROAGGRESSIONS

The act of depriving individuals of civil liberties, including access to housing, education, and employment, has historically been the understated legacies for people of color (American Psychological Association, 2007; Takaki, 1993). The experiences of discrimination, oppression, and racism have typically been the backdrop to the everyday life engagement of Latino and African American men (Organista et al., 2010; D. W. Sue et al., 2007). These challenging life events often come in the form of psychological insults or microaggressions. Certain conscious and unconscious attitudes from individuals, social environments, and institutions as well as unexpected personal occurrences serve to diminish or dehumanize one's personhood. Further, interpersonal episodes are characteristically life-altering, influencing entire life trajectories relative to one's mental and emotional functioning. These episodes often contribute toward internalized racism that subsequently leads to self-destructive behaviors (Pinderhughes, 1989).

The recent introduction of new language to explain the often subtle expressions of racism on individuals, *racial microaggressions*, has been helpful in describing the process of continuous emotional, psychological, and spiritual assaults, and their impact on the lives of people of color primarily (D. W. Sue, 2010). D. W. Sue et al. (2007) defined *microaggression* as brief, everyday exchanges that send denigrating messages to

TABLE 13.1   Concept, Characteristics, and Clinical Relevance

Concept	Characteristics	Relevance to Practice
Discrimination	• Can denote favorable or unfavorable actions toward a social group as a result of a group membership (Jones, 2002) • Context is experienced as negative where noninclusivity and daily reminders of one's diminished and often unequal social status is emphasized (Boyd-Franklin, 1989; Gorman-Smith & Tolan, 1998; Organista, Marin, & Chun, 2010)	• Observe relevant emotional and behavioral consequences • Discuss perceptions of event(s) on one's self esteem and feelings of self competency • Review impact of event on couple and family relationship
Oppression	• Act of feeling powerless in a situation, environment, personal, or ethnic/cultural standing (Pinderhughes, 1989) • Diminished capacity for self-competency, worthwhileness, and feeling unvalued • Sociopolitical forces primarily framed through experiences of sexism, ethnocentrism, homophobia, racism, and classism (Marsiglia & Kulis, 2009; Sue, 2010)	• Examine how marginalized status has been defined • Explore context of how experiences of feeling powerless has defined one's status • Has perceptions of diminished capacity impacted other areas of functioning • Review impact of event on couple and family relationships

(Continued)

TABLE 13.1   Concept, Characteristics, and Clinical Relevance (Continued)

Concept	Characteristics	Relevance to Practice
Racism	• Any attitude, action, or institutional arrangement that results in the subordination of another group based offensively upon grouplike physical characteristics (Jones, 2002) • As a result of socially constructed biological differences, some groups will prove to be directly superior to others reinforcing a base of validated social inferiority and social stigma (Robinson, 2005) • Potential for internalized perceptions of self-disgust, self-depreciation, self-hatred (Miller & Garran, 2008; Willie Kramer, & Brown, 1973)	• Explore whether experiences of racism have become one's image of self • Evacuate the past and current presence of recurring aggression and experiences of violence in the partner relationship • Assess for related self-destructive behaviors • Review impact of experience on couple and family relationships

people of color because they belong to a racial minority group (p. 3). These authors go on to describe this pattern as involving underrespected and devalued attitudes, and disregard as a result of one's race or gender. Further, they indicate that subtle, often aggressive exchanges are typically conducted through gestures, tones, and seemingly inconsequential snubs that serve to disrespect or disempower individuals. D. W. Sue, Capodilupo, and Holder (2008) go on to highlight the presence of racial microaggression on African Americans and provide examples that frequently occur in racial encounters.

In contrast to microaggressions, many men of color also tend to experience increased assaultive behavior, which is more impactful and not subtle, such as unjust employment terminations, community violence, and direct confrontations based on one's ethnicity and race. These experiences, now labeled as *macroaggressions,* refer to a direct disqualification of an individual's sense of personhood. Macroaggressions also refer to experiences such as lack of access to health and employment due to one's marginalized status, a commonly reported reality for Latino and African American men. These examples suggest that racism, discrimination, and oppression are less likely to be disguised and covert adding to the greater assault on one's emotional and behavioral functioning (Miller & Garran, 2008). Consider the impact of these experiences on men of color who have been tolerating these every day occurrences of disrespect. Clinical practice has demonstrated that the psychological and behavioral consequences are often negative and subsequently define the stability and wellness of one's couple and family relationships (Flores-Ortiz, 2004; Gallardo & McNeill, 2009; White & Cones, 1999).

Pinderhughes (1989) provides relevant examples detailing the consequences of oppression and racism on individuals. In her commentary, the direct experience of helplessness is likely to result in creating dependency and vulnerability in one's intimate relationships. Psychological and behavioral instabilities, such as drug and alcohol abuse, domestic violence, child abuse, and anger management issues, underscore the embedded imprint of internal, couple, and family violence, which can lead to the frequent pathologizing of men of color. We have long understood that behavioral and emotional instability often originates in childhood and adolescence as a result of emotional and spiritual wounds prompted by histories of community and gang violence, diminished social status in the school system, and possibly migratory histories that have caused social, residential, and neighborhood displacement (Ceballo, Ramirez, Heary, & Maltease, 2003; Coperland-Linder, Lambert, & Ialongo, 2010; Gorman-Smith & Tolan, 1998; Lambert, Ialongo, Boyd, & Cooley, 2005; Wilkerson, 2010).

The developmental experiences and social forces of oppression, micro- and macroaggressions often become a dehumanizing process that fuels a powerlessness in one's individual and collective lives (D. W. Sue, 2010; D. W. Sue et. al., 2007). This powerlessness and subsequent emotional wounding lead to experiences of anger and rage and subsequently to acting out these behaviors in intimate partner violence and other self-destructive behaviors (Freire, 1992). The consequences of relationship distress can often stem from many contributory factors; however, for Latino and African American men, those factors are often centered in the experiences of racial and oppressive social forces that have become internalized.

PROFESSIONAL LENS

Following over three decades of practice, my understanding of clinical situations, particularly in regard to families of color, has been defined by a family psychology and family systems perspective (Pinsof & Lebow, 2005), the increased multicultural literature particularly in the area of gender (Levant, 1996; Rabinowitz & Cochran, 2002), and the incorporation of a psychospiritual healing perspective that is consistent with my own cultural underpinnings (McNeill & Cervantes, 2008). In brief, understanding the structure of a family's internal functioning and the multiple layers of relational and generational history form a core aspect of how I conceptualize behavior. In addition, the relevant cultural belief systems, and socioeconomic and sociopolitical issues that are particular to communities of color along with related spiritual and religious practices add to the incorporation of what this means for me relative to psychological intervention.

This integration of family psychology, multicultural considerations, and psychospiritual reference points are encapsulated within a humanistic perspective that supports an orientation toward acceptance of the person, a nonjudgmental attitude, and a belief in possibilities. Following a gradual seasoning as a practitioner, I have become more colloquial and yet professional in how I interact with clients. As a result, I have learned to utilize self-disclosure, appreciation for the emotional suffering and disempowerment of one's life history, and harnessing the strengths that a client brings to help increase motivation and follow through in a client's change process. For example, two cases are presented in this chapter where I as the treating therapist support clients to advocate for themselves in order to increase their own experiences of empowerment and to help resolve some of the primary issues that are impacting their present life circumstances.

Perhaps the prominent aspect of my practice with families of color has been my own ethnic and cultural background as a Latino with Mexican Indian identity. Having a sharpened awareness for my Mexican American and Mexican Indian ancestry, and growing up in a community where I perceived myself as having marginal status have increased my sensitivity to disempowered communities. Familiarity with cultural norms, related sociocultural life experiences, and routine interaction of families with low socioeconomic status have been fundamental to the collective shaping of myself as a man, psychologist, and community advocate.

STRATEGIES FOR EFFECTIVE TREATMENT FOR LATINO AND AFRICAN AMERICAN MEN

Some of the primary insights that I have gained in practice with men of color across diverse socioeconomic status histories are noted next. These strategies are intended to provide guidance for practitioners regardless of gender or ethnic and cultural identity in order to support clinically meaningful and effective psychological understanding and intervention with these male populations.

Despite the lack of writing about men of color and their experiences with couples therapy, there are salient recommendations with regard to the development of an affirming therapeutic relationship with Latino and African American men. These recommendations can support an effective professional relationship and therapeutic process. While these strategies are not meant to be exhaustive, they do comprise some fundamental principles that I have incorporated into my own practice and which I have found essential toward establishing a meaningful dialogue and understanding with these client populations.

Strength-Based Approach

A salient consideration in the treatment of Latino and African American men has been to focus on strengths and minimize stereotypes, assumed weaknesses, and perceived cultural deficits that could distract from effective professional care. Evidence-based treatment continues to be a prominent aspect in psychotherapy, yet difficult to practice with populations of low socioeconomic status, poverty, and challenging community issues, such as violence and drug and alcohol abuse (Goodheart, Kazdin, & Stenberg, 2006). As such, it is important when treating these male populations in couples work that the therapist understands their unique personal and family situations though contextualizing their complaints and life experiences. An acknowledgement of history will likely find that episodes of rage, discrimination, and racism are an important dimension to their everyday functioning (Clark, Anderson, Clark, & Williams, 1999; Pinderhughes, 1989; D. W. Sue et al., 2008). I have learned as a psychotherapist to evaluate the level of stress while acknowledging those areas where they have coped well. A meaningful strategy is to have the client talk out what they had to do concretely to facilitate participation in couples therapy (i.e., willingness to confront one another, rearrange work schedules, child care, disrupted home routine). In addition, as it becomes relevant to the case, having the client describe any experiences that he has had with discrimination and racism, and the impact it had on self or couple relationships can be helpful toward determining how they have coped with those circumstances. This information can be invaluable relative to learning an initial foundation for helping men of color to increase their perceptions of ability and "ableness," and open the opportunity for assignment of therapeutic tasks that can increase these abilities.

Evaluate for Experiences of Micro- and Macroaggression

Effective practice with communities of color often includes a diverse approach, incorporating a realistic assessment of the client's psychological issues, and a psychoeducation approach that is often the undercurrent to the therapeutic process (Acosta, Yamamoto, & Evans, 1982; Cornish et al., 2010). Consequently, educating clients about the roles

that contextual factors (i.e., low socioeconomic status, unsafe neighborhoods, self-obstructive behavior) may play in their behavior can
be an important intervention particularly with Latino and African
American families (Minuchin et al., 2007). Some of this education
can include therapist acknowledgment of experiences of racism and
discrimination that have become embedded in psychological complaints, thereby shadowing some of the evolution of couples' relational
issues (Robinson, 2005). For example, it is important to deal with
racial microaggressions, which often are numerous in the everyday
lives of Latino and Black men: how they accumulate and impact the
interpersonal relationship (D. W. Sue et al., 2007, 2008). An often-
cited example is that of an African American male who enters an
elevator as White occupants take double looks about whether they
feel safe, leading some to exit prematurely; this kind of episode can
contribute to anger and resentment on the part of the client who
has had this experience. Over time the accumulation of these racial
micro- and macroaggressive experiences can lead to the compromising
of one's attitudes and behaviors, and the development of an unhealthy
anger that becomes interwoven in the daily routine of a couple (Boyd-
Franklin & Franklin, 1998; Carter, 1995; White & Cones, 1999). As
a consequence, feeling powerless and developing a diminished capacity for self competency and worth may influence one's level of coping
and the manner in which one handles frustration, life challenges, and
ultimately any partner relationship.

Examine One's Personal and Professional Biases

As it has often been described by various multicultural writers (D. W.
Sue & Sue, 2003), being aware of one's assumptions and implicit biases
is an ethical and professional practice consideration (D. W. Sue et al.,
1992). All psychotherapists develop a particular mindset, cultural reality, and awareness of one's life-span experiences. As such, these implicit
biases will direct the level of care and involvement, which could have
an impact on the therapist–couple relationship. Some of these potential
discrepancies are influenced by socioeconomic status, gaps in economic
stability, unexamined psychological issues for the therapist, one's history
of racism, and the combination of psychological issues that the couples
themselves brings to the therapeutic encounter (Liu, Soleck, Hopps,
Dunston, & Pickett, 2004). As such, these implicit biases will influence
the level of care and involvement that proceeds as well as the distinct
attributes that will affect the interpersonal encounter (Dovidio, Glick,
& Rudman, 2005). A critical self-examination of our own prejudices is
an expectation that comes with our profession (American Psychological
Association, 2003), particularly as this awareness is coupled with client populations who challenge the cultural beliefs and lifestyle of the
counseling professional.

Review One's Personal and Private Behavior Relative to Biased Attitudes and Actions

As a psychotherapist is reviewing the experiences of discrimination, oppression, and racism in the lives of clients, particularly communities of color, it is important for the professional to equally explore how one has contributed toward these attitudes through their own actions (La Roche, 2002; D. W. Sue, 2005). The negative and unjustified feedback to a carwash attendant, insensitive remarks made to a server in a restaurant who may be African American or Latino, or simply reviewing a clinical case with a colleague or supervisee in which Latino and African American men are negatively described, is an important personal and professional awareness that should be considered.

It has been suggested in this chapter that the psychotherapist can have stereotypes about Latino and African American men that can be unhelpful and destructive in the therapeutic process (La Roche, 2002). Recall the discrepancy between therapist and client that can frequently exist relative to ethnicity and race, gender sexual orientation, and socioeconomic status (Liu et al., 2004). A critical awareness of the therapist's values relative to environmental and contextual differences will permit Latino and African American men a more meaningful relationship encounter and, subsequently, more effective treatment.

Become Familiar with the Community of the Client System

It is important when treating Latino and African American men in couples therapy that the therapist becomes aware of the socioenvironmental and community experiences that frame complaints and their life experience (Conner & White, 2006; Gorman-Smith & Tolan, 1998; Lambert et al., 2005). A review of history will find that experiences of discrimination and racism may be the backdrop to their everyday functioning. As such, I have found it helpful to evaluate the level of stress and accompanying distress that may have contributed by these destructive social forces on the couples' relationship directly and particularly on the psychosocial functioning of the male in this dyad. There is something to be said about knowing the neighborhood that a client comes from and allowing that knowledge to infuse one's awareness about the couples' complaints and the potential issues that may be framing their lives (Liu et al., 2004). It is not being suggested that a psychotherapist develop a road map to an individual's community. Rather, asking sensitive questions about one's neighborhood, the friendships and family that may be part of their support system, and any potential issues that they view as significant in their lives may be important clinical material to integrate for the practitioner.

Religious and Spiritual Life Experiences

I have learned that in practicing with communities of color, particularly Latino and African American men, experiences of empowerment, hope, and inspiration have historically been supported through a combination of prayer, belief in the intercession of a higher spirit, and participation in a church community (Cervantes & Ramirez, 1992; Cervantes & Parham, 2005; Levin, 1984; Matovina & Riebe-Estrella, 2002). Boyd-Franklin and Lockwood's writing on spirituality and families (1999) provides an important understanding for the connection between spirituality and moral conduct. The juncture of religion and spirituality for Latino and African American men facilitate a common meeting ground for a dialogue of empowerment, mutual alignment of energy and goals, and the opportunity to utilize this dimension as a useful bridge toward resolution of violence, oppression, and self-hatred. I have found it helpful with these male populations to acknowledge the importance of a meaningful spirituality; this acknowledgment may help clients disclose not only personal limitations but also past community experiences that may have contributed to esteem and self-acceptance issues. When appropriate, initiating this dialogue for men of color can help clients develop their own version of a spiritual, connecting force. This dialogue may include developing a meaningful personal prayer; attendance at church; consulting with a minister, rabbi, or priest; or simply acknowledging the larger spiritual forces that may be at play in their own lives (Aponte, 1999; Matovina & Riebe-Estella, 2002; Stevenson, 1990).

Teach Advocacy Skills

Education can have a significant role in the therapeutic process with men of color, particularly as the practitioner is orienting clients to incorporate empowerment skills. As stated by Pinderhughes (1989), families of color undergo significant life stressors that are complicated by sustained experiences of helplessness and disempowerment. Knowing that these factors may be relevant life experiences for many Latino and African American men of color may provide a therapeutic opportunity toward increasing self-advocacy and ability to manage life circumstances more effectively (Connor & White, 2006; Velasquez & Burton, 2004; White & Cones, 1999). Experiences of discrimination, oppression, and racism can marginalize emotional and social standing, subsequently compromising feelings of security and relational stability. Exploring the context of how experiences of feeling powerlessness have defined one's personal and relational identity can open up the conversation between therapist and client fostering further perceptions of client trust, and meaningful disclosures that could build effective therapeutic momentum. Providing direction and education consultation in practice with the couple could lead toward a more positive outcome and a model of success relative to men of color and their role as caretakers and protectors.

Consider Clinically Meaningful Self-Disclosure

An important dimension that may be considered in practice with men of color has been the utilization of self-disclosure as an affirming approach to developing effective therapeutic trust (Carter, 1995; Cervantes, 2005; Franklin, 2010; Ridley, 1995). The use of this process has been repeatedly discussed in other writings demonstrating its efficacy when utilized in a manner that underscores the primacy of the client (Hill & Knox, 2002; Watkins, 1990). Admission of therapist vulnerability where it is conducted in service to the client primarily and where said disclosure is consistent with the complaint, can maximize an affirming therapeutic encounter. In brief, the exchanging of relational stories between therapist and client provides an interesting bond that levels a playing field while still acknowledging a respectful client–professional relationship and the clinician's authoritative presence. When experiences of racism and discrimination have been a reported aspect of a client's past history, these events can sometimes sour the building of effective trust even between an ethnically similar therapist and client. However, the display of vulnerability and willingness to disclose a personal story that underlies a therapist experience relative to the client's life history may provide a needed point of contact, grounding the relationship in a trusting and affirming manner.

CASE STUDIES

Two cases are now described that reflect the author's typical practice and the therapeutic interactions that are an important part of this process. Each of these cases are viewed within a family psychology perspective that integrates the relevant contextual factors and meaningful life experiences that help to frame my understanding of the couples' concerns. The clinical material presented is summarized with the salient issues that impacted the case and a brief transcription of how I responded to a selected issue. I follow each case with a commentary that reflects what occurred from my perspective and how I managed the issues that were revealed by these respective couples.

Robert and Elena

Robert and Elena Flores are a second generation Mexican American couple, married 10 years and are the oldest of their respective families of origin. Robert has a landscape business that he inherited from his father who still works with him. Elena recently received her cosmetology license and is employed full time at a beauty salon. They share three children (ages 4, 6, and 10) and the 10-year-old has recently had difficulties due to his aggressive stance with other peers and potential involvement with gang-related activity. The primary reason for referral was due to the parenting problems they are experiencing particularly with their 10-year-old. In addition, Elena has complained about Robert hosting too many barbecue parties at their home where he is consuming extensive alcohol leading to arguments between them.

Initially, the therapeutic relationship focused on a combination of child and family therapy due to the aggressiveness of 10-year-old Mario. It quickly became evident that this couple's rapport with each other and their day-to-day routine were becoming increasingly disruptive due to Robert's aggressiveness and his alcohol difficulties, which were now extending beyond the barbecue parties. As a result, Mario was referred to another therapist for counseling, and Robert and Elena became the focus in marital therapy.

A brief family of origin history found that Robert had worked with his father for several years cutting lawns, trimming trees in upscale neighborhoods, and learning how knowledge of different vegetation could create an affirming space for a particular home. Within this context, Robert commented on the frequent verbal assaults and disrespect that his father would endure, and by association, himself, from the various homeowners who would often look down on them. They were often referred to as wetbacks and dirty Mexicans while they were working and the clients would often exploit his father for hours of work where he would not be compensated fairly. As Robert inherited the landscape business, he also took on many of the landscape jobs that his father had worked for several years. Consequently, Robert inherited the verbal assaults and attempts to exploit his work from many of the homeowners, whom he described as White and ignorant.

Robert stated that the impact of the abusive language and racist remarks that he has received daily had started to wear on him causing frustration and anger and increased alcohol consumption. He also acknowledged that he had been increasingly angry with his family and felt that his wife did not understand him nor the stressors that he would often undergo as part of his daily abuse. Robert indicated that the harsh verbal discipline toward his children, particularly his 10-year-old son, Mario, was intended to "toughen him up" and prepare him for the role that he too would inherit as he became older.

During counseling visits, Robert complained of feeling anger and confusion over the individuals who have historically mentally abused his father and himself growing up. He admitted to sometimes talking to his wife regarding these various episodes following his return from work, however, in the last few years, he would keep these reactions to himself. Elena commented that she had become more frightened over his accelerating anger toward her and the children, particularly at the verbal abuse he would show toward Mario. The relational cycle that had now ensued was initiated by Robert's aggressive behavior toward his family, his wife's protective measures to redirect his anger, and Robert's own resolution of increased alcohol consumption.

Interestingly, the alcohol abuse resulted in verbally abusive episodes and not in domestic violence. Rather, his reactions following ingestion of alcohol were to become calmer and eventually fall asleep. As the couple's therapist of record for Robert and Elena, I found that this couple accepted me immediately due to the similarity of our ethnic and cultural backgrounds that we shared, and the fact that I also spoke Spanish. Although the majority of the counseling was conducted in English and my no-nonsense approach toward his alcohol use and the aggressive behavior he was displaying toward his family, a therapeutic relationship continued to grow. As their family therapist with a strong existential and systemic perspective, I focused particularly on the relationship between the macroaggression assaults that he had learned to endure during his workday, his subsequent behavior at home, and his understanding of this sequence. Cognitively, Robert appeared to understand the connection; however, the psychological and verbal assaults he would endure from his job and the subsequent discharge of these long-embedded reactions at home would prove to be a salient challenge for him.

The following is an example of how I responded to Robert.

Robert: Look doc, I am tired of the bullshit that I get from these people ... don't you know what it feels like to be told that you are not worth anything as you are doing your job as best as you can?

Therapist: We talked about this before, Robert. These are putdowns that these guys are doing to you so that they can make themselves feel better and more important. But the important point here is to look at what you are doing to yourself and your family each time that you come home ... you are beating yourself up on the drive home, wanting to forget what happened and then you get home and you take it out on your family either through your drinking or through the verbal abuse toward your wife. (*Wife agrees with a nonverbal sign.*)

Robert: Yeah, I know what's going on. I just don't know what to do and how to make this better for myself and my family.

Therapist: Look, you and I have talked about this before and remember when we discussed the kind of man and husband you want to be to your wife and children, you really described yourself as a person of integrity, somebody who knew right from wrong and could handle himself with more confidence in who you are.

Robert: You're right doc. I just know that if I pick up my voice and say that I am not going to be treated like this anymore, I might lose my job but I guess I have to deal with that. I have to understand that what is more important is how my family sees me and what my children are learning from me.

Therapist: That's right, Robert ... *si se puede* (yes, it is possible) you are a man that knows better and now more eyes are on you to do the right thing for yourself and your family.

This couple was seen for more than 20 visits and by midway in the counseling, Elena had taken a position that unless her husband did something about his drinking, she would no longer condone these reactions at home and would consider a separation. Although Robert had been prompted on several occasions by the therapist to participate in Alcoholics Anonymous (A.A.), he was finally motivated following the ultimatum given by his wife. The combination of Robert's participation in A.A. three to four times per week, the increased communication between him and his wife, the termination of alcohol use at home, and a more loving rapport between himself and the children, started to make a difference. At visit 13, Robert was in a position to begin taking more active management of his circumstances with those whose homes he landscaped and was standing up for himself despite risking the potential loss of work with one of his clients.

Although only having a high school education, Robert was intellectually bright yet lacked self-confidence likely as the result of his experiences with his father in the landscape business. His bright and alert style was commented on several occasions by the therapist as well as highlighting the caring and stable family he and his wife had developed in their marriage. Robert was well intentioned and even tempered, which made him personable when he was not drinking and this characteristic was also emphasized. The toughening up of his son was redefined so that the intent of teaching his son about life was accomplished in a more positive and affirming way rather than through an abusive and aggressive style.

Over the course of the 6 months that Robert and Elena were seen for couples counseling, Robert was found to be more confident and affirming in his relating with Elena and the children. He was attending A.A. religiously and had fully terminated any alcohol use. In addition, Robert had commented in the last two visits that his team of six employees has also been instructed about how to protect themselves from verbal assaults. He reported that they began standing up in a more proactive way and affirming their self worth as immigrant workers who were trying to stabilize themselves and their respective families in the United States.

Jamal and Lorraine

Jamal and Lorraine Jones are an African American couple whose families moved from New Orleans approximately 15 years ago. They met each other as high school seniors and married approximately 4 years ago. This couple reported that their families of origin experienced several generations of poverty, which was the primary reason for their geographic move to the West Coast. Lorraine stated that they have one child, a precocious 5-year-old who seems to want to know everything. Jamal is a police officer in a large metropolitan city, and Lorraine is employed as a secretary for a dental office on a part-time basis and attends a local community college. Their entry into couples counseling was due to the anger management problems that have been most evident with Jamal following his shift in the neighborhood he patrols and his accusations of unfaithfulness toward his wife who attends classes after work at the dentist office.

Jamal was referred by his supervisor due to his having uncooperative behavior with his fellow officers, angry outbursts, and tardiness at work over the past month. Jamal expressed the strong feeling of not trusting any "mental health people," indicating to me that "I'm not crazy." He stated that several of his fellow officers were racist and he just became tired of their remarks and comments. Further, Jamal indicated that as a patrol officer, he frequently was involved in incidents where there were racial insults aimed at him by both the Black perpetrators whom he would have to arrest as well as by White and Latino individuals who had broken the law and would also have to be arrested. Regardless of their ethnic and racial background, Jamal reported that he was feeling abused and tired of being called racist names, a sellout, and an Uncle Tom. He further stated that his wife needed to be more attentive to him as she is becoming increasingly distant and not available to listen to his stories after work, which she used to do prior to her starting classes at the community college the past year.

Lorraine commented that the world that they live in is unfair and unjust and to a degree understands her husband's feelings. She herself reported experiences of harassment from patients at the dental office who would sometimes become angry because they could not be seen immediately and would have to wait past their appointed time for at least a half hour. As a result, their negative comments would often be directed to her suggesting that she was incompetent and not mentally equipped to handle the demands of this job. At least this was the interpretation that Lorraine felt, which she subsequently interpreted as racial bias and felt attacked by those individuals she was trying to serve.

Jamal and Lorraine each described their own individual experiences with racism on the job and their attempts to cope with this daily confrontation. Jamal reflected that the instances of racial remarks and insults were just as prominent in New Orleans when living there and thought that by moving to the West Coast there would be less discrimination. Lorraine echoed these same sentiments. This couple confirmed that their lives seemed to revolve around coping with racial hatred and managing their lives with some normality despite the presence of negative comments that have come to make up their daily work experience. Early on in the counseling visits, Jamal questioned me relative to my ability to help them as a couple and demonstrated a short-lived suspicion over whether I also would mistreat them in some way or label him with a "diagnostic code" that could place him at risk with his employer. I chose to manage this relevant therapeutic question with self-disclosure by commenting on some of the racial and ethnic abuse I had experienced in the past in order to try to forge a secure and therapeutic relationship with this couple. This couple was relieved following my disclosure, which seemed to give them permission to describe other events where they felt helpless, vulnerable, and powerless over the racial assaults that they frequently had learned to endure.

The following is an example of how I responded to Jamal.

Jamal: I don't know if I can really trust you because even though I came to see you with my wife, I don't really know what you can do for me or what you even know about me.

Therapist: Jamal, you are right. I don't really know you other than the little bit of information that you have given me about your life story and the history with discrimination that you experienced throughout your life. It is a history that I know about too personally.

Jamal: What do you mean? What do you know about people talking behind your back because you're Black? And forming opinions without even knowing you and just treat you bad because of who you are. I mean sometimes I don't even know whether it's because I'm a Black man or a cop.

Therapist: You make a good observation, Jamal, about whether it is that you are a Black man or you as a cop and how people treat you. But I know that before you were a cop, there were many times when you felt mistreated because of being a Black man. Some people just have a lot of learning to do about their neighbor and I think you know what I mean. As a Latino, I can remember several experiences growing up when I felt similar to what you indicated to me. (*Relays specific life experiences where discrimination and racism were evident.*)

Jamal: I appreciate you saying that about yourself, man. I didn't mean to disrespect you. I just wanted to make sure you understood my deal and I think you do.

Jamal's position as a police officer often placed him in dangerous situations and in front of a public audience where his actions would always be scrutinized. As a result, he often felt pressure trying to control a crisis in the streets where the public was not on their best behavior. While the racial assaults were more manageable when conducting his patrol, it was the verbal assaults he was receiving at work that made life more difficult.

Jamal and Lorraine were seen for 12 visits generally every other week. He was encouraged to address the issues related to inappropriate verbal comments about his ethnic and cultural background to his supervisor and subsequently to file a formal complaint if the comments were not terminated. In addition, it was recommended to Jamal that he pursue the possibility of multicultural awareness training for his fellow workers through the human resources department. A similar approach was taken with Lorraine who was directed to speak with her employer regarding the verbal assaults by patients and enact a policy relative to appropriate language to use in the office.

Jamal was able to acknowledge that given his prior experiences of racist attitudes, he had become prone to expect these reactions from White people and possibly misperceive one's intent sometimes due to this inherent bias. Jamal attended anger management sessions along with outpatient counseling, which helped him to increase his awareness and modify his reactions. The combination of my self-disclosure, and the acknowledgement of the impact of discrimination and racism on Jamal's psyche were relevant dimensions to the healing process for this couple.

A final issue that was left unresolved was Jamal's accusations of unfaithfulness regarding his wife. While acknowledging that perhaps he may have overreacted to her classes at a community college, he nevertheless was unable to resolve the fact that his wife, through her education, was becoming more independent, had less time for him, and wanted a career. Jamal and Lorraine without resolution of this last issue, however, appeared to be more proactive with regard to managing their feelings of powerlessness at their respective work settings.

CASE COMMENTARY

Robert Flores and Jamal Jones, while of different ethnic and cultural groups, each shares very similar experiences relative to discrimination, experiences of depression and helplessness, and racism. In addition, they were socialized in low-income families who settled in the same geographic area following their respective migrations. They were found to be committed and stable couples, share at least one child, and are gainfully employed. The treatment of these cases each evoked a unique therapeutic response. With Robert, the attachment was almost immediate as a result of my similar gender, ethnic, and cultural background as the treating psychotherapist. Robert became responsive quickly to assumptions he made about our mutual Latino heritage, which was reinforced through my own demonstration of cultural familiarity, bilingual ability, and awareness of the negative experiences of discrimination. This last aspect proved to be a pivotal issue in the formation of the therapeutic alliance as well as in the selection of treatment goals.

The therapeutic attachment with Jamal Jones was more challenging due to what appeared to be healthy skepticism and distrust of the therapist's intentions and his having minimal confidence in mental health professionals. The quality of self-disclosure for the author proved to be a helpful, unplanned intervention that helped to win over trust and confidence from Jamal and Lorraine (Hill & Knox, 2002). This self-disclosure involved the relating of direct, personal experience regarding my own history of discrimination and racism. As a result of laying this unintended foundation, the underlying message was that we were on the same side and understood each other's past experiences, namely, disclosures for Jamal about his past experiences of overt racism. This dialogue allowed me to empathize and begin serving as a validated example for how to manage the negative assaults that confronted all of us as *brothers of color,* a term that Jamal now used to describe our relationship. As is true with clinical practice, the presenting problems and development of effective and meaningful professional contact need to be matched by the creativity of the psychotherapist (Sadeghi, Fischer & House, 2003; La Roche, 2002). This creativity may permit one to be eclectic while utilizing one's personal life experiences to help couples cope with difficult circumstances such as low-income status, social marginalization, and destructive social forces (Minunchin et al., 2007).

The development of empirically validated treatments toward efficacy in practice with communities of color still lags in the professional literature (Gallardo & McNeill, 2009; Goodheart et al., 2006). I have found that meaningful pacing of the relationship between client and therapist, and the identification of issues that are most immediate to be an effective component of my approach. In addition, my training as a systems and family therapist has proven to be invaluable relative to viewing the broader arena of roles, relationships, hierarchy, alliances, and boundaries in understanding the more detailed yet broader landscape of family functioning (Goldenberg & Goldenberg, 2008).

Each of these cases required the building of effective therapeutic rapport, however, the cultural and relational dynamics in each case relative to intervention was unique and distinct. With Robert and Elena, therapeutic change occurred as a result of establishing a base of empathy for understanding with regard to cultural similarity (Falicov, 1998; Santiago-Rivera et al., 2002). Subsequent development of a firm, professional relationship permitted the teaching of effective guidelines to managing the inappropriate, abusive behavior from some homeowners at his job sites. In addition, making the connection between the internalization of anger and the subsequent abuse of alcohol and its effect on his family was a relevant behavioral sequence for Robert to understand.

In contrast, for Jamal and Lorraine Jones, major therapeutic change was accomplished through self-disclosure, the implication of similar cultural experiences that allowed the bonding process to deepen, and the direction to approach his superiors about managing the ethnic and racial remarks he was experiencing. This direction also provided the opportunity for having Jamal take responsibility for initiating multicultural training in his police unit. The combination of established cultural similarity and life experiences between therapist and client, self-disclosures, teaching effective ways to manage abusive behavior, and having Jamal address the racial insults and negative attitudes to his superiors all proved to be effective interventions in helping Robert and Jamal and their respective partners (Franklin, 2004; White & Cones, 1999).

Perhaps the most salient aspect of treatment in these two cases was the identification of distrust and racism as the base of their anger, and the appropriate labeling of self-injurious behavior and presence of depression for these men. Failure to have understood the impact of racism for both Robert and Jamal and their respective partners could have undermined a more integrative and meaningful outcome in the couples counseling (Miller & Garran, 2008). As a result, the importance of recognizing the impact of discrimination and racism in the lives of men of color may prove a significant backdrop to the relational ties of couples who as persons of color may likely be responding to a life-span history that has incorporated ineffective coping and potentially, self-destructive behaviors (D. W. Sue, 2010; D. W. Sue et al., 2007).

CONCLUDING REMARKS: ON BECOMING A BROTHER OR SISTER OF COLOR AS A PSYCHOTHERAPIST

This chapter has attempted to illuminate reasons why Latino and African American men have been stereotyped into a perception that they are uncooperative in the counseling process. Some of the examples and studies cited refer to these population of men as invisible and prone to display of relational problems with their partners, likely to undermine the outcome of psychological care, and showing tendencies that would perceive them as unwilling family members with self-destructive tendencies (Coley, 2001). Each of these stereotypical descriptions have likely contributed to negative attitudes and lowered expectations by therapists, and a decreased likelihood to have these male populations participate actively in professional intervention. Although it is acknowledged that there are individual differences among all clinical populations and that no cultural group is immune to pathologizing its male gender, this chapter has affirmed the belief in men of color as being resilient, committed to the well-being of their families, and open toward an invitation to be active participants along the healing journey with their partners.

An observation that I have noted in working with Latino and African American men is the similarity of my early life experiences, a commonality that has strengthened my belief in the importance of cultural competence with these populations. Furthermore, my professional association over the years with Latino and African American men has shaped who I have become as a psychotherapist. However, there are various ways to build respectful relationships that do not necessitate a cultural similarity between therapist and client (Fowers & Davidov, 2006; La Roche, 2002). Authentic recognition of the emotional suffering in one's life circumstances, a willingness to go the extra mile in being helpful, the installation of hope and sacredness in the therapeutic bond, and a strength-based approach that acknowledges all forms of effective coping can go a long way toward a therapist of any gender or ethnicity being designated as a brother or sister of color. In brief, culturally specific knowledge with treating populations is essential in the establishment of any effective therapeutic attachment and competent practice (Sadeghi, Fischer, & House, 2003).

I have learned that becoming a brother or sister of color is not necessarily about being a person of color. Rather, a belief in the interdependence of relationships, acknowledgment of cultural belief systems relative to health and illness, and awareness of the socioenviromental background in contextualizing one's therapeutic relationship are some of the primary ingredients toward effective practice with men of color. In addition, self-disclosure where by one allows personal vulnerability and humility to be present, goes a long way toward establishing credibility as a professional counselor. Being granted the label of brother or sister of color is not a title that is given due to one's professional degrees, analysis of a clinical situation, or expert understanding of psychological dysfunction. Rather, this title is earned through authentic and open dialogue that recognizes the vulnerability between and within people and how we experience related existential dilemmas.

It has been the intent of this chapter to provide not only a strong reminder of the impact of discrimination and racism on Latino and African American men, but also to review old stereotypes about these male populations, leading to new insights for the treating psychotherapist (Gonzalez, 1997). It is incumbent on each of us to acknowledge any resistances that may exist, and subsequently integrate novel and creative ways in which to provide effective psychological care (American Psychological Association, 2003, 2007; American Psychological Association Task Force on Socioeconomic Status, 2007; Miller & Garran, 2008).

REFERENCES

Acosta, F. X., Yamamoto, J., & Evans, L. A. (1982). *Effective psychotherapy for low-income and minority patients.* New York: Plenium Press.

American Psychological Association. (1993). Guidelines for providers of psychological services to ethnic, linguistic, and culturally diverse populations. *American Psychologist, 48*, 45–48.

American Psychological Association. (2003). Guidelines on multicultural education, training, research, practice, and organizational change for psychologists. *American Psychologist, 58*, 377–402.

American Psychological Association. (2007). Resolution on prejudice, stereotypes and discrimination. *American Psychologist, 62*, 475–481.

American Psychological Association Task Force on Socioeconomic Status. (2007). *Report of the APA Task Force on socioeconomic status.* Washington, DC: Author.

Aponte, H. J. (1999). The stresses of poverty and the comfort of spirituality. In F. Walsh (Ed.), *Spiritual resources in family therapy* (pp. 76–89). New York: Guildford Press.

Billingsley, A. (1992). *Climbing Jacob's ladder: The enduring legacy of African American families.* New York: Simon & Schuster.

Boyd-Franklin, N. (1989). *Black families in therapy: A multisystems approach.* New York: Guildford Press.

Boyd-Franklin, N., & Franklin, A. J. (1998). African American couples in therapy. In M. McGoldrick (Ed.), *Re-visioning family therapy: Race, culture and gender in clinical practice* (pp. 268–281). New York: Guildford Press.

Boyd-Franklin, N., & Lockwood, T. W. (1999). Spirituality and religion: Implications for psychotherapy with African American clients and families. In F. Walsh (Ed.), *Spiritual resources in family therapy* (pp. 90–103). New York: Guildford Press.

Caldwell, L. D., & White, J. L. (2001). African-centered therapeutic and counseling interventions for African American males. In G. R. Brooks & G. E. Good (Eds.), *The new handbook of psychotherapy and counseling with men* (pp. 737–753). San Francisco, CA: Jossey Bass.

Carter, R. T. (1995). *The influence of race on racial identity in psychotherapy.* New York: John Wiley & Sons.

Casas, J. M., Turner, J. A., & Ruiz de Esparza, C. A. (2001). Machismo revisited in a time of crisis: Implications for understanding and counseling Hispanic men. In G. R. Brooks & G. E. Good (Eds.), *The new handbook for psychotherapy and counseling with men* (pp. 754–779). San Francisco, CA: Jossey Bass.

Ceballo, R., Ramirez, C., Heary, K. D., & Maltese, K. L. (2003). Community violence and children's psychological well-being: Does parental monitoring matter? *Journal of Clinical Child and Adolescent Psychology, 32,* 586–592.

Cervantes, J. M. (2005). A new understanding of the macho male image: Exploration of the Mexican American man. In M. Englar-Carlson & M. A. Stevens (Eds.), *In the room with men: A casebook approach to psychotherapy with men* (pp. 197–224). Washington, DC: American Psychological Association.

Cervantes, J. M. (2010). Mestizo spirituality: Toward an integrated approach to psychotherapy for Latina/os. *Psychotherapy: Theory, Research, practice, Training, 47*(4), 527–539.

Cervantes, J. M., & Parham, T. A. (2005). Toward a meaningful spirituality for people of color: Lessons for the counseling professional. *Cultural Diversity and Ethnic/Minority Psychology, 11,* 69–81.

Cervantes, J. M., & Ramirez, O. (1992). Spirituality and Family Dynamics in Psychotherapy with Latino Children. In L. Vargas & J. Kross-Chianio (Eds.), *Working with culture: Psychotherapeutic interventions with ethnic minority children and adolescents* (pp. 103–128). San Francisco, CA: Jossey-Bass.

Cervantes, J. M., & Sweatt, L. I. (2004). Family therapy with Chicana/os. In R. J. Velasquez, L. M. Arellano, & B. W. McNeill (Eds.), *The handbook of Chicana/o psychology and mental health* (pp. 285–322). Mahwah, NJ: Lawrence Erlbaum Associates.

Clark, R., Anderson, N., Clark, V., & Williams, D. (1999). Racism as a stressor for African Americans: A biopsychosocial model. *American Psychologist, 54,* 805–816.

Coley, L. R. (2001). (In)visible men: Emerging research on low income, unmarried, and minority fathers. *American Psychologist, 56,* 743–753.

Comas-Diaz, L. (2001). Hispanics, Latinos, or Americans: The evolution of identity. *Cultural Diversity and Ethnic Minority Psychology, 7,* 115–120.

Connor, M. E., & White, J. L. (Eds.). (2006). *Black fathers: An invisible presence in America.* Mahwah, NJ: Lawrence Erlbaum Associates.

Cornish, J. A. E., Schreier, B. A., Nadkarni, L. I., Metzger, L. H. & Rodolfa, E. A. (2010). *Handbook of multicultural counseling competencies.* New York: John Wiley & Sons.

Coperland-Linder, N., Lambert, S. F., & Ialongo, N. S. (2010). Community violence, protective factors and adolescent mental health: A profile analysis. *Journal of Clinical Child & Adolescent Psychology, 39,* 176–186.

Dovidio, J. F., Glick, P. G., & Rudman, L. (Eds.). (2005). *On the nature of prejudice: Fifty years after Allport.* Malden, MA: Blackwell.

Falicov, C. J. (1998). *Latino families in therapy: A guide to multicultural practice.* New York: Guilford Press.

Franklin, A. J. (2004). *From brotherhood to manhood: How Black men rescue their relationships and dream from the invincibility syndrome.* New York: Wiley.

Franklin, A. J. (2010). *Another side of invincibility: Present and responsible Black fathers.* In C. Z. Oren & D. C. Oren (Eds.), *Counseling fathers* (pp. 121–140). New York: Routledge.

Flores-Ortiz, Y. G. (2004). Domestic violence in Chicana/o families. In R. J. Velasquez, L. M. Arellano, & B. W. McNeill (Eds.), *The handbook of Chicana/o psychology and mental health* (pp. 267–284). Mahwah, NJ: Lawrence Erlbaum Associates.

Fowers, B. J., & Davido, B. J. (2006). The virtue of multiculturalism: Personal transformation, character and openness to the other. *American Psychologist, 61,* 581–594.

Freire, P. (1992). *Pedagogy of the oppressed.* New York: Continuum.

Gallardo, M. E., & McNeill, B. W. (Eds.). (2009). *Intersections of multiple identities: A casebook of evidence-based practices with diverse populations.* New York: Routledge.

Goldenberg, H., & Goldenberg, I. (2008). *Family therapy: An overview.* Belmont, CA: Thomson Brooks/Cole.

Goodheart, C. D., Kazdin, A. E., & Stenberg, R. J. (Eds.). (2006). *Evidence-based psychotherapy: Where practice and research meet.* Washington, DC: American Psychological Association.

Gorman-Smith, D., & Tolan, P. (1998). The role of exposure to community violence and developmental problems among inner-city youth. *Development and Psychopathology, 10,* 101–116.

Gonzalez, G. (1997). The emergence of Chicanos in the twenty-first century: Implications for counseling, research and policy. *Journal of Multicultural Counseling and Development, 25,* 94–106.

Gutman, M. C. (2007). *The meanings of macho: Being a man in Mexico City.* Berkeley: University of California Press.

Hill, C. E., & Knox, S. (2002). Self-disclosure. In J. C. Norcross (Ed.), *Psychotherapy relationships that work: Therapist contributions and responsiveness to patients* (pp. 255–265). London: Oxford University.

Jones, M. (2002). *Social psychology of prejudice.* Upper Saddle River, NJ: Prentice Hall.

La Roche, M. J. (2002). At the crossroads: Managed mental health care, the ethics code, and ethnic minorities. *Cultural Diversity and Ethnic Minority Psychology, 8,* 187–198.

Lambert, S. F., Ialongo, N. S., Boyd, R. C., & Cooley, M. (2005). Risk factors for community violence exposure in adolescence. *American Journal of Community Psychology, 36,* 29–48.

Levant, R. F. (1996). The new psychology of men. *Professional Psychology: Research and Practice, 27,* 259–265.

Levin, J. S. (1984). The role of the Black church in community medicine. *Journal of the National Medical Association, 76,* 477–493.

Liu, W. M., Soleck, G., Hopps, J., Dunston, K., & Pickett, T. Jr. (2004). A new framework to understand social class in counseling: The social class worldview model and modern classism theory. *Journal of Multicultural Counseling and Development, 32,* 95–122.

Marsiglia, F. F., & Kulis, S. (2009). *Diversity, oppression and change.* Chicago, IL: Lyceum Books.

Matovina, T., & Riebe-Estrella, G. (Eds.). (2002). *Horizons of the sacred: Mexican traditions in U.S. Catholicism.* Ithaca, NY: Cornell University Press.

McNeill, B. W., & Cervantes, J. M. (Eds.). (2008). *Latina/o healing practices: Mestizo and indigenous perspectives.* New York: Routledge.

Miller, J., & Garran, A. M. (2008). *Racism in the United States: Implications for the helping professions.* Belmont, CA: Thomson Brooks/Cole.

Minunchin, P., Colapinto, J., & Minunchin, S. (2007). *Working with families of the poor.* New York: Guilford Press.

Mirande, A. (1997). *Hombres Y machos: Masculinity and Latino culture.* Boulder, CO: Westview Press.

Organista, P. A., Marin, G., & Chun, K. M. (2010). *The psychology of ethnic groups in the United States.* Thousand Oaks, CA: Sage.

Parham, T. A. (1989). Cycles of psychological nigresence. *The Counseling Psychologist, 17,* 187–226.

Parham, T. A., White, J. L., & Ajamu, A. (2000). *The psychology of Blacks: An African centered perspective.* Upper Saddle River, NJ: Prentice Hall.

Pinderhughes, E. (1989). *Understanding race, ethnicity, & power: The key to efficacy in clinical practice.* New York: The Free Press.

Pinsof, W. M., & Lebow, J. L. (Eds.). (2005). *Family psychology: The art of the science.* New York: Oxford Press.

Rabinowitz, F. E., & Cochran, S. V. (2002). *Deepening psychotherapy with men.* Washington, DC: American Psychological Association.

Ridley, C. R. (1995). *Overcoming unintentional racism in counseling and therapy.* Thousand Oaks, CA: Sage.

Robinson, T. L. (2005). *The convergence of race, ethnicity, and gender.* Upper Saddle River, NJ: Pearson/Prentice Hall.

Sadeghi, M., Fischer, J. M., & House, S. G. (2003). Ethical dilemmas in multicultural counseling. *Journal of Multicultural Counseling and Development, 31,* 179–191.

Santiago-Rivera, A. L., Arredondo, P., & Gallardo-Cooper, M. (2002). *Counseling Latinos and la familia: A practical guide.* Thousand Oaks, CA: Sage.

Stevenson, H. (1990). The role of the African-American church in education about teenage pregnancy. *Counseling and Values, 34,* 131–133.

Sue, D. W. (2005). Racism and the conspiracy of silence: Presidential address. *The Counseling Psychologist, 33,* 100–114.

Sue, D. W. (Ed.). (2010). *Microaggressions and marginality: Manifestation, dynamics, and impact.* San Francisco, CA: John Wiley.

Sue, D. W., Arredondo, P., & McDavis, R. J. (1992). Multicultural counseling competencies and standards: A call to the profession. *Journal of Counseling and Development, 70,* 477–483.

Sue, D. W., Capodilupo, C., & Holder, A. (2008). Racial microaggressions in the life experience of Black Americans. *Professional Psychology: Research and Practice, 39,* 329–336.

Sue, D. W., Capodilupo, C. M., Torino, G. C., Bucceri, J. M., Holder, A. M., Nadal, K. L., & Esquilin, M. (2007). Racial micro-aggressions in everyday life: Implication for clinical practice. *American Psychologist, 62,* 271–286.

Sue, D. W., & Sue, D. (2003). *Counseling the culturally diverse.* New York: Wiley.

Sue, S., Zane, N., Hall, G. C. N., & Berger, L. K. (2009). The case for cultural competence in psychotherapeutic interventions. *Annual Review of Psychology, 60,* 525–548.

Takaki, R. (1993). *A different mirror: A history of multicultural America.* Boston: Little, Brown & Co.

Torres, J. B., Solberg, S. H., & Carlstrom, A. H. (2002). The myth of sameness among Latino men and their machismo. *American Journal of Orthopsychiatry, 72,* 163–181.

Velasquez, R. J., & Burton, M. P. (2004). Psychotherapy of Chicano men. In R. J. Velasquez, L. M. Arellano, & B. W. McNeill (Eds.), *The handbook of Chicana/o psychology and mental health* (pp. 177–192). Mahwah, NJ: Lawrence Erlbaum Associates.

Watkins, C. E. Jr. (1990). The effects of counselor self-disclosure: A research review. *The Counseling Psychologist, 18,* 477–500.

White, J. L., & Cones, J. H. (1999). *Black man engaging: Facing the past and seizing a future in America.* New York: Routledge.

Wilkerson, I. (2010). *The warmth of other suns.* New York: Random House.

Male-Sensitive Therapy for the Returning Veteran and his Partner

GARY R. BROOKS

The returning male* military veteran† is situated at the intersection of a myriad of cultural, institutional, sociopolitical, and family systems impediments to successful participation in couples therapy. This chapter advances the effort to make couples therapy more gender sensitive by identifying these special impediments and offering adaptations to common counseling practices. First, a case example.

---

* Perhaps the most relevant aspect of the returning veteran's cultural heritage is his "maleness." Although women have served honorably in the U.S. military in all conflicts since the Revolutionary War (Goldstein, 2001; Street, Vogt, & Dutra, 2009), it is only recently that female troops have represented (been allowed to represent) a sizable portion of military forces. In Vietnam, women's enlistment was capped at 2% of total forces, but women's participation climbed to 11% in the Gulf War and 14% of deployed forces in Operation Enduring Freedom (OEF) in Afghanistan and Operation Iraqi Freedom (OIF) in Iraq. It is recognized therefore that the term veteran is not synonymous with male, and military burdens are more shared across genders than ever.
† This chapter attempts to address challenges common to all military veterans. It must be recognized, of course, that there are multiple variants of veteran status dependent upon era, site of conflict, enlisted man versus officer, career versus single tour, and drafted versus volunteer (as well as those differences rooted in race and ethnicity). As a result, only a generalized description of the experience of veterans is possible.

CASE ILLUSTRATION

My first meeting with Travis (age 28) came several weeks after I had first been contacted by his wife, Jessica (age 26). After Travis had refused to return to the local Veterans Affairs (VA) outpatient clinic for any of his scheduled outpatient appointments, he had "holed up" in his bedroom, refusing all efforts by Jessica to encourage interaction with her and their two sons (ages 9 and 7). Other than smoking cigarettes in the backyard and occasionally visiting his Vietnam vet father-in-law, Travis remained isolated and withdrawn. The family was subsisting on Jessica's income from work as a teacher and Travis's 50% service-connected disability (for headaches and hearing loss). I met twice with Jessica, hearing her concerns that Travis had become increasingly moody and preoccupied with e-mailing his former buddies from the Iraq conflict (Operation Iraqi Freedom, OIF). Although Jessica had pleaded with Travis to accompany her to the therapy sessions, he had refused: "Who needs all that talking and whining crap?" Only after I encouraged Jessica to take a more insistent stance with Travis ("something has to change or the boys and I are going to stay with my parents"), did he agree to attend one couples session.

The first conjoint meeting was a predictable disappointment. Jessica was outspoken in her concerns; Travis was minimally involved and contentious. After repeated efforts by Jessica to provoke some engagement from Travis, he blurted, "Look, there is no f-----g point to this ... You people back here have no f-----g idea what went on over there ... I probably need to re-up and get back there with my guys ... that was when I felt like I knew who I was and what I was doing!" Rising from his chair and moving toward the door, he challenged, "Would it be a big problem to you if I just got the f--k outta here?"

Taking advantage of some hesitation from him, I asked Travis to allow me just a few minutes to give him my take on the situation. I explained that I was not a combat veteran, but that I had spent more than 30 years listening intently to the incredible stories of vets from Korea, Vietnam, the Persian Gulf, Iraq, and Afghanistan. Thanks to them, I had gained some sense of what they had gone through and what they had lost. "If you would give me a chance, I'd be deeply grateful for a chance to hear your story ... I gotta tell ya, it has been clear to me that holding these stories inside does nobody any good and eventually tears a guy apart."

Although somewhat tentative, Travis agreed to at least one individual follow-up meeting. It didn't take long. After opening the door about his conversations with his Vietnam vet father-in-law, Travis passionately described his deeply felt connection with the men who fought beside him and those "still over there who won't come back." Before long his rising anger gave way to silence as he struggled to control his tears and his breathing. "Do you have any f-----g idea what it's like to have a god-damn IED explode beside your vehicle when you can't hear a goddamn thing! Your partner is f-----g bleeding and half-his f-----g face is blown the f--k off!"

For several more sessions, I listened as Travis described and reexperienced some of the trauma of his Iraq experiences. Some sessions were intense, some were listless and emotionally avoidant. Eventually, Travis agreed to sign up on the wait list for the nearby VA posttraumatic stress disorder (PTSD) outpatient program. As he became better able to understand his mood swings and he was less fearful of his repressed memories, he felt more able to share his hidden self with Jessica.

It is not surprising that the couple's sessions were subdued at first as I cautiously encouraged Travis to discuss his inner life with Jessica, and as she patiently and empathically listened, Travis' fears of her reactions were lessened. To a great extent, Jessica's compassion and understanding had been enabled by supportive individual sessions, attendance at PTSD spouse support groups, and selected readings about combat PTSD.

Eventually, Travis became able to contain his fixation with his Iraq memories, put aside his ruminative dwelling on his days in Iraq, and commit himself to investing in his civilian life. At this stage, the couple's sessions shifted into a more balanced process, whereby Travis and his PTSD issues receded and here-and-now couple issues became the primary focus. Jessica became better able to describe her own suppressed concerns and needs, and Travis had no choice but to abandon his previous self-justification of "Don't expect anything from me ... I'm just a f----d-up crazy vet!"

This very brief overview of the work with Travis and Jessica illustrates many of the impediments inherent in work with returning vets and their partners. Many of these obstacles merit further elaboration.

CULTURAL IMPEDIMENTS: MALE CULTURE

Since most returning veterans are men (and the focus of this volume is on male populations), it is therefore not inappropriate to examine the role that a soldier's "maleness" plays in his accommodation to the military environment and his eventual efforts to reenter civilian settings. Over the past four decades, a burgeoning men's studies literature has allowed for far greater appreciation of male socialization and the hazards of the male gender role (David & Brannon, 1976; Kilmartin, 2009; Levant & Pollack, 1995; Pleck, 1995). Of this exhaustive literature, the most immediately relevant aspects are those that touch upon the relationship of men to the help-seeking process in general, and to counseling/psychotherapy in particular.

In a comprehensive review of men and help seeking, Addis and Mahalik (2003) noted that "a large body of empirical research supports the popular belief that men are reluctant to seek help from health professionals" (p. 5). More specifically, it has also been well established that men experiencing emotional distress are much less likely than women to be found in the office of a psychotherapist (Gove, 1984; Vessey & Howard, 1993). Scher (1990) has long held that men enter therapy only when they are desperate and when they believe there is no alternative. Brooks (1998, 2010) carried this observation further in claiming that at some level most men "hate" psychotherapy.

Several reasons were cited for this antipathy. First, psychotherapy has most always been portrayed fairly negatively in the media (Sleek, 1995; Wedding & Niemiec, 2003). Second, Brooks argued, many men perceive the world of therapy to be the province of women and therefore fear that a therapy session will be used to shame a man or create a triangulation between the therapist and woman partner against him. Additionally, the qualities of the "ideal" therapy client are quite different than the qualities of the "real man." Traditional masculinity emphasizes the virtues of dominance, power, and interpersonal control, while, to most men therapy seems to demand that the client cede control, let others take charge and allow oneself to be in a "one-down" position. Further, male socialization teaches men to be highly competitive and to think hierarchically. Unfortunately, men often view the counseling office as a sign of competitive failure. Historically, psychotherapy has been portrayed as a venue to "get in touch with feelings," whereas men have been taught to hide their inner emotions and are frequently alexithymic (having no words for feelings; Levant, 2003). Finally, the heightened intimacy commonly part of the therapy process can be threatening and confusing to men who have been taught to sexualize their feelings of intimacy (Brooks, 1995; Levant & Brooks, 1997).

CULTURAL IMPEDIMENTS: MILITARY CULTURE

Most all men are exposed to fairly similar socialization experiences and throughout their lives are expected to participate in the "doing or making of gender" (Gilbert & Scher, 1999, p. 159). Yet, dependent upon happenstance and variations in cultural context, the intensity and degree of variance in expression of masculinity can be lessened or it can be dramatically heightened. With the military veteran, the latter situation is very much the case. Military socialization and veterans' experiences, from boot camp until discharge, exponentially intensify traditional masculine values and perspectives. In terms of military culture, Keith and Whitaker (1984, p. 149) noted, "In the last two decades it has become very difficult to stay 'macho'... the military services provide some opportunity." This should not come as a surprise since one primary mission of the military has always been to take a select group of young men and turn them into "warriors and fighting machines" (Egendorf, 1985, p. 6). In his historical analysis of male roles, Doyle (1989) notes that warrior manhood in the form of the "epic male" has always had the dominant position in our understanding of men's place in most all cultures. The price of this process is highlighted by Sammons and Batten (2008) who observe, "Since the beginning of human combat, warriors have been adjusting to their home lives through personal strengths, with the support of communities, loved ones, and religious traditions … However, we must also recognize that a substantial minority of returnees will experience mental health problems" (p. 926).

In his efforts to integrate men's studies literature with the literature on treatment for returning veterans, Brooks (1990, 2005) called attention to the many ways that military culture reinforces traditional male socialization and increases the gender role strain of most veterans. First, and perhaps most prominent, the military is inherently about violence whereby soldiers become conditioned to its pervasive presence. In the military, violence is central, the world is sharply divided into allies and enemies, and enemies are depersonalized as justifiable targets of violent impulses (Carlson, 1987). Soldiers must adapt to a context in which violence is a highly legitimate mechanism, a means to serve moral goodness (Egendorf, 1985).

But it is not only the violent missions of the military that create problems for returning veterans, as other aspects of military life also exacerbate male gender role strain. Many men's problematic issues with limited emotional sensitivity and empathy deficits (Levant, 1995; Lisak, 2001) are made more severe by the emotional suppression and *psychic numbing* (Lifton, 1973), frequently a survival mechanism for combat soldiers. Erbes et al. (2008) refer to this relationally maladaptive emotional process as *experiential avoidance,* a major component of problems among veteran couples. Shatan (1978) noted than from the beginning of their basic training, soldiers are taught to suppress their compassion by dehumanizing the enemy and ultimately distorting their own humanity. Psychic numbing, of course, is one of the primary features of posttraumatic stress syndrome, one of the most common symptomatic outcomes of combat in the Vietnam war and in the more recent Iraq and Afghanistan wars (Jakupchak et al., 2009; Tanielian & Jaycox, 2008).

Military situations contribute to a tendency for men to develop a suspicious and distrustful approach to others. Keith and Whitaker (1984) referred to the military as the "paranoid edge of the culture" (p. 150). Hendin and Haas (1984) reported that *paranoid adaptation* is a common residual effect for combat veterans. The Vietnam counterinsurgency combat was characterized by the lack of frontlines, further adding to the continual guardedness of combat veterans (Leventman & Camacho, 1980). Nearly identical situations in Iraq and Afghanistan produce "little respite from the constant vigilance required in such settings" (Sammons & Batten, 2008, p. 922). In Iraq (OIF) and Afghanistan (OEF), the paranoid tendency continued because of a minimal capacity to recognize enemies, with the additional dimension of great danger presented by hidden improvised explosive devices (IEDs; Chard, Schumm, Owens, & Cottingham, 2008; Sollinger, Fisher, & Metscher, 2008).

One of the most problematic aspects of traditional masculinity has been the proclivity for men to cope with emotional distress through alcohol and drug abuse (Brooks & Silverstein, 1995; Dawson, 1996; Isenhart, 2005). Sadly, the military has a long and troubled relationship with alcohol. Stanton (1980) observed that the use of alcohol has a long history in the military. Jelinek and Williams (1982) charged that the military actively condones alcohol abuse. The addition of marijuana and heroin to this problematic equation became especially troublesome for Vietnam veterans (Frenkel, Morgan, & Greden, 1977). Although less is known as yet about hazardous alcohol use among OEF and OIF veterans, a recently published study found that 40% of a VA outpatient clinic population was found to be positive for hazardous alcohol use and 22% screened positive for possible alcohol use disorder (Calhoun, Elter, Jones, Straits-Troster, & Kudler, 2008). In light of the study's authors recommending "increased vigilance and action," it remains apparent that the association between military experience and susceptibility to substance abuse is ongoing.

In an era when the misogynistic features of traditional patriarchy are changing in most areas of civilian culture, the military remains as a relatively anachronistic environment of sexism and negativity toward women. The frequent male problems with pornography and nonrelational sexuality (Brooks, 1995; Levant & Brooks, 1997; Paul, 2005; Stock, 1997) are worsened in military culture. For example, Egendorf (1978) reported that "the military world denigrates women and treats sex as a commodity even more blatantly than the civilian world does" (p. 240). The increased presence of women in the military has added a new dimension to problematic relations with women. Consistent with workplaces that are traditionally male dominated and characterized by relatively large power differentials between organizational levels, the military is a place where poor treatment of women, sexual harassment, and sexual assault are far too common. While 9% of military women have reported experiencing some form of sexual coercion, 31% have reported some other form of unwanted sexual attention, and 52% have reported experiencing other forms of offensive sexual behaviors (Street et al., 2009). Obviously, not all (or even a majority of) male soldiers engage in these behaviors. Nevertheless, exposure to environments so hostile to women cannot help but have a deleterious impact on young men's interactions with women in their military time and when they return to civilian life.

Overemphasis on the good provider role and neglect of relationships has been central components of all characterizations of traditional male problems (David & Brannon, 1976; Brooks & Silverstein, 1995; Levant, 1995; O'Neil, 1982). This issue is nowhere more insidious than in the military where all else is secondary to loyalty to mission and duty to country (Ridenour, 1984). Keith and Whitaker (1984) observed that all families in the military are indoctrinated with the ethos that military comes first, with the resultant gulf between the soldier and his family, "one of the most hopeless troubles in family therapy" (p. 151). Dunning (1996) quoted the oft-heard military maxim, "if the military had wanted you to have a family, it would have issued you one" (p. 198). For male veterans in Iraq and Afghanistan, this struggle to adapt one's traditional role in his family has been exacerbated by the special *cycle of deployment* problems inherent in these conflicts (Sheppard, Malatras, & Israel, 2010). Lincoln, Swift, and Shorteno-Fraser (2008) describe the enormous problems for the returning parent-partner (usually a husband-father) to reestablish his customary roles: "This readjustment changes how the family has functioned during the period in which the parent-soldier was deployed and may create unanticipated difficulties in adapting to the new family constellation and roles" (p. 986).

Many observers of contemporary men have noted the prominence of bitterness, resentment, and occasional angry backlash against groups thought to be infringing upon traditional male privilege (Clatterbaugh, 1997; Faludi, 1991). To some extent, the anger of many men can be attributed to a general loss of some men's relative power base resulting from the gains from the women's movement, civil rights movement, and gay rights movements (Kimmel, 1996). However, an entirely separate source of bitterness seems to be the province of modern military veterans. Unlike their predecessors, Vietnam veterans have been shortchanged by a generalized lack of national recognition of their service and contributions (Figley & Leventman, 1980). For Iraq and Afghanistan veterans, the national mood is far more supportive, but other unique circumstances generate considerable dissatisfaction and bitterness. Unlike any previous military engagements, the OEF and OIF campaigns have been fought with an all-volunteer force, with a higher proportion of the armed forces being deployed, with deployments being longer, redeployment to combat being common, and breaks between deployments being infrequent (Hosek, Kavanagh, & Miller, 2006). Although a degree of anger and resentment has been described as the heritage of *all* returning soldiers (Waller, 1980), the contemporary returning veteran seems to have even greater cause for negativity toward his country and the civilian community (Chard et al., 2008; Erbes et al. 2008).

INSTITUTIONAL IMPEDIMENTS

As has been noted earlier, the heritage of traditional manhood is a generalized aversion to all forms of help seeking, with particular distaste for counseling and psychotherapy. The military's reinforcement of this go-it-alone attitude is manifested not only in terms of internalized values of individual service members but also in terms of broad institutional barriers to treatment. The Department of Defense Task Force on Mental Health (2007) identified the stigma of mental illness as a significant issue, noting that service members are reluctant to seek help for mental health problems. Institutional-level stigma, defined by

Sammons (2005) as institutional policies or practices that unreasonably limit an individual's opportunities, is present in the military in several forms. In reviewing the military's institutional barriers inhibiting access to mental health care, Tanielian and Jaycox (2008) cited (a) attitudes and beliefs about mental health and treatment seeking; (b) unit cohesion; and (c) unit dynamics (p. 276). The latter two factors relate to the special circumstances of military service, whereas the first involves a sort of hypermasculine value orientation.

In military settings, the bond among comrades is exceptionally critical, as the *culture of independence* (Tanielian & Jaycox, 2008, p. 278) may mediate between death and survival. This interconnective bond, referred to as *unit cohesion* (National Defense Research Institute, 1993), enhances morale, motivation, and psychological resilience, particularly under adverse combat situations. In fact, Helmus and Glenn (2005) stated that most military experts consider unit cohesion to be the most important protective factor in preventing psychiatric breakdown. Another observer noted, "When morale is high, stress casualties are low, and vice versa" (Labuc, 1991, p. 475). Unfortunately, this "protective factor" may have a downside. When help seeking is equated with abandonment of comrades, even the most extreme psychic distress may be denied or managed with alcohol and drug use. Further complicating matters has been the pervasive distrust between service members and mental health providers (Hoge, Auchterlonie, & Milliken, 2006), with identification of a mental health problem viewed as the first step toward discharge from the service (Sammons, 2005).

The second special circumstance of the military service situation impeding mental health access relates to the dynamics of military units. As noted by Tanielian and Jaycox (2008), the "accountability" aspect of military units requires noncommissioned officers to know the whereabouts of their soldiers at all times. It becomes virtually impossible for a trouble soldier to seek help confidentially, and any mental health diagnosis will frequently have negative career implications (Hoge et al., 2004).

The third type of institutional barrier identified by Tanielian and Jaycox (2008)—attitudes and beliefs—relates to the manner in which the military services reinforce and amplify traditional masculine values that run counter to self-care and help seeking. These authors note, "Every war fighter has a culture of toughness, independence, not needing help, not being weak, and expecting to handle stress without problems ... soldiers, sailors, airmen, and marines are encouraged to develop inner strength and self-reliance ... to shake off ailments and injuries" (Tanielian & Jaycox, 2008, p. 276). In a survey from the Office of the Surgeon General's Mental Health Advisory Team (U.S. Department of the Army, 2005) it was found that half of all service members who screened positive for mental disorders cited treatment inhibiting concerns about appearing weak, being treated differently, and losing the confidence of other unit members.

In sum, men who serve in the military and ultimately return to civilian life can be expected to experience a variety of major value clashes and culture shocks. Their previous socialization into traditional masculinity has not only been reinforced by military culture, but any psychic distress and impulse to reach out to a mental health professional has been strongly discouraged by widespread institutional impediments within the armed services. But these are not the only factors making it difficult for returning veterans to participate effectively in couples therapy.

SOCIOPOLITICAL AND FAMILIAL IMPEDIMENTS

In the effort to find more effective ways to understand the complexities of their clients' presenting problems, family therapists and couples therapists continually broadened their conceptual lenses from an intrapsychic, to an interpersonal, and to a family systems paradigm, until more recently moving toward an *ecosystemic* paradigm (Goldberg & Goldberg, 2008). This ecosystemic perspective widens consideration beyond intrafamilial functions to the various social contexts in which couples and families are embedded (Robbins, Mayorga, & Szapcznik, 2003). One such larger ecosystem, the major focus of this volume, is that system organized around gender. This gender ecosystem not only structures the world according to fairly fixed (although shifting) social roles for women and men, but it also has been highly affected by vast discrepancies in access to power and influence. To operate effectively in couples counseling with returning male veterans, counselors need to be aware of the various sociopolitical forces impinging upon these couples. Returning veterans are subject to ecosystemic influences from their role and position within two primary systems: the VA health care system and the family system to which they return. Each of these systems affect, and are affected by, the returning veteran. Furthermore, these reciprocal influences can facilitate or hamper couples treatment.

For many decades, the VA health care system has publicly presented itself as loyal to a mission first articulated by President Abraham Lincoln in his second inaugural address: "To care for him who shall have borne the battle and for his widow, and his orphan" ("The Origin," n.d.). Although there has recently been some concern within the U.S. Department of Veterans Affairs expressed on blogs that this motto is no longer appropriate because of its sexist, exclusionary, and anti-family implications, ecosystemic forces remain within the VA that impinge upon the returning veteran's ability to be effectively treated within the couples counseling modality.

Brooks (1991a) noted that up until that point in time there had been some efforts to shift treatment focus for veterans beyond pure intrapsychic factors to interpersonal systems aspects of veterans stress responses (Figley & Sprenkle, 1978). However, Brooks (1991a) then asserted that therapists wishing to intervene with Vietnam veterans (the majority of veterans requesting treatment at that time) would face therapy pitfalls from "linearity, contextual naïveté, and gender role blindness" (p. 446).

One aspect of the argument presented by Brooks is that there had been a pervasive tendency to view the veteran couple and family from a linear causality position. That is, the returning veteran with military-related problems was consistently viewed as the principle cause of the couple's issues, with minimal attention to systemic factors that might have inhibited the veteran's reintegration with his family. Mental health practitioners have generally recognized that families reorganize when a military father is absent and face a major reintegrative challenge when he returns (Lincoln, Swift, & Shorteno-Fraser, 2008; Ridenour, 1984; Strange, 1984). However, most publications on treatment of veterans have "punctuated" the problems as residing within the veteran. For example, Marrs (1985) described family work with Vietnam veterans as primarily focused upon "what the family can do to help" (p. 85). This historical tendency to focus too narrowly on the veteran alone has been recently critiqued by Sammons and Batten (2008) when they noted, "PTSD cannot be treated in a vacuum … the effects on couples or families of a multifaceted and often chronic disorder must be considered to optimize recovery" (p. 925). In seeking to understand this systemic blindness of previous work with veterans, Sammons and Batten attribute the problems to earlier reductions in military mental health staffs. Fortunately, they also describe a "recent acknowledgement by the military of the necessity of directly integrating the family into treatment." (p. 925).

This criticism of treatment recommendations for returning veterans is not intended to impugn the highly commendable and positive intentions of mental health practitioners in the military or the VA health care system. In fact, the early emphasis on individual veteran-centered treatment may be inevitable in a treatment system designed principally to help veterans. However, this should not mean that couples therapists limit themselves to a linear view of a veteran couple's relationship problems. As noted by Brooks (1991a), "Although the veteran's extraordinary experiences must be acknowledged as a critical element in long-standing adjustment problems, family interactions must not be ignored as mediating factors" (p. 456). For example, structural therapy practitioners could focus on how the couple's boundary characteristics, subsystem functioning, and hierarchical rules are affected by the veteran's post-military problems (e.g., PTSD) as well as how these factors contribute to the same problematic issues. Strategic therapists might be interested in how a family's faulty "solution behaviors" (Watzlawick, Weakland, & Fisch, 1974) might stimulate or perpetuate a veteran's symptoms. Another therapist, such as Madanes (1991) might see the relationship between the veteran and the spouse as comprising an "incongruous hierarchy," in which the veteran's symptoms are both an indication of his weakness as well as a method of gaining interpersonal control.

In addition to therapy pitfalls from an overly linear conceptual paradigm, couples counseling with returning veterans can be derailed by ignorance of the context in which most veterans function, that is, the VA health care system and the veteran subculture. It wasn't until the late 1980s that literature began to appear regarding the larger context of veterans' treatment and reintegration. Frey, Swanson, and Jacob (1987) explored the role of the VA as the significant contextual variable in treatment of Vietnam veterans. In their study they described the VA as a system burdened with complicated issues of secondary gain, in which "the VA becomes not only a treatment facility, but a source of potential or real income" (p. 225). The authors then built upon the concept of *therapeutic triangulations,* noted by Stanton, Todd, and Associates (1982), to consider more than compensation issues and they highlighted several isomorphic transactional sequences that maintain the veteran's position as the problem family member.

> The benevolent and accepting attitude may entice an impaired veteran to seek solace amidst understanding staff and peers rather than to work through conflict in his home and family. Second, the level of comaraderie [sic] among VA patients in terms of war and services experiences, and the shared experience of being a VA patient, combine to promote enmeshment. (Frey et al., 1987, p. 226)

This concern about enmeshment with the VA and other veterans is especially problematic for the returning veteran when it contributes to any withdrawal and estrangement from his marital partner. In this regard, Fleming (1985) noted:

> The creation of a minuscule ghetto-like environment isolates the maladjusted veteran from society and serves to reinforce deviant trends. In such a setting, alienated veterans may in effect form a subculture in which sustaining group comfort provides rationalization for inadequacies. Concurrently, adverse reactions from mainstream society become a new stress, which generates new maladaptive responses and further insulates the environment. (p. 138)

A final point must be made about possible sociopolitical impediments to counseling returning veteran couples. The foregoing material describes situations in which the male veteran partner is handicapped or disadvantaged in his ability to participate in couples counseling. This is quite in keeping with the central purpose of this volume: to extend gender sensitivity to male partners. However, just as some men may have a type of power disadvantage in a couple counseling situation, there also must be recognition that counseling takes place in a larger culture in which men generally have more power than their female partners. In brief, couples counseling can be ineffective when men have too little feeling of competence and personal power, but it also can be sabotaged when men have too much power (i.e., relatively greater power than their partner such that they are able to control or sabotage couples treatment). Therefore, power differentials between partners can become a fundamental issue that requires deep appreciation in any therapy effort. This matter is highlighted in the conversations about the similarities and differences of "gender-sensitive therapy" and "feminist" therapy.

Silverstein (2003) differentiated between feminist approaches to families and couples and those describing themselves as "gender sensitive." According to her analysis, gender-sensitive approaches call for recognition of ways that both genders are restricted by gender role strain (Pleck, 1995) but do not necessarily pay attention to the power inequities in patriarchal culture. A key difference between the two views of family and couples work is that feminist approaches make explicit calls for men to give up power to embrace equality in their relationships. Further, men are encouraged to recognize coercive and illegitimate forms of power, and to use alternative ways to express their needs and caring (Dienhart & Avis, 1994). Brooks (1991b) described the multiple ways that a more powerful, yet threatened male partner may seek to derail therapy by utilizing a range of political maneuvers to undercut his partner's empowerment.

These feminist positions regarding the need to correct power imbalances are not inconsistent with gender-sensitive therapy, nor do their practitioners see power sharing as a bad thing for male partners. In fact, the primary thrust of the "feminist therapy for men approach" (Brooks, 2003; Levant & Silverstein, 2001) is that men's efforts to project overdeveloped images of personal power and maintain relationship control are ultimately toxic to their physical, psychological, and relational health.

ISSUES IN SELECTING COUPLES THERAPY FOR RETURNING VETERANS

The first obvious question in determining the wisdom of selecting couples therapy for returning veterans is that related to the efficacy of this modality of treatment; that is, does couples therapy work? Although once unchallenged in claims about the usefulness of their therapy interventions, counselor and therapists have increasingly been expected to provide some form of empirical validation for their therapies (APA Presidential Task Force on Evidence-Based Practice, 2006; Barlow, 2006; Westen, Novotny, & Thompson-Brenner, 2004). Fortunately, many variations of couples intervention modality have been demonstrated to have positive effects (Baucom, Shoham, Mueser, Daiuto, & Stickle, 1998). Although Gottman, Ryan, Carrere, and Erly (2002) questioned the durability of the changes produced in many couple therapies, there is accumulating evidence that therapies with couples produce positive outcomes. For example, Gottman et al. noted, "In a very short time we can dramatically change most distressed marital interactions ... we have been surprised to find that about 30% of the time the changes made in marital interaction seem to last" (p. 69).

The apparent good news about the likely salutary effects of couples therapy must be tempered by some unfortunate realities. By its very nature, scientific research must be conducted under rigorously controlled conditions with explicitly designed and regulated interventions. Most all outcome research is therefore based upon interventions with persons who agree to enter the research program and continue to participate until conclusion. As noted by Silverstein and Brooks (2010) in their comments about evidence-based treatments, "Marital therapy that never begins cannot have a successful outcome. Moreover, couples intervention will not be helpful if one partner comes reluctantly, participates minimally, and ultimately abandons the process" (p. 260).

Because of the multiple impediments for work with returning veteran couples, this additional issue of securing and maintaining a veteran's therapy participation becomes even more problematic. Therefore, as illustrated in the couples work with Jessica and Travis cited earlier, a primary step in couples work with returning veterans is that of engaging the veteran and developing a therapeutic alliance with him. Thereafter, the therapy will benefit greatly by the adoption of a male-friendly therapy format (Brooks, 2010; Kiselica & Englar-Carlson, 2008) that is both gender sensitive (Philpot, Brooks, & Lusterman, 1997) and feminist informed (Silverstein & Brooks, 2010). The following section will address those issues.

OVERCOMING IMPEDIMENTS FOR THERAPY WITH RETURNING VETERANS

If we grant that returning military veterans are subject to multiple sources of resistance to help seeking, it becomes quite likely that their partners will be the ones pressing for treatment. Successful treatment, therefore, typically begins with a therapist utilizing the leverage provided by the motivation of the veteran's partner. A critical issue here is to alert the troubled partner to the many change-sabotaging maneuvers that might be utilized by the change-resistant veteran. Among the maneuvers identified by Brooks (1991b) are those involving (a) various forms of intimidation and coercion; (b) winning favor; (c) creating confusion and manipulating others; and (d) provoking guilt and appealing to feminine nurturing" (pp. 55–57). When the therapist effectively aids the motivated partner to anticipate and counter these potentially sabotaging maneuvers, it can then become possible for the therapy to move forward with engagement of the veteran and provision of therapeutic interventions sensitive to his needs and preferences. (Obviously, not all veterans will be resistant and many will be determined to overcome the gender-based and institutional impediments, and will bravely seek help. For these men, the therapy can move forward more quickly).

It would seem to be ideal if couples treatment could begin with each partner equal in psychological ability to participate. Unfortunately, this is often not the case. Gender studies literature has made it clear that women typically are more comfortable with the relational communication and expression of feelings integral to psychotherapy (Levant, 2001; Tannen, 1990). Therefore, immediate immersion in couples therapy is frequently premature for most veterans since they will be involved in an activity in which they have fewer skills, may feel triangulated against, and have a poor grasp of the long-term therapy benefits and goals. For this reason, Brooks (1998) proposed a "sequence of change" for men in therapy. In this formulation, participation in couples therapy is not initiated until an initial period of individual work is completed with a therapist committed to developing a therapeutic alliance with the male veteran (while maintaining his therapeutic alliance with the woman partner). In addition to conveying appreciation of the veteran's suffering and empathy for his struggles, the therapist arranges for consciousness-raising about masculinity and gender role strain, akin to that central component of feminist therapy of the 1960s and 1970s (Worrell & Johnson, 2001). This consciousness raising is best accomplished by participation in a men's group, but can also be accomplished through selected readings and experiential activities (Brooks, 2010).

Many other recently described male-friendly individual therapy interventions may also be useful prior to, or concurrent with, couples therapy. Levant (1998) has described a communication skills-oriented program to help men improve in terms of empathic listening and better understanding nonverbal communications. Rabinowitz and Cochran (2002) have described a range of experiential exercise and activities to help men gain greater appreciation of repressed emotions. Mahalik (2005a, 2005b) has outlined adaptations to interpersonal psychotherapy and cognitive therapy that make these approaches better suited to men's needs. Jakupchap et al. (2006) have described the effectiveness of a behavioral activation program for veterans suffering from PTSD.

Brooks (2010) has proposed a model of male-friendly therapy that seems quite applicable to work with veterans and partners. He notes,

> This model of male-friendly psychotherapy has several distinguishing characteristics: It is informed by in-depth knowledge of men's lives; attuned to political issues and the ambiguous role of power in men's lives; broad and catholic in its consideration of modes of intervention; positive and focused on enhancement; eclectic, integrative, and transtheoretical; sensitive to a variety of diversities among men; and demanding of therapist self-awareness. (p. 12)

Of particular importance in this context is the author's emphasis of appreciation of diversity among men. With the increasing numbers of ethnic minority men serving in the U.S. military— 11% in Vietnam but more than 25% ethnic minority service members as of the past 5 years

(Sollinger et al., 2008)—it becomes even more critical that recognition of *hegemonic masculinity* (Connell, 1995) not supplant appreciation of the ways that ethnic minority men experience oppression and cultural disadvantage in the military (Latty & Tarver, 2004; Montemayor & Mendoza, 2004).

Once couples therapy is initiated, several additional therapy strategies are indicated. Gottman has made major contribution to couples work with his identification of "diffuse physiological arousal" as a significant problem for men and has demonstrated the utility of "softened start-up" and "soothing" activities (Gottman, 1994, p. 432). Given the experiences of OEF and OIF veterans, this may be an especially important aspect of treatment since "autonomic hyperarousal," that is, difficulty monitoring the level of emotional arousal and returning to emotional baseline, is a common problem for combat veterans (Brooks, 1998; Galovski & Lyons, 2004).

In their book, *Bridging Separate Gender Worlds*, Philpot et al. (1997) described several specialized therapy strategies for improving comprehension of each partner's gender-based life experiences. The *empathic interview* and *gender inquiry* are structured techniques for each partner to listen noncritically to each person's description of his or her gender role experiences and pressures. *Intergender translating and reframing* is the process whereby the therapist reformulates previously contentious attributions of partner behavior and replaces them with those more positive and contextually sophisticated. Ultimately, this effort to heighten mutual understanding and empathy sets the stage for exploration of gender roles more enhancing for each partner. This approach to couples work seems especially applicable to work with returning veterans and their partners since, as noted earlier, military socialization reinforces traditional gender roles, heightening disconnections between partners and creating a need for greater understanding of other-gender experiences.

In the end, feminist therapy, gender-sensitive therapy, and male-friendly couples therapy should incorporate the several characteristics that are completely consistent with the model of multicultural competence provided by Sue and Sue (2008). First, this therapy must be informed by substantial *knowledge* of the common life experiences and gender role pressures of women and men. Second, it must incorporate a range of *skills* or intervention styles congruent with the help seeking style of both partners. Third, it should be characterized by *awareness* in terms of therapists understanding the personal strengths and weakness, biases, as well as possible blind spots that they bring into work with women and men clients.

When applied to work with veterans and partners, multicultural competence would call for therapists to have in-depth knowledge of military culture, the unique challenges of each military engagement, and the resultant stresses upon all military family members. It would require flexibility in therapy interventions, with a capacity to accommodate the many factors impeding help seeking within military culture.

Finally, therapists and counselors would need to have a thorough appreciation of their personal comfort level for work with veterans in times of a wider gulf between civilian and military value systems. Naturally, the national ambivalence about the wisdom of military actions must not seep into the therapist's interventions.

CONCLUSION

Couples work with military veterans and their partners is complicated by multiple obstacles inherent in male socialization and in military culture. However, a gender sensitive intervention model that is informed by feminist and men's studies perspectives will allow for compassionate engagement with couples in this environment. With knowledge of the military context, flexibility in intervention approaches, and awareness of one's assets and reactivities, a therapist can make a substantial difference in the reintegration (coming home) process for veterans and their partners.

REFERENCES

Addis, M. E. & Mahalik, J. R. (2003). Men, masculinity, and the contexts of help seeking. *American Psychologist, 58*(1), 5–14.
APA Presidential Task Force on Evidence-Based Practice. (2006). Evidence-based practice in psychology. *American Psychologist, 61*, 271–285.
Barlow, D. H. (2006). Psychotherapy and psychological treatments. *Clinical Psychology: Science and Practice, 13*, 216–220.
Baucom, D. H., Shoham, V., Mueser, K. T. Daiuto, A. D., & Stickle, T. R. (1998). Empirically supported couples and family interventions for adult mental health problems. *Journal of Consulting and Clinical Psychology, 66*, 53–88.
Brooks, G. R. (1990). Post-Vietnam gender-role strain: A needed concept? *Professional Psychology: Research and Practice, 21*, 18–25.
Brooks, G. R. (1991a). Therapy pitfalls with Vietnam veteran families: Linearity, contextual naïveté, and gender role, blindness. *Journal of Family Psychology, 4*, 446–461.
Brooks, G. R. (1991b). Traditional men in marital and family therapy. In M. Bograd (Ed.), *Feminist approaches for men in family therapy* (pp. 51–74). New York: Haworth.
Brooks, G. R. (1995). *The centerfold syndrome: How men can overcome objectification of women and achieve true intimacy.* San Francisco, CA: Jossey Bass.
Brooks, G. R. (1998). *A new psychotherapy for traditional men.* San Francisco, CA: Jossey Bass.
Brooks, G. R. (2003). Helping men embrace equality. In L. B. Silverstein & T. J. Goodrich (Eds.), *Feminist family therapy: Empowerment in social context* (pp. 163–176). Washington, DC: American Psychological Association.
Brooks, G. R. (2005). Counseling and psychotherapy for male military veterans. In G. E. Good & G. R. Brooks (Eds.), *A new handbook of counseling and psychotherapy with men* (pp. 206–228). San Francisco, CA: Jossey Bass.

Brooks, G. R. (2010). *Beyond the crisis of masculinity: A transtheoretical model of male-friendly therapy.* Washington, DC: American Psychological Association.

Brooks, G. R., & Silverstein, L. B. (1995). Understanding the dark side of masculinity: An integrative systems model. In R. H. Levant & W. S. Pollack (Eds.), *A new psychology of men* (pp. 280–336). New York: Basic.

Calhoun, P. S., Elter, J. R., Jones, E. R., Straits-Troster, K., & Kudler, H. (2008). Hazardous alcohol use and receipt of risk-reduction counseling among U.S. veterans of the wars in Iraq and Afghanistan. *Journal of Clinical Psychiatry*, 69(11), 1686–1693.

Carlson, T. A. (1987). Counseling with veterans. In M. Scher, M. Stevens, G. Good, & G. Eichenfeld (Eds.), *Handbook of counseling and psychotherapy with men* (pp. 343–359). Newbury Park, CA: Sage.

Chard, K. M., Schumm, J. A., Owens, G. P., Cottingham, S. M. (2010). A comparison of OEF and OIF veterans receiving cognitive processing therapy. *Journal of Traumatic Stress, 23*, 25–32.

Clatterbaugh, K. (1997). *Contemporary perspectives on masculinity: Men, women, and politics in modern society.* (2nd ed.). Boulder, CO: Westview Press.

Connell, R. W. (1995). *Masculinities.* Berkeley: University of California Press.

David, D. S., & Brannon, R. (1976). *The forty-nine percent majority: The male sex role.* Reading, MA: Addison-Wesley.

Dawson, D. (1996). Gender differences in the risk of alcohol dependence: United States, 1992. *Addiction*, 91, 1831–1842.

Department of Defense Task Force on Mental Health. (2007). *An achievable vision: Report of the Department of Defense Task Force on Mental Health.* Falls Church, VA: Defense Health Board.

Dienhart, A. & Avis, J. M. (1994). Working with men in family therapy: An exploratory study. *Journal of Marriage and Family Therapy, 20*, 397–417.

Doyle, J. A. (1989). *The male experience.* (Second Edition) Dubuque, Iowa: Wm. C. Brown Company.

Dunning, C.M. (1996). From citizen to soldier: Mobilization of reservists. In R. J. Ursano & A. E. Norwood (Eds.), *Emotional aftermath of the Persian Gulf War: Veterans, families, communities, and nations* (pp. 197–225). Washington, DC: American Psychiatric Press.

Egendorf, A. (1978). Psychotherapy with Vietnam veterans: Observations and suggestions. In C. R. Figley (Ed.), *Stress disorders among Vietnam veterans* (pp. 231–253). New York: Brunner/Mazel.

Egendorf, A. (1985). *Healing from war: Trauma and transformation after Vietnam.* Boston: Houghton Mifflin.

Erbes, C. R., Polusny, M. A., MacDermid, S., & Compton, J. S. (2008). Couple therapy with combat veterans and their partners. *Journal of Clinical Psychology: In Session, 64*(8), 972–983.

Faludi, S. (1991). *Backlash: The undeclared war against American women.* New York: Crown.

Figley, C. R., & Leventman, S. (Eds.). (1980). *Strangers at home.* New York: Praeger.

Figley, C. R., & Sprenkle, D. H. (1978). Delayed stress response syndrome: Family therapy indications. *Journal of Marriage and Family therapy, 4*, 53–60.

Fleming, R. H. (1985). Post-Vietnam syndrome: Neurosis or sociosis? *Psychiatry, 48*, 122–139.

Frenkel, S. I., Morgan, D. W., & Greden, J. F. (1977). Heroin use in the United States and Vietnam: A comparison in retrospect. *International Journal of the Addictions, 12,* 143–154.

Frey, J., Swanson, G., & Jacob, M. (1987). Structure, self-regulating sequences, and institutional third parties in therapy: The Veterans Administration as a model. *Family Process, 26,* 223–233.

Galovski, T., & Lyons, J. A. (2004). Psychological sequelae of combat violence: A review of the impact of PTSD on the veteran's family and possible interventions. *Aggression and Violent Behavior, 9,* 477–501.

Gilbert, L. A., & Scher, M. (1999). *Gender and sex in counseling and psychotherapy.* Boston: Allyn & Bacon.

Goldberg, H., & Goldberg, I. (Eds.). (2008). *Family therapy: An overview* (7th ed.). Belmont, CA: Thomson.

Goldstein, J. S. (2001). *War and gender: How gender shapes the war system and vice versa.* Cambridge, MA: Cambridge University Press.

Gottman, J. M. (1994). *What predicts divorce: The relationship between marital processes and marital outcomes.* Hillsdale, NJ: Lawrence Erlbaum.

Gottman, J. M., Ryan, K. D., Carrere, S., & Erly, A. M. (2002). Toward a scientifically based marital therapy. In H. A. Liddle, D. A. Santisteban, R. F. Levant, & J. H. Bray (Eds.), *Family psychology: Science-based interventions* (pp. 147–174). Washington, DC: American Psychological Association Books.

Gove, W. R. (1984). Gender differences in mental and physical illness: The effects of fixed roles and nurturant roles. *Social Science and Medicine, 19,* 77–84.

Helmus, T. C., & Glenn, R. W. (2005). *Steeling the mind: Combat stress reactions and their implications for urban warfare.* Santa Monica, CA: RAND Corporation.

Hendin, H., & Haas, A. P. (1984). *Wounds of war: Psychological aftermath of combat in Vietnam.* New York: Basic Books.

Hoge, C. W., Castro, A., Messer, S. C., McGurk, D., Cotting, D. I., & Koffman, R. L. (2004). Combat duty in Iraq and Afghanistan, mental health problems, and barriers to care. *New England Journal of Medicine, 351,* 13–22.

Hoge, C. W., Auchterlonie, L., & Milliken, C. S. (2006). Mental health problems, use of mental health services, and attrition from military service after returning from deployment to Iraq or Afghanistan. *Journal of the American Medical Association, 295,* 1023–1032.

Hosek, J., Kavanagh, J., & Miller, L. (2008). *How deployments affect service members.* Santa Monica, CA: RAND Corporation.

Isenhart, C. (2005). Treating substance abuse in men. In G. E. Good & G. R. Brooks (Eds.), *A new handbook of counseling and psychotherapy with men* (pp. 134–146). San Francisco, CA: Jossey Bass.

Jakupcak, M., Roberts, L. J., Martell, C., Mulick, P., Michael, S., Reed, R., ... McFall, M. (2006). A pilot study of behavioral activation for veterans with posttraumatic stress disorder. *Journal of Traumatic Stress, 19,* 387–391.

Jelinek, J. M., & Williams, T. (1982). Post-traumatic stress disorder and substance abuse: Treatment problems, strategies, and recommendations. In T. Williams (Ed.), *Post-traumatic stress disorder* (pp. 103–118). Cincinnati, OH: Disabled American Veterans.

Keith, D. V. & Whitaker, C. A. (1984). C'est la guerre: Military families and family therapy. In F. W. Kaslow & R. I. Ridenour (Eds.), *The military family: Dynamics and treatment* (pp. 147–166). New York: Guilford.

Kilmartin, C. T. (2009). *The masculine self* (4th ed.). Cornwall-on-the Hudson, NY: Sloan.

Kimmel, M. (1996). *Manhood in America: A cultural history.* New York: Free Press.

Kiselica, M. S., & Englar-Carlson, M. (2008). Establishing rapport with boys in individual counseling and psychotherapy: A male-friendly perspective. In M. S. Kiselica, M. Englar-Carlson, & A. M. Horne (Eds.), *Counseling troubled boys: A guidebook for professionals* (pp. 49–65). New York: Routledge.

Labuc, S. (1991). Cultural and societal factors in military organizations. In R. Gal & D. Mangelsdorff (Eds.), *The handbook of military psychology* (pp. 471–489). New York: Wiley.

Latty, Y & Tarver, T. (2004). *We were there: A celebration of African American veterans from World War II to the War in Iraq.* New York: HarperCollins.

Levant, R. F. (1995). Toward the reconstruction of masculinity. In R. F. Levant & W. S. Pollack (Eds.), *A new psychology of men* (pp. 229–251). New York: Basic Books.

Levant, R. F. (1998). Desperately seeking language: Understanding, assessing, and treating normative male alexithymia. In W. S. Pollack & R. F. Levant (Eds.) *New Psychotherapy for men.* (pp. 35–56). New York: Wiley.

Levant, R. H. (2001). Desperately seeking language: Understanding, assessing, and treating normative male alexithymia. In G. R. Brooks & G. E. Good (Eds.), *The new handbook of counseling and psychotherapy with men* (pp. 224–443). San Francisco, CA: Jossey Bass.

Levant, R. H. (2003). Treating male alexithymia. In T. J. Goodrich & L. B. Silverstein, (Eds.), *Feminist family therapy: Empowerment in social context* (pp. 177–188). Washington, DC: American Psychological Association.

Levant, R. H. & Brooks, G. R. (Eds.). (1997). *Men and sex: New psychological perspectives.* New York: Wiley.

Levant, R. H. & Pollack, W. S. (Eds.). (1995). *A new psychology of men.* New York: Basic.

Levant, R. F., & Silverstein, L. B. (2001). Integrating gender and family systems theories: The both/and approach to treating a post-modern couples. In S. H. McDaniel, D.-D. Lusterman, & C. L. Philpot (Eds.), *Casebook for integrating family therapy. An ecosystemic approach* (pp. 245–252). Washington, DC: American Psychological Association.

Leventman, S., & Camacho, P. (1980). The "Gook" syndrome: The Vietnam War as racial encounter. In C. R. Figley (Ed.), *Stress disorders among Vietnam veterans* (pp. 55–70). New York: Brunner/Mazel.

Lifton, R. (1973). *Home from war.* New York: Simon & Schuster.

Lincoln, A., Swift, E. & Shorteno-Fraser, M. (2008). Psychological adjustment and treatment of children and families with parents deployed in military combat, *Journal of Clinical Psychology, 64,* 984–992.

Lisak, D. (2001). Male survivors of trauma. In G. R. Brooks & G. E. Good (Eds.), *The new handbook of counseling and psychotherapy with men* (pp. 263–277). San Francisco, CA: Jossey Bass.

Madanes, C. (1991). Strategic family therapy. In A. S. Gurman & D. P. Kniskern (Eds.), *Handbook of family therapy* (Vol. 2, pp. 396–416) New York: Brunner/Mazel.

Mahalik, J. R. (2005a). Cognitive therapy for men. In G. E. Good & G. R. Brooks (Eds.), *A new handbook of counseling and psychotherapy with men* (pp. 217–233). San Francisco, CA: Jossey Bass.

Mahalik, J. R. (2005b). Interpersonal therapy for men. In G. E. Good & G. R. Brooks (Eds.), *A new handbook of counseling and psychotherapy with men* (pp. 234–247). San Francisco, CA: Jossey Bass.

Marrs, R. (1985). Why the pain won't stop and what the family can do to help. In W. E. Kelly (Ed.), *Post-traumatic stress disorder and the war veteran patient* (pp. 85–101). New York: Brunner/Mazel.

Montemayor, R. & Mendoza, H. (Eds.) *Right before our eyes: Latinos past, present, & future.* Tomas Rivera Policy Institute: Tempe, AZ.

National Defense Research Institute. (1993). *Sexual orientation and the U.S. military personnel policy: Options and assessment.* Santa Monica, CA: RAND Corporation.

O'Neil, J. M. (1982). Gender-role conflict and strain in men's lives. In K. Solomon & N. Levy (Eds.), *Men in transition: Theory and therapy* (pp. 5–44). New York: Plenum.

Paul, P. (2005). *Pornified: How pornography is transforming our lives, our relationships, and our families.* New York: Times Books.

Philpot, C. L., Brooks, G. R., Lusterman, D., & Nutt, R. L. (1997). *Bridging separate gender worlds.* Washington, DC: American Psychological Association.

Pleck, J. H. (1995). The gender role strain paradigm: An update. In R. H. Levant & W. S. Pollack (Eds.), *A new psychology of men* (pp. 11–32). New York: Basic.

Rabinowitz, R. E., & Cochran, S. V. (2002). *Deepening psychotherapy with men.* Washington, DC: American Psychological Association.

Ridenour, R. I. (1984). The military, service families, and the therapist. In F. W. Kaslow & R. I. Ridenour (Eds.), *The military family: Dynamics and treatment* (pp. 1–17). New York: Guilford.

Robbins, M. S., Mayorga, B. A., & Szapocznik, J. (2003). The ecosystemic "lens" for understanding family functioning. In T. L. Sexton, G. R. Weeks, & M. S. Robbins (Eds.), *Handbook of family therapy: The science and practice of working with families and couples* (pp. 23–40). New York: Brunner-Routledge.

Sammons, M. T. (2005). Psychology in the public sector: Addressing the psychological effects of combat in the US Navy. *American Psychologist, 60,* 899–909.

Sammons, M. T. & Batten, S. V. (2008). Psychological services for returning veterans and their families: Evolving conceptualizations of the sequelae of war-zone experiences. *Journal of Clinical psychology: In Session, 64*(8), 921–927.

Scher, M. (1990). Effect of gender-role incongruities on men's experience as clients in psychotherapy. *Psychotherapy, 27,* 322–326.

Shatan, C. F. (1978). Stress disorders among Vietnam veterans: The emotional content of combat continues. In C. R. Figley (Ed.), *Stress disorders among Vietnam veterans* (pp. 43–56). New York: Brunner/Mazel.

Sheppard, S. C., Malatras, J. W., & Israel, A. C. (2010). The impact of deployment on U.S. military families. *American Psychologist, 65,* 599–609.

Silverstein, L. B. (2003). Classic texts and early critiques. In L. B. Silverstein & T. J. Goodrich (Eds.), *Feminist family therapy: Empowerment in social context* (pp. 17–36). Washington, DC: American Psychological Association.

Silverstein, L. B & Brooks, G. R. (2010). Gender issues in family therapy and couples counseling. In J. C. Chrisler & D. R. McCreary (Eds.), *Handbook of gender research in psychology* (pp. 253–277). New York: Springer.

Sleek, S. (1995). Psychology and society: The media isn't always kind to mental health providers. *Monitor on Psychology, 26,* 7.

Sollinger, J. M., Fisher, G., & Metscher, K. N. (2008). The wars in Afghanistan and Iraq: An overview. In T. Tanielian & L. H. Jaycox (Eds.), *Invisible wounds of war: Psychological and cognitive injuries, their consequences, and services to assist recovery* (pp. 19–31). Santa Monica, CA: Rand Corporation.

Stanton, M. D. (1980). The hooked serviceman. In C. R. Figley & S. Leventman (Eds.), *Strangers at home* (pp. 279–292). New York: Praeger.

Stanton, M. D., Todd, T.C., & Associates. (1982). *The family therapy of drug abuse and addiction.* New York: Guilford.

Stock, W. E. (1997). Sex as commodity: Men and the sex industry. In R. F. Levant & G. R. Brooks (Eds.), *Men and sex: New psychological perspectives* (pp. 100–132). New York: Wiley.

Strange, R. E. (1984). Retirement from the service: The individual and his family. In F. W. Kaslow & R. I. Ridenour (Eds.), *The military family: Dynamics and treatment* (pp. 217–225). New York: Guilford.

Street, A. E., Vogt, D., & Dutra, L. (2009). A new generation of women veterans: Stressors faced by women deployed to Iraq and Afghanistan. *Clinical Psychology Review, 29,* 685–694.

Sue, D. W., & Sue. D. (2008). *Counseling the culturally diverse: Theory and practice* (5th ed.). New York: Wiley.

Tanielian, T., & Jaycox, L. H. (2008). *Invisible wounds of war: Psychological and cognitive injuries, their consequences, and services to assist recovery.* Santa Monica, CA: Rand Corporation.

Tannen, D. (1990). *You just don't understand: Women and men in conversation.* New York: Morrow.

"The origin of the VA motto: Lincoln's second inaugural address." (n.d.). Retrieved from http://www1.va.gov/opa/publications/celebrate/vamotto.pdf

U.S. Department of the Army, Office of the Surgeon General, Mental Health Advisory Team (MHAT-II). (2005). *Operation Iraqi Freedom (OIF-II), MHAT Report,* U.S. Army Surgeon General, January 30.

Vessey, J. T., & Howard, K. I. (1993). Who seeks psychotherapy? *Psychotherapy, 30,* 546–553.

Watzlawick, P., Weakland, J. H., & Fisch, R. (1974). *Change: Principles of problem formation and problem resolution.* New York: Norton.

Wedding, D., & Niemiec, R. M. (2003). The clinical use of films in psychotherapy. *Journal of Clinical Psychology, 59,* 207–215.

Westen, D., Novotny, C. M., & Thompson-Brenner, H. (2004). The empirical status of empirically supported psychotherapies: Assumptions, findings, and reporting in controlled clinical trials. *Psychological Bulletin, 130,* 631–663.

Worrell, J. & Johnson, D. (2001). Therapy with women: Feminist frameworks. In Unger, R. K. (Ed.). *Handbook of the psychology of women and gender* (pp. 317–329). New York: Wiley.

15

Male-Sensitive Couples Counseling

Fathering Issues

DAVID B. WEXLER

Men seeking help.
In the format of couples therapy.
Working on their issues as fathers.

That's what this chapter is about, and I review all three of these issues
and how, as therapists, we can all get even better at what we already do
with men in this situation.

First, I review the issues that men face in seeking help and engaging
in the counseling or therapy process. Next, I address the profound role
of shame sensitivity, or what I call *shame-o-phobia*, in male psychology and fathering issues, and then identify ways of engaging men that
respect this sensitivity. Then, I review the case of Lewis and Amy, which
includes recommendations for how to integrate a man's partner to help
him bring out his own best qualities as a father. Finally, I identify special
issues that emerge when a female therapist attempts to help a man dealing with fathering issues within the context of couples therapy.

It is actually unusual for men to come into a clinical setting announc-
ing their goal of "I need help being a better father to my kids." Men
typically do not initiate counseling or therapy under any circumstances.
Only one-third of voluntary psychotherapy clients are men (Vessey &
Howard, 1993), and we now have extensive findings demonstrating

something that many of us have known all along: Men are less likely than women to seek help for their emotional, interpersonal, and psychological problems (Addis & Mahalik, 2003). "The man who comes into the consulting room is usually there because he believes there is no alternative. Very few men come for therapy because they subscribe to its life-enhancing qualities. Even if they did they would likely not see it as something for them anyway. Men are in therapy because something, internal or external, has driven them to it" (Scher, 1990, p. 323).

And parenting issues are not the most likely motivator even when a man does come in for counseling. The focus on helping with his skills or issues as a parent usually comes out later in the process. In the couples therapy context, the primary focus is usually on the conflict and unhappiness between the two partners, which is sometimes triggered by conflicts over parenting issues and specifically the woman's unhappiness with the ways her partner is not parenting effectively.

Men most often enter some form of counseling (group, individual, couples, psychoeducational workshops, or substance abuse treatment) because someone else told them to. Sometimes the outside pressure comes from social institutions, as when men are ordered into treatment for domestic violence, parenting classes, sexual offender programs, or anger management programs. Other times men are pressured to seek services by their workplace, such as when they are required to attend sexual harassment counseling, a substance abuse program, or stress management. And, last but not least, many men are "ordered" into some form of treatment by the women in their lives. In an intake session, when I ask men my standard question, "What are you doing here?" the answer I hear most often is "my wife told me I needed to be here."

One of the most powerful advantages of working with men's parenting issues in the couples therapy format is quite simple: He might not come in otherwise! At least if they are both there, he can deflect some of his anxiety and some of his shame about being viewed as the identified patient.

MEN'S RESISTANCE TO TREATMENT

One of the fears that many men have about even entering counseling or therapy involves stigmatization. It's tough enough for a man to admit to having a problem. Even if he recognizes that something is wrong, this man must admit that he needs help. Most men have trouble asking for directions, let alone seeking assistance for psychological or relational distress. Even reading a self-help book about the problem creates some stigmatization. And taking medication often elicits an even more intense level of stigmatization for being really "defective" in some way.

Furthermore, even if this man is able to deal with these issues and still seek help, he then must rely on a professional to help fix his problems.

Although there are certainly many men who are quite comfortable turning to a professional for advice in many situations, there are plenty of other men who perceive this particular help-seeking behavior as a sign of weakness, dependency, and inadequacy. The very structure of this help-seeking relationship functions as a signal of inadequacy: "If I am relying on someone else to fix me, I must be failing at being a man."

Another issue often overlooked by even the most informed and experienced therapists: the confusion and anxiety many men have about how the strange and mysterious counseling process actually works. Many of the men whom we treat are entering uncharted territory. They are anxious about what they should disclose. They are not sure what is being asked of them. As a result they avoid coming in the first place or, when they do make it in, they are defensive and wary just being in the counseling setting.

MEN, SHAME, AND FATHERING

In working with the parenting issues that emerge for men in the context of couples therapy, one of the most central tasks is telling the right story, to ourselves and to our clients, about men as fathers. I find one of the most valuable "stories" for many men to be what I call the *broken mirror syndrome* (Wexler, 2004, 2009)

Self psychology theory highlights how the *mirroring of self object* plays a primary role in developing and maintaining a cohesive sense of self. The response from the other, the "object," serves as a mirror reflecting back a picture of the individual that may be positive or negative, worthy or unworthy, valuable or degraded. From a theoretical perspective, we understand this process very well in terms of how children are affected by parents (or how clients are affected by therapists).

But this particular process takes place the other way around as well. Parents, too, rely on their kids to make them feel good about themselves. They shouldn't, but they do. The child is a self object mirror to the adult. The dysfunctionality of this mirroring process from child to parent leads parents to overreact to the behaviors, achievements, mood states, and even core personalities of their kids. It's as if the parent is constantly scanning the behavior of his or her child and secretly asking the question, What does this say about me? And thus the parent is extremely vulnerable to narcissistic injuries when the child fails at a task, acts shy at a birthday party, doesn't keep his room clean, or simply voices autonomous opinions.

One of the key factors in problematic father–son relationships is the father's unresolved hurt feelings from his own childhood (Sanford & Lough, 1988). This type of father lives with a hurt little boy within himself, one who is always ready to be rejected, and this makes the father oversensitive to what he perceives as rejection.

Many fathers see themselves as lacking parenting skills (Pleck, 1997) or positive parental role models, which may result in shame and low confidence and may reduce fathers' involvement (Oren & Oren, 2010). The conclusion of this sequence, way too often, is that the parent either withdraws or turns against the child aggressively for making the parent feel ineffective or anxious.

In our clinical work with men who are confronting their issues in being a father, this is one of the first places to go. The man who *needs* something from his children in order to feel whole, loved, or successful himself will inevitably get tripped up by the complex demands of parenting. It is normal (at least once in a while) to reap the rewards of parenting and feel more whole, loved, or successful; it is neither normal nor functional when the man needs these too much. It sets him up to try too hard, to expect too much, and to be much too sensitive to perceived failures or the inevitable moments of incompetence as a father.

Helping men identify the ways that their children function as a mirroring self object (and how easily this can trigger the broken mirror sequence) helps them become better fathers. When a perceived broken mirror reflects a fragmented image back on a father, he is likely to lose access to his wiser judgment about what is happening with his child and what to do about it. Suddenly—and, most dangerously when it is unconscious—the psychological task becomes one of validating and protecting his own sense of self. At those junctures, he is quite capable of rationalizing the destructive response to his child as being justified, deserved, or for the kid's own good when it is really only to make the father feel temporarily better or temporarily less powerless.

A classic example of the broken mirror story is this: A man, previously wounded, turns to another person—this time his child—as a mirror to confirm his self-worth and to offer him a sense of well-being. Sanford and Lough (1988) point out that fathers who are laboring with these personal issues tend to either avoid relating to their children or go out of their way to be good fathers, but then feel hurt when they don't feel properly appreciated or rewarded. They experience the child's rejection of their help or their values as a fundamental rejection of their own self. And, in their own overt or covert way, they blame the child. They blame the mirror for breaking on them.

GETTING THROUGH TO MEN: GUY TALK

I find it particularly helpful to reframe the requests for new behavior from men in language and metaphors in ways that honor the best of masculinity and ways that respect the sensitivity to shame. This allows a man to "feel like a man" and still branch out to new behaviors that are more prorelationship and promental health. It's called *guy talk*.

The therapist who is attuned to the broken mirror sequence, the male *shame-o-phobia*, and the defenses that men activate as they deal with the emotional demands of their relationships and meaningful life issues, develops language, imagery, and strategies with men so they are more likely to understand. And helping their partners understand this is a crucial component of this process as well.

Male-Friendly Motivations

When I work with fathers to react more maturely and rationally in the face of the demands of parenting, I will often frame for them what we are looking for.

> We want you to really take charge. We want you to be really powerful. Not over others, but over yourself. We want to make sure that the everyday crap that comes up for all of us does not control you or provoke you into reactions that are not good for you or the others around you. We want you to be in charge, not the stuff outside of you.

Male-Friendly Language and Metaphors

As already described, men often feel stigmatized by the labels assigned in the mental health world. This is especially evident in the label applied for the help-seeking process. Men (and the others around them) certainly don't have to call it *psychotherapy*. They don't even have to call it *counseling*. They can call it *stress management*, a *psychological tune-up*, *coaching, consulting*. Or, in the case of men who need help with fathering, simply *parent education*. They may balk at being called a *patient* or, in some cases, may not even want to be called a *client*. As long as they walk in the door and start doing the work, it does not matter what they choose to be called or how they label the process.

Male-friendly metaphors for change also come in very handy in capturing men's imagination and activating motivation (Englar-Carlson & Shepard, 2005):

> I want to make sure that you are navigating your own ship. (For yacht club members and active duty Navy.)
>
> It seems like this family is coming in here with two strikes and two outs in the bottom of the ninth. (For baseball fans.)
>
> It appears to me that the foundation of your relationship with your kids may need to be repaired. (For men in the construction industry.)
>
> I wonder how you analyze the benefits and costs of continuing with the same patterns in your relationship with your kids? (For men in the financial industry.)
>
> I think the way you parent needs a tune-up, but you can be relieved to know that it doesn't need an overhaul! (For the automotive crowd.)

Communicating Respect: Empathic Responses

When a man in a couples therapy session that is focused on his parenting issues is called upon to respond with affect but he seems blocked, there are a number of user-friendly and engaging responses that can disarm resistance (Englar-Carlson & Shepard, 2005):

When a man freezes up in response to a demand to express affect, the therapist can validate: *You're feeling a kind of blankness right now, is that it?*

When a man is reluctant to talk about his emotional states, the therapist can acknowledge the man's anxiety: *It's got to be difficult to talk about feelings in front of a woman who is "experienced" at this and a therapist who does this all the time.*

If a man has a hard time expressing emotions and the therapist is male, the therapist can normalize with self-disclosure: *We were not trained for this, were we?*

When a man describes failing at the task of offering his kids an empathic response, the therapist can reframe for positive intentions: *You want to let your daughter know you care but it's just hard to find the right words.*

If a man is ashamed of himself for being too critical or controlling with his kids, the therapist can identify the positive component in this negative behavior: *If you didn't care about these kids, you wouldn't be reacting like you do.*

Communicating Respect: Respect Resistance

There is a time and place to directly identify and confront male resistance and defensiveness. However, it is usually much more productive to offer respect for the defenses that we observe, keeping in mind constructs about the vulnerability that men experience. Typically, when we adapt some of our styles to give men a little room to activate their defenses, they don't feel like they have to perform upon demand. The therapeutic outcome is better in the long run.

For example, it works best with men to give them *permission to disclose gradually*: It is easy for therapists to get impatient when men take a while to warm up to the counseling experience. But it is essential that we respect, at least for a while, his anxiety or his unfamiliarity with plunging right into the emotionally laden issues at hand. Men also seem to be put at ease when there is a certain amount of *folksiness and humor,* and that the therapist seems "real" (what Latinos refer to as *personalismo* or Jews might call *schmoozing*). Furthermore, men are most likely to lower their defenses and hear the message when they perceive *therapeutic transparency*: They want to be reassured that they will know what the therapist is thinking of them and what the plan is, no secrets or mind games.

CASE STUDY: LEWIS

Lewis was a 46-year-old Caucasian man who came in to see me under intense pressure from his wife, Amy—like many other men that I see. Almost all of the time, with men more than with women, something specific happens that sets off alarms practically demanding that he get some help: infidelity, violence or abuse, a DUI, or feedback from a boss or coworkers. The trigger for Lewis was an explosion with one of his kids.

Lewis had been married to Amy for 18 years. They had three children, ranging in age from 4 to 11. Both he and Amy were practicing attorneys. Lewis was quite successful in his career but dreaded most of the tasks that his job demanded of him, especially the performance role in the courtroom. He often spent many sleepless, anxiety-ridden nights anticipating a trial, obsessing about making a mistake, missing something important, failing and looking foolish.

The family in which Lewis grew up was especially important for us to examine. His father had many traits similar to Lewis: a hard time making friends and connecting with people, and an occasionally volatile temper. Lewis described his mother as angry a lot and quite passive-aggressive and undermining. He looks back upon her as being a martyr and never joyful. She saw her life, as Lewis recalled it, as a series of burdens, and he was one of them. She found fault with him all the time; everything had to be "just so." He went to Catholic school—and he remembers always feeling that "anything I did was not good enough ... I never took satisfaction in my accomplishments because I always 'could have done better.'" As a child, he remembers feeling valued for what he did *not* do: for not causing trouble, for not failing, for not causing embarrassment to his parents.

Growing up, Lewis developed his own negative, pessimistic perspective on the world. He expected bad things to happen and had a hard time, by his own admission, experiencing much joy: "I have never really been comfortable in my own skin knowing who I am ... I'm always trying to please somebody and I always know I am going to fail." He had never really liked himself and he didn't believe that anyone else could like him either.

Just before Amy contacted me about making an appointment, she had come close to calling child protective services. Lewis had been trying to get their 4-year-old daughter dressed in the morning. This particular daughter was definitely on the fussy side: she obsessed and deliberated, trying on outfit after outfit in the morning, never quite satisfied. Lewis knew this about her, Amy knew this about her, they both often got frustrated with her, but they kept trying creative strategies to defuse the frustrating situation.

On the morning in question, Lewis was especially impatient. He was anxious about an upcoming trial, he had not slept well, and he was plagued by an underlying (even more than usual) doubt about his overall competence as a man. So his daughter fussed, he got more demanding with her, she got a little mouthy, he ordered her into timeout, which she ignored. He then proceeded (as frustrated parents are known to do) to "take charge": by grabbing her, throwing her into her bed, pinning her down, and screaming inches away from her face: "You are such a stupid brat! Is this what you want? Is this what you want?"

Amy came bursting into the room, pushed Lewis away, and grabbed the hysterical child and comforted her. She told Lewis to get out. He stormed outside into the backyard and started sobbing.

Engaging Lewis

Although Lewis had resisted Amy's "encouragement' that he seek out some kind of counseling at previous times, this dramatic incident convinced him, and it also illustrated a common, crucial event that has been described in contemporary theories of transtheoretical models regarding the stages of "readiness to change" (Proschaka, 1984, 2003). The catalyst that moves someone from the *precontemplation* stage (not even identifying the behavior as a problem and therefore not seeing it as something that needs to be changed) to the *contemplation* stage (realizing that there is a problem and it is now time to at least consider possible courses of action) and then on to the *preparation* stage (characterized by the desire to change in the immediate future, with the initiation of small steps toward change) usually requires a dramatic event: a wake-up call. This is especially true for many men, who are typically adept at denial and minimization, and suffer from a profound fear of seeking help. The identification of problems is feared, because change is feared, because attempts at change may generate failure and shame.

So this incident emboldened Amy, because she knew she now had Lewis's full attention. She told him that he needed to see an individual therapist, alone, to figure out his "issues"; but for two reasons they decided to come in together. For one thing, Lewis was still reluctant to be the identified patient (not his words) and insisted that they be seen together to work out their "mutual" problems. Second, Amy wisely anticipated that Lewis might not be able or willing to present the full story on his own. Although Amy was tempted to insist that "it's your problem, you deal with it," she chose the pragmatic route instead and agreed to go in for couples counseling. In my experience, pragmatism rules.

From the barebones background that Amy gave me when she made the appointment, I was prepared to encounter a reluctant man who was out of his element, the type of man I see very often: a good man who had been behaving badly. I made sure that there were copies of sports and business magazines in plain view in the waiting room in the hope that these would appeal to his male interests and help him to feel comfortable in my work setting.

Lewis entered my office with Amy, looking apprehensive. I made small talk about whether they had been able to find the office building and how they had done with parking. I congratulated them on being able to successfully navigate our small parking lot in back and told them (turning to Lewis) that anybody who could do that on the first try had a lot going for them.

I made sure to very deliberately spell out all the basic rules and expectations of therapy: confidentiality, cancellation policy, length of session, and so forth. All of this seemed to help, as it usually does. It is especially valuable to anticipate the uneasiness that many men have in this new situation where other people seem to know the rules and they don't—and to design some initial structure accordingly.

I also made it clear at the end of the first session how much I respected their decision to come in and get help with this; only people who really cared about their family would go through the time, expense, and emotional energy that this takes. I have seen way too many therapists forget to congratulate men for managing this step.

To frame the work we had ahead, I appealed to Lewis' need for a positive image of himself: "I know you are the type of man who wants to be a wonderful father and usually is." I turned to Amy for her endorsement of this description of her husband. Fortunately, she enthusiastically agreed. "And I know that you do not like yourself when you slip, and you want to do everything you can to be your best self with them. Right?" He nodded, tearfully. "Then let's go after this problem with everything we've got. First step is to figure out what triggers the times when you get off your good track." Lewis took a deep breath: "OK, let's go for it." He looked over at Amy, carefully scanning her face and body language for her evaluation of how he was doing. The look must have been good enough, because he turned back to me and said, "I want to do better at this."

Recognizing "Broken Mirror" Issues

The work began with my explanation to Lewis about the broken mirror sequence, and I assigned him the first chapter of my book, *When Good Men Behave Badly* (Wexler, 2004) to make sure he got the basics. He got it right away, as most men do: "That's exactly what happens to me. It's like I'm looking everywhere for signs that I am screwing up somewhere, or that people see me like that. And the closer I am to someone, like Amy or the kids, or my dad, the worse it is."

I gave him the homework assignment of keeping track of broken mirror experiences, "justified" or not, and to scan his memory for times in the past when it really flared up. The couple' format allowed us to enlist Amy as his ally in this process. With my encouragement, he invited Amy to let him know when it seemed like he had entered the broken mirror zone. We worked with her on the most effective ways for her to pass on this feedback (more on this later).

One of the first incidents he recognized was a small conflict with his oldest daughter, Arielle. She told him something about what happened to her at school that day. Lewis didn't exactly hear her (he is a little hard of hearing but not much). He asked her to repeat it: "Arielle, I'm sorry, say that again. What happened?" Dead silence. No response from Arielle. "Arielle, I just didn't hear you. Can you just tell me again what you said?" "No, forget it," Arielle replies. Lewis says, "I just didn't hear you. Don't be like that. What did you say?" Arielle walked off without a word.

Lewis pouted. He described his self-talk: "My daughter broke the 'contract.' She treated me disrespectfully. I thought we had a good relationship, and good people in good relationships don't treat other good people this way. It's like she's saying there is something wrong with me. And if I don't take charge of this, I will be accepting this and I will be weak! Just like I always felt with my father."

Fortunately, because Lewis was now more conscious and paying attention, he was able to catch himself before he acted out in response to this classic broken mirror experience. We opened up a bottle of champagne (figuratively speaking) in the couples session when he described his choice to let the incident go.

I helped Lewis generate a new narrative for the frustrating encounter with his daughter:

This hurt my feelings.
And it was frustrating because I really couldn't hear her and she just blew me off like I didn't care.
But ... I have to remember that she is a terrific kid—who sometimes acts likes a bratty 14-year-old. That's her job description.
If I really love her, and if I really want to have good relationship with her, I will blow off the small frustrations like this.
It's not really about me.
Repeat: It's not really about me.

We talked further about the broken mirror issues, and Amy was an invaluable resource in generating examples. Here is one description she offered:

I see exactly how this works. You go into this withdrawn state where we can all tell that you just start feeling like you are isolated and unimportant. It's like you are looking for signs that this is true! Then our life keeps going and it's like you're saying to yourself, "You see, they don't really need me! I don't really matter!" But you do! You do.
Remember a couple of weeks ago when we were all talking about going to a movie, and the kids got excited. Then we agreed on the movie—and all of a sudden you announced that you were going to the gym to work out! Everybody looked at you like you were nuts. We were all hurt.

I had to slow Amy down because I could see she was working up a big head of steam and about to launch into example after example of his mistakes. And I knew this would flood Lewis.

He was still taking all this in. He didn't say anything for a few moments and looked away. Then he looked up and said: "You were all hurt? You were all hurt? I didn't know you even cared."

This is the good man behaving badly personified. He feels vulnerable and needs to feel important, doesn't realize how he accidentally distances himself, then either withdraws or blames others (or both) for his unhappiness. All it looks like on the outside is that he is acting like an ass. But there is more to it than that, and he—as a whole person—is not an ass.

Amy admitted that she often took over in planning things with the kids and probably excluded Lewis from this process, and it was valuable for Lewis to hear that he was not crazy and not the only one contributing to this problem. But it had never occurred to him how much he was creating his own experience of alienation and disconnection.

"Many fathers do not hear—nor do they feel—that they are important in the lives of their children and may even wonder if they matter" (Oren & Oren, 2010, p. 31).

The Lewis Strategies

When all was said and done, the most meaningful intervention for Lewis turned out to be developing his new consciousness of the broken mirror sequence. The more he understood about his propensity to feel shamed and unsuccessful, and how easily this was activated in his most intimate family relationships, the better he got at interpreting and handling these situations differently.

I assigned as homework for both Lewis and Amy to watch the movie *Parenthood*, where the pattern of men overidentifying with the fate of their own children is dramatically and hilariously portrayed (Howard, 1989). The father imagines his son appreciating his efforts at helping him play baseball, then thanking him for being the world's greatest dad at his college valedictorian speech. Then the opposite fantasy emerges: Maybe his son will hate him for pressuring him, then becomes a mass murderer and blame his farther! The moral of the story for Lewis and for all fathers:

> Your kid is who he is. Your role is to be the best father you can be, which means deeply appreciating him as he is. If his behavior does not match your standards, adjust your standards. If your own issues about proving yourself as a man take over when it is time to offer yourself to your kid, think first and act second. Parenting is not about you.

But there were several other key pieces to this puzzle. One valuable lesson Lewis learned was how to avoid conflict with kids by simply structuring the environment differently. If your 2-year-old opens up cabinets, put a lock on the cabinets. If your teenager's friends like to raid your liquor cabinet, put a lock on that too. Amy had a more pragmatic sense of how to engineer things like this, and now Lewis was open to hearing her ideas and doing this with Arielle.

Another piece involved an adjustment of Lewis's expectations of this child and his other children. We worked on keeping his expectations of his children as developmentally realistic as possible. Furthermore, he learned to adjust his expectation based on the unique temperament of his children. Lewis and Amy both developed a richer understanding for the high-intensity child that they had on their hands with Arielle. I directed them to authors who helped parents think of their "problem" kids as *spirited* or *high energy* (Greene, 1998; Kurcinka, 1991; Nelsen & Lott, 1994), and we generated exercises in which Lewis wrote out voluminous lists of gratitudes about each of his children.

Behavioral assignments were also central to our work. Amy came in one time and said that their 11-year-old had complained that "Dad has that 'angry face' on again." Lewis was shocked. (Again, we would not have been able to address this situation in such detail if she were not included in these sessions—the information may never have even surfaced.) He had no clue about his "angry face" and had no memory of feeling angry at that time.

I asked Lewis, "Do you want your kids to think of you as the guy with the 'angry face'?"

That was a softball question, designed to activate his cooperation with the assignment. "Of course not," he replied.

"Then let's try this: Ask your kids to let you know when they notice the 'angry face' or the harsh tone that everyone seems to notice. Tell them this is your homework and you need their help. Make it a family project. Bug them daily to make sure they are doing their job at giving you feedback."

Lewis joked about opening up Pandora's box but agreed to give it a try. At first, he "forgot." Then he remembered but only talked to one of his kids. And he "mis-remembered" the assignment: He thought it was for overall feedback about how he was doing as a communicator, which is way too general. Finally he got it straight and actually got some feedback from the kids. More important than any specific feedback was his increased consciousness of this target behavior (the observer effect) and the meta-message to his kids: Daddy really cares and Daddy is really trying. And "real men" ask for help to do better in their lives.

A key component in the ultimate success of this intervention was Lewis's increasing ability to take in feedback from his wife. In the past, Amy had often given up trying to point out her observations of Lewis's fathering styles and to offer suggestions. His broken mirror issues derailed the potential value of this constructive criticism. But now he was choosing to perceive Amy's feedback as "influence" rather than "control" (Gottman, 2000). I gave Lewis an instruction to thank Amy for her feedback (very counterintuitive) rather than snap at her defensively. She was relieved to be able to have these conversations—and his ability to welcome them reduced her edge and critical tone in delivering them.

USING COUPLES THERAPY TO
PROMOTE GOOD FATHERING

Often, a woman will enter couples therapy complaining of her husband not being involved enough with their children. In many cases, this is a very legitimate complaint.

Many women perceive themselves as the resident expert on parenting. Often, this is well deserved, because they often have spent more time with the children, have read more parenting books, and have more advanced levels of certain kinds of emotional intelligence. However, women often unconsciously discourage men from being more active and involved. Because mothering is their realm, some women micromanage fathers and expect them to do things their way. And it often serves an unconscious need on the part of the mother to help maintain her role as the expert—alienating and discouraging the father from more involvement.

Contemporary research tells us that fathers do things differently but not necessarily in ways that are worse for the children (Pruett, 2009). Fathers do not mother, they father. They tend to discipline differently, use humor more, and use play differently. Fathers foster the separation–individuation process and help get their kids ready for the outside world. Sometimes fathers are not as attentive or as empathic with their children as are mothers, and fathers are viewed as being irresponsible. But just as often, fathers play a crucial role in encouraging risk taking and problem solving.

Furthermore, a mother's support of the father turns out to be a critical factor in his involvement with their children. Fathers are more likely to be engaged with their children when they experience more respect, support, affection, and positive communication from their partner. And, when couples can learn about these dynamics especially informed by the broken mirror self object issues for most males, the marital relationship becomes an especially valuable vehicle to help the man become a better father, and to help the kids get more of what they deserve.

Based on these perspectives, here are some of the most valuable couples-based strategies that facilitated the treatment of Lewis and Amy:

1. Perhaps the most valuable role that Amy played in helping Lewis work on the parenting issues was simply her ability to be a valuable informant and reporter. Many men that I work with are crummy reporters about their own behavior—not because they are consciously lying or engaged in impression management, but simply because they are not aware of how they are coming across or don't quite have the language to accurately describe it.
2. We focused on the importance of demonstrating mutual respect in front of children and generating a collaborative parenting approach. In her resentment and pessimism, Amy had slipped into a subtle

pattern of passive-aggressively undermining Lewis in front of the children.

3. We helped Amy generate respect for Lewis's male shame-o-phobia: Amy had never really grasped how vulnerable Lewis felt to feeling like a failure as a husband and father, and how easily her words or actions could activate these feelings in him. The couples sessions helped her develop a narrative of Lewis as a "good father sometimes acting badly," and the more she believed that, the more clearly she communicated that to him. And, because men are extremely influenced by the way in which the most important woman in their life views them (Wexler, 2004), Amy's narrative helped Lewis have more compassion for himself and believe in his ability to change.

One time several months into our treatment, Lewis asked Amy if she thought he was doing better in the way he was dealing with the kids. She took a deep breath, hesitated a moment, then offered a rather lukewarm yes. The hesitation stung. But of course Lewis didn't say anything, then or later at home. When I next met with him for an individual session, I asked him about how he had felt when Amy responded like that. He looked away and said: "What's the point? I'll never get credit. I'll never please anybody. I just have to do things for myself anyway." This was followed by the most succinct expression of his interpersonal attitude, carefully crafted throughout most of his 46 years: "Screw it."

He said that the message from Amy (or so he perceived) was that "you'll never make up for the mistakes of the past."

I pointed out to him the obvious:

1. He was entitled to feel hurt by Amy's withholding comment.
2. It was an exaggeration and overreaction to go into "screw it" mode.
3. Much could be undone if he talked to her about this rather than withdraw as usual.

This is what he proceeded to do in the next couples session, and Amy was appropriately apologetic for being more withholding than she really needed to be. She especially appreciated that Lewis approached her on this issue in the first place—and that he framed it as his feelings being hurt rather than focusing on her character issues.

4. Amy was able to recognize and reduce her unintentional *statements of diminshment*.

One of the patterns in couples counseling that often derails progress occurs when the woman complains about a man's behavior and requests that he change. He integrates this (sometimes reluctantly and defensively) and actually tries to make some movement in the requested direction. And then she finds fault with him and his efforts. She usually finds fault because of her anxiety that the changes are not real or likely to last. No matter what the understandable reason for her criticism and skepticism, it kills his momentum. Here are some classic negative reactions from a woman in response to the changes a man is trying to make (Wexler, 2006):

- He never would have done this on his own.
- I don't think I can forgive him for letting me down so much in the past.
- What good is it to me if he doesn't do it the way I think it should be done?
- Of course you're listening to me talk more about my feelings now, but that's only because I'm watching you so carefully. As soon as I take the pressure off, this will all go back to the way it used to be.

5. Amy also developed the use of the *softened start-up* (Gottman, 2000).

Women who are "informed" about broken mirror issues and the particular sensitivities that men have about feeling unimportant or disrespected are in a better position to approach their partners. She can contribute to the health of the relationship, and to the likelihood of drawing out the good man rather than the good man behaving badly, by perfecting the art of the softened start-up. These might otherwise be described as old-fashioned good manners.

The harsh start-up sounds like this: "Why am I the only one who ever does any cleaning up around here?" It may seem true at the moment, but it is an exaggeration of the truth, it does not honor the positive qualities of her partner, and it is usually communicated in a hostile tone of voice.

The softened start-up sounds more like this: "I am really feeling overwhelmed with how messy the house is—can we spend some time tonight working on this together?" Isn't that how anyone would like to be addressed? Although many men need a shove sometimes, most men do best if they feel fundamentally respected and appreciated. Then they are much more likely to feel generous.

The softened start-up is concise. It may register a complaint but without much blame or accusation. It comes with a softened tone of voice and nonconfrontational body language. And it is much less likely to activate any broken mirrors.

SPECIAL ISSUE: WHEN THE COUPLES THERAPIST IS FEMALE

If a female therapist is working with a couple, she has a few built-in advantages—and potential disadvantages—in terms of working with the man's issues. Men tend to see women as the experts on relationships (particularly on issues about raising children), and men are often more likely to trust a woman's judgment, just like they might turn to a man if they needed consultation about subjects that they assumed men would know better (business advice, auto repair, financial investment, etc.). And the soft, nurturing touch (or certainly the man's projection of these qualities onto a female therapist) often reaps enormous therapeutic benefits and allows input that would otherwise be deemed too threatening.

However, men may also feel like the female therapist just doesn't quite get it or get his experience. He may feel ganged up by the two females in the room who are trying to force some feminized version of relationships down his throat and turn him into something that he is not. It is also hard for a female therapist to activate the "twinship" response in ways that a male therapist can more naturally do with a male client.

It is common for female therapists, especially, to want to help men be more emotionally expressive. However, when a male client slowly begins to share his inner experiences, he frequently feels a rush of relief, followed by a wave of anxiety and vulnerability (Scher, 1990). As a female therapist, it is vital to recognize that expressing his feelings breaks male tradition and may activate fears about his loss of manliness.

Female therapists especially need to recognize that (although there are plenty of exceptions) many men do not respond well to typical therapy talk like "getting in touch with your feelings." It is often very helpful to use metaphors and images that are user friendly to men, and both male and female therapists can facilitate treatment by having some available to help capture his attention and get the message across. Another form of guy talk is humor. Because therapy can be too emotionally intense for many men, humor serves to normalize the interpersonal experience and offer men some emotionally acceptable detachment from their feelings. It helps bond the client and therapist as equals: the "twinship" experience (Sweet, 2006).

Perhaps most important, it is extremely important for female therapists to recognize the tremendous anxiety and shame-o-phobia that many men experience in the counseling environment. So when a man enters the therapy office, it helps to anticipate that he feels this way and to prophylacticly reinforce his effort: "I know how hard it must be for you to be here, and I really respect your decision to come in and work on these issues despite that. That tells me that you are a good man and a man committed to helping his family."

SUMMARY

We know that men, in general, often don't talk about feelings frequently or easily, and are more reluctant to seek help when they could really use it—and these patterns are not usually in their best interest in becoming better men and better fathers. But it is good news in one sense: When they enter the counseling setting, however they have gotten there, they are especially likely to benefit from talking things over, because it is so new and foreign. A man who is struggling in trying to live up to his own high standards as a father often benefits enormously and quickly by getting feedback that he has never allowed himself to get before. He benefits from recognizing issues within himself, like the broken mirror sequence, that have never been clear before. He benefits from learning new parenting skills that had never occurred to him before.

The couples therapy format offers an outstanding format for him to move forward on these issues—because he feels like he is working on this in partnership and because he is able to get valuable feedback and insight not only from a professional but also from a loving person who is in the best position to know him and observe him. If the couple, with the therapist's help, can generate a fundamentally trusting and respectful atmosphere, the man we are trying to help can grow in ways that never seemed possible before.

REFERENCES

Addis, M. E., & Mahalik, J. R. (2003). Men, masculinity and the contexts of help seeking. *American Psychologist, 58,* 5–14.

Basch, M. F. (1980). *Doing psychotherapy.* New York: Basic Books.

Carlson, M. J., Pilkauskas, N. V., McLanahan, S. S. and Brooks-Gunn, J. (2011), Couples as partners and parents over children's early years. *Journal of Marriage and Family, 73,* 317–334. doi: 10.1111/j.1741-3737.2010.00809.x

Englar-Carlson, M., & Shepard, D. S. (2005). Engaging men in couples counseling: Strategies for overcoming ambivalence and inexpressiveness. *The Family Journal, 13*(4), 383–391.

Gottman, J. M. (2000). *The seven principles for making marriage work: A practical guide from the country's foremost relationship expert.* New York: Three Rivers Press.

Greene, R. (1998). *The explosive child: A new approach for understanding and parenting easily frustrated, "chronically inflexible" children.* New York: HarperCollins.

Howard, R. (Director). (1989). *Parenthood* [Motion picture]. United States: Imagine Entertainment.

Kurcinka, M. (1991). *Raising your spirited child.* Chicago: University of Chicago Press.

Nelsen, J., & Lott, L. (1994). *Positive discipline for teenagers.* Rocklin, CA: Prima Publishing.

Oren, C. Z., & Oren, D. C. (2010). *Counseling fathers.* New York: Routledge.

Pleck, J. H. (1997). Paternal involvement: Levels, sources, and consequences. In M. E. Lamb (Ed.), *The role of the father in child development* (3rd ed., pp. 61–103). New York: Wiley.

Prochaska, J. O., & DiClemente, C. C. (1984). *The transtheoretical approach: Crossing the traditional boundaries of therapy.* Homewood, IL: Dow Jones-Irwin.

Prochaska, J. O., & Norcross, J. C. (2003). *Systems of psychotherapy: A transtheoretical analysis.* Pacific Grove, CA: Brooks/Cole.

Pruett, K., & Pruett, M. (2009). *Partnership parenting: How men and women parent differently–Why it helps your kids and can strengthen your marriage.* Cambridge MA: Da Capo Lifelong Books.

Sanford, J. A., & Lough, G. (1988). *What men are like.* New York: Paulist Press.

Scher, M. (1990). Effect of gender role incongruities on men's experience as clients in psychotherapy. *Psychotherapy, 27,* 322–326.

Shapiro, S. (1995). *Talking with patients: A self psychological view of creative intuition and analytic discipline.* Lanham, MD: Jason Aronson.

Sweet, H. B. (2006). Finding the person behind the persona: Engaging men as a female therapist. In M. Englar-Carlson & M. A. Stevens (Eds.), *In the room with men: Casebook of therapeutic change* (pp. 69–90). Washington, DC: American Psychological Association.

Vessey, J. T., & Howard, K. I. (1993). Who seeks psychotherapy? *Psychotherapy: Theory, Research, Practice, Training, 30*(4), 546–553.

Wexler, D. B. (2004). *When good men behave badly: Change your behavior, change your relationship.* Oakland, CA: New Harbinger.

Wexler, D. B. (2006). *Is he depressed or what: What to do when the man you love is irritable, moody, and withdrawn.* Oakland, CA: New Harbinger.

Wexler, D. B. (2009). *Men in therapy: New approaches for effective treatment.* New York: W.W. Norton.

INDEX

A

Abandonment, childhood, 39
Addiction, sexual. *See* Sexual addiction
Adler, Alfred, 60–61, 81, 125
Adlerian couples therapy
    assessment, 83–84
    case example, boxer's daughter and
        momma's boy, 88–89, 90–92,
        92–95, 95–96, 97–98, 98–99
    interpretation and insight, 84
    marriage/committed relationships
        focus, 82–83
    masculine culture, exploring, 85–86
    overview, 81–82
    patriarchy, identifying, 85
    relationship building, 83
    reorientation, 84–85
    social inequality, addressing, 85,
        86–87
    social interest, concept of, 87
Adrenaline, 185
Alcohol abuse, 284
Alexithymia, 133–134, 136–137
Altruism, 92

B

Behavior change requests (BCRs), 118–122
Behavior exchange, 172
Behavioral marital therapy (BMT),
    156–157, 158
Being *versus* doing, 52–53, 62–62
Blaming, 199
Bonding, 206
Broken mirror syndrome, 303, 309–311
Bullying, 5

C

Castration, fear of, 81
Childhood events, male
    abandonment issues, 39
    case study, Andrew and
        Julie, 65–73
    eliciting, in therapy, 63–64
    father, identification with, 38–39
    memories, early-life, 63–64
    memories, forms of, 59
    memories, meaning-
        making, 60–62
    object-relations approach to, 61
    origins, examining, 38
    presentation of findings, in
        therapy, 64–65
    unresolved, 303
Christie, Agatha, 62
Communication training, 172–173
Coping strategies, 50
Cortisol, 185
Counseling environment, 44
    safety, 130, 131
Countertransference, 15, 18–19
Couples therapy. *See also specific*
    models of
    challenges of, 13
    efficacy of, 1–2
    Latino and African American
        men, couples counseling
        with. *See* Latino and
        African American men,
        couples counseling with
    male-sensitive. *See* Male-sensitive
        couples therapy
    need for, 1

unified detachment, promoting, 170, 171
Intergender translating and reframing, 293
Intimacy, male
  childhood abandonment issues and, 39
  childhood origins, 38
  independence, *versus,* 42–44, 49
  vignette, 39–40
  withdrawal, male. *See* Withdrawal, male
Intimate partner violence (IPV)
  defensiveness regarding, 31
  dynamics of violent marriages, 184
  intake assessment, 27–28
  need to address in couples therapy, 14, 26–27
  underreportage, 27
  vignette, 28–31

L

Latino and African American men, couples counseling with
  advocacy skills, teaching, 264
  biases, therapist's, 262, 263
  case study, Jamal and Lorraine (African American couple), 268–271, 271–272, 273
  case study, Robert and Elena (Mexican American man), 265–268, 271, 272–273
  community of client system, 263
  macroaggressions, racial, 259, 261–262
  microaggressions, racial, 256, 258–259, 261–262
  overview, 253–254
  professional literature on, lack of, 254–256
  religious and spiritual life, 264
  self-disclosure, 265
  stereotypes, 255–256
  strengths-based approach, 261

M

Macroaggressions, racial, 259, 261–262
Male-sensitive couples therapy. *See also specific therapeutic models*

case study, James and Ruth, 239, 240–248
defining, 13–14
fathering issues. *See* Fathering issues
gender considerations (therapist), 237–238
history, intake, 235
Latino and African American men, couples counseling with. *See* Latino and African American men, couples counseling with
male resistance to therapy, 291, 302–303, 306
masculinity, relationship between, 4, 13–14
need for, 2–5
predisposing factors, examining, 235
rapprochement, 235–236
therapeutic alliance. *See* Therapeutic alliance in couples therapy
treatment models, 236
unfaithful men, with. *See* Unfaithful men, male-sensitive couples therapy with
veterans and their partners. *See* Male-sensitive couples therapy, veteran and his partner
Male-sensitive couples therapy, veteran and his partner
  case study, 280–281
  cultural impediments to, maleness, 281–282
  cultural impediments to, military, 282–285
  efficacy, 290–291
  familial impediments, 287–290
  institutional impediments, 285–287
  overview, 279
  resistance to help, 291
  sociopolitical impediments, 287–290
  VA system, 287
Masculine culture, 85–86
Masculine gender role stress, 133–134
Masculine protest, 125
Memory. *See* Childhood events, male
Microaggressions, racial, 256, 258–259, 261–262
Mindfulness meditation, 97
Mirroring of self objects, 303